Meeting the Challenge of 9/11

About the Academy

The National Academy of Public Administration, like the National Academy of Sciences, is an independent, nonprofit organization chartered by Congress to identify emerging issues of governance and to help federal, state, and local governments improve their performance. The Academy's mission is to provide "trusted advice"—advice that is objective, timely, and actionable—on all issues of public service and management. The unique source of the Academy's expertise is its membership, including more than 650 current and former Cabinet officers, members of Congress, governors, mayors, legislators, jurists, business executives, public managers, and scholars who are elected as Fellows because of their distinguished contribution to the field of public administration through scholarship, civic activism, or government service. Participation in the Academy's work is a requisite of membership, and the Fellows offer their experience and knowledge voluntarily.

The Academy is proud to join with M.E. Sharpe, Inc., to bring readers this and other volumes in a series of edited works addressing major public management and public policy issues of the day.

The opinions expressed in these writings are those of the authors and do not necessarily reflect the views of the Academy as an institution.

Meeting the Challenge of 9/11
Blueprints for More Effective Government

Edited by **Thomas H. Stanton**

Foreword by **Admiral James Loy**

NATIONAL ACADEMY OF
PUBLIC ADMINISTRATION

TRANSFORMATIONAL TRENDS IN
GOVERNANCE AND DEMOCRACY

M.E.Sharpe
Armonk, New York
London, England

Copyright © 2006 by M.E. Sharpe, Inc.

Library of Congress Cataloging-in-Publication Data

Meeting the challenge of 9/11 : blueprints for more effective government /
edited by Thomas H. Stanton.
    p. cm. — (Transformational trends in governance & democracy)
  Includes bibliographical references and index.
  ISBN–13: 978-0-7656-1758-3 (cloth : alk. paper)
  ISBN–10: 0-7656-1758-7 (cloth : alk. paper)
  ISBN–13: 978-0-7656-1759-0 (pbk. : alk. paper)
  ISBN–10: 0-7656-1759-5 (pbk. : alk. paper)
  1. Public administration—United States. 2. United States—Politics and government—2001–
3. National security—United States. I. Stanton, Thomas H., 1944– II. Series.

JK275.M28 2006
352.3'750973—dc22   2006005559

| BM (c) | 10 | 9 | 8 | 7 | 6 | 5 | 4 | 3 | 2 | 1 |
| BM (p) | 10 | 9 | 8 | 7 | 6 | 5 | 4 | 3 | 2 | 1 |

This book is dedicated to the proposition that
effective government is an essential response
to the challenge posed by September 11.

Contents

Foreword

The United States is engaged in a conflict unprecedented since the early days of the Republic. For the first time in recent memory, a foreign enemy struck the continental United States causing massive civilian casualties and harm to our economy.

We have organized to defeat this enemy, both at home and overseas. In March 2003, we created the Department of Homeland Security, merging twenty-two disparate federal agencies with more than 180,000 employees and a combined budget of $36 billion. We are beginning the difficult but essential process of designing and implementing new government programs in border and immigration control; infrastructure security; hardening of transportation systems; protection of people and agriculture against bioterrorism; and, in the wake of the Hurricane Katrina disaster, emergency responses to man-made and natural disasters.

This reorganization of government presents the biggest "change management" challenge of all time, dwarfing even the creation of the Department of Defense after World War II. Never before has a consolidation of this size occurred with such national importance and urgency and in such a short amount of time—the Environmental Protection Agency (EPA) and Department of Transportation (DOT) were major reorganizations, but insignificant when compared to DHS.

This effort requires looking beyond old agendas, missions, cultures, histories and processes and coming together as one holistic enterprise. It required—and I would emphasize, finally enabled—a once-disjointed civil service to rally around an enormously complex mission: to gather, analyze, and distribute information (intelligence) more efficiently; prevent and deter terrorist attacks and remediate their effects in the aftermath; to protect the critical infrastructure of America; to secure our borders but also keep the open doors so characteristic of, and essential to, this welcoming and economically thriving country; and to manage the crisis and recovery of incidents heretofore unimaginable in America.

At the same time, from the start, we were immersed in the other half of our work…building the organizational structure and relationships to accomplish that mission. That meant integrating the numerous support functions of the new department. It meant working swiftly to get servers up, systems consolidated, and a stapler on every desk—all without moving forces from the protection of the country.

Homeland Security is about much more than the horizontal melding of twenty-two agencies and multiple systems. Attacks of September 11, and lessons learned from the management of Hurricane Katrina, require a new philosophy of how we secure the country—a philosophy of shared leadership and shared responsibility—in essence, a new notion of federalism. It's clear that the protection of this nation cannot be micro-managed from Washington, DC. Instead, it must be a priority in every state, city, every neighborhood, and every home across America. Homeland security in the twenty-first century is really about the integration of a nation—led by national leaders, but also governors, mayors, county officials, airline personnel, border patrol agents, law enforcement, business leaders—citizens everywhere.

It's about partnerships and networks. Immediately following September 11, we began working with state and local partners to improve coordination and delineate chains of command. The response to Hurricane Katrina illustrated to us that our nation has a long way to go if we are to be effective protectors to our citizens. We have a large collaborative agenda, ranging from sharing and responding to threat information to building up emergency preparedness capabilities.

Many steps have been taken at the Department of Homeland Security to become effective at addressing the issue of terrorism, and its first cousin, the natural disaster. This book points out the need for effectiveness to permeate all government programs and agencies. In homeland security, as in other aspects of government, effective design and implementation must be the keys to success.

While our attention has understandably centered on issues of homeland security, we also recognize that we are part of the larger executive branch and its management requirements, also undergoing significant transformation independent of homeland security. President Bush has instituted management reforms to hold all federal programs accountable for performance. The President has extended performance even to foreign assistance where developing countries must demonstrate that they can achieve results from aid received. Prior personnel systems have been superseded, allowing policymakers to craft systems that better suit the customized needs of their agencies. Work traditionally accomplished by civil servants has been contracted out to private companies and in some cases to federal employees who may reorganize their work processes to become more efficient. Much of the inter-action of citizens with our government is now electronic. We at Homeland Security now better appreciate how we must integrate our organizational, personnel, financial, evaluation, and information technology systems with the rest of the government. Indeed, this latter focus occupies the attention of many of the contributors to this volume.

As President Bush has said, "good beginnings are not the measure of suc-cess. What matters in the end is completion. Performance. Results. Not just making promises, but making good on promises. In my Administration, that will be the standard from the farthest regional office of government to the highest office in the land."

As this book shows, there are many lessons from the past that, combined with thoughtful new approaches, can help government become more nimble and capable. We have much to do and the security of America's citizens demands that it be done quickly. The first decade of this first century of the new millennium was deemed by Pope John Paul II to be the time we would usher in a new and peaceful world. Even his peaceful reach mandates that we work hard to sustain that peace by designing those protective and preventive systems and those response and recovery capabilities required. Those are the guarantees our generation owes our children and grandchildren. This book challenges us to get to work and that's precisely what we each must do.

Admiral James Loy
former Deputy Secretary of the Department of Homeland Security

Preface and Acknowledgments

This book is a product of the Standing Panel on Executive Organization and Management of the National Academy of Public Administration.[1] The Academy is an independent, nonprofit organization, chartered by Congress to identify emerging issues of governance and to help federal, state, and local governments improve their performance. It exists to help organizations to achieve excellence in the provision of public services.

The distinctive source of the Academy's expertise is its membership, which includes 550 current and former Cabinet officers, members of Congress, governors, mayors, legislators, jurists, business executives, public managers, and scholars who are elected as Fellows because of their distinguished contributions to the field of public administration through scholarship, civic participation, or government service. Participation in the Academy's work is a requisite of membership, and the Fellows offer their experience and knowledge largely on a voluntary basis. The Academy is supported by a professional staff of experienced former federal officials, academics, and others with extensive knowledge of federal, state, and local government programs, organization, and management.

The Academy's Standing Panel on Executive Organization and Management is a unique institution. Established in 1971, it serves as a meeting place and sounding board for Academy Fellows and others to exchange views on approaches to improving the structure, capacity, management, and performance of public institutions. The panel meets monthly and frequently hears presentations from leading federal officials and experts on public administration. Speakers at the panel have included David Walker, the comptroller general of the United States, two postmasters general of the United States, deputy secretaries and undersecretaries of cabinet departments, heads of agencies, and other senior officials. Panel members have submitted testimony and supporting analyses on government organization and management issues on numerous occasions, including on the reorganization of the nation's intelligence functions and legislative proposals to create a Department of Homeland Security.

The panel consists of experienced federal managers and management analysts who know that government can improve its performance and who in many cases have helped federal departments and agencies to increase the quality of their organization and management. The authors thus bring a combination of political wisdom, administrative principles, and practical experience to this book.

This is the second book produced by the panel. The first was *Making Government Manageable: Executive Organization and Management in the Twenty-First Century,* published by Johns Hopkins University Press in 2004. The present book and *Making Government Manageable* sound many similar themes. Many panel members are concerned about the federal government's loss of management capabilities in recent years. Chapters in both books include lessons from times in the twentieth century when government needed to respond to challenges by increasing its effectiveness. Other chapters show how new forms of organization and management, and other improvements, are needed to make government more effective so that we can properly address the critical challenges posed by the terrorist threat against the American homeland.

Based in part on the success of *Making Government Manageable,* the Academy has entered into an agreement with M.E. Sharpe, Inc., to publish a series of books on *Transformational Trends in Governance and Democracy,* edited by Terry F. Buss. Each edited book will answer the questions: How is governance or democracy being transformed? What impact will transformation have? Will forces arise to counter transformation? Where will transformations take governance and democracy in the future? Books planned in the series include: *IT and the Transformation of Government, Federalism after September 11, Citizen Participation and Engagement in the Information Age, Voting in America, Performance-Based Management and Budgeting, Privacy,* and more. The present book is the first in that series.

Acknowledgments

The National Academy of Public Administration would like to thank James Carroll, George Fredrickson, Steve Redburn, and Terry Buss for reviewing the manuscripts in this edited book. The Academy would also like to thank Adam Gardner and Amy Odum for their expert work preparing the manuscript for publication. The Academy is grateful to Harry Briggs at M.E. Sharpe, Inc. for his support and encouragement.

Thomas H. Stanton
Terry F. Buss
Washington, D.C.

Note

1. This panel's Web page is www.napawash.org/eom.

Meeting the Challenge of 9/11

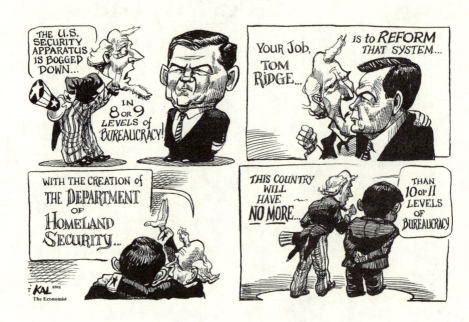

Introduction

Meeting the Challenge of September 11

Thomas H. Stanton

The Challenge

From the perspective of institutions of government, September 11 hit the United States at a very difficult time. The public and private sectors, working together, need to organize to meet a new and unprecedented challenge. Government must play a critical role. Yet, the organizational strength of many parts of government, and of the federal government in particular, has been in decline for some time. The challenge of September 11 demands not only new policies, programs, systems, and organizational relationships to deal with the threat, but also the revitalization of old programs and agencies to carry out their missions more effectively.

How to make government more effective, especially in the realm of national and homeland security, is the subject of this book. Its thrust is not that we always need to spend more money, although that is the case with many aspects of homeland security, but rather that we must improve the organization and management of government, both generally and as it relates to the urgent need to strengthen homeland defense. This requires restoration of the capacity that once existed in the Executive Office of the President to learn and adapt lessons on how to make government more effective, and then apply these lessons to critical areas of government involvement.

The decline in quality of executive branch institutions has occurred over several decades. In 1988 then-comptroller general Charles A. Bowsher delivered a major address to the National Academy of Public Administration (NAPA) in which he warned of an emerging crisis, what he called the "disinvestment of government" (Bowsher 1988). He pointed to the increasing gap between the responsibilities of government agencies to carry out their missions and their capacity to do so.

By the 1990s, the crisis foretold by Bowsher began to emerge. Budget and staff cuts turned many agencies into hollow organizations (Goldstein 1992). Prosperity in the private sector attracted many capable government officials and their departure further lowered the tone of organizations. The United States Commission on National Security/21st Century looked at the activities of agencies relating to homeland security and found that the Department of State was "starved for resources" (U.S. Commission on National Security 2001, 47). Moreover, "The Customs Service, the Border Patrol, and the Coast Guard are all on the verge of being overwhelmed by the mismatch between their growing duties and their mostly static resources" (U.S. Commission on National Security 2001, 16).

The commission reported that the problem of hollow government was widespread, and not confined merely to the domestic side of government: "As it enters the 21st century, the United States finds itself on the brink of an unprecedented crisis in competence in government. . . . Both civilian and military institutions face growing challenges . . . in recruiting and retaining America's most promising talent" (U.S. Commission on National Security 2001, xiv).

September 11 showed that the commission's warnings were not misplaced. We must revitalize the government's capacity to deal effectively with the threat to our homeland security. In areas such as border and immigration control, cybersecurity, and the need to strengthen first responders, September 11 and later disasters such as the botched response to Hurricane Katrina in 2005 revealed shortcomings in organization, people, and systems. We must improve our systems and infrastructure to prevent or mitigate hostile acts, increase our capacity to detect potential threats, and be able to deliver an effective response. To do so, we must upgrade government's ability—at the federal, state, and local levels—to act intelligently, both alone and in concert with the private sector.

In addition to improvements in systems and infrastructure, organizational changes are needed. An overarching theme of this book is that traditional hierarchical government departments and agencies alone are no longer adequate to meet the challenges of effective governance, much less those after September 11. Although traditional public administration has concerned itself with hierarchical and governmental organizational models, an effective response to terrorism also will require design, creation, and management of nonhierarchical networks that include private as well as public actors.

This is an acceleration of a development that was perceptible before September 11. As Harold Seidman has observed,

The principles . . . which call for straight lines of authority from the President down through department heads with no entity exercising power independent of its superior are not adapted to current circumstance. Straight lines of authority and accountability cannot be established in what has become in major degree a non-hierarchical system. Federal agencies now rely for service delivery on third parties who are not legally responsible to the President and subject to his direction. Federal powers are limited to those agreed upon and specified in grants and contracts. (Seidman 2004, x)

The need to manage a nonhierarchical system that includes governments and private-sector organizations is especially pronounced in homeland security. Coordination, which has always been difficult for government agencies, is now an imperative:

- Biodefense: The Center for Disease Control (CDC) is funding states to create a Health Awareness Network to centralize and strengthen state and local responses to bioterrorism. The recommended systems would include secure high-speed Internet connections for local health care officials, capacity for rapid, secure communications for first responders, electronic laboratory reporting of infectious diseases, drug inventories and biological agents, distance learning systems to provide training for health care workers and response teams, and early-warning broadcast systems. Figure I.1, from the Government Accountability Office, shows the many actors whose coordinated participation is needed for effective early detection and response to an incident.
- Agrodefense: We need the capacity to detect a threat to our food supply and respond by isolating the affected part of the food system without disrupting unaffected parts. This requires seamless communication between agricultural areas and firms in the food-supply chain and central monitors who have the ability to detect and act on early warning signals.
- Border Security: In 2002 the Customs Service processed some 6 million cargo containers arriving at U.S. seaports. Inspectors at over 300 ports of entry inspected nearly 450 million travelers. The Border Patrol apprehended nearly 960,000 aliens trying to enter the United States illegally between ports of entry (GAO 2003). Resources alone cannot deal with this problem. Also needed are organizational changes that result in better coordination among agencies and functions such as the U.S. Coast Guard, customs, immigration officials, the Border Patrol, and state and local officials, at and between ports of entry.

Figure I.1   Local, State, and Federal Entities Involved in Response to the Covert Release of a Biological Agent

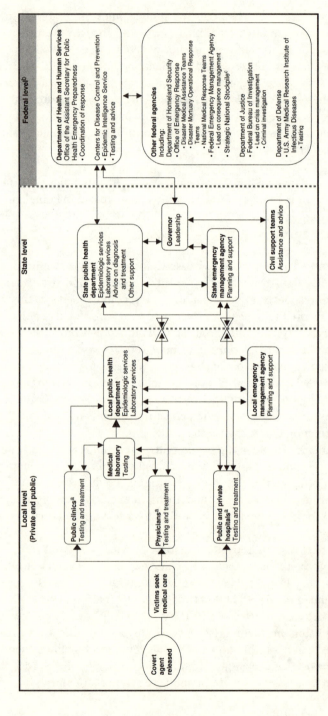

Source: GAO.

a. Health care providers can also contact state entities directly.

b. Federal departments and agencies can also respond directly to local and state entities.

c. The Strategic National Stockpile, formerly the National Pharmaceutical Stockpile, is a repository of pharmaceuticals, antidotes, and medical supplies that can be delivered to the site of a biological (or other) attack.

- Immigration Control: The processes for granting visas, checking them at points of entry, and monitoring temporary visa holders is anything but seamless. The U.S. Consular Service needs to be able to detect fraudulent applications while accommodating legitimate visitors. Immigration authorities need computer systems that accurately identify visitors and monitor the length of their stay. Federal officials need to improve coordination with local police officers, who can detect and apprehend dangerous visitors.
- Infrastructure Protection: Many parts of the country's infrastructure and systems, ranging from chemical and nuclear facilities to seaports, rail systems, and the Internet, require upgrading to protect against potentially serious incidents. Voluntary efforts will not be enough and proposed mandatory solutions are complicated by the unresolved question of which parties should bear the costs. Yet in major areas the federal government has failed to bring the affected governmental and private parties together to determine (1) the most cost-effective approaches for making high-priority improvements to infrastructure and systems and (2) a reasonable approach for sharing the costs. Unless these issues are addressed, efforts to coordinate protective measures are not likely to succeed.

The federal government must play a crucial role on these issues, but not necessarily as the manager of a hierarchical organization. Instead, the federal government must help to align the actions of multiple federal, state, and local agencies, and private-sector organizations, which can contribute to coping with problems that single actors cannot address by themselves.

Harold Seidman, who characterized government attempts at coordination as "the search for the Philosopher's Stone" (Seidman 1998),[1] is among those who have pointed out the difficulty of coordinating autonomous organizations. Yet coordination is imperative if we are to respond effectively to ongoing terrorist threats. An entirely new organizational form may be needed, one that provides a template for coordinated organizations to trade off their individual interests against those of the larger whole and be compensated for their losses. Such an organizational form would rival in achievement the development of the joint stock company in the seventeenth century (Davis 1905; Williston 1888; Lyon, Watkins, and Abramson 1939) and the general-purpose corporation charter in the nineteenth century (Lyon, Watkins, and Abramson 1939). Meanwhile, we will need to muddle through, but quickly.

The Lessons of This Book

The authors in this book have long experience in managing government organizations at a senior level or in analyzing government organization and management. Most are fellows of the National Academy of Public Adminis-tration (NAPA) and active participants in NAPA's Standing Panel on Execu-tive Organization and Management. Their analyses of government organizations would have been important at any time; on September 11 they gained special salience.

Public Administration since September 11

The book begins with Thomas Stanton's overview of organizational forms that enhance the capacity of government to carry out public purposes. These forms range across governmental and private organizations. Critical criteria for assessing the quality of an organization include (1) capacity, (2) flexibil-ity, (3) accountability, and (4) the organization's life cycle (Stanton 2003; NAPA 2004).[2] It turns out that when government uses departments or agen-cies to deliver public services such as homeland security, the key issues re-volve around capacity and flexibility. Government agencies are usually subject to annual appropriations and have often been subjected to the process of disinvestment described by Charles Bowsher years ago. Law- and rule-bound systems of personnel, budgeting, procurement, and asset management may promote accountability to elected officials in the executive and legislative branches, but they may also restrict flexibility of the organization to carry out its mission, especially when compared to private-sector organizations.

On the other hand, when government uses third parties to provide public services, the critical issues revolve around accountability. Privately owned firms must obey the law and honor their contracts. This aside, their first and foremost responsibility is to their owners, even if they also have a responsibility to carry out their public purposes. Nonprofit organizations, such as state public authorities,[3] sometimes may gain autonomy from the political process to the point that they are not accountable on many issues to anyone except their managers. Life cycle is a dynamic force that besets all organizations, public and private: They may peak, stagnate, or undergo mutations over time. Effective organizational design seeks to anticipate such forces, maximize the benefits, and reduce the likelihood of serious dysfunction or stasis.

This chapter makes another point: Good organizational design is not a universal panacea. Reorganization alone will not solve many problems of interagency coordination, which can continue to pose major challenges even within a single department such as the Department of Homeland Se-curity (DHS). Also, poor leadership, unmotivated staff, insufficient re-sources, and glacial or irrational procedures will not be overcome merely by restructuring.

As the creation of the DHS has shown, reorganization is not a cure for poor coordination and can make matters worse, at least during the shakedown period. This was seen with tragic consequences in the failure of the Federal Emergency Management Agency (FEMA) to respond appropriately to the destruction of New Orleans by Hurricane Katrina and the subsequent flooding. The reduction of FEMA from a cabinet-level agency to become a small part of the new DHS, combined with a shift in emphasis to homeland security from FEMA's mission of responding to natural disasters, demoralized FEMA staff and led to an exodus of capable people from the agency. When Katrina hit, FEMA had become a shadow of the effective agency that it once was. The cartoon at the beginning of this book, questioning the wisdom of adding yet another layer of bureaucracy on top of agencies such as FEMA, is right on the mark.

The chapter closes with the observation that the federal government has lost much of its former capacity to design organizations and manage programs so that they might operate more effectively. Neither the Executive Branch nor the Congress now possesses the wealth of design talent that once existed. This theme recurs in different ways throughout the book.

James Carroll argues in the second chapter that the form of the American state is evolving. The old administrative state was superseded by an entitlement state in which many federal outlays were fixed in law rather than being left to agency discretion. The entitlement state now is being superseded by what he calls the "domestic security state," in which issues of coordination are paramount: "The administrative core of the domestic security state is mutuality of understanding, unity of purpose, and interoperability of systems in sharing and using information across boundaries to anticipate, prevent, respond to, and recover from terrorist action and cataclysmic events." In the past, government usually dealt with known actors and defined threats. By contrast, in the domestic security state, a continuous process of identifying and defining the threat is central. This places a premium on government's ability to develop and share information on changing circumstances and events in real time.

Carroll sees the elements of this critical intelligence function as forming a triangle. At its base are extensive intelligence gathering and sharing of information across governmental and national and public-private boundaries. It is critical to obtain a fast and comprehensive view of developments. On one side of the triangle, intelligence must be transmitted to a central point so that apparently unconnected pieces of information can be scrutinized and patterns recognized. On the other side of the triangle, intelligence is transmitted from the apex to the base so that timely investigation, prevention, or remedial action can be taken.

In biodefense, for example, a single point in government, probably the federal Centers for Disease Control and Prevention, must have access to information about a surge in doctor or pharmacy visits by people reporting flu-like symptoms. The central agency must unleash a team of experts to diagnose the cause and determine a response. Time is of the essence. Given the speed at which some pathogens can spread, early diagnosis and wide dissemination of a response protocol can help to contain an outbreak.

This was one of several lessons from the SARS outbreak. Another was that biodefense is likely to need to be international in scope, which again makes Carroll's point about the need for the domestic security state to operate across traditional boundaries. Perhaps the most serious lesson from the SARS outbreak, relating to anticipating an emergency rather than to the response, is the need to assure that we have invested in the needed infrastructure—properly equipped and staffed hospitals, laboratories, and state and local public health agencies—in anticipation of an outbreak.

Carroll closes with a warning: The domestic security state must learn to meet the needs of security while doing the least possible damage to our precious liberties. "The challenge is stark. It is whether governance in a system of constitutional democracy, separated powers, and individual liberty can develop methods of countering terrorism that are consistent with the principles and values of this system. Public administration in America has never faced a greater challenge."

Organizing for More Effective Government

The second section of the book includes three chapters on government organization. Chapter 3, by Frederick Kaiser, takes up where James Carroll's chapter left off. If, as Carroll contends, the old hierarchical model is facing obsolescence, then why create a Department of Homeland Security to meet the challenges of September 11? Frederick Kaiser's chapter presents a conceptual and historical overview of the decisions that led to the creation of the department. He contends that the creation of the department was not a foregone conclusion.

The new DHS combined 22 federal agencies with 170,000 employees and a total budget of $37.5 billion. In employees, it is the second-largest Cabinet department, behind the Defense Department; in budget, it is fourth, behind Defense, Health and Human Services (HHS), and Education. The DHS absorbed the Coast Guard, the Border Patrol, the Customs Service, the Transportation Security Administration, the Federal Emergency Management Agency, functions of the Immigration and Naturalization Service, and over a dozen smaller entities such as the Secret Service and the Animal and Plant

Health Inspection Service of the U.S. Department of Agriculture. On the other hand, Kaiser points out that more than 100 other agencies, from the Agriculture Department (USDA) and the Central Intelligence Agency (CIA) to the Federal Bureau of Investigation (FBI) and the U.S. Postal Service (USPS), have responsibilities and jurisdiction in homeland security.

The creation of the department involved contending ideas and issues. The core debate concerned the choice between coordinative mechanisms and creation of a new department. Interests as well as concepts were at stake. Kaiser reminds us that the organizational arrangements have implications for political power and control. President George W. Bush initially opted to create two coordinative mechanisms, an Office of Homeland Security and a companion Homeland Security Council. This approach allowed the president to specify organization, operations, and management, without sharing control with the Congress. The president determined the membership and leadership of the two bodies and their budgets, responsibilities, jurisdiction, authority, activities, operations, and the extent of their power. A clear signal of this independence from Congress came when the director of the Office of Homeland Security refused to testify before the Senate Appropriations Committee about antiterrorism funding.

Legislation creating the DHS changed everything. Although the president's design for the department largely prevailed, Congress altered particular elements. The use of enabling legislation to authorize the new department opened the door for Congress to apply its influence at later points. Congress had a say in the particular agencies and functions to be included in the department, their degree of autonomy, their responsibility for preexisting missions other than homeland security, and funding levels and resources. Congressional authority over expenditures and the confirmation process for top officials also applies, and these officials must report to and testify before Congress.

The chapter closes with a review of eight coordinative mechanisms that have been employed among homeland security agencies both before and after September 11. We have come full circle: The new department changed the locations of functions that need to be coordinated; it did not change the need for such coordination and in some instances made coordination more difficult by creating new organizational relationships.

In chapter 4 Alan Dean and Dwight Ink endorse a feature of the new department that they believe should be widely replicated across the executive branch. This is the position of undersecretary for management, which the legislation spells out in careful detail. The DHS enabling law, they say, gives the new undersecretary authority over "the broadest scope [of subject areas] ever specified by law for a management official in a federal department."

The office was created to establish a center for comprehensive management leadership. The lack of such a focal point is a serious omission in most executive departments, resulting in the dispersion of responsibility for promoting effective management among numerous second- and third-tier officials (Wamsley 2004). As Dean and Ink conclude, "Only by creating a post at the undersecretary level with this broad scope of authority could a DHS secretary hope to shape this extraordinarily complex department into an organization that could operate effectively under stress."

The DHS was unwilling, for some reason, to share details of the undersecretary's first year of operation with the authors, who apply their long experience with federal organizations to set forth factors that will be critical if the office is to live up to its potential:

- Keeping the office strong: This will require high-quality appointments to the undersecretary position, preferably of professionals who will serve through a change in political administration. The DHS secretary, the OMB, and committees of the Congress should work to support the undersecretary.
- Overcoming fragmentation: The authority of the office should be kept broad so that it can overcome the tendency, found in other government organizations, of fragmenting administrative functions. For example, it makes no sense for one set of officials to have responsibility for designing the department's headquarters structure and another set for organizing its field offices. Yet there are disturbing signs that such fragmentation is beginning to occur.
- Broader use of the audit function: Although the audit function is a key part of the responsibility of a departmental inspector general, the undersecretary also needs this capability. In the hands of the undersecretary, the audit function can be an important management tool for identifying and responding to weaknesses in departmental practices or for addressing an emerging scandal before it escalates into the public domain.
- Strengthening management analysis: This function can help the new department break down the walls of its component organizations through design of organizations, operating systems, and improved processes that cut though organizational barriers.
- Program management: The office should assist program leaders to develop effective program systems and should provide leadership in the management dimension of designing and improving DHS programs.
- Monitoring: The secretary should hold this office responsible for identifying deficiencies in the department's organization and management systems, and designing measures to bring about improvements.

- Departmental culture: The office can offer critical support in the secretary's effort to create a cohesive and vital organizational culture. It can block "stovepiping" and parochial concepts that undermine teamwork. It can establish both formal and informal incentives for recognizing and improving performance.

In chapter 5, Ronald Moe calls for another major step in improving the capacity of government to organize and manage itself. Moe calls for an Office of Federal Management (OFM) in the Executive Office of the President (EOP) to strengthen the capacity of the president in his role as chief manager of government.

Moe seeks to restore a capacity that once existed in the EOP. In 1970, the management side of the OMB had 224 employees. By 1980, when President Jimmy Carter left office, the number had fallen to 111. The Reagan administration's concentration on budget cutting and regulatory review further reduced the management staff to only 47. Finally, the Clinton administration implemented a reorganization in 1994 that simply eliminated most of the management positions and integrated the management function into the budget side of the agency. This was a complete departure from the Nixon administration's view that the budget should be part of management, not vice versa.

Moe proposes that the new Office of Federal Management would exercise authority in at least the following areas:

- organizational design and management oversight
- central legislative review and advice
- information technology policy
- financial systems management
- regulatory review and clearance
- procurement, contracting policy, and privatization
- government corporations and enterprises
- real and personal property management
- federalism and intergovernmental relations

Moe argues that career federal officials should largely staff the office, noting that most management issues, unlike most budgetary issues, lack high political saliency and rarely follow party lines. There are no Republican or Democratic principles for structuring field offices or for creating a government corporation. Reliance on career staff would help provide some continuity in executive branch management in support of politically accountable officials. New administrations want to begin their initiatives early; this office can help.

Moe makes the same point as Dean and Ink, that many management functions have become stove piped, leading to an unhealthy fragmentation of functions. Personnel, financial management, procurement, and information management should be considered together in designing and improving government organizations and programs.

To illustrate the costs of not having an Office of Federal Management, Moe points to the shortcomings in the process of creating the DHS and the problems that inadequate design have created.

> It is difficult not to conclude that if an OFM had been in existence, it would have begun on September 12, 2001, to develop the organizational and management issues and options available to the president and other executive decision makers on how best to organize to meet this new national challenge. Having institutional memory of other reorganization challenges and what complex issues are involved in bringing together, in this instance, twenty-two separate agencies, would have put the White House ahead of the management curve rather than behind.

Moreover, Moe points out, the absence of such an office as a lead player in designing the DHS means that there will not be one agency where the lessons learned can be kept, studied, and integrated into administrative doctrine to serve in the future.

Managing for More Effective Government

The third section of the book addresses management as well as organization. In chapter 6, Murray Comarow offers insights based on his half-century of public and private service on public issues, backed by knowledge gained both as an academic and as executive director of President Nixon's Council on Executive Organization (Ash Council). His observations are instructive for the reorganization of homeland security functions:

- The core principle [of government organization] on which most practitioners and organizational theorists agree . . . is that an enterprise should be organized in a way best calculated to achieve its purpose, its goals. This requires that those goals be clear and consistent, unlike those in the Agency for International Development or the old Atomic Energy Commission (AEC). In the latter case, AEC's mission to promote the use of nuclear energy conflicted with and sometimes overrode its safety mission.
- No structural arrangement can reconcile all interests or resolve all conflicts; nevertheless, there is no substitute for organizing according to

purpose, logical assignment of functions, and establishment of centers of accountability.

- Opposing interests should be drawn together at the right levels of government, so that the vast majority of conflicts can be resolved below the level of the Executive Office of the President.
- The objectives of the agencies involved must be plainly set out and must respond to a distinct and enduring public need.
- There must be some assurance that the functions to be grouped under one head not only belong together, but that, collectively, they can be managed efficiently.
- The agencies should be so structured that a high order of public interest is served in making policy rather than narrower advocacy positions.
- There is no perfect arrangement that will mediate among all interests, much less resolve all conflicts. Admit mistakes ungrudgingly, and make adjustments as required.

Comarow criticizes presidents Carter, Reagan, and Clinton for their demeaning treatment of career federal officials. He says that their contempt for "bureaucrats" has seeped into public consciousness and has become embedded in our culture. The consequences are grave, but they have remained largely unexamined.

This chapter's observations about leadership provide the distilled wisdom of years of direct experience. Comarow says that good leaders:

- Share responsibility with their managers;
- Have the courage to take reasonable risks;
- Do not rely on formal communications systems; they go among the troops and listen hard;
- Are scrupulously fair, have integrity, and avoid the appearance of conflict of interest or favoritism;
- Where possible, will establish mutually agreed-upon goals, not objectives imposed without consultation;
- Will insist that their managers act like managers by wiping out unnecessary functions, controlling costs, and removing marginal or incompetent people; and
- Care about their employees as people and visibly show that they care.

Comarow places some of the blame for government inefficiency on Congress, citing the DHS as an example:

On August 8, 2004, the *New York Times* reported that since January 2003, Department of Homeland Security officials "testified before 300 Congressional hearings and held 2,000 briefings for members of Congress or their staffs . . . an average of 4 hearings and 25 briefings a week." No fewer than 88 committees and subcommittees were involved. The drain upon executive energy was enormous. Congress, impatient with inefficiency in the executive branch, thus contributes to inefficient management. One committee in each house should be established [for homeland security].

In chapter 7, Dwight Ink presents strategies for achieving meaningful change. From watching a multitude of reforms that more often failed than succeeded, Ink culls five examples of change that made a difference. He personally played a leading role in four of these as a top career civil servant; in the fifth he was an invited evaluator. Each of these case studies provides important lessons for today's managers. "In developing new approaches," says Ink, "it is a mistake to neglect past experience that can be of great help when adapted to new circumstances."

This chapter is a must-read for officials at the beginning of each new administration. The facts of the five case studies help to illustrate the management strategies that Ink extracts:

- *Rapid Action.* Delays can increase costs and weaken support for major management initiatives. If an incoming administration can rely on proven management strategies, it can move quickly, mobilize for broad reforms, and institutionalize major changes before the next election.
- *Political-Career Partnerships.* Sharply contradicting the conventional wisdom about career people allegedly resisting change and lacking innovation, each case study involves the political leadership's benefiting from the experience of the career leadership and developing a working partnership. Within this framework, political leadership sets broad policy and may withdraw delegated authorities, should that become necessary. Conversely, effectiveness of career men and women depends heavily on good political leadership.
- *Innovative Design.* All major presidential initiatives for change occur under conditions, and with objectives, that differ from past initiatives. Managers need to be skilled and grounded in basic management concepts to permit innovations to succeed. Otherwise, innovations run a much greater risk of causing expensive mistakes whose consequences may emerge later.
- *Openness and Outreach.* An important component of the five initiatives was the close working relationship with key congressional committees and the openness and level of consultation between the executive branch and those committees. A heavy investment of effort in working with

Congress saves time, usually reduces the extent to which Congress changes presidential management initiatives, and results in a more supportive congressional attitude.

In contrast to these proven management strategies, Ink sees management reforms in recent years as neglecting critical issues, such as the need to strengthen internal departmental communication systems and contract management capacity, both of which are woefully inadequate in many departments. He finds that departmental organizations and operations often are designed and implemented ad hoc, with insufficient attention to accountability, to the relationship between headquarters and field offices, or to intergovernmental and interagency management. Ink adds his experience to the observations of Carroll, Kaiser, and others in this book concerning these areas of special significance for effective homeland security.

Beryl Radin, in "Developments in the Federal Performance Management Movement: Balancing Conflicting Values in GPRA and PART," chapter 8, provides a striking contrast to Dwight Ink's chapter. While Ink shows how to carry out major successful management initiatives, Radin explores currently fashionable exercises such as those of the Government Performance and Results Act (GPRA) and the Performance Assessment Rating Tool (PART).

GPRA is the law enacted in 1993 that requires all federal agencies to develop strategic plans, annual performance plans, and performance reports. PART is a Bush administration initiative that began with a pilot program in 2003 as an effort to integrate budget and performance assessments. GPRA applies to departments and agencies; PART applies to government programs. PART rates program effectiveness according to four dimensions: program purpose and design, strategic planning, program management, and program results. OMB budget examiners complete questionnaires on agency programs for which they have responsibility.

Radin notes that, although performance is an appealing idea, it may be misleading because performance criteria often fail to reflect conflicting values inherent in government agencies and programs. Indeed, users of performance information include people and organizations with positive, neutral, and negative agendas concerning the agencies and programs whose performance is to be measured. Radin argues that both GPRA and PART, because of their virtually total focus on efficiency, do not easily fit into the conflicting structures, values, and political realities of the American system of government.

Radin concludes that GPRA and PART operate largely as rhetorical devices and lack influence over substantive policy and budgetary processes. Of the multiple functions within the performance rubric—planning, budgeting, and management—each contains its internal contradictions, beyond the conflicts across the functions: "The one-size-fits-all, government-wide approach to management reform that is illustrated by both GPRA and PART does not fit easily into the reality of policy design and politics."

Radin also observes difficulties with the implementation of PART and GPRA:

- The relationship between PART and GPRA requirements is not clear and is often confusing to program officials.
- PART focuses only on the president's budget and is thus limited to an executive branch perspective.
- The assessment of program purpose and design by OMB staff has been viewed by some critics as an attempt to preempt the role of the Congress.
- While program goals often include several purposes and multiple values, PART appears to focus only on the achievement of efficiency goals. There is little in the process that highlights broader goals of program effectiveness, and basically nothing that assesses the achievement of equity goals within programs. This is similar to the GPRA experience.
- In order to satisfy both GPRA and PART requirements, agencies would need to collect new data. They are constrained, however, by the mandates of the Paperwork Reduction Act, by budget limitations, and by the difficulty of collecting program performance data that involve block grants to states.
- The autonomy of OMB budget examiners has created a highly variable pattern of dealing with PART.

Radin concludes that there is little to suggest that GPRA and PART have improved agency or program performance.

Addressing Critical Issues

The final section of the book includes five chapters that address issues that have gained in significance since September 11.

In chapter 9 Michael Maccoby addresses in greater depth the issue of organizational culture that Dean and Ink raised earlier. In Maccoby's view, cultural factors primarily determine organizational behavior and effectiveness. The DHS leadership would be well advised to address cultural aspects of the effort to combine so many disparate organizations. Cultural differences not only divide the various organizations but also create a gulf between the political leadership of an agency or department and its career civil servants. Such differences need to be managed, and are ignored only at peril.

Maccoby argues that the DHS leadership should not try to impose a uniform organizational culture: "The subcultures of Homeland Security are unlikely to shed the histories and sense of identity that provide pride and meaning for people. To attempt to blot out these identities would provoke resistance and undermine positive motivation for work." Instead, DHS leadership should aim to develop effective collaboration among the different subcultures and across the organizational boundaries.

How should this be done? Maccoby turns to the experiences of leading companies that have successfully addressed similar cultural challenges. They utilize "network leaders" who develop relationships of trust. The DHS should use career civil servants for these roles and should select those people whose social attributes most lend themselves to playing such a role.

Managers must learn how to lead organizational cultures into effective collaboration: "This requires not only designing new leadership roles but also developing new leadership skills, and selecting people whose social character motivates them to build relationships of trust and facilitate participative decision making. It requires aligning measurements and rewards to support the strategy."

How well is the DHS doing? Although extensive information is not available, it appears that DHS managers are meeting resistance. In addressing problems of communications across organizations, Maccoby reports, the "easy part was to install communication technology. The hard part was getting people to communicate in a timely way. Another problem was determining who was in charge when there was need for collaboration across organizational barriers. Here the political and civil service cultures clashed."

Chapter 10, by Dan Guttman, also raises a warning, about the rush to contract out important functions of government. Guttman argues that government agencies can and do lose the ability to supervise their contractors and hold them accountable. The result can be wastefulness or worse, as in some U.S.-administered prisons in Iraq. The resulting management challenges can be immense. A major concern is the disregard of the principle that certain governmental activities must be performed by agencies and officials, and should not be delegated to nongovernmental actors. The state is subject to a different body of law than that applicable to private individuals. If we continue to blur the boundaries between the public and private workforces we may lose the very qualities that we most value in each.

Guttman believes that the root of the contractor accountability issue is conceptual. Developments have pyramided on top of one another to the point where the U.S. government has become substantially dependent on its contractor workforce: "[B]ipartisan limits on the number of civil servants ('personnel ceilings') assured that as government grew, third parties would be increasingly needed to perform its basic work—planning, policy and rule drafting, managing the nation's nuclear weapons complex, serving as go-betweens in dealings with citizens and other governments, and managing the federal official and contractor workforce themselves."

In the process the nation has lost any useful theory about the legal and political basis of the relationship between government and its citizens on the one hand and the contractor workforce on the other. Guttman asks how we will know if muddling through without an organizing concept is not good enough. He proposes a research agenda to obtain solid information about the extent and nature of contracting out and the extent to which contractors in fact are accountable for their performance. It is time, he warns, for the United States to develop a clear concept of the boundaries between the use and misuse of contractors to carry out the public's work.

Cindy Williams, in chapter 11, reviews the military personnel system. Especially with the added strains in coping with the war on terrorism, weaknesses in the military personnel system are beginning to show. The pay disparity has continued to grow between critical military specialties and the comparable civilian occupations. This is exacerbated by increased use of contractors to perform functions that military personnel could perform. An additional complication is the concept of equal pay across all military specialties, which prevents the military from offering increased pay to attract and retain people with critical skills in short supply. The military may be able to get by in peacetime, "[b]ut in wartime, even modest setbacks in filling the ranks with the right people can ripple rapidly through the force and its leadership, increasing the risks to fielded troops and making it more difficult for them to achieve military aims."

Williams lists seven major problems with the military personnel system and proposes improvements for each. For example, reforms of pay and benefits of the National Guard and the Reserve are especially important because of their essential role in homeland security, besides being called upon for combat service. The unusual military pension system is another problem. Military personnel who serve for twenty years receive an annuity tied to the cost of living. Those who decide to leave earlier receive no pension at all. This all-or-nothing approach results in retaining unneeded people and losing others who are at the peak of their experience.

Reform is not yet on the horizon. The military is a conservative institution and pay and pay equity issues are especially sensitive. Stakeholders include members and committees of Congress, civilian leaders in the Pentagon and the White House, military family and retiree associations, veterans' organizations, contractors that provide goods and services to military members and their families, and political figures who treat military pay and benefits as campaign issues.

In chapter 12 Enid Beaumont and Bruce McDowell look at the critical role of intergovernmental relations in homeland security. In their view, the nation can either use the imperative of homeland security to improve upon federal relations with state and local governments or else may simply adopt ad hoc approaches, for example, to providing grant funds, that replicate past problems.

Past problems have been substantial. The federal government manages itself through hierarchical administration that often involves a command-and-control approach; yet, intergovernmental relations within our constitutional system are best managed through a collaborative approach that emphasizes problem solving. States and localities are a prime example of the types of third parties that Seidman believed required a relationship other than through the traditional hierarchical model.

Beaumont and McDowell call for a collaborative approach. They cite NAPA panel studies showing how federal managers may neglect collaboration, even when the traditional hierarchical approach is not helpful. To work together successfully, diverse groups require four ways of approaching problems: trust-building, skill at crossing organizational boundaries, flexible funding, and the all-hazards approach championed by the former Federal Emergency Management Agency (FEMA).

Federal officials will need training in the first two of these skills. Flexible funding will require a new approach to relations between DHS and states and localities. The all-hazards approach will be critical in dealing with sporadic and, one hopes, infrequent homeland security incidents so that first responders and the practice of intergovernmental coordination can keep their tone between incidents.

Legislation causes many problems of intergovernmental relations. Beaumont and McDowell point to the fragmentation of federal grants. Federal grants for first responders display considerable overlap: Funding for seven of the sixteen relevant grant programs can be used for equipment; twelve for training; eight for exercises; and twelve for planning. Grant funding formulas frequently bear little relation to the security needs of particular states and localities. Long experience with federal grant programs has generated lessons to apply to give states and localities greater flexibility, within guidelines, to use their grant money more effectively. It is not clear whether DHS and other federal grant-making agencies will apply that experience, despite the importance of these scarce funds to developing state and local capabilities.

Beaumont and McDowell conclude that it is not clear whether homeland security will increase the centralizing tendencies of a stronger federal government vis-à-vis states and localities or—because of the need to get homeland security right—will serve as a model for improving intergovernmental relations in other areas: "All of the governmental partners will need to be extraordinarily vigilant as this new program unfolds to make sure that its centralizing tendencies do not overrun and dampen the vitality and essential capabilities that come with the dispersed responsibilities in our federal system of government."

The inability of the City of New Orleans and the State of Louisiana to respond appropriately to the 2005 Katrina disaster, combined with an inadequate federal response, led to many avoidable casualties. The result of that demonstration of weakness in the federal relationship, involving, for example, a breakdown in collaboration between the governor and the federal government regarding disaster relief, is likely to tip the balance even further in the direction of the centralizing tendencies that are the subject of concern in this chapter.

Chapter 13 concludes this book with a new template for an organized process of enhancing the design and management of stakeholder networks. Thomas Stanton proposes applying to selected homeland security issues the "Stakeholder Council Model" of collaboration of federal agencies, state and local governments, and private organizations. Two good candidates for the model are the development of interoperable identity management systems and interoperable systems for container and port security.

Stanton cites Harold Seidman's caution that "Agencies are most likely to collaborate and network when they are in agreement on common objectives, operate under the same laws and regulations, and do not compete for scarce resources." This poses challenges; policymakers need to determine (1) where the Stakeholder Council Model is most applicable and (2) under what conditions.

The Stakeholder Council Model is similar to standards-setting groups in many sectors of the economy. The most relevant case is the Electronic Benefits Transfer (EBT) Council, which began in 1995 as an organization composed of federal agencies, states, merchants, payments networks, financial institutions, and other EBT service providers, including consultants and processors. The OMB encouraged these stakeholders to develop operating rules for the electronic delivery of government benefits, including food stamp and cash benefits. Instead of giving beneficiaries food stamp coupons or paper checks, state governments provide them with a debit-type card that contains the value of their food stamp or cash benefits and that can be used at retailers and in ATMs.

The process took many years, but forty-eight states now offer statewide EBT programs. As the use of the EBT Council's operating rules has expanded, states are adding to functions that are served through their EBT card systems, including payments for Temporary Assistance for Needy Families, Medicaid, and child care. The U.S. Department of Agriculture announced in 2004 that food stamp delivery has moved completely to electronic form, and is seeking to rename the program because "food stamps" has become an anachronism.

Stanton reviews the applicability of this model to another issue involving interoperability, the development of identity management systems. The weakness of the driver's license and other identification such as the Social Security Number has led governmental and private organizations to design and implement their own identity management systems. However, if these systems are not interoperable, the result can be confusion, loss of time in having one's identity verified, and creation of potential gaps across systems that can be exploited in undesirable ways,.

When backed by adequate high-level support, the Stakeholder Council Model can bring governmental and private parties to the table to devise standards of trust for identity documents based on their quality. However, it remains to be seen whether this process can generate the needed degree of collaboration among the parties to achieve a useful and timely outcome. Experience will determine the conditions under which it is most effective.

This book, then, is a compilation of analyses that show the state of executive organization and management as the country gears for effective governmental action. Each chapter highlights a different area where government can and should be better organized and managed both generally and with respect to homeland security.

Notes

The author would like to acknowledge the many insights contributed by members of the NAPA Standing Panel on Executive Organization and Management, and especially the valuable comments provided by Murray Comarow, the panel's vice chair. The author is solely responsible for the contents of this introduction.

    1. One chapter in Seidman 1998 is titled "Coordination: The Search for the Philosopher's Stone." The Philosopher's Stone was a medieval fantasy that was believed to catalyze the transformation of lead into gold.

    2. These criteria can be applied to a variety of governmental and private organizations. Compare Stanton 2003 and NAPA 2004.

    3. Public authorities are described in Walsh 1978 and Mitchell 1999.

References

Bowsher, Charles A. 1988. "An Emerging Crisis: The Disinvestment of Government." James E. Webb Lecture. Washington, DC: National Academy of Public Administration, December 2.

Davis, John P. 1905. *Corporations: A Study of the Origin and Development of Great Business Combinations and of Their Relation to the Authority of the State.* New York: G.P. Putnam's Sons.

Goldstein, Mark L. 1992. *America's Hollow Government*. New York: McGraw-Hill.
Government Accountability Office (GAO). 2003. *Homeland Security: Challenges Facing the Department of Homeland Security in Balancing its Border Security and Trade Facilitation Missions*. Washington, DC: Government Accountability Office.
Louis K. Liggett Co. v. Lee. 1933. 233 U.S. 517 at 541 (1933) (dissent of Justice Brandeis).
Lyon, Leverett S., Myron W. Watkins, and Victor Abramson. 1939. *Government and Economic Life: Development and Current Issues of American Public Policy*, vol. I, chapter 4. Washington, DC: The Brookings Institution.
Mitchell, Jerry. 1999. *The American Experiment with Government Corporations*. New York: M.E. Sharpe.
National Academy of Public Administration (NAPA). 2004. *Grid West: An Assessment of the Proposed Governance Structure*. Washington, DC: NAPA.
Seidman, Harold. 1998. *Politics, Position and Power*, 5th ed. New York: Oxford University Press.
————. 2004. "Foreword," In *Making Government Manageable*, eds. Thomas H. Stanton and Benjamin Ginsberg, x. Baltimore, MD: Johns Hopkins University Press.
Stanton, Thomas H. 2003. "The Administration of Medicare." *Washington and Lee University Law Review* 60 (Fall). 1373–1416
U.S. Commission on National Security/21st Century. 2001. *Road Map for National Security: Imperative for Change*. Washington, DC: US Commission on National Security, xiv, 47.
Walsh, Annmarie Hauck. 1978. *The Public's Business: The Politics and Practices of Government Corporations*. Twentieth Century Fund. Cambridge, MA: MIT Press.
Wamsley, Barbara. 2004. "Technocracies: Can They Bell the Cat?" In *Making Government Manageable*, eds. Thomas H. Stanton and Benjamin Ginsberg, chapter 9. Baltimore, MD: Johns Hopkins University Press.
Williston, Samuel. 1888. "History of the Law of Business Corporations before 1800." *Harvard Law Review* 2.

Part 1

Public Administration since September 11

1

Moving toward More Capable Government

A Guide to Organizational Design

Thomas H. Stanton

The September 11 attack on the United States, followed by the poor governmental response to Hurricane Katrina four years later, turned issues of government capacity and organizational design into national priorities. Almost immediately after September 11, proposals to create a Department of Homeland Security and a new organization to take charge of airport security commanded the attention of policymakers. These officials faced urgent questions: (1) whether to create new entities, (2) whether these entities might be agencies or offices or nongovernmental organizations, and (3) how best to design the organization once the larger questions had been answered.

This guide for organizational design attempts to provide a framework to assist policymakers and others who may face such questions. As the dust settles after September 11, and now Katrina, it is likely that Americans will press for a more effective government than was required earlier. Sound organizational design is an important part of more capable federal, state, and local government.

When organizational change is appropriate, restructuring can have a profound and beneficial impact on the performance of an organization. On the other hand, many of the problems that beset government agencies may not be susceptible to being solved by organizational redesign. Reorganization alone will not solve many problems of interagency coordination. Poor leadership, unmotivated staff, insufficient resources, and glacial or irrational procedures also will not be overcome just by restructuring.

Box 1.1 shows six means of improving the performance of organizations that carry out public purposes. This guide addresses only the issue of the design and restructuring of an organization. Other approaches may prove more valuable in solving the particular types of problems that now face many agencies; also, they may be less disruptive than reorganization.

Box 1.1

Improving the Delivery of Public Services

- Redesign the Program
- Redesign Administrative Systems
- Provide Additional Resources
- Improve the Organization's Leadership
- Improve Coordination of Activities of Multiple Organizations
- Redesign the Organization's Structure (the subject of this chapter)

This introduction is the first section of this chapter. The second presents the context for the need for redesign of many parts of government. It looks at the nature and causes of stress on government organizations and programs that can make their current organizational structure inappropriate. The third presents a basic premise of organizational design: The key is to identify the organizational problem or problems that need to be remedied, and then to determine whether or not there is a beneficial and achievable organizational solution to that set of problems. The section identifies when reorganization might be helpful and also notes shortcomings of reorganization. The focus of this chapter is on the government agency or bureau rather than on the organizational structure within agencies or bureaus.

The fourth provides a guide to levels of analysis, from the need to obtain added managerial flexibility, to the desire to change the form of government organization, to the consideration of creating a private organization to carry out the intended public purposes. As a general rule, lower-level changes are easier to implement in less time.

The fifth presents a guide to analysis of private organizations that carry out public purposes. This section introduces the concept of the instrumentality, an organization that is not part of government and that carries out public purposes. Instrumentalities can take a variety of forms, including the for-profit company, the cooperative, and the nonprofit organization. For-profit federal instrumentalities include large shareholder-owned companies such as Fannie Mae and Freddie Mac, cooperatives such as the Farm Credit System, and nonprofits such as the American Red Cross. For-profit instrumentalities of state governments include investor-owned utility companies and state-chartered banks and thrift institutions. Nonprofit instrumentalities of state government include housing finance organizations and student loan secondary markets in some states, while in other states these functions may be carried out by agencies of state government rather than by instrumentalities. Although instrumentalities are private organizations, they carry out public purposes that are defined in federal or state law. If capacity has been a major issue confronting many government agencies, the question of accountability is critical for instrumentalities.

Unfortunately, government has lost much of its former capacity to improve the design of organizations and programs so that they might operate more effectively. For the federal government, neither the Executive Branch nor the Congress currently possesses the wealth of design talent that once existed to help policymakers and legislators create or update the legal structures that support effective administration and delivery of public services. The chapter concludes by recommending that the federal government take steps to improve its capacity to design effective organizations and programs as an essential step in improving the capacity of government.

Organizational design in government is often a political process, and a growing body of literature exists concerning the politics of organizational design (Zegart 1999; T. Moe 1989). As Harold Seidman states, "[D]ecisions on program design, institutional type, organizational jurisdiction, and management systems may well determine who will control and benefit from a program and, ultimately, whether national objectives are achieved" (Seidman 1998, 219).

This chapter does not deal with the politics of government design, except to note that the scope of any intended organizational transformation will involve considerations of the constituencies that favor or oppose particular changes. In chapter 3, Frederick Kaiser provides useful insights in that regard, with respect to creation of the Department of Homeland Security. Instead the purpose of this guide is more modest: to assure that policymakers have access to a conceptual framework that helps them to make wise decisions about organizational changes to enhance the capacity of government to perform well.

Government Organizations under Continuing Stress

Many government organizations today are falling behind in the effort to keep up with demand for their services. A mere mention of some of these services, such as medical care for the elderly, tax collection, and financing for low-income housing, helps validate the observation that many government agencies are being asked to meet increasing public needs with fewer resources. Not all agencies and programs are in decline, and some people would argue that—to the extent that the private sector is taking up the slack—not all of the decline is bad. Nonetheless, the trend is disturbing, especially in light of the new demands for increased national security since September 11, and for improved responses to natural disasters.

In architecture, form follows function. Similarly, in organizational design, form should follow purpose. Many government agencies and programs are under stress because government must carry out new purposes and functions while many old activities no longer appear appropriate. Issues of purpose are in flux in three different dimensions: (1) political disagreements about the proper role of government that can call into question the current purposes of a program or agency, (2) technological developments that can change the way that purposes are carried out, and (3) economic developments that can affect the need for government to carry out some purposes in the old ways.

Each of these effects makes itself felt differently. Issues of the proper role of government are reflected in the many pieces of legislation that have sought to increase the government's capacity to respond after the September 11 attack. These new proposals follow a quite different period in the 1980s and 1990s when many policymakers had suggested that Congress should zero out or privatize or devolve some or all of many agencies' existing program activities.

As of this writing, the public purposes of many agencies remain in flux. Policymakers still do not know, for example, how many agencies or programs have a significant role to play in assuring the national defense against a new form of warfare. For an agency with security responsibilities, such as the Immigration and Naturalization Service (INS), the increased priority placed on homeland security called its old organizational form into question. INS has now been reorganized within the Department of Homeland Security. For an agency without a clear security role, the mere fact that its purposes are called into question can have significant consequences, especially in the budgeting and appropriations process. If the Office of Management and Budget and congressional appropriators begin to question certain activities, they are likely to try to reduce their funding, in favor of higher-priority programs such as those that relate directly to national security.

Technology acts to take apart old purposes and ways of doing business, and put them back together in new ways. Driving forces of some technology-based systems include new economies of scale and the superiority of information-based technologies over older approaches. The economy of the Internet and toll-free (800) numbers means that government agencies often can provide more extensive service from centralized service centers compared to traditional face-to-face meetings at a local federal office; the availability of optical imaging and electronic data interchange similarly can make many paper filing systems—and the tasks of the people who maintain them—obsolete.

Finally, the economic context for many government activities is changing at a rapid pace. Many services that the federal government provides now find themselves threatened by new forms of competition. Thus, increased consumer use of electronic transactions is eroding the Postal Service's once profitable service in delivering bills and financial payments by mail. In one area of service delivery after another, private companies are able to use new technologies to skim off customers who would have been part of the government's customer base in earlier years.

The private sector also is adept at screening customers to attract the most profitable segments among consumers of power, housing, or financial services. Thus, automated underwriting systems allow private mortgage insurance companies to attract borrowers who formerly might have been served by the Federal Housing Administration through an FHA-insured mortgage. The screening process leaves government with a smaller customer base composed of borrowers that the private sector considers too costly to serve. For the agencies and programs that bear the brunt of such adverse selection, a downward spiral is possible, with diminished resources available to serve an increasingly needy segment of the population.

If an organization's form should follow its purposes and purposes are up for grabs in several major dimensions—political, technological, and economic—the results can be devastating for government agencies and programs that had been organized around old ways of doing business. It is not surprising that departments such as Housing and Urban Development (HUD) and agencies such as the Centers for Medicare and Medicaid Services (CMS) have been hammered by waves of change (Stanton 2003). The questions then become (1) whether redesign of the organization will solve the agency's most important problems, and (2) if so, what type of organizational redesign would be most beneficial.

The Decision to Change Organizational Structure

Deciding When a New Structure Is Appropriate

There are a number of sound reasons to create a new organization or to reorganize. These include the need (1) to combine related programs from disparate governmental units to provide an organizational focus and accountability for carrying out high-priority public purposes, (2) to help assure that information flows to the proper level of government for consideration and possible action, (3) to change policy emphasis and assure that resources are more properly allocated to support high-priority activities, and (4) to determine who controls and is accountable for certain governmental activities.

Consider each of these in turn.

Combining Related Programs

A panel study of the National Academy of Public Administration presented a useful set of questions to help decide when it might be beneficial to combine programs into a single department or agency (Jasper 1997):

- Are the agency's programs, along with other programs that might be added from other agencies, closely related in terms of achieving broad national goals?
- Would the combination of related programs improve service delivery? Would it save money, either for the taxpayers or for those affected by the programs? Would it prevent one constituency group or profession from dominating the agency?
- Does the agency warrant independent status, whether in the cabinet or not, as compared to other agencies?
- Would cabinet status improve the leadership, visibility, and public support for the programs?
- Does the public interest require that it remain in the government (even if many of its functions are contracted) or should it be devolved or privatized?

There are a number of success stories in this regard, including creation of the Department of Housing and Urban Development (HUD) and the Department of Transportation (DOT). The creation of the DOT as a cabinet agency was the result of careful analysis and twenty years of waiting until the conditions were right to bring together disparate programs from departments including Commerce (e.g., the Civil Aeronautics Administration) and Treasury (the Coast Guard), independent agencies (the Federal Aviation Administration) and commissions (the Civil Aeronautics Board and the Interstate Commerce Commission), and one government corporation (the St. Lawrence Seaway Development Corporation). Although the reorganization was a large-scale effort, the sound design of the new department (see Box 1.2) mitigated the disruption caused by the change. Alan Dean writes, "An executive department is usually called for when programs related to some definable government purpose become so numerous, so large, and so complex that an official of secretarial rank with enhanced access to the president is needed to provide effective oversight and coordination of program management" (Dean 2004, 157).

In stark contrast, it took just over a year to create a Department of Homeland Security on the basis of limited planning and analysis. On November 25, 2002, President Bush signed legislation to create a Department of Homeland Security. The new department includes a large number of organizations with responsibilities relating to homeland security, including major organizations such as the Coast Guard, the Border Patrol, the Customs Service, the Transportation Security Administration (TSA), the Federal Emergency Management Agency (FEMA), the Immigration and Naturalization Service (INS), and over a dozen smaller entities such as the Secret Service and the Animal and Plant Health Inspection Service of the U.S. Department of Agriculture.

The new Department of Homeland Security combined twenty-two federal agencies with 170,000 employees and a total budget of $37.5 billion. Based on the number of people, this is the second-largest department in the Cabinet, behind the Defense Department; in budget, it is fourth in size, behind Defense, Health and Human Services (HHS), and Education. The president explained that the purpose of the reorganization was, in his words, "not to increase the size of government, but to increase its focus and effectiveness." Although the purpose of the new department was to underscore the seriousness of the priority that the government assigns to homeland security, the design of the department does not yet assure its success in coordinating the myriad of homeland security functions within and outside of its organizational boundaries (Kettl 2004).

Assuring that Information Flows to the Proper Level
of Government

The creation of the position of the director of the Office of National Homeland Security in the White House immediately after September 11 is a classic example of this type of reorganization. The president sought to create in one place a focus for the information that would flow from several dozen federal agencies that, until September 11, had not necessarily emphasized issues of homeland security.

Many observers urged that the director's position be established formally by law to assure the accountability of the office to Congress and also to give it more strength in the inevitable turf battles that arise when government begins to focus on new urgent priorities. In this regard, the Office of National Homeland Security would come to resemble the Office of National Drug Control Policy (ONDCP), which was established by law to help focus the efforts of numerous agencies on the issue of drug control. Besides its position in the White House, the ONDCP has authority to review budgets of federal agencies to determine the extent that they are consistent with the antidrug policies of the president. In fact, the president chose to create an entirely new Department of Homeland Security with authority over a number of the functions relating to homeland security. Frederick Kaiser explores these issues more fully in Chapter 3.

Box 1.2

**The United States Department of Transportation:
A Well-Designed Department**

After World War II, the Office of Management and Organization of the Bureau of the Budget and the Hoover Commission began to consider the idea of creating a single department to consolidate transportation activities that were spread across numerous cabinet departments and independent agencies. When President Lyndon Johnson became interested in a legislative initiative to improve transportation, the political context was right for creation of the new department (Redford and Blisset 1981; Dean undated).

The Department of Transportation Act of 1966 embodied a carefully designed structure that built upon many of the constituent units that were transferred from other parts of the government. The statutory constituents were largely based on modes of transportation. They originally included the Federal Aviation Administration, the Coast Guard, the Federal Highway Administration, the Federal Railroad Administration, and the St. Lawrence Seaway Development Corporation. Later additions included the Federal Transit Administration and the Federal Maritime Administration. Also, the National Highway Transportation Safety Administration was separated from the Federal Highway Administration, where it had been located for a short time. Except for the Coast Guard, which was transferred to the Department of Homeland Security (DHS), principal operations of the Department of Transportation are conducted through these administrations (Dean 2004).

The secretary of transportation is the president's chief adviser on transportation policy. The secretary sets policies for the administrations, supported by the deputy secretary and by several assistant secretaries. Currently there are assistant secretaries for transportation policy, aviation and international affairs, governmental affairs, budget and programs, and administration. While the law specifies the responsibilities and powers of the modal administrations, the assistant secretaries function solely in a staff capacity; they do not have authority to direct the administrators who head each administration.

The secretary is free to change the duties and functions of the assistant secretaries. This allows the department to adjust to changing circumstances and priorities over the years. The statutory structure of DOT conforms to

(continued)

Box 1.2 *(continued)*

the precepts urged by the NAPA Standing panel on Executive Organization and Management: "Legislation establishing executive departments or agencies or addressing aspects of general management should to the maximum feasible extent avoid the prescription of statutory detail and should empower the agency head to make the internal arrangements best suited to the effective execution of the laws" (EOM Panel 1997).

The strength of the administration-based operating structure of the department is that each of the administrations possesses the staff and budget resources to carry out its mission. By contrast to some other departments, notably the Department of Energy with its tightly centralized structure, each of the larger DOT administrations has the ability to manage its own systems for personnel, procurement, and legal support, for example, according to policies that often may be set by the parent department. The missions of the modal administrations are different enough to merit operations through distinct organizational units. For example, the Federal Aviation Administration has quite different responsibilities and activities from the Federal Transit Administration, the Federal Rail Administration, or the St. Lawrence Seaway Development Corporation.

On the other hand, the autonomy of the modal administrations has had disadvantages too. It has taken years to improve intermodal transportation activities so that, for example, rail and urban transit systems link with airports in a manner that is familiar to travelers in Europe. Successive intermodal transportation acts have helped to address this concern, especially by promoting cooperation between the Federal Highway Administration and the Federal Transit Administration.

After September 11, the government enacted the Transportation and Airport Security Act, creating a new Transportation Security Administration (TSA) headed by an under secretary of transportation for security. Closer study of the structure of the department instead would have led to creation of an administrator for transportation security in DOT, and the lodging of greater power in the secretary, with authority to delegate. This provides a useful lesson in organizational design: be sure to study the organizational context before proposing changes. Knowledge of the context can help to prevent confusion and problems in implementing organizational changes. In this case the effects were short lived because the TSA was transferred to the Department of Homeland Security when DHS was created in 2002.

Placing Policy Emphasis on High-Priority Activities

Many times, the creation of a major new program may be accompanied by a proposed change in organization. Thus, the Clinton administration successfully sought creation of the Corporation for National and Community Service as a part of the proposal to create AmeriCorps. The Bush administration first approved creation of the new Transportation Security Administration in the DOT as a response to the events of September 11 and the weaknesses revealed in aviation security. Later the Bush administration also urged creation of the new Department of Homeland Security. It is not certain that a new organization was needed in any of these instances; however, the creation of a new organization was a part of the emphasis given to the new activities and a way to demonstrate the administration's commitment to assuring that resources would support those activities.

The creation of the Office of Federal Housing Enterprise Oversight (OFHEO) as the safety and soundness regulator of Fannie Mae and Freddie Mac took place in part to demonstrate a new government priority on safety and soundness in the aftermath of the savings and loan debacle and also as an implicit statement that the regulatory responsibilities of the new office would have a higher priority and would gain greater resources than had been the case earlier (Stanton 2004). Subsequent management and accounting failures at both Fannie Mae and Freddie Mac are likely to persuade the government to create a new stronger regulator of the two government-sponsored enterprises (GSEs), although that has not happened as of this writing.

Determining Control and Accountability

The creation of the Transportation Security Administration represented a significant shift in control and responsibility for aviation security, from the airlines that had hired low-cost low-performance contractors, to direct federal administration of the airport and airplane security functions of some 28,000 officials in a newly created organization. The debate in Congress concerned whether the government should contract for security services or whether federal employees should carry them out. In either event, there was substantial agreement on creating a Transportation Security Administration to assure that the government, rather than private airlines, controlled and was accountable for aviation security.

The reorganization of the U.S. Post Office Department also represented a change in control and accountability of important aspects of administration. The Postal Reorganization Act of 1970 transformed the organization from a cabinet department into an organization with the attributes of a wholly owned government corporation. This changed the method of financing and allowed the U.S. Postal Service to exercise increased control over funding and operations. The new law also ended congressional control over appointments of postmasters. It depoliticized appointments, promotions, and management decisions, thereby allowing the USPS to increase its control over personnel and to make significant gains in productivity. The law also created a postal ratemaking process that, with all of its faults, is superior to the congressional ratemaking that was in place before 1970. The reorganization thus shifted accountability for major decisions concerning rates and appointments from the Congress to the U.S. Postal Service and the new Postal Rate Commission. Even though the reorganization was flawed in some respects, notably the creation of the Postal Rate Commission, it did provide a substantial increase in capacity for the U.S. Postal Service that served the public well for many years (Comarow 2004).

A very difficult reorganization to accomplish politically was the Goldwater-Nichols Department of Defense Reorganization Act of 1986. That act transformed the Joint Chiefs of Staff (JCS) from a weak coordinating body into a source of influence that could promote serious interservice cooperation. The act accomplished this by (1) increasing the authority of the JCS chairman, (2) improving the quality of the JCS staff by requiring joint service for promotion to flag or general officer rank, and (3) granting unified and specified combatant commanders (CINCs) increased autonomy and authority over their joint field commands. Observers attribute a significant increase in U.S. military capabilities, including combined service operations in the Persian Gulf War, to the 1986 Goldwater-Nichols Act and the reform of the JCS (Zegart 1999).

In summary then, while creation of new organizations such as the DOT and reorganizations such as the Postal Reorganization Act of 1970 or the 1986 Goldwater-Nichols Act sometimes may be difficult to enact, they can have substantial positive benefits so long as the change in organizational structure solves a real problem that had been impeding more effective performance.

Fitting the Solution to the Problem

In organizational design, the key is to fit the appropriate organizational form to the purposes to be achieved. This is not always easy. Policymakers frequently reach for organizational answers that may compound rather than alleviate issues of capacity, including the creation of governing boards. This happened to the Internal Revenue Service in 1998, for example. Policymakers often find ready constituencies for such organizational "quick fixes" that can complicate rather than solve the fundamental problems that beset an agency or program. Harold Seidman and Alan Dean have pointed out that there is no organization that cannot be made worse through a poor reorganization.

Many problems do not have solutions that involve organizational design. Elements such as leadership, quality of personnel and systems, level of funding, and freedom from unwise legal and regulatory constraints may be as important as organizational structure in the search for solutions to many problems that confront government agencies and programs.

As Frederick Kaiser points out in chapter 3, problems of interagency coordination, in an operational sense, sometimes may require quite different solutions than a consolidation or interagency reorganization does. Thus, a major concern behind the recommendation to create the Department of Homeland Security was that so many of our border agencies—including Customs, the Coast Guard, and the Immigration and Naturalization Service—did not share common communications systems or databases with one another, or with the FBI, the CIA, and other involved agencies, that would allow them to exchange information promptly and to assemble that information into patterns that could signal the likely entry into the United States of dangerous people or cargo (Flynn 2001). The creation of a common Department of Homeland Security to contain some but not all of these organizations is likely to prove much less effective than a more straightforward concerted effort to design the appropriate systems along with the provision of adequate resources, over a period of years, to develop the needed systems and integrate them into day-to-day operations of all of the relevant frontline agencies, including state and local government and private organizations, that must help to detect and respond to major types of terrorist attack.

Agencies also may seek to reorganize based on the belief that they can increase their ability to carry out their responsibilities. Budget and staff cuts have turned many agencies into hollow organizations. The United States Commission on National Security/21st Century found that the Department of State was "starved for resources" (U.S. Commission on National Security 2002, 47). Moreover, "The Customs Service, the Border Patrol, and the Coast Guard are all on the verge of being overwhelmed by the mismatch between their growing duties and their mostly static resources" (U.S. Commission on National Security 2002, 16).

The problem is not confined to agencies and departments with national security responsibilities. In 1999, a bipartisan group of fourteen health care experts published an open letter calling for increased resources to be devoted to the Health Care Financing Administration (now renamed the Centers for Medicare and Medicaid Services): "[N]o private insurer, after subtracting its marketing costs and profit, would ever attempt to manage such large and complex insurance programs with so small an administrative budget" (Butler et al. 1999).

The United States Commission on National Security/21st Century stated the general problem in stark terms: "As it enters the 21st century, the United States finds itself on the brink of an unprecedented crisis in competence in government. . . . Both civilian and military institutions face growing challenges . . . in recruiting and retaining America's most promising talent" (U.S. Commission on National Security 2002, xiv).

Reorganization is not a substitute for adequate resources in areas such as budget, staffing, or systems. Consolidation of activities into a new larger organization, for example, may not help an agency obtain greater resources. On the other hand, carefully targeted organizational redesign sometimes can enhance the capacity of a governmental organization by fitting the structure more closely to an agency's mission and changing the method of financing. That was the case with the change in financing of the U.S. Postal Service that resulted from the Postal Reorganization Act of 1970 and its establishment as an organization with the attributes of a wholly owned government corporation.

Organizational redesign also may make a substantial contribution to enhancing an agency's flexibility, for example, by removing layers of review and delegating responsibility for personnel, contracting, and budgeting to subordinate organizational units. In the mid-1990s the Federal Housing Administration sought to become more autonomous through transformation into a wholly owned government corporation. That initiative failed because of the opposition of key constituencies. Had it gone into effect, the FHA might have gained substantial flexibility in its operations. Indeed, as is discussed below, the government corporation is an especially flexible organizational form that is intended to be able to respond to market demand for an agency's services.

On the other hand, many issues of flexibility can be addressed without going through a process of major organizational redesign. Simple delegations of authority, for example from a department to its major subordinate organizations, can relieve many agencies of layers of review that add little value to the quality of staffing, procurement, or budget decisions. The President's Management Agenda of 2002 adopted a focused approach. It called upon agencies to design and implement removal of redundant layers from their organizational hierarchies, although this recommendation does not seem to have been implemented.

Life cycle is also an important issue to consider in the design or redesign of government organizations. One issue is capture. As Marver Bernstein (1955) and others have pointed out, some agencies (Bernstein wrote about independent regulatory commissions) are susceptible to capture by particular constituencies. The result can be to direct the activities of an agency or program to serve selected purposes in a different manner than if underrepresented interests had a more effective voice. Thus, as Harold Seidman observes, when designing an organization it is useful to consider whether its constituency is likely to be broad based, or whether it will represent narrow interests potentially antithetical to some of the public purposes to be accomplished.

Another life-cycle issue might be called ossification. Some agencies gain and maintain so much autonomy that they lose sensitivity to their external environment. Robert Mueller, the head of the FBI, has been actively trying to address this problem. Much of the frustration of the United States Commission on National Security/21st Century at the lack of coordination among agencies with security responsibilities would seem to relate to this issue. Amy Zegart, who studied the organizational design of the CIA, Joint Chiefs of Staff, and National Security Council, argues that national security organizations may find themselves beset by issues of bureaucratic "turf" that can be even more substantial than those among domestic agencies of government.

Harold Seidman notes the importance of organizational culture in organizational design. He asks two questions: (1) What is the culture and tradition of the administering department or agency? and (2) Will it provide an environment favorable to program growth or will it stunt development?

It can be difficult to anticipate and address issues of life cycle when creating or redesigning an organization. Nonetheless, these issues can be essential in determining the quality of an agency's performance at critical moments such as the weeks and months after September 11. They deserve thought as a part of the process of organizational design.

Selecting an Appropriate Organizational Form

Once policymakers have identified the intended goals and purposes of an agency, they can look to existing organizations for possible models that they might adapt as a goal for the agency's transformation. A range of organizational forms can be constructed, from the usual government department or agency at one end to the completely private firm at the other.[1] Intermediate points along the organizational range would include independent agencies, wholly owned government corporations, and private instrumentalities of government. Note however that precise distinctions sometimes can be elusive. The political process tends to generate a variety of organizational types, such as the Smithsonian Institution or the Federal Reserve System, that do not fall clearly into any single organizational category.

Figure 1.1 presents a continuum of organizational forms ranging from public (i.e., governmental) to private. This continuum includes some of the

Figure 1.1   **The Continuum of Organizational Forms**

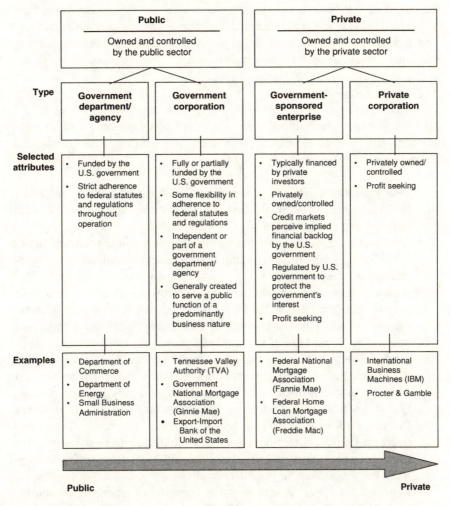

Source: Adapted from *Government Corporation: Profiles of Existing Government Corporations* (General Accounting Office, GAO/GGD-96-14).

intermediate types of organization, such as the government corporation and the government-sponsored enterprise; other forms, and especially other forms of government instrumentality, could have been included as well.

For officials of an agency that is enmeshed in restrictive laws and regulations and limited by scarce resources, it is inviting to dream of the organizational freedom that is enjoyed by entities such as the Federal Reserve System or the Tennessee Valley Authority. Similarly, when a public priority such as airline security suddenly becomes urgent, some policymakers may grasp at the model of a government corporation or even a government-sponsored enterprise to provide the organizational answers. However, caution is merited. Few federal purposes enjoy either the policy justification or the political constituency to take on such organizational forms.

The Costs of Reorganization

Besides providing benefits, even a good reorganization can involve costs. Herbert N. Jasper, an expert on government organization, has summarized some of those limitations (Jasper 1997):

- Reorganization can be costly and disruptive; it may immobilize an agency for one to three years while the proposal is being formulated, debated, enacted, and implemented.
- Abolishing a government department or agency without terminating or consolidating the programs administered by the organization may cost more than preserving it.
- Although there may be benefits from reorganization, there may also be losses—not just costs. That is, reorganization is a way to emphasize certain values or goals, but this means downgrading other values or goals. The Coast Guard, for example, has many responsibilities—for safety, search and rescue, maritime pollution, high seas fishing, and oceanographic research, for example—that have little to do with border security. According to one rough estimate only perhaps one-fifth of Coast Guard functions may relate directly to homeland security. Merging the Coast Guard into the Department of Homeland Security thus risked downgrading the other important Coast Guard functions in the effort to upgrade border security. These issues require careful analysis and judgment before making an organizational change.
- Reorganization per se seldom saves money. For example, combining two executive departments, without other actions, would save little more than the salaries of a handful of presidential appointees and their immediate staffs. Often program redesign can be much more cost effective than reorganization.
- Efficiency, cost savings, and improved service can best be accomplished by program simplification or consolidation, rather than by merely vesting the authorities of two or more agencies in a single one. On the other hand, vesting overlapping functions in a single agency may permit the agency head to develop sound legislative proposals to rationalize the related functions.

Some of the costs of organizing the DHS, involving tragic consequences, were seen in the failure of the Federal Emergency Management Agency (FEMA) to respond to the destruction of New Orleans by Hurricane Katrina and the subsequent flooding. The reduction of FEMA from a cabinet-level agency to a small part of the new DHS, combined with a shift in emphasis to homeland security from FEMA's mission of responding to natural disasters, demoralized FEMA staff and led to an exodus of capable people from the agency. When Katrina hit, FEMA had become a shadow of the effective agency that it once was.

This problem of downgrading other important agency missions was foreseen before the creation of DHS. The author of this chapter testified before a Senate committee in October 2001, for example, that:

> Merging of disparate organizations such as the Federal Emergency Management Agency, Customs, the Border Patrol, and the Coast Guard, will increase the priority that national security is given in these organizations. On the other hand, each of these agencies has important functions that do not relate to national security that must be considered in any reorganization proposal. (Stanton 2001)

In the case of the Coast Guard, the reorganization act protected the Coast Guard's performance of those other missions; in the case of FEMA, its absorption into the new department meant downgrading FEMA's ability to deal with a natural disaster. The reorganized FEMA was instructed to give the highest priority to dealing with a homeland security event, the mission of the new department, rather than retaining its capability to deal with a hurricane such as Katrina.

Executive reorganization proposals often fail because they would lead some to propose corresponding revisions in congressional committee jurisdictions. On occasion, deference to jurisdictional issues has led to the need for an agency appointee to be confirmed by two different Senate committees; this is preferable to trying to change lines of authority within the Congress, which is politically very difficult.

Finding Organizational Solutions: Government Departments and Agencies

When initial analysis indicates that an organizational solution may be appropriate for the problem at hand, it may be useful to continue the analysis through different levels of organizational concern. This design guide can only begin to highlight some of the matters that must be considered in finding solutions to problems caused by flawed organizational structure.

Box 1.3

Levels of Analysis for Government Organizations

- What operational flexibilities does the organization require?
- If the organization is governmental, where should it be located?
- What governance structure is appropriate?
- If a single administrator heads an agency, should there be a fixed term?
- If the organization is a government agency, should it be a government corporation?
- If the agency is not a government corporation, should its funding be changed in any other way?
- Should the organization be part of government or private?

However, accepting that this chapter must adopt a high level of generality, some observations can help to illuminate the issues and tradeoffs that must be considered.

Some problems are larger than others, and organizational design needs to take this into account. In many, but not all, cases, the smaller the organizational change that will solve the most pressing problems, the easier the change may be to implement. One useful approach is to consider a series of questions that can help guide the search for an appropriate organizational solution. As can be seen in Box 1.3, the questions start with the most common issues of lack of resources, capacity, and managerial flexibility, and move upward to the highest level of question, whether the organization should be located in the public or private sector. This section looks at options for governmental organizations. The following section looks at options for organizations in the private sector that carry out public purposes.

Consider each question in turn.

What Operational Flexibilities Does the Organization Require?

Over the years, governmental organizations have become enmeshed in a web of legal restrictions that combine to limit their ability to carry out their missions. Some of these restrictions result from program failures that policymakers then address through tight financial controls that begin to impede program operations far beyond the scope of the original problem. Other restrictions come about when a crosscutting law inadvertently covers programs for which it is not suitable. The Federal Credit Reform Act, which requires complex accounting on the basis of annual appropriations, applies by its terms also to financially self-sustaining government corporations that are supposed to achieve operating flexibility through multiyear budgeting. The result of this otherwise beneficial law is to force some government corporations into the constraints of funding through the annual appropriations process, which is counterproductive for this organizational form.

The Bush administration recognizes the importance of addressing legal constraints that may not add value to the operations of a particular organization. The President's Management Agenda for fiscal year 2002 proposed legislation that would create expedited procedures so that the administration could submit requests for legislative relief that could be addressed promptly by the Congress.

The Clinton administration also recognized this problem. One proposal of the Vice President's National Performance Review was to create a new organizational form, known as the performance-based organization, or PBO. Only two PBOs were enacted into law, the Office of Student Financial Assistance of the Department of Education and the Patent and Trademark Office of the Department of Commerce. In practical effect for many agencies, the consideration of PBO status involved an invitation to obtain needed management flexibilities, especially in personnel actions and contracting, in return for a commitment to achieving performance goals.

For the Office of Student Financial Assistance, the conversion to PBO status has provided an opportunity to reorganize the office and to experiment with new contracting approaches. On the other hand, the creation of a PBO has proved tricky in one major respect. The PBO concept is premised on the assumption that policy issues, which remain with the larger department, can be separated from operations, which are the province of the PBO. Unless designed correctly, the details of a PBO statute can create bureaucratic fault lines between the PBO and its parent department that create tensions and confuse rather than streamline organizational relationships. Both current PBOs would seem to manifest this difficulty.

For many government agencies, the achievement of operating flexibilities will not require such a large-scale redesign of the organization. Again the solution must fit the problem. An organizational solution is not appropriate merely to alleviate some statutory or departmental constraint that impedes effective operations. Rather, as the President's Management Agenda for FY 2002 suggests, a more targeted solution is called for, such as specific improvements in administrative or program delivery systems or perhaps some form of de-layering of the department to remove redundancies in tasks between the larger department and the subordinate agency. Congress recently has shown itself open to providing increasing numbers of excepted service positions for agencies that otherwise might not be able to recruit needed specialists with important technical or financial skills, for example. In obtaining such relief, it is wise to consider the admonition of public administration expert Ronald Moe, who counsels that—as with organizational redesign—targeted relief should rest upon well-considered principles rather than a simple desire to rid oneself of constraints that may have been intended to promote accountability in the operations of government as a whole (Moe 2004).

If the Organization Is Governmental, Where Should It Be Located?

As a general rule, it is preferable to link a governmental organization to a cabinet department, rather than leaving it independent. That said, organizational change might be appropriate when an activity becomes an orphan within its cabinet department. Competition among organizations within a department can deprive an agency or activity of access to funding, personnel, contracts, or other needed resources. This was a problem for the U.S. Coast Guard, for example, when it was a part of the Treasury Department. Once the agency transferred to the then-new Department of Transportation, the Coast Guard underwent a significant transformation in role and mission. As the United States Commission on National Security/21st Century properly pointed out, after some years the Coast Guard once again became neglected in the competition for resources, this time within the Department of Transportation.

A strong cabinet secretary can defend the department against encroachment from outside forces. By contrast, an independent agency cannot call on a larger department to try to offset the pull of narrow interests that may have influence over the relevant congressional subcommittees. Independent agencies may have other difficulties as well. With exceptions, such as the Social Security Administration, NASA, and the Small Business Administration, Congress may place a board structure at the top of an independent agency. Thus, independent agencies with operating responsibilities, such as the Export-Import Bank of the United States, the Tennessee Valley Authority, the Pension Benefit Guaranty Corporation, and the Federal Retirement Thrift Investment Board, all are governed by boards of directors. In most cases the creation of a board reduces rather than enhances the capacity and accountability of a government agency.

What Governance Structure Is Appropriate?

As a general rule, a single administrator rather than a multimember board best governs a federal agency. An agency governed by a board can lose capacity in several ways. The process of filling political appointments can be very slow. When seats on a board remain vacant, an agency can find its activities constrained by the inability to obtain a quorum to vote on important matters.

Harmful vacancies also can occur if a board consists of ex officio members who are too busy to attend regular board meetings. Alternatively, ex officio members of a government board will send subordinates who may lack the authority to act on their own. The Pension Benefit Guaranty Corporation (PBGC), for example, is supposed to be governed by a board consisting of three cabinet secretaries. Virtually none of these secretaries has the time or inclination to attend meetings of the PBGC board. Instead, the secretaries routinely send subordinates who lack the power to vote or otherwise act for the PBGC without obtaining guidance from their individual departments. This can greatly impair the ability of a board to serve as a forum for exchanging views to arrive at a consensus on an issue of importance to the organization that the board is supposed to guide.

As a general rule, the board structure in government functions much less effectively than a board of directors in the private sector. Members of the board of directors of a private corporation have a fiduciary responsibility to represent the interests of shareholders, and often hold a financial stake in the company. This creates a significant incentive to come to agreement about the desired direction for the organization. By contrast, members of a government board have no such incentive to act in a collaborative fashion. Indeed, the appointees to a government board are likely to have divergent views on some major issues. The lack of a working consensus can create delay and impede the ability of agency managers to act in the best interests of the organization and its mission.

Problems also can arise if appointments to a government board do not possess the requisite backgrounds, experience, or stature. This issue can be addressed by writing some minimal qualifications into the authorizing statute, but such language still does not assure high-quality appointments.

The board structure can impede accountability of a government organization. Without any one person who is fully responsible for decisions, board members and the agency's senior managers all can assign blame to each other for parts of a discredited decision or for inaction.

This said, there are some times when a board structure is appropriate or even necessary for a government agency. Multimember boards are found in some regulatory agencies. For regulatory agencies, and in contrast to operating agencies, some consider the fact of divergent opinions among board members to be helpful in assuring the fairness of a decision.

Multimember boards also are helpful in insulating some agencies from potential political interference in their operations. Here the Board of Governors of the U.S. Postal Service and the Federal Retirement Thrift Investment Board come to mind. In both cases, the board is charged with appointing the chief executive of the agency. The insertion of a multimember board between the CEO and the political process is considered valuable in helping to insulate the agency's operations from the kind of untoward political intervention that characterized the Post Office Department, for example, before its reorganization after 1970.

If a single administrator heads an agency, should there be a fixed term?

Generally, the preferred choice is to allow the president of the United States to appoint the agency head and to have the appointee serve at the pleasure of the president. The key issue in deciding on a fixed term is whether the position involves significant policy decisions or whether its functions tend to be more technical and nonpartisan in nature. If the position involves issues of policy, then there are costs to keeping someone in office who has no rapport with a new administration. Thus, the head of one organization, who nominally served for a fixed term of years, was asked to resign several times during a two-year period after the Bush administration came into office. Although the position is a presidential appointment and therefore the president could dismiss the incumbent, the person declined to depart amicably; this contributed to a state of considerable friction between the organization and the leadership of the larger department.

On the other hand, if a position is largely technical and nonpartisan, for example in a position relating to national security, then there may be some benefits to a fixed term. Most important, the government doesn't lose a skilled professional just because a new president takes office. There is time to arrange a more careful transition or to reappoint the incumbent.

If the organization is a government agency, should it be a government corporation?

One kind of government agency deserves special attention. The government corporation is an organizational form that can be quite helpful in supporting the operations of an agency that provides business-type services (similar to the U.S. Postal Service, mentioned above). President Harry Truman, in his 1948 budget message, stated the criteria for creating a government corporation: "Experience indicates that the corporate form of organization is peculiarly adapted to the administration of government programs which are predominately of a commercial character—those which are revenue producing, are at least potentially self-sustaining and involve a large number of business-type transactions with the public. In their business operations such programs require greater flexibility than the customary type of appropriations budget ordinarily permits" (U.S. House of Representatives 1948).

The essence of the government corporation is its ability to keep its accounts and manage its affairs on a businesslike basis. In other words, a government corporation that is financially self-sustaining does not need annual appropriations; it funds itself instead from revenues that it generates from its activities. The U.S. Postal Service sells mail delivery services, the Tennessee Valley Authority sells power, and the Government National Mortgage Association (Ginnie Mae) charges a fee for guaranteeing mortgage-backed securities. The Government Accountability Office has issued a legal opinion indicating that wholly owned government corporations are exempt from the limitations imposed by many of the laws that apply to agencies funded by appropriations (GAO, 1979).

State and local governments in the United States have established literally thousands of government authorities and enterprises, especially in areas such as transportation (e.g., airport, highway, or port authorities), power production, and finance (e.g., housing finance agencies or student loan finance agencies). They are supposed to be financially self-sustaining from revenues that they derive from operations. Often the states establish these organizations as a way to avoid constitutional limitations upon borrowing. When they issue bonds to finance construction and other capital-intensive activities, these organizations may benefit from a federal government subsidy in the form of the federal tax exemption, and possibly a state and local exemption of income on the bonds from taxation. The result is to lower borrowing costs substantially, so long as the particular enterprise manages itself in a financially prudent way or otherwise maintains its credit rating (Mitchell 1999).

Some government corporations, such as the Federal Deposit Insurance Corporation (FDIC) and the Tennessee Valley Authority, benefit from considerable autonomy.[2] Other government corporations, such as Ginnie Mae, the Pension Benefit Guaranty Corporation, and the St. Lawrence Seaway Development Corporation, have less autonomy in their operations. Even these less autonomous corporations benefit from some management flexibilities that noncorporate government agencies would envy.

At the state and local level, independent authorities have played to mixed reviews. On the one hand, for example, Robert Moses constructed bridge and highway and development authorities in New York State that built impressive infrastructure over several decades from the 1930s to the 1960s. On the other hand, these authorities often were immune from democratic processes, which meant that neither ordinary citizens nor state and local officials were able to exert sufficient influence to deflect potentially disruptive or unwise projects.[3] A costly and misguided effort by the Tennessee Valley Authority to engage in a large-scale nuclear power program, including many facilities that failed to be completed or even built, would seem to be a federal example of this problem.

When a government corporation is appropriate for the intended mission, the organization is able to develop an institutional culture that can be quite businesslike. For example, a survey in the early 1990s of federal agencies that provide loans and guarantees showed that government corporations had established a practice of obtaining clean audit opinions year after year. These corporations—Ginnie Mae, the Overseas Investment Corporation (OPIC), and the Export-Import Bank of the United States (ExImBank)—achieved an organizational tone and operational effectiveness that allowed them to use relatively small staffs to manage significant programs. By contrast, other federal credit agencies at the time were unable to generate auditable financial statements and often were unable to achieve the businesslike culture that characterized the government corporations.

On the other hand, when a government corporation is an inappropriate organizational form, the result can be confusion. Inappropriate designation as a government corporation complicated accounting, budgeting, and reporting for the Corporation for National and Community Service, which does not conduct commercial activities and is not financially self-sustaining. Rather, it is a government agency that funds itself entirely from annual appropriations. The designation of the agency as a government corporation was intended to give the organization a corporate aura, rather than because the design was appropriate. As a result of the designation, however, the agency initially was forced to keep its books both as a federal agency based upon appropriated funds and also as a government corporation.

If the agency is not a government corporation, should its funding be changed in any other way?

Especially for agencies that obtain revenues from their activities, changes in funding present an attractive way to obtain management flexibility. On the other hand, annual budget and appropriations rules provide accountability; policymakers must be careful that they do not free an agency from much of its accountability if they change the funding rules.

Agencies have obtained a variety of funding changes. The United States Mint obtained authority to retain its revenues and make its expenditures out of a special public enterprise fund. This fund, similar to the authority of government corporations to retain and utilize revenues without regard to fiscal year limitation, has provided the mint with significant flexibility. The mint may pay major expenses from the fund, including the cost of metals used in coin production, fabrication and transportation costs, costs related to research and development, purchases of equipment, and capital improvements. This is a form of flexibility not available to most agencies.

Some other federal agencies have managed to obtain more extensive exemptions from federal budget and appropriations rules. The federal bank regulators, for example, obtain their funding from fees that are imposed by law on the banks that they supervise. The bank regulatory agencies are authorized to deposit these fees in accounts outside of the Treasury and to retain and use them without regard to annual limitations. The U.S. Constitution states, in Article I, Section 9, that, "No money shall be drawn from the Treasury, but in consequence of appropriations made by law. . . ." The ability to keep and use their funds outside of the Treasury thus helps to exempt the federal bank regulators from the annual appropriations process.

Budget considerations have driven a number of organizational transformations. In 1968 Fannie Mae was converted from a government corporation into a government-sponsored enterprise, in large part as a way to remove the corporation from the "vagaries" of the budget situation (Weaver 1968). Given the way that many federal agencies today find themselves squeezed for administrative expenses such as salaries, overhead, travel, and training, one can imagine that off-budget funding is very attractive.

On the other hand, the appropriations process serves the critical function of allocating scarce budget resources across competing public purposes. As some federal agencies obtain relief from budget limitations, other agencies may find themselves squeezed even more. This means that, in many cases, proposals to remove agencies from either the budget or the appropriations processes (1) may be bad public policy and (2) may run into substantial political resistance. Policymakers should not assume that changes in the funding structure for an agency would be easy to achieve.

Should the organization be part of government or private?

From the perspective of organizational design, the choice between creating a governmental or private entity raises issues beyond pure economics. First, some inherently governmental functions, and especially those that involve the exercise of discretion in applying government authority or making decisions for the government, are not suitable candidates for delegation to a private organization (GAO 1989).

Second, if the government turns an activity over to the private sector, the performance of that activity will change in response to the incentives created by private ownership. Investor-owned companies will seek to carry out only those activities that are profitable. Thus, when the United States converted the U.S. Enrichment Corporation into a private shareholder-owned company, that company behaved quite differently from a government agency in adopting economy measures that conflict with some of the public policy commitments that the organization made when it became private. As is discussed below, policy considerations may suggest that some privatizations might better be turned over to nonprofit or cooperative organizations rather than to investor-owned companies; the performance of these organizations too will differ from government agencies.

Third, as attorney Dan Guttman, an authority on public-private relationships and privatization, points out in chapter 10, the choice between a governmental or private entity to carry out public purposes determines the rules that will apply to the organization. Most government agencies are subject to a range of procedural and due process requirements, for example, that do not bind private organizations (Guttman 2000; Gilmour and Jensen 1998).

Thus, the choice between using a governmental or private entity to carry out public purposes involves tradeoffs. On the one hand, capacity could be significantly greater for the private organization. Government departments and agencies are subject to a panoply of controls over organizational inputs. These controls include prescriptions about staffing and personnel processes, procurement and contracting, and—above all—budget and other resource limitations. Subjecting an agency to input controls, especially over resources, means that, with exceptions such as some government corporations, its capacity will be limited compared to many private companies.

On the other hand, accountability of a government organization to Congress and the Executive Branch is fairly direct; by contrast, the private organization can exert influence through the political process so that private instrumentalities, authorized by government to carry out public purposes, are likely to play a major role in determining the nature of their own authorized activities. Thus, Ginnie Mae, a government agency, is a subordinate part of the Department of Housing and Urban Development; by contrast, Fannie Mae, a privately owned company, is one of the most influential financial institutions in the United States (Stanton and Moe 2002).

Private Instrumentalities of Government

The instrumentality of government is an organizational category that includes a variety of nongovernmental organizations that carry out public purposes as defined by law. The instrumentality is an important category for organizational design because efforts to privatize government functions can involve

Box 1.4

Governance of an Operating Agency:
The Choice between a Single Administrator and a Board

The National Academy of Public Administration submitted a report to the Congressional Panel on Social Security Organization in which it stated that: "[T]o the extent that management needs dictate the form of leadership, it is strongly advocated that a single commissioner be appointed and that the use of a board be avoided as neither necessary nor desirable."

The report made the following points about the choice between a single administrator and a board:

1. In management terms, the most important point is that it is almost universally agreed that single administrators are far more effective and accountable than multiperson boards or commissions, bipartisan or otherwise.

2. Again in management terms, a board is not a necessity and is not desirable. Even if a board's role is carefully defined and its membership carefully selected, history strongly suggests that it is almost impossible to keep such a board from interjecting itself into the management of the organization that it governs. Although such involvement is occasionally useful, the likelihood is that it would confuse and undercut the authority of the agency head, creating conflict for the staff, and becoming another layer of management that adds little if any value. Furthermore, the composition of such boards becomes an issue in itself, and all too often breeds preoccupation with diversionary issues of balance, representativeness, or political fairness, rather than the ability of such boards to contribute to the success of the program.

3. Where boards attempt to manage programs directly without an authoritative manager (administrator, executive director) they have proved most often to be ineffective (NAPA 1984).

creation of an instrumentality, or use of an existing organization as an instrumentality, to carry out purposes that previously were carried out by a government agency.

Private instrumentalities of the federal government are privately owned and managed. As with government organizations, the features of private instrumentalities involve their capacity to carry out public purposes, their accountability for carrying out those purposes, and the life cycle of the organization. Like government, and unlike ordinary private firms, private government instrumentalities are permitted to engage only in those activities that are authorized by their enabling legislation. Table 1.1 summarizes some of the distinctions among government agencies, government instrumentalities, and completely private companies. The distinctions are not always sharply drawn. As Ronald Moe points out, the law creates many hybrid organizations that resist easy categorization (Moe 2001).

For purposes of clarity, one should hasten to add that the typical private firm that contracts with government does not become an instrumentality merely because of the contractual relationship with a government agency. Rather, an instrumentality is a private company, cooperative, or nonprofit that is authorized by law or whose activities are directed by law so that it serves public purposes.

Federal instrumentalities tend to be prevalent in the financial sector. They include Federal Reserve Banks, the Securities Investor Protection Corporation, government-sponsored enterprises, and commercial banks. Nonfinancial instrumentalities have included the Communications Satellite Corporation and some nonprofits such as the Corporation for Public Broadcasting, the Legal Services Corporation, the American Red Cross, and the National Park Foundation. Again, the importance of instrumentalities is that they represent an important organizational alternative to carrying out public purposes through a government department or agency.

The choice between using government agencies or instrumentalities to carry out public purposes is seen most clearly at the state and local levels. Although some states have selected the government agency form to serve as state housing finance agencies or state student loan finance agencies, other states use nonprofit organizations, chartered by state law, to carry out similar purposes.

One study of student loan secondary markets found that government agencies tend to be subject to significant state control, varying among the states, including civil service or other personnel and staffing restrictions, procurement requirements, freedom of information disclosures, and direct accountability to state oversight agencies. By contrast, student loan secondary markets that are organized as nonprofit corporations are free from most such restrictions; they have considerable flexibility to deal with changing market conditions. One notable advantage is their ability to offer attractive salaries and benefits to obtain and retain employees with critical skills. Many variations are possible. Some states have established nonprofit corporations under specific state statutes with sufficient state control to qualify as governmental authorities and benefit from special advantages under the tax laws (Stanton 1989).

Another option should be noted. The federal government may enact legislation that authorizes state and local government organizations to carry out

Table 1.1

Institutional Differences: Government Agencies, Private Instrumentalities, and Ordinary Private Companies

Government agency	Private instrumentality of government	Ordinary company
Political factors predominate; the market affects some government corporations	External environment includes the market, but political factors tend to dominate	External environment is more market-based than political
Subject to controls on resources that often include annual appropriations limits; a tendency exists to maintain agency functions despite inadequate resources or capacity	Stream of revenues and federal subsidies generates needed resources to build capacity	Stream of profits generates needed resources to build capacity
Accountable to multiple parts of government and, in varying degrees, to influential constituencies	Accountable to private owners (except for nonprofits); often regulated by government as well	Accountable to private owners
Some public disclosure; often less financial disclosure than is required of private firms	Financial disclosure (less than for the ordinary company) to private owners and possibly to government regulators	Financial disclosure to private owners; if a publicly held firm, also required public disclosures
Heavy controls on inputs (e.g., budget and staffing) and procedures; government corporations may have greater autonomy	Market-based external controls may be offset by federal subsidies; some regulatory controls	Market-based external controls based upon financial performance
Diffuse political pressures lead to serving multiple purposes that often may not be articulated	Mix of profit-oriented goals and regulated service; cooperatives serve their members	Profit-oriented goals often force focus upon particular activities, market segments, and strategies
May stagnate over time, as public priorities change, without ceasing to exist	Some have government backing at start-up; sometimes may gain monopoly or market power; may stagnate over time; government backing, if present, can forestall easy exit	Life cycle: thrives or goes out of business; forced exit of failed firms

public purposes under federal law; these organizations also then may become federal instrumentalities whose activities and powers are shaped by federal law. The idea of devolution of federal activities can involve arrangements with state or local government organizations that, by virtue of their responsibilities under federal law, may become federal instrumentalities. The devolution alternative is not discussed further here.

As might be expected, given the quite different legal frameworks of government and private organizations, the questions for private instrumentalities are quite different from those for government departments or agencies. Government agencies frequently seek added managerial flexibility and organizational capacity to carry out their programs. By contrast, private organizations that carry out public purposes often possess capacity, and the questions tend to focus more on promoting accountability to carrying out their public purposes. As Harold Seidman warns, "Intermingling of public and private purposes in a profit making corporation almost inevitably means subordination of public responsibilities to corporate goals. We run the danger of creating a system in which we privatize profits and socialize losses" (Seidman 1998, 213). Any instrumentality, whether for-profit, cooperative, or nonprofit, must be designed with careful attention to accountability if it is to succeed in serving its public purposes.

Box 1.5 presents a series of questions that can help policymakers to decide on the appropriate design of private organizations that are responsible for carrying out public purposes.

Consider each of these questions in turn.

Does the Organization Carry out Public Purposes or Only Private Ones?

The threshold question is whether the activities carried out by a private organization are deemed to embody public purposes. Most companies and other private organizations do not conduct activities that are considered to involve public purposes. However, when the government charters or otherwise authorizes an organization to carry out specified purposes under law and also provides that organization with special benefits under law, then that organization takes on the status of a federal instrumentality. Federal instrumentalities may be immune from certain statutes such as antitrust or securities laws, may benefit from preemption of some state laws and taxes, and may receive special government support under applicable law. State and local instrumentalities may be authorized to issue bonds that benefit from federal, state, and local tax exemption.

The courts have long acknowledged the federal government's authority to use private institutions to serve public purposes. In an early case, the chief

---

Box 1.5

**Levels of Analysis for Private Instrumentalities
that Serve Public Purposes**

- Does the organization carry out public purposes or only private ones?
- Is the organization likely to be financially self-sustaining?
- Does the government plan to provide support (i.e., a subsidy) for the organization? If so, what form is appropriate for the public purposes to be served?
- Who should own the organization, or should it be a nonprofit?
- What governance structure is appropriate?
- What types of accountability are appropriate?
- Which agency of government should be responsible for holding the organization accountable?
- What should happen when the organization ceases to serve a high-priority public purpose?

---

justice of the United States, John Marshall, explained the role of the privately owned Bank of the United States, the nation's first central bank, as a federal instrumentality as follows: "The bank is not considered as a private corporation, whose principal object is individual trade and individual profit; but as a public corporation, created for public and national purposes. . . . [T]he bank is an instrument which is 'necessary and proper for carrying into effect the powers vested in the government of the United States'" (*Osborn v. Bank of the United States* 1824).

From the perspective of organizational design, the first question is whether the purposes carried out by a private organization are considered to embody public purposes. Thus, with respect to the National Consumer Cooperative Bank, the government decided that an organization that once was considered an instrumentality that carried out public purposes should be converted to a purely private company. The government allowed the Bank to repay a low-interest federal loan, one of the forms of support that government may provide to an instrumentality, over many years. The organization changed its name to National Cooperative Bank, altered its focus to serve more profitable types of cooperative such as larger producer cooperatives, and no longer functions as a federal instrumentality.

The question of whether an organization should be an instrumentality or not will face the Rural Telephone Bank (RTB) as it contemplates its transition from being a government agency. The federal budget calls for privatization of the RTB. The question then becomes what type of financial services charter will best allow the RTB to carry out its activities while satisfying the concerns of stakeholders and the government. Here a range of alternatives might be explored, including taking a commercial bank charter and becoming a federal instrumentality or becoming a completely private company such as a general financial services company, or possibly even a specially chartered private company similar to the National Cooperative Bank

Is the Organization Likely to Be Financially Self-Sustaining?

Assuming that a decision is made to create a private government instrumentality to carry out public purposes, the next question is whether that organization can earn enough revenues to cover its costs. Only then can it be financially viable. If an organization is expected to be profitable, that is, to cover its expenses, be able to pay taxes, and provide returns to investors, then it can be structured as a for-profit company or (as will be discussed below) a cooperative. If an organization is expected to earn a surplus, but not necessarily enough to pay taxes and provide returns to shareholders, then it might be structured as a nonprofit. If the organization is not expected to earn a surplus, then it will not be viable unless the government provides a subsidy.

Does the Government Plan to Provide Support (i.e., a Subsidy) for the Organization?

The nature of government subsidy, if any, for private organizations deserves careful consideration. This involves considerations of both the amount of the subsidy and the form of the subsidy. If the government provides too little subsidy, then some organizations may not be willing or able to carry out public purposes. On the other hand, if the subsidy is too large, then the subsidized organization can grow at the expense of private organizations that are not favored with government support. If the government does provide a subsidy, it should not provide so much that the favored organization displaces its competitors. This may not be an easy balance to strike.

The other issue that deserves careful thought is the form that the subsidy should take. For many institutions, the form of government support helps to define the organizational form. Insured depository institutions—banks, thrift institutions, and credit unions—are defined by their access to federal deposit insurance. Each of these institutions is considered to serve an important public purpose by providing people with access to place their money safely in federally insured deposits.

Government-sponsored enterprises (GSEs) are defined by their access to a unique bundle of attributes that creates a perception of implicit government backing. They are expected to use their benefits to serve the public purposes defined in their charters. Fannie Mae and Freddie Mac, the two largest GSEs, can use their preferential borrowing costs to lower mortgage rates for homebuyers.

Nonprofits, and categories of nonprofits such as charities and foundations, are defined by their tax exemptions. For state and local instrumentalities, the authority to issue tax-exempt obligations has become a fairly standard feature for some types of activity. To the extent that a nonprofit such as the American Red Cross or a state housing finance organization or a nonprofit hospital or health insurance company is considered to have a public purpose, it is supposed to use its special benefits to lower costs and permit access to services that otherwise might not be available on affordable terms. Some nonprofit instrumentalities, such as the Corporation for Public Broadcasting and the Legal Services Corporation, receive federal appropriations to carry out their work.

When policymakers contemplate an organizational transformation—for example, when a 1968 law authorized Fannie Mae to convert from a government corporation into a GSE or if the Rural Telephone Bank today contemplates converting from a federal agency to become a private instrumentality—the choice of whether to have a subsidy and, if so, what type, is very important in determining how the organization will develop and how it will serve public purposes in addition to its private interests.

Who Should Own the Organization or Should It Be a Nonprofit?

Private instrumentalities fall into three basic organizational types: (1) the investor-owned for-profit company, (2) the cooperative, and (3) the nonprofit organization. Examples would be commercial banks, the Farm Credit System, and the American Red Cross, respectively.

Each organizational type has strengths and limitations. Profit-seeking investor-owned companies are subject to the discipline and incentives of a financial bottom line by which to measure success. The advantages of using an investor-owned firm to carry out public purposes relate to their ability to use resources efficiently in search of profits. When necessary to achieve profitability, private firms can invest in high-quality personnel and systems that may be far more productive than those found in government. A disadvantage of using profit-seeking companies is the principal-agent problem and the need to deal with the divergent interests of private owners vis-à-vis the government's interests in promoting service for public purposes.

The distinguishing design feature of the cooperative is that it is owned and controlled by the people or institutions that use its services. That means that the benefits of a cooperative organization flow to its members, in the form of services and, generally to a lesser extent, as dividends. To coin a phrase, investor-owners of a private company want to create a racehorse—to perform well and return dividends to the shareholders. By contrast, the owners of a cooperative want to create a milk cow—to pass through benefits to the owners, even at the cost of its own performance in the marketplace. In particular, cooperatives are unlikely to compete with their user-owners.

These unusual characteristics make the cooperative a distinctive instrument for carrying out public purposes. To the extent that government provides a subsidy through a cooperative, those subsidy benefits will flow through to the member-owners. On the one hand, this makes it possible to use the cooperative to target selected constituencies, e.g., farmers, rural communities, or certain kinds of financial institutions. On the other hand, targeting of benefits to the most needy constituents can be difficult; some cooperative organizations may end up serving primarily their strongest members, that is, those that are the most affluent and influential, with their government-supported benefits.

Nonprofit organizations are a distinct organizational type. Nonprofit instrumentalities vary considerably in size and purpose. The common elements of all nonprofit organizations are (1) tax-exempt status under the Internal Revenue Code and (2) the absence of shareholders or other owners of the organization (Boris and Steuerle 1999; Orlans 1980). In addition, some state or local instrumentalities may be authorized to issue tax-exempt obligations. Not all nonprofits are government instrumentalities; the distinction again rests on whether the organization is carrying out activities that are deemed to involve a public purpose.

Unlike investor-owned companies or cooperatives, nonprofits do not have shareholders. This plays a role in the behavior of nonprofits. On the one hand, the absence of investors means that nonprofits can save money that otherwise would be paid as returns to shareholders. On the other hand, the absence of shareholder returns may make it difficult for nonprofits to raise capital needed to assure the financing of the organization's objectives. Indeed, many nonprofits have established for-profit affiliates to provide a source of income beyond donations and the remuneration from services provided. Like government agencies, nonprofit organizations can be torn between trying to do good and trying to do well enough to survive and grow.

In terms of capacity and flexibility, nonprofit organizations sometimes may lag their investor-owned counterparts. Thus, many nonprofit hospitals or health insurance plans justify their conversion to for-profit status on the grounds that they need the greater access to the capital markets that is available to private firms, and also that they need to be able to pay greater compensation to highly skilled professionals than is possible in a nonprofit organization.

What Governance Structure Is Appropriate?

All three types of instrumentality use a board of directors to govern the organization. Directors and officers of each have a fiduciary responsibility of care and loyalty to the organization and—except for nonprofits—to shareholders. However, the different ownership structure does have implications for the performance of the organization.

The officers and directors of shareholder-controlled instrumentalities are expected to owe their primary allegiance to shareholders rather than to the federal government that charters them. In other words, as in a private company, the interests of the private owners come first in the minds of company directors and officers. Unlike the ordinary private company, service to public purposes arises from the laws and regulations that government uses to assure that the institution serves public interests as well as private ones. This creates a significant tension between private profits and the public purposes that the instrumentalities are supposed to serve, discussed further below.

Sometimes, the enabling legislation for an instrumentality will prescribe that there be a minority of publicly appointed directors on the board. This was true for Comsat, the Communications Satellite Corporation, and for the boards of most of the GSEs. Often the president of the United States appoints the minority of public directors. Such appointments are unlikely to greatly change the behavior of a private instrumentality. Like the shareholder-elected directors, the publicly appointed directors owe a fiduciary responsibility to the organization and its owners. Often an investor-owned instrumentality may reinforce the identification of interests between the directors and owners by awarding generous stock options that benefit the directors to the extent that the organization is a financial success.

For the cooperative, governance by a board of directors means attention to the needs of the owners that use the cooperative's services. Thus, a cooperative such as the Farm Credit System in the past showed a tendency to underprice its services to members, compared to the pricing that would be expected if the instrumentality had been structured to be investor owned. Another distinctive feature is that some cooperative boards of directors may be very large, as a way to promote shareholder involvement. This can lead to overhead expenses that are large compared to the investor-owned company; also, the cooperative board may find it difficult to have the focus and flexibility that may be found in a comparable investor-owned company.

Nonprofits are different from the other two organizational types. Although directors and officers of a nonprofit do have a fiduciary responsibility of care and loyalty to the organization, there are no shareholders to enforce property rights that might be infringed by any violation of that responsibility. The absence of shareholders can mean that board oversight of the managers of a nonprofit can be weak or unfocused, and that board members may lack adequate independence from management. Without the need to serve shareholders, officers and directors of a nonprofit are free to guide the organization to serve their conceptions of the public interest.

What Types of Accountability Are Appropriate?

The government tends to have two interests in the instrumentalities that it uses to carry out public purposes: (1) to assure that high-priority public purposes are carried out and (2) to assure that the organization operates in a prudent financial manner. The latter issue is especially important for depository institutions and GSEs because of the government backing of insured deposits and the perception of government backing for GSE obligations.

Box 1.6 shows some of the ways that government can promote accountability of instrumentalities. Under applicable legislation, government has a number of ways to try to assure that instrumentalities serve public purposes. These include provisions that limit the scope of authorized powers that an instrumentality may possess, governance or organizational requirements, and government oversight of the activities that instrumentalities carry out under their enabling legislation. Some of these approaches, such as the supervision of safety and soundness of banks, seem to work fairly well; others, such as the government's power to appoint directors of some private instrumentalities, may add little if anything to the accountability of the organization to serve its public purposes.

When a cooperative is an instrument for providing public services, the issue of accountability to government is quite similar to the issues raised by investor-owned companies. If the government lacks the capacity to protect its own interests, then the cooperative will go its own way. At the time that the Farm Credit System failed in the mid-1980s, for example, in a period of ruinous agricultural conditions, the government had largely lost control over the safety and soundness of the system and its member financial institutions. After providing taxpayer assistance, the government restructured the cooperative's federal regulator to have powers comparable to those of a federal bank regulator.

The issue of accountability of nonprofits is complex. On the one hand, nonprofits may have a service ethos that allows them to serve less-profitable

Box 1.6

**Promoting Accountability of Private Instrumentalities
that Serve Public Purposes**

- Limitations in the enabling legislation on authorized powers
  - permitted functions
  - limited market segments
  - restricted members or borrowers
  - requirement to serve designated market segments

- Governance/organization requirements
  - inclusion of directors to represent particular constituencies
  - specification of investor or cooperative or nonprofit structure

- Supervision by a government agency
  - oversight and regulation of activities
  - required approval of new activities
  - supervision of safety and soundness

people and public purposes than would be expected from a for-profit firm. On the other hand, some nonprofits (and Medicare contractors come to mind here) may require careful supervision to try to assure good performance and financial integrity, much as if they were investor-owned firms. Nonprofit public authorities, which may have considerable flexibility under their charters, may not be easy for state or local governments to hold accountable (Axelrod 1992).

Some government agencies, especially in the Department of Defense, have improved the accountability of nonprofits by developing long-term relationships. Thus, federally funded research and development centers (FFRDCs) such as units of the RAND and MITRE corporations operate under special long-term contracts that allow for an especially close relationship between the agency and its nonprofit partner (Moe 2001, 295–96). Because of the long-term relationship, an agency traditionally was able to insist that the FFRDC dedicate itself primarily to the interests of the government. To the extent that an FFRDC has relationships, such as interlocking directors, with a private for-profit firm with a range of other clients and interests, its accountability to the government in this respect may diminish.

Once instrumentalities have become established, both the Executive Branch and the Congress can find it difficult to influence their activities, either with respect to serving new and evolving public priorities or with respect to reducing financial exposure from their activities. Because private instrumentalities can live or die according to the terms of their enabling legislation, they have an incentive to use resources to influence the Congress or state legislatures, their designated regulators, and others in government who might threaten their legal franchise or otherwise impose policies at variance with the interests of the private owners or, in the case of nonprofits, the managers (Stanton 2002).

Which Agency of Government Should Be Responsible for Holding the Organization Accountable?

The congressional committee structure is likely to determine which federal agency is responsible for overseeing the public purposes served by a federal instrumentality. Thus, during the congressional deliberations that led to the creation of the Office of Federal Housing Enterprise Oversight (OFHEO), a regulator of Fannie Mae and Freddie Mac, the House Ways and Means Committee preferred that the Treasury Department, with which the committee had a close working relationship, should undertake this role. By contrast, the congressional housing subcommittees insisted that OFHEO be a part of HUD, the department whose activities they authorize.

Sometimes, as in the case of OFHEO or the federal bank regulators, supervisory authority may be split among two or more agencies. In the case of OFHEO, HUD was left with responsibility for overseeing the two GSEs' service to affordable housing goals and other public purposes, while OFHEO is responsible for overseeing financial soundness. The history of federal bank regulation has led to a convoluted regulatory structure involving the federal or state agency that charters commercial banks, the Federal Deposit Insurance Corporation, and the Federal Reserve Board.

Once a regulatory agency has been selected, an important organizational issue relates to the capacity of the agency to carry out its responsibilities. This raises the question of funding for the regulator. On the one hand, many financial regulators are funded from fees assessed on the regulated institutions. This has the advantage of freeing the regulator from the vagaries of the appropriations process and the possibility that unexpected budget cuts could hamper the agency's effectiveness. On the other hand, an agency needs some way to fund itself in case the regulated companies get into financial trouble, which could reduce available fees just at a time when the regulator needs to be most active.

What Should Happen When the Organization Ceases to Serve a High-Priority Public Purpose?

Sallie Mae is a government-sponsored enterprise that decided to give up its government sponsorship in favor of obtaining a broader array of authorized activities. A Sallie Mae report discusses the life cycle of GSEs; the report could just as well refer to other instrumentalities of government in its suggestion that when an organization has served its public purposes, or when those purposes no longer have a high public priority, then a transition is called for:

> In creating the various GSEs, Congress did not contemplate the need at some point to unwind or terminate their federal charters. However, Congress did not assume the perpetual existence (and continual expansion) of individual GSEs in the context of changing social and economic priorities. The missing element in the GSE concept is the notion of a life cycle for government sponsorship. GSEs are *created* to increase the flow of funds to socially desirable activities. If successful, they grow and *mature* as the market develops. At some point, the private sector may be able to meet the funding needs of the particular market segment. If so, a *sunset* may be appropriate. (Sallie Mae 1994)

A few organizations have outlived the perceived need for their services as federal instrumentalities. In 1981, the government arranged for a transition of the National Consumer Cooperative Bank from an instrumentality to an ordinary private company that does not carry out public purposes. Legislation in 1996 removed instrumentality status from the College Construction Loan Insurance Association (Connie Lee). Also in 1996 the government enacted legislation to remove government sponsorship from Sallie Mae. After a transition period, the company became a completely private organization rather than a GSE.

Nonprofits raise special issues with respect to the transition to private status. Some seek to convert to or merge with for-profit companies that may not be instrumentalities. Managers of a nonprofit organization may have strong personal incentives to convert into a for-profit company. Yet, attractive as conversion may be for some stakeholders, conversions in fields such as health care often can leave a gap in public purposes that had been served by a nonprofit. The track record of such nonprofit conversions shows that the potential of this life cycle event deserves more consideration from organizational designers than it has received so far.

Enhancing the Government's Capacity to Design Effective Organizations and Public-Private Relationships

The events of September 11 have brought into sharp focus the limitations on the federal government's ability to design effective organizations and working relationships with other partners, whether in the private sector or among

Box 1.7
The Government-Sponsored Enterprise

One type of federal instrumentality deserves special mention. This is the government-sponsored enterprise. (Stanton 2002).The government-sponsored enterprise, as distinct from the wholly owned government corporation, is a government-chartered, privately owned, and privately controlled institution that, although lacking an express government guarantee, benefits from the perception that the government stands behind its financial obligations. In return for statutory privileges, including tax benefits and regulatory exemptions, as well as reduced borrowing costs, the GSE is confined by its charter to serving specified market segments through a limited range of services. (For a comparison of GSEs and government corporations, see Stanton and Moe 2002).

GSEs are some of the largest financial institutions in the United States. Fannie Mae and Freddie Mac each fund over two *trillion* dollars of home mortgages. The Federal Home Loan Bank System, nearly a trillion-dollar group of cooperative institutions, provides funding on favorable terms to the banks and thrift institutions that own the individual banks. The smaller GSEs are multibillion-dollar financial institutions. The Farm Credit System and a small GSE known as Farmer Mac provide loans to agricultural borrowers.

Three of the GSEs—Fannie Mae, Freddie Mac, and Farmer Mac—are investor owned. The other two—the Farm Credit System and the Federal Home Loan Bank System—are structured as systems of cooperative organizations.

Thanks to their federal support, GSEs can grow rapidly. Taken together, GSEs have more than doubled in size every five years since Freddie Mac was chartered in 1970. Both Fannie Mae and the Farm Credit System became troubled in the 1980s and the Farm Credit System required direct government assistance. Freddie Mac's accounting systems and internal controls failed starting in the late 1990s and the company was unable to issue suitable financial statements for several years. Fannie Mae's accounting systems and internal controls also are poor, as its regulator has reported at the time of this writing. One GSE, Sallie Mae, which funds student loans, has made the transition to becoming a completely private company without the status or public purposes associated with a federal instrumentality.

state and local governments. Many years ago, the Executive Office of the President (EOP) included an Office of Management and Organization (earlier a part of the Administrative Management Division), housed first in the Bureau of the Budget and then in the new Office of Management and Budget (OMB), with responsibility for enhancing the management and organization of government organizations and programs.

As Ronald Moe points out in chapter 5, that office had responsibility for enhancing the institutional capacity of the presidency and, by extension, the rest of the Executive Branch. On issues of interagency coordination, for example, the office had the capacity to develop a cognitive map of a problem, overlay a map of the available jurisdictions of constituent organizations, and then help those organizations to plug the gaps. In cases such as housing and community development, the scope of analysis also included the relationship of federal agencies and programs with state and local governments. Today, the capacity of such an office could help to address homeland security issues.

The danger of many urgent proposals in the aftermath of September 11 is that they seek to apply this salutary analytic approach to homeland security, but generally leave the rest of the government's programs in the same sorry state of neglect that was the case for many security functions before September 11. The federal government needs to restore its strategic organization and management capability to provide help for agencies and programs across the government, from provision of Medicare services to an improved organizational structure for energy programs to federal housing programs to any of a number of other major government commitments that are being implemented by troubled agencies or departments.

The new office might have the following general responsibilities (Moe 1999; Jasper 1999):

- *Government Organization:* Review government-wide organizational structure on a continuing basis, periodically reporting to the president and Congress on the state of government organization and proposals to improve the performance and efficiency of federal programs and the capacity of federal agencies.
- *Cooperation and Coordination:* Facilitate interagency and intergovernmental cooperation and assist in developing effective coordinating mechanisms throughout the government.
- *Systems Improvement:* Provide leadership for improvement of agencies' administrative and program delivery systems, including those that can help to make the Government Performance and Results Act a success. Administrative systems include personnel, procurement, and information resources, for example.

- *Early Warning:* Analyze agency capacity and operations, for example with respect to national homeland security, public health, or financial vulnerabilities, to detect potentially damaging gaps and shortcomings.
- *Special Organizations:* Oversee the overall operations and management of government corporations, government-sponsored enterprises, quasi-governmental entities, and other institutions with a governmental interest.
- *Reorganization and Management Legislation:* Develop criteria and standards to be met prior to the submission of legislation to establish new or reorganize existing government corporations, enterprises, and other entities with a government interest; provide advice on the workability of proposed programs and legislation as they are being developed.
- *Fostering Management Analysis Capacity:* Help departments and agencies to develop internal management analysis capabilities.

The question of location of organizational expertise in the Executive Office of the President has been a matter of considerable debate within the National Academy of Public Administration. On the one hand, Fellows of the academy who are current or former OMB officials argue that organization, management, and budget are inseparable; the design of programs and agencies must be accomplished with close attention to the resources that may be required (DeSeve 1999). On the other hand, other academy fellows argue that there is a fundamental conflict between the management and budget functions. In their view the primacy of budget constraints since at least the 1980s has meant that the budget function inevitably dominates over the issues of government effectiveness that the organization and management function must address. They point to a general neglect of the management function at OMB, especially in the past few years, and urge that the organization and management function be in a separate office from OMB (Moe 1999; Jasper 1999). Although the budget function requires OMB to wield power to constrain resources that agencies and programs would like to have, the organization and management function is more supportive in nature and calls for the establishment of collaborative working relationships with agency officials that could be jeopardized by budget conflicts.

With appropriate top-level support, the organization and management function could operate well within OMB, as it did historically in the Bureau of the Budget; unfortunately, as a practical matter, and with some notable exceptions, OMB has not been able to prevent budget considerations from seriously undermining the management function.

Traditionally, the influence of the Division of Management and Organization of the Bureau of the Budget rested on its support from the president and organizational knowledge and competence. The effectiveness of such an office today similarly would depend on (1) support from the president for its work, (2) other demand for its services, and (3) the abilities of its leadership and staff.

It can be seen that, if such an office existed today, it would greatly add to the president's capacity to address the critical issues of organization, management, and coordination that are a national priority with respect to assuring homeland security.

To some extent the effectiveness of the new office will depend on actions on Capitol Hill. In recent years, the governmental affairs and government reform committees of both houses have lost much of their traditional capacity to deal with issues of government organization and management. In the aftermath of September 11, this could change. Especially if Congress restores provisions for presidentially initiated reorganizations under a general Executive Branch reorganization act, the governmental affairs committees will gain clear jurisdiction over many of these matters.

Expanded authority and capability among the committees, in turn, is likely to prompt the U.S. Government Accountability Office (GAO) to enhance its ability to deal with organizational design issues. As the congressional committees and GAO begin to generate hearings, inquiries, and reports that highlight shortcomings and solutions with respect to executive organization and management, then the role of the new office will increase as well. It is likely that demand for solid analysis of executive organization and management issues will continue to be strong for quite some time. We have far to go in dealing with the major issues before us.

Notes

The author would like to acknowledge the considerable assistance he received in preparing this guide to organizational design. The PricewaterhouseCoopers Endowment for the Business of Government provided a grant to conduct this work and write an earlier research report. Mark Abramson and John Kamensky helped to shape the conception and provided valuable comments on the first draft. Members of the Standing Panel on Executive Organization and Management contributed extensively to the author's understanding of these issues. Special gratitude is owed to reviewers of earlier drafts of this material, including Jonathan Breul, Murray Comarow, Alan Dean, Herbert Jasper, Dwight Ink, Bernard Martin, and Harold Seidman. Others who contributed insights include Dan Guttman, Ronald Moe, and Charles Kause. Although the author benefited immeasurably from these contributions, he remains solely responsible for the contents of this chapter.

1. The author is indebted to Alan Dean, one of the nation's leading authorities on government organization, for this insight.

2. Under the Government Corporation Control Act, the FDIC is a so-called "mixed ownership" government corporation, an organizational form with even greater statutory autonomy than is provided for wholly owned government corporations. See 31 U.S.C. Chapter 91.

3. On the issue of accountability and the performance of public authorities, compare Doig 1983 with Mitchell 1999.

References

Axelrod, Donald. 1992. *Shadow Government: The Hidden World of Public Authorities—and How They Control Over $1 Trillion of Your Money.* New York: St. Martin's Press.

Bernstein, Marver. 1955. *Regulating Business by Independent Commission.* Princeton: Princeton University Press.

Boris, Elizabeth T., and C. Eugene Steuerle. 1999. *Nonprofits & Government.* Washington, DC: Urban Institute Press.

Butler, Stuart M., et al. 1999. "Crisis Facing HCFA & Millions of Americans, an Open Letter to Congress and the Executive." *Health Affairs* 18, no. 1 (January/February): 8–10.

Comarow, Murray. 2004. "The Future of the Postal Service." In Stanton and Ginsberg 2004, 88–111.

Dean, Alan L. 2004. "The Organization and Management of Executive Departments." In Stanton and Ginsberg 2004, 156.

DeSeve, G. Edward. 1999. Deputy Director for Management, Office of Management and Budget's Statement before the House Committee on Government Reform, Subcommittee on Government Management, Information, and Technology, February 4.

Doig, Jameson W. 1983. "If I See a Murderous Fellow Sharpening a Knife Cleverly: The Wilsonian Dichotomy and the Public Authority Tradition." *Public Administration Review* 43 (July/August): 292–304.

Flynn, Stephen E. 2001. Statement before the Committee on Governmental Affairs, United States Senate, October 12.

Gilmour, Robert S., and Laura S. Jensen. 1998. "Reinventing Government Accountability: Public Functions, Privatization, and the Meaning of 'State Action.'" *Public Administration Review* 58 (May/June): 247–58.

General Accounting Office (GAO). 1979. Decision of the Comptroller General of the United States, B-193573, January 8, 1979, concerning the St. Lawrence Seaway Development Corporation.

———.1989. "Opinion of the Comptroller General," B-237356, December 29, letter to Senator David Pryor.

———. 1996. Federally Funded R&D Centers: Issues Relating to the Management of DOD-Sponsored Centers. GAO/NSIAD-96-112.

Guttman, Dan. 2000. "Public Purpose and Private Service: The Twentieth Century Culture of Contracting Out and the Evolving Law of Diffused Sovereignty." *Administrative Law Review* 52 (Summer): 859–926.

Jasper, Herbert N. 1997. "Making Reorganization of the Executive Branch Work." National Academy of Public Administration, Standing Panel on Executive Organization and Management, working paper, January.

———. 1999. Statement before the House Committee on Government Reform, Subcommittee on Government Management, Information, and Technology, February 4, 2.

Kettl, Donald F. 2004. *System under Stress: Homeland Security and American Politics.* Washington, DC: CQ Press.

Mitchell, Jerry. 1999. *The American Experiment with Government Corporations.* Armonk, NY: M.E. Sharpe.

Moe, Ronald C. 1999. "Office of Management Act of 1999," Congressional Research Service, Statement before the House Committee on Government Reform, Subcommittee on Government Management, Information and Technology, February 4, 10.

———. 2001. "The Emerging Federal Quasi Government: Issues of Management and Accountability." *Public Administration Review* 61, no. 3 (May/June): 290–312.

———. 2004. "Governance Principles: The Neglected Basis for Federal Management." In Stanton and Ginsberg 2004, 21–39.

Moe, Terry M. 1989. "The Politics of Bureaucratic Structure." In *Can the Government Govern?* eds. John E. Chubb and Paul E. Peterson. Washington, DC: Brookings Institution Press.

National Academy of Public Administration (NAPA). 1984. "Management Reforms as a Part of Organizational Independence," Report to the Congressional Panel on Social Security Administration, May, 1–2.

Orlans, Harold, ed. 1980. *Nonprofit Organizations: A Government Management Tool.* New York: Praeger Publishers.

Osborn v. Bank of the United States. 1824. 22 U.S. (9 Wheat.), 738, at 860.

Redford, Emmette S., and Marlan Blisset. 1981. "The Department of Transportation: Integration of Old Functions." In *Organizing the Executive Branch: The Johnson Presidency,* ed. Emmette S. Redford, chapter 3. Chicago, IL: University of Chicago Press, 46–76.

Sallie Mae. 1994. *The Restructuring of Sallie Mae: Rationale and Feasibility.* Washington, DC. Student Loan Marketing Association.

Seidman, Harold. 1998. *Politics, Position and Power: The Dynamics of Federal Organization.* 5th ed. New York: Oxford University Press, 213–19.

Standing Panel on Executive Organization and Management. 1997. "Principles of Federal Organization." Washington, DC: National Academy of Public Administration.

Stanton, Thomas H. 1989. *Legal and Institutional Factors Affecting Competition in the Secondary Market for Guaranteed Student Loans.* Prepared for the U.S. General Accounting Office, pp. 4–5.

———. 2001. Statement before the Senate Committee on Governmental Affairs on Legislative Options to Strengthen National Homeland Defense, October 12. The author wishes to credit the experienced members of the Standing Panel on Executive Organization and Management of the National Academy of Public Administration for suggesting a number of the insights that he presented in this testimony.

———. 2002. *Government Sponsored Enterprises: Mercantilist Companies in the Modern World.* Washington, DC: AEI Press.

———. 2003. "The Administration of Medicare: A Neglected Issue." *Washington and Lee University Law Review* 60, no. 4 (Fall): 1373–1416.

———. 2004. "When Government Isn't Exactly Government." *Journal of Public Administration Research and Theory* 14, no. 3 (July): 435–37.

Stanton, Thomas H., and Benjamin Ginsberg. 2004. *Making Government Manageable.* Baltimore: Johns Hopkins University Press.

Stanton, Thomas H., and Ronald C. Moe. 2002. "Government Corporations and Government Sponsored Enterprises." In *Tools of Government: A Guide to the New Governance,* ed. Lester M. Salamon, chapter 3. New York: Oxford University Press.

U.S. Commission on National Security/21st Century. 2002. *Road Map for National Security: Imperative for Change.* Wilkes-Barre, PA: Kallisti Publishing.

U.S. House of Representatives. 1948. Budget Message of the President of the United States. House Document 19, 80th Congress.

Weaver, Robert. 1968. Quoted in "Fannie Mae and the Secondary Mortgage Market," by Richard Bartke, *Northwestern University Law Review* 66 (March/April 1971): 833–64.

Zegart, Amy B. 1999. *Flawed by Design: The Evolution of the CIA, JCS, and NSC.* Stanford, CA: Stanford University Press.

2

Developing the Domestic Security State

James D. Carroll

From Administrative to Entitlement to Domestic Security State

As the administrative state—"big government"—developed in the United States in the twentieth century, Congress delegated extensive discretionary power to the executive branch to work on economic and social and technological problems within broad statutory frameworks (Waldo 1948; Rosenbloom 2000; Stillman 1991). This power took many forms, including regulation and service provision. As a result of World War II and the Cold War it was extended to military and foreign as well as domestic affairs.

From a centrally bureaucratized form of direct action, the administrative state in domestic matters in the late twentieth century evolved into a mix of direct and indirect action, including third-party government and various forms of privatization. Through use of such instrumentalities as contracting and assistance and other programs such as subsidies, the administrative state spread throughout American society (Mosher 1980; Salamon 1981; Kettl 1988; Donahue and Nye 2002; Suleiman 2003; Singer 2003).

In the late twentieth century the entitlement state became the predominant form of public action, measured by money spent and tax expenditures allocated.[1] The entitlement state now commands approximately 60 percent of federal outlays.

In such programs as Social Security and Medicare, Congress invests rights to benefits and services enforceable in court to designated classes of individuals, often but not always bypassing the states. Entitlement programs limit the discretionary judgment of administrators and bureaucracies. Definitions of need as well as of appropriate responses are primarily legislative as distinguished from administrative in character. Entitlement programs function like logarithms by establishing sequences of rules to be followed in determining eligibility and establishing levels and types of benefits. Although in these

71

programs rules established in law replace the discretion that characterizes many programs of the administrative state, substantial managerial challenges characterize these programs. By the late twentieth century a substantial part of public administration—federal, state, local, and intergovernmental—was involved with administering programs of the entitlement state. In the entitlement state Congress also allocates extensive benefits in the form of tax expenditures to qualifying individuals and organizations.

In the domestic/global security state that is emerging, the central purpose is developing, sharing, and using information and intelligence in domestic/global matters to reduce the vulnerability of people and complex systems to catastrophic disruption and destruction through intentional and accidental acts (*Public Administration Review* 2002).[2] The term "domestic/global security state" is an analytical construct for use in identifying and analyzing a set of trends. At this time many of these trends are emergent. They are not a fully realized reality.

While the administrative state is being diffused throughout society, the emergent domestic security state is being developed and unified in a conceptual, virtual way under the imperative of developing, sharing, and using information for domestic security in a global context. Although the administrative state of old presupposed organizational unity and command and control, the domestic security state presupposes conceptual unity and strategy and purpose across many organizational and technical systems. It presupposes mutual understanding and cooperative action. It requires a new virtual, conceptual structure of mission and organization and operations not limited to Weberian and other forms of organization theory and practice. It requires new ways of anticipating and responding to continuous change in the organization, methods, and tactics that are the core of terrorism and technological interdependencies.

The administrative core of the domestic security state is mutuality of understanding, unity of purpose, and interoperability of systems in sharing and using information across boundaries to anticipate, prevent, respond to, and recover from terrorist action and cataclysmic events (Arquilla and Ronfeldt 1997; Davis et al. 2004).[3]

The development of the domestic security state portends fundamental changes in the mission and roles of government in American society, in public and private values, and in significant aspects of public administration. It portends new relationships and structures based upon new purposes and missions. The critically important factor is that it portends new relationships in and between foreign and domestic affairs, intelligence and law enforcement, defense and military powers and civilian police powers, the federal government and state and local governments, and the public and private sectors. It portends changes in the operational cultures of many parts of government operations.

Evolution

The domestic/global security state has both evolutionary and revolutionary elements. It is evolutionary in that it is rooted in the American system of government, with that system's distinctive emphasis on constitutionalism, liberty, separation of power, pluralism and countervailing power, federalism, due process of law, equal protection of the law, and individual rights. The domestic security state is in the tradition of responses to previous real and perceived internal threats to the nation, such as the Civil War, civil unrest and labor strife in various periods of American history, racial strife and urban riots, natural and human error disasters, distrust of citizens of German origin and foreign nationals in World War I and citizens of Japanese descent and foreign nationals in World War II, fear of internal subversion in the Cold War, and many incidents of terrorism affecting America prior to September 11, domestic and international.

Responses to these events have taken many forms, such as suspension of "ordinary" law, activation of the National Guard and civil defense systems, occasional use of military tribunals, development of emergency management systems, and development of counterterrorism organizations systems in government (Rehnquist 2000; Doary 2003; Duncan 2003; Wilson 1994; Brake 2003; Best 2001; U.S. GAO 2004). It should be noted that the domestic security state is rooted in responses to technological and other disasters, as well as to terrorism (Roenthal, Boin, and Comfort 2001; Waugh 1999; Platt 1999; Wermuth 2004). From the perspective of immediate response and recovery, the response to an event can be as important as the cause.

Revolution

The domestic security state is revolutionary in several ways. First, the context and challenges are different from the circumstances that contributed to development of the administrative and entitlement states. The context is a new form of technological terrorism—global terrorism—as part of extensive interactions among global and local technological, economic, and cultural realities (Berger and Huntington 2002).[4] Although terrorism is an old phenomenon, global terrorism is not. The emerging global reality, of which the new terrorism is a central part, includes new interdependencies and somewhat inconsistent tendencies—evolution and revolution, universalizing technologies and intensified search for local identity, and simultaneous centralization and devolution.

The combination of these forces makes it increasingly difficult to separate domestic concerns and jurisdictions from global developments. For example, in combating terrorism on non-American soil, the United States is increasingly dependent on other nations because much of what is called terrorism is rooted in other countries (Stern 2003; Rosenau 2003; Squassoni 2004; Benshel 2003; Ochmanek 2003). To some extent the same point applies to international crime. The entire conceptual, political, and legal architecture of much of government is disjointed between matters that government must deal with and the jurisdiction, authority, power, and capability of doing so, a point raised by Daniel Bell and others some years ago (Bell 1999).[5] As a result, much of public management is management of mission across organizations as distinguished from management of organizations.

Non-State "Sharks"

Second, the use of force has changed. Non-state actors have become threats to the nation-state from within and from without (Cragin and Daly 2004). For well over a century, the nation-state has been the primary form of organized political power in the world, including the power to exercise force in a particular territory. Although revolutionary groups have often struggled for control of the nation-state, the nation-state has remained the primary form of political power, even when taken over by evolutionary force. Today non-state terrorist and other groups are challenging the dominance of the nation-state through the exercise of force in selective but sometimes highly effective ways.

The Cold War was primarily a struggle among states relying heavily on military and diplomatic power, and to some extent technological, economic, and ideological competition. The question was the balance of power and coalition building and diplomacy among states. The objective was to define the challenge posed by a nation-state and its allies—in the Cold War the Soviet Union vis-à-vis the United States—and to construct a defense against the challenge, such as the doctrines of containment and of mutually assured destruction. In this sense, the context was a stable one, a known universe with a known enemy.

In the emerging context of the domestic security state, the central concern is not solely or even primarily with the threat posed by another nation-state, although this concern continues to be important. The concern also is identifying and responding to patterns of activity undertaken by groups that use violence outside the structures of governments. Some of these groups may have the support of states, while others may not. Established concepts such as those expressed in the Geneva Conventions do not apply easily to this evolving reality (Elsea 2002; White House 2002; U.S. Department of Justice—Office of the Inspector General 2003b). Terrorism is constantly changing and evolving, a factor that makes even the definition of terrorism a challenge. In Bruce Hoffman's words, "The terrorist campaign is like a shark in water: it must keep moving forward—no matter how slowly or incrementally—or die" (Hoffman 2001, 162). In this context governments must keep adapting as well.

The threat is constant and ubiquitous, but also shifting and elusive in scope, location, and nature. Uncertainty is the most powerful weapon of terrorists. As noted in previous contexts, government usually dealt with known actors and defined threats. In the evolving context, continuously identifying and defining the threat is central. As a result, real-time development and sharing of information on changing circumstances and events has become critical to government's role of maintaining public security and order (Dacey 2003). Such real-time information is the core of the domestic security state.

Combining Power

Third, in this context the domestic security state is blurring and commingling the military, defense, and diplomatic systems and functions of government with the traditional domestic police powers of the state. The distinctions between these forms of action are part of the broader separation of powers of the American system of government, which stresses countervailing power in the form of separate institutions and levels of government (Carroll 2003b). The system is a deliberate restraint on the consolidation and unification of power. The police power includes public health, safety, welfare and morals, civil defense, and emergency management. Historically, state and local governments have had extensive responsibility for exercising much of the police power in the United States, although in some matters, such as those affecting interstate commerce, the federal government has had a major role.[6]

The terrorist threat cuts across all jurisdictions and distinctions between domestic and foreign and public and private. It requires consolidating power. The result is a mismatch between jurisdiction and capability and threat. Among other things the result is uncertainty about who is responsible for what and a blurring of traditional legal jurisdictions and standards.[7] Action across organizational and other boundaries that rapidly shifts in focus and scope to meet emergent events—action on the edge—moves from the periphery of organizations to the center.

In this context, public administration's overriding challenge is how and by whom threats to domestic order and acts of terrorism or catastrophic accident should be anticipated, prevented, and if necessary acted upon. Who is responsible for what phases and stages of threat prevention, detection, and response (Chalk and Rosenau 2004; Bowman 2003; Bolkcom, DeSerisx and Kapp 2003)? What rules and norms of behavior apply? Do normal rules apply in extraordinary circumstances?

To what extent and under what circumstances are threats and acts of disruption a matter of civil order, within the traditional police powers of the state to protect public health, safety, welfare, and morals? To what extent do threats and acts raise criminal system questions? To what extent are the threats and events within the defense, war, and intelligence powers of the president and Congress? To what extent do normal limitations on domestic military action and other forms of government activity affecting liberty, due process of law and equal protection of the law, and individual rights and private property apply (Stevens 2002; U.S. Senate Committee on the Judiciary 2002; USDOJ—Office of Legislative Affairs 2002; and Schulfofer 2002)?[8] Who is responsible and empowered to sort out missions and roles?

"Persons of Interest"

These questions raise further questions regarding issues such as the rights and appropriate procedures applicable to a "person of interest" who comes under suspicion, or the rights, if any, of a person who is incarcerated—a detainee—but not charged with a crime, or the rights of members of groups and organizations that are regarded with distrust and subjected to unusual surveillance. Deciding when civil, criminal, and military jurisdiction applies involving what units of government and other parties has substantial implications for governmental jurisdictions and resources, for the parties affected, and for constitutional law and democracy.

Without strategic thought, analysis, and management, these questions will be increasingly difficult to answer. The questions are apt to be handled through ad hoc administrative action or the politics of partisan advantage and denial, in which issues may be obscured in the confusion of manipulated media moments and other forms of misdirected attention. In matters of such fundamental import ideology and chance are poor substitutes for careful thought.[9]

Triangulation

Fourth, the domestic security state involves a distinct form of management—triangulation. This form of administration combines elements of traditional hierarchical administration with elements of the lateral, network administration emphasized in the new public management (Brudney, O'Toole, and Rainey 2001). Triangulation administration combines traditional hierarchy, evolving networks, and lateral action. At the base the domestic security state requires extensive intelligence gathering and sharing across governmental, national, and public-private boundaries. A central objective is combining defense, foreign policy, and domestic intelligence to obtain a comprehensive view of developments. Networks may be particularly valuable in developing information (Mandell 2001; McGuire 2002; Arquilla and Ronfeldt 2001).

On one side of the triangle, intelligence is transmitted to a central point so that unconnected pieces of information can be scrutinized and patterns recognized and acted upon. This is the unifying, jigsaw phenomenon— "connecting the dots"—in which patterns emerge from seemingly disconnected pieces.[10] It is the core of the centralizing nature of triangulation administration. On the other side of the triangle, intelligence is transmitted from the apex to the locus at the base of the perceived concern or anticipated action so that timely investigative, preventive, or remedial action can be taken. All three elements—collection, pattern recognition, and response—are—or should be—inter-operationally connected.

As noted, triangulation administration combines elements of orthodox hierarchical administration—movement of information upward—with elements of the non-hierarchical, lateral, network administration often associated with the new public management and related conceptual approaches to public action.[11] In many ways triangulation administration transcends the boundaries of state and local governments and the federal government as well as barriers between public and private activities and property and national boundaries. In this sense information is a sweeping, all-encompassing, and unifying phenomenon that does not respect most conventional boundaries of the modern world, including legal and political boundaries (See Arquilla and Ronfeldt 1997).[12] Triangulation administration encompasses vast swaths of global activity. It also raises formidable questions of accountability and control.

Intelligence as Decision Making

Fifth, the domestic security state depends on decision making based on processes of intelligence. To some extent processes of intelligence are becoming the locus of decisions in some domestic matters as distinguished from processes of public deliberation and debate—for example, should some groups be targeted for special surveillance? In traditional defense and foreign policy matters decision making in the context of intelligence is not new. In the evolving mix of global/local and defense and domestic affairs it is new because norms of secrecy have not applied in domestic matters as fully or overtly as they have applied in foreign affairs and military matters (Lowenthal 2000; Watson 1990; Krizan 1999; Powers 2002).[13]

In the United States two primary forms of intelligence traditionally have been recognized, (1) intelligence applicable to defense and foreign affairs and (2) intelligence applicable to domestic, particularly criminal, matters. Each category has subcategories. Counterterrorism intelligence is sometimes defined as another major category (Permanent Select Committee on Intelligence 1996). The forms have corresponded roughly to organizational jurisdiction and function and cultures with extensive organizational division of labor and struggles over turf, particularly in national security. The result has been stovepipe intelligence—intelligence flowing upward in carefully controlled routes (Richelson 1999; U.S. Department of Justice—Office of the Inspector General 2003a; Cumming 2004). Integrating intelligence across organizational barriers has been a major problem, in many contexts.

Generally, defense and foreign policy intelligence, and domestic intelligence are different cultures, encompassing many subcultures. Defense and domestic intelligence are governed by different principles, laws, regulations, and processes. Terrorism and potential catastrophic technological systems failures spanning the globe require combining these types of intelligence in many ways. Sharing is central. What is discovered as a matter of defense intelligence can be of crucial significance for domestic action and vice versa. The central objective is reducing the nation's vulnerability to terrorist attack and catastrophic systems failure.

Combining defense and domestic intelligence and power does not fit the American constitutional distinction between jurisdictions in defense and domestic matters, or the system of countervailing powers. Information must be brought together in a way that is neither purely defense based nor purely domestic based—a third way. What is involved is a different realm of policy and action than those built into the constitutional structure of the American system of power, or the organizational structure established in earlier eras. A third force is involved—a fusion of domestic and military and diplomatic jurisdictions, for which there are no agreed-upon concepts, words, or labels in American thought or practice.

The natural tendency is to treat this new reality through established categories of thought, labels, and jurisdiction, as the automobile was initially called the "horseless carriage." Although there is some precedent for combining foreign and military and domestic intelligence, for example, in combating international crime (Nadelmann 1993), these precedents have been exceptions to the general rule of separate intelligence systems, and to distinctions between military and public safety and law enforcement operations.

Public Participation

By convention and to some extent by law, in the United States significant decisions affecting most domestic matters are supposed to be made with an opportunity for public participation, or at least knowledge, and public representation. Under democratic norms decisions are supposed to be subject to public accountability, notwithstanding the reality that many legislative and executive decisions are made in secret (Crenson and Ginsberg 2002; Theoharis 1998; GAO 2003). Because of the ethos of secrecy inherent in many forms of intelligence, the technical nature of some intelligence, threats to sources, and other concerns, democratic processes of well-informed deliberation, choice, and representation in matters of domestic security and significant issues of domestic policy can easily be subordinated to other concerns. Public administration faces a great and grave challenge of developing new concepts, institutions, and processes that will manage tensions between the military and defense and domestic challenges of public life (Campbell Institute 2003).

Liberty

Sixth, the domestic security state poses serious questions of individual liberty, the powers of government, and responsibility for advancing liberty as well as security.[14]

These questions are particularly important:

- Can public institutions and officials develop new ways of protecting both liberty and security without damaging both (Heyman 1998, 2003; Weich 2001)? How? Who should be "in charge" of advancing liberty in specific ways? Who is "in charge" of protecting domestic liberty? Can public administration as a field contribute to the reconciliation of liberty and security?
- What are the limits on government's powers in what circumstances to conduct surveillance and collect and use information (Rosenzweig 2003)? Can reasons of intelligence (reasons of state) substitute for limits in some circumstances?
- What are the due process rights of persons—citizens and others—suspected of terrorist conspiracies or acts (U.S. House, Subcommittee on the Constitution 2003)?
- What are the rights of government, under what circumstances, to detain people without charge (Elsea 2002)?
- What are the rights of government to use military law and tribunals to charge and try people? What people? Under what circumstances (Elsea 2001; Olshensky 2002)?
- To what extent and under what circumstance can "normal" civil liberties be suspended (Farber 2003)?

Rule of Law

Seventh, the domestic security state raises significant questions about the meaning of the rule of law, particularly about the meaning of "war" and of separation of powers (Stern and Halperin 1994; Stevens 2002). Can a president unilaterally declare that a state of "war" exists against an indeterminate enemy for an indefinite duration and invoke exceptional "war" powers to conduct the "war"?

What is the meaning of "terrorism"? How can terrorist acts be distinguished from other acts? How and why does this matter? To what extent can considerations of a war on terrorism override other concerns such as federalism and separation of powers? Will state and local governments be reduced to agents of the federal government in domestic security matters, because of scarcity of resources and the centralizing, unifying imperative of domestic intelligence? Can the reason of "war" be used as a reason of state to establish a form of federal executive power greater than any explicitly or implicitly given the president or the federal government as a whole under the constitution?

Implications for Public Administration

The advent of the domestic security state requires a searching reexamination of the conceptual cultures of public administration. Conceptual cultures consist of the implicit perceptions, ideas, beliefs, and worldviews that underlie the overt doctrines and practices of a field. Like all cultures, conceptual cultures are expressed and reinforced by symbols, language, narratives, and the like.

In theory and practice the conceptual cultures of public administration have been formed by answers to Woodrow Wilson's three questions about public administration: purpose, values, and methods (Carroll 2003a). Orthodox public administration of the mid-twentieth century defined the purpose and central value of public administration as efficiency and accountability. Scientific management, hierarchy, and related concepts formed the core methods of management.

The new public administration of the late twentieth century supplemented efficiency by defining the purpose of government as delivering services. Customer satisfaction and "results" became central values (Crenson and Ginsberg 2004). Methods centered primarily on non-hierarchical forms of action.

The central purpose of public administration in the domestic security state is to develop and use intelligence to reduce the vulnerability of people, systems, and infrastructure to advertent or inadvertent debilitation or destruction. This purpose cannot be achieved by assigning responsibility to one organization. The core value is survival, consistent with the pluralism of values of the American system. Conceptually and methodologically the management of intelligence is based on vulnerability analysis. How and where and in what ways are the nation's systems subject to intentional or in some instances unintentional attack, and from what sources?

Vulnerability Analysis

The challenge can be thought of by analogy to the challenge of the environment in the 1960s. At that time, concern with the environment was at the fringe of public policy. Publication of Rachel Carson's *Silent Spring* and other developments contributed to a fundamental change in public understanding, public policy, and public action. Concern with the environment moved to the center of public policy (Carson 2002). Congress enacted the National Environmental Policy Act in 1969.[15] The act included a requirement for environmental impact statements, an ingenious invention of a policy/administrative instrumentality (Bregman 1999). The impact statement requires extensive analysis of the potential impacts of an action, and remedial action if possible. The requirement applies to most publicly funded projects, and is enforceable in court.

The domestic security state requires an analogue—a vulnerability analysis concept, methodology, process, and statement requiring assessment of all technological and human behavior and systems, public and private, that are potentially subject to sabotage or catastrophic accident (Relyea 2004a, 2004b; Gorman 2004). It is critically important to stress that responsibility cannot and should not be assigned to a central organization, although a central organization such as the Department of Homeland Security may perform important functions. The terrorist threat—"the shark in the water"—is multidimensional, ubiquitous, and omnipresent. Prevention, anticipation, and response cannot be contained by a centralized bureaucracy. Pervasive action across levels of government and public-private boundaries is required.

Chaos and Complexity

Historically, much of public administration has proceeded on the assumption that relatively stable economic and social and other forms of order exist. With the exception of the Civil War, most administration has not been designed to anticipate and respond to the destruction of domestic social and technical systems. With some exceptions in public safety and disaster/emergency management, social and technical chaos has been peripheral to the field.

Terrorism and technological complexity are changing this perception of reality. Reality now includes the ongoing potential of extensive disruption or destruction of social, economic, and technological systems, often in simple ways such as disruption of a computer on a desk. In the ricin episode, a seemingly small incident became the center of extensive chaos management and vulnerability reduction. In that incident, "The Senate shut down its three office buildings . . . disrupting the work of lawmakers and thousands of their aides, after a powder identified as the deadly poison ricin was found in the office suite of the Senate majority leader, Bill Frist" (Johnston and Hulse 2004). In the domestic security state the form and nature of the threat is constantly changing, requiring a mind-set and approach that itself is constantly changing. Historically, public administration has sought regularity and stability in the conduct of public business. In the domestic security state elements of irregularity and instability and a search beyond bureaucratic norms will be required to comprehend and meet the threat. At this time, how this can and should be done is unclear (Brown and Eisenhardt 1998).

The Agenda

The challenge is stark. It is whether governance in a system of constitutional democracy, separated powers, and individual liberty can develop methods of countering terrorism that are consistent with the principles and values of this system. Public administration in America has never faced a greater challenge (Gormley 2002).

Notes

1. Entitlement spending as of 2003 was about 60 percent of all direct federal spending. If tax expenditures were included as a form of "spending," the total was considerably higher—perhaps 70 to 80 percent of all dollar value allocated. For current data on entitlement spending, see www.cbo.gov. See Joint Committee on Taxation (1999) for a recent review of tax expenditures. See Steuerle (1998) and Fox (2001) for background on the entitlement state. The standard description of entitlement programs is the "Green Book" (Committee on Ways and Means 2000, King 2000, Smith 2002, Jost 2003, Peterson 2004).

2. This present paper defines "vulnerability" to include disruption and destruction from both intentional acts and accidental system failures. The concept of domestic security as used in this paper is broader than the concept of homeland security as used in many government documents, because this paper includes natural and accidental catastrophes as elements of domestic security (as some other government documents do). The *National Strategy* stipulates: "Homeland security is a concerted national effort to prevent terrorist attacks within the United States, reduce America's vulnerability to terrorism, and minimize the damage and recover from attacks that do occur" (Office of Homeland Security 2002, 2). The subject of disasters and emergencies and other events is discussed in part in Rubin (2004) and Kirschenbaum (2003).

3. A new Terrorist Threat Integration Center had been established in the Central Intelligence Agency to integrate foreign and domestic intelligence as of May 30, 2004 (Office of Homeland Security 2002; OMB 2003, 2004). As of that date, the National Commission

on Terrorist Attacks upon the United States had issued the following staff reports, which analyze many of the dimensions of terrorist attacks upon the United States. These reports are valuable background:

No. 1. Entry of the 9/11 Hijackers into the United States
No. 2. Three 9/11 Hijackers: Identification, Watchlisting, and Tracking
No. 3. The Aviation Security System and the 9/11 Attacks
No. 4. The Four Flights
No. 5. Diplomacy
No. 6. The Military
No. 7. Intelligence Policy
No. 8. National Policy Coordination
No. 9. Law Enforcement, Counterterrorism, and Intelligence Collection in the United States Prior to 9/11
No. 10. Threats and Responses in 2001
No. 11. The Performance of the Intelligence Community
No. 12. Reforming Law Enforcement, Counterterrorism, and Intelligence Collection in the United States
No. 13. Emergency Preparedness and Response
No. 14. Crises Management

   See: http://www.9-11commission.gov/; the RAND Corporation maintains a terror-ism database; see also http://db.mipt.org/mipt_rand.cfm.

   4. Walter Laqueur observes: "Terrorism became truly global for the first time in his-tory in the 1990s, as local conflicts turned into a worldwide campaign" (Laqueur 2003). Robert S. Mueller, the director of the FBI as of June 2004, projected that the FBI will become part of an "official international terrorism alliance similar to NATO." He has stated "I envision the F.B.I. of tomorrow as a highly trained, electronically sophisticated, internationally networked organization that has terrorism as its principal target. ... Soon all counterterrorism functions will be intelligence-driven operations with law enforce-ment sanctions as an ancillary aspect" (Johnston 2004).

   5. This disjunction has long been noted in urban affairs and metropolitan government (Schmandt and Bollens 1982). In recent years a similar point has been raised by George Frederickson (Frederickson and Smith 2003; Kettl 2002). It can be argued that most peri-ods of American history have been marked by a mismatch between social and economic problems and the jurisdiction, authority, and capacity of governments to respond. See Friedman (2000) and Rosenau (2003) for two studies of simultaneous centripetal/cen-trifugal action.

   6. The Patriot Act appears to strengthen and extend federal criminal laws applicable to terrorism. Section 802 defines domestic terrorism as activities that "(A) involve acts dangerous to human life that are a violation of the criminal laws of the United States or of any State; (B) appear to be intended—(i) to intimidate or coerce a civilian population; (ii) to influence the policy of a government by intimidation or coercion; or (iii) to affect the conduct of a government by mass destruction, assassination, or kidnapping; and (C) occur primarily within the territorial jurisdiction of the United States." Section 808, a lengthy section, defines a federal crime of terrorism. It appears to establish a long list of what were previously separate crimes into one general crime of terrorism, with many different parts, if the elements of Section 802 are present (H.R. 3162 2001).

   7. The congressional joint inquiry of 2003 into 9/11 highlights these and many other questions. As one example, see S. Report No. 107-351, H. Report No. 107-792 (2003) and OMB (2003). Doary (2003) offers an analysis of a potential solution drawing on the tradition of civil defense.

8. For example, a Department of Defense directive established a Counterintelligence Field Activity program. It is authorized among other things to "Conduct Domestic Threat Analyses and Risk Assessments in support of DOD Force Protection and DOD Critical Infrastructure Protection efforts" (Department of Defense 2002). See also Brennen (2002).

9. RAND recently published a summary of policy recommendations from many sources that would be elements to consider in a strategic plan for homeland security, beyond current plans, and to some extent elements for a strategic plan for the government as a whole. See Parachini, Davis, and Liston (2003).

10. "Data Mining" is one form of relevant action. See Pear (2004).

11. The logic underlying the Defense Advanced Research Projects Agency's 2002 Total Information Project (TIP), renamed the Terrorism Information Awareness Program in 2003 and then suspended, is a strong example of designing technologies to collect information at a very broad and deep base across almost all jurisdictional lines and transmit it to an apex to "connect the dots." See Poindexter (2003). For an extensive discussion of data mining and related subjects see Technology and Privacy Advisory Committee (2004). Since September 11, the Defense Advanced Research Projects Agency (DARPA) has stressed developing technology to detect, prevent, and respond to terrorism through such projects as information assurance and survivability programs, self-forming networks, and several counterterrorism projects. See DARPA (2003).

12. See Carroll (1969) for a discussion of knowledge and information as a form of authority and power in the context of Max Weber's analysis of organization and administration.

13. For a discussion of the increasing use of intelligence as a tool in domestic matters, see Sparrow (2000, 255–78). The question of how intelligence "fits" homeland security is a somewhat open one. See Best (2002), Senate Committee on Governmental Affairs (2003), and Schulfofer (2002).

14. The following site has a clear summary of four of the most important legal issues involving liberty, detention, Fourth Amendment protections, prisoners of war and military tribunals, and electronic surveillance: FACSNET: "Making Sense of Terrorism Laws," www.facsnet.org/issues/specials/terrorism/pepperdine.php3.

15. The act is codified at 42 USC §§ 4321–47.

References

Arquilla, John, and David Ronfeldt, eds. 1997. *In Athena's Camp: Preparing for Conflict in the Information Age.* Santa Monica, CA: RAND.
———. 2001. *Networks and Netwars.* Arlington, VA: RAND.
Bell, Daniel. 1999. *The Coming of Post Industrial Society.* New York: Basic Books.
Benshel, Nora. 2003. *The Counterterror Coalitions: Cooperation with Europe, NATO, and the European Union.* Santa Monica, CA: RAND.
Berger, Peter L., and Samuel Huntington. 2002. *Many Globalizations.* Cambridge: Oxford University Press.
Best, Richard A., Jr. 2001. *Intelligence and Law Enforcement: Countering Transnational Threats to the United States,* Washington, DC: Congressional Research Service.
———. 2002. *Homeland Security: Intelligence Support.* Washington, DC: Congressional Research Service, updated November 18.
Bolkcom, Christopher, Lloyd DeSerisx, and Lawrence Kapp. 2003. *Homeland Security: Establishment and Implementation of Northern Command.* Washington, DC: Congressional Research Service.
Bowman, Steve. 2003. *Homeland Security: The Department of Defense's Role.* Washington, DC: Congressional Research Service.

Brake, Jeffrey D. 2003. *Terrorism and the Military's Role in Domestic Crisis Management.* Washington, DC: Congressional Research Service.

Bregman, Jacob. 1999. *Environmental Impact Statements.* 2d ed. New York: Lewis Publishers.

Brennen, Richard. 2002. *Protecting the Homeland: Insights from Army Wargames.* Santa Monica, CA: RAND.

Brown, Shona L., and Kathleen M. Eisenhardt. 1998. *Competing on the Edge: Strategy as Structured Chaos.* Boston, MA: Harvard University Press.

Brudney, Jeffrey L., Lawrence J. O'Toole Jr., and Hal G. Rainey, eds. 2001. *Advancing Public Management: New Developments in Theory, Methods and Practice.* Washington, DC: Georgetown University Press.

Campbell Institute of Public Affairs. 2003. *National Security and Open Government: Striking the Right Balance.* Syracuse, NY: The Maxwell School of Syracuse University.

Carroll, James D. 1969. "Noetic Authority." *Public Administration Review* 29 (September/October), 492–500.

———. 2003a. "The Future of Public Action: From the Administrative to the Entitlement to the Domestic Security State." In *Government Foresight: Myth, Dreams, or Reality,* ed. David Rejeski. Washington, DC: Woodrow Wilson International Center for Scholars.

———. 2003b. "The Right to Privacy vs. the Right to Protection: The Question of Countervailing Power." *Public Administration Times* (January), 26.

Carson, Rachel. 2002. *Silent Spring 40th Anniversary Edition.* New York: Houghton Mifflin.

Chalk, Peter, and William Rosenau. 2004. *"Confronting the Enemy Within": Security Intelligence, the Police, and Counterterrorism in Four Democracies.* Santa Monica, CA: RAND.

Committee on Ways and Means, U.S. House of Representatives. 2000. *The 2000 Green Book: Background Material and Data on Programs within the Jurisdiction of the Committee on Ways and Means.* 17th ed. Washington, DC: U.S. Government Printing Office.

Cragin, Kim, and Sara A. Daly. 2004. *The Dynamic Terrorist Threat.* Santa Monica, CA: RAND.

Crenson, Matthew A., and Benjamin Ginsberg. 2002. *Downsizing Democracy: How America Sidelined Its Citizens and Privatized Its Public.* Baltimore, MD: Johns Hopkins University Press.

———. 2004. "Citizens into Customers: How America Downsized Citizenship and Privatized Its Public." In *Making Government Manageable: Executive Organization and Management in the 21st Century,* eds. Thomas H. Stanton and Benjamin Ginsberg. Baltimore, MD: Johns Hopkins University Press.

Cumming, Alfred. 2004. *FBI Intelligence Reform since September 11, 2001: Issues and Options for Congress.* Washington, DC: Congressional Research Service.

Dacey, Robert. 2003. *Homeland Security: Information Sharing Responsibilities, Challenges and Key Management Issues.* Washington, DC: General Accounting Office.

Davis, Lynn E., Gregory F. Treverton, Daniel Byman, Sara Daly, and William Rosenau. 2004. *Coordinating the War on Terrorism.* Santa Monica, CA: RAND.

Defense Advanced Research Projects Agency (DARPA). 2003. *FACT FILE: A Compendium of DARPA Programs.* Washington DC: DARPA.

Department of Defense. 2002. "Directive No. 5105.67." Section 6.2.11.6, February 19. Available at www.fas.org/irp/doddir/dod/d5105_67.htm.

Doary, Amanda J. 2003. *Civil Security.* Washington, DC: Center for Strategic and International Studies.

Donahue, John D., and Joseph Nye Jr., eds. 2002. *Market-Based Governance: Supply*

Side, Demand Side, Upside, and Downside. Washington, DC: Brookings Institution.

Duncan, Stephen M. 2003. *Citizen Warriors: America's National Guard and Reserve Forces and the Politics of National* Security. New York: Presido Press.

Elsea, Jennifer. 2001. *Terrorism and the Law of War: Trying Terrorists as War Criminals before Military Commissions.* Washington: Congressional Research Service, updated December 11.

———. 2002. *Treatment of "Battlefield Detainees" in the War on Terrorism.* Washington, DC: Congressional Report Service, April 11.

Farber, David. 2003. *Lincoln's Constitution.* Chicago, IL: University of Chicago Press.

Fox, John O. 2001. *If Americans Really Understood the Income* Tax. Boulder, CO: Westview Press.

Frederickson, H. George, and Kevin B. Smith. 2003. *Public Administration Theory Primer.* New York: Westview Press.

Friedman, Thomas. 2000. *The Lexus and the Olive* Tree. New York: Anchor Books.

General Accounting Office. 2003. *Homeland Security: Information Sharing Responsibilities, Challenges, and Key* Issues. Washington, DC: General Accounting Office.

———. 2004. *Reserve Forces: Observations on Recent National Guard Use in Overseas and Homeland Missions and Future Challenges.* Available at www.gao.gov/new.items/d04670t.pdf.

Gorman, Siobhan. 2004. "Second-Class Security." *National Journal* 36 (May): 1303–74.

Gormley, William. 2002. "Reflections on Terrorism and Public Management." In *Governance and Public Security.* The Campbell Public Affairs Institute. Syracuse, NY: The Maxwell School.

H.R. 3162. 2001. The Patriot Act (Uniting and Strengthening America by Providing Appropriate Tools Required to Intercept and Obstruct Terrorism). October 24, Sections 802, 808.

Heyman, Philip B. 1998. *Terrorism and America: A Commonsense Strategy for a Democratic Society.* Cambridge: MIT Press.

———. 2003. *Terrorism, Freedom, and* Security. Cambridge: MIT Press.

Hoffman, Bruce. 2001. *Inside Terrorism.* Santa Monica, CA: RAND, 162.

Johnston, David. 2004. "F.B.I. Chief Sees NATO-like Antiterror Alliance." *New York Times* (June 23), A12

Johnston, David, and Carl Hulse. 2004. "Ricin on Capitol Hill: The Overview; Finding of Deadly Poison in Office Disrupts the Senate." *New York Times* (February 4), A1.

Joint Committee on Taxation. 1999. *Estimates of Federal Tax Expenditures for Fiscal Years 2000–2004.* Washington, DC: U.S. Government Printing Office.

Jost, Timothy Stoltzfus. 2003. *Disentitlement?* Oxford: Oxford University Press.

Kettl, Donald F. 1988. *Government by Proxy: (Mis?)Managing Federal Programs.* Washington, DC: Congressional Quarterly Press.

———. 2002. *The Transformation of Governance.* Baltimore, MD: Johns Hopkins University Press.

King, Roderick. 2000. *Budgeting Entitlement.* Washington, DC: Georgetown University Press.

Kirschenbaum, Alan. 2003. *Chaos Organization and Disaster Management.* New York: Marcel Dekker.

Krizan, Lisa. 1999. *Intelligence Essentials.* Washington, DC: Joint Military College.

Laqueur, Walter. 2003. *No End to War.* New York: Continuum, 49.

Lowenthal, Mark M. 2000. *Intelligence: From Secrets to Policy.* Washington, DC: Congressional Quarterly, Inc.

Mandell, Myrna P., ed. 2001. *Getting Results through Collaboration: Networks and Net-*

work Structures for Public Policy and Management. New York: Greenwood Publishing Group.

McGuire, Michael. 2002. "Managing Networks." *Public Administration Review* 62 (September/October): 599–609.

Mosher, Frederick C. 1980. "The Changing Responsibilities and Tactics of the Federal Government." *Public Administration Review* 40 (November/December): 541–48.

Moynihan, Daniel Patrick.1998. *Secrecy: The American Experience*. New Haven, CT: Yale University Press.

Nadelmann, Ethan A. 1993. *Cops across Borders: The Internationalization of U.S. Criminal Law Enforcement*. University Park: Pennsylvania State University Press.

Ochmanek, David. 2003. *Military Operations against Terrorist Groups Abroad*. Santa Monica, CA: RAND.

Office of Homeland Security. 2002. *National Strategy for Homeland Security*. Washington, DC: Office of Homeland Security, July. Available at www.whitehouse.gov/homeland/book/.

Office of Management and Budget (OMB). 2003. *Report to Congress on Combating Terrorism*. Washington, DC: Office of Management and Budget, September. Available at www.whitehouse.gov/omb/inforeg/2003_combat_terr.pdf.

———. 2004. *Budget of the United States Government, Analytical Perspectives*. Washington, DC: Office of Management and Budget. Available at www/whitehouse.gov/omb/budget/fy2005/pdf/spec.pdf.

Olshensky, Barbara. 2002. *Secret Trials and Executions: Military Tribunals and the Threat to Democracy*. New York: Seven Stories Press.

Parachini, John V., Lynn E. Davis, and Timothy Liston. 2003. *Homeland Security: A Compendium of Public and Private Organizations' Policy Recommendations*. Santa Monica, CA: RAND.

Pear, Robert. 2004. "Survey Finds U.S. Agencies Engaged in Data Mining." *New York Times* (May 27).

Permanent Select Committee on Intelligence, U.S. House of Representatives. 1996. "Intelligence and Law Enforcement." In *IC21: The Intelligence Community in the 21st Century*, 13. Available at www.access.gpo.gov/congress/house/intel/ic21/ic21013.html.

Peterson, Peter G. 2004. *Running on Empty*. New York: Farrar Straus, & Giroux.

Platt, Rutherford H. 1999. *Disaster and Democracy: The Politics of Extreme Natural Events*. Washington, DC: Island Press.

Poindexter, John M. 2003. "Finding the Face of Terror in Data." *New York Times* (September 10), reprinted at http://foi.missouri.edu/terrorintelligence/findingface.html.

Powers, Thomas. 2002. *Intelligence Wars: American Secret History from Hitler to Al-Qaeda*. New York: New York Review of Books.

Public Administration Review. 2002. "Democratic Governance in the Aftermath of September 11, 2001." *Public Administration Review* (September–October).

Rehnquist, William. 2000. *All the Laws but One*. New York: Vintage Books.

Relyea, Harold C. 2004a. *Homeland Security: Department Organization and Management—Implementation Phase*. Washington, DC: Congressional Research Service.

———. 2004b. *Homeland Security: The Presidential Coordination Office*. Washington, DC: Congressional Research Service.

Richelson, Jeffrey J. 1999. *The U.S. Intelligence Community*. Boulder, CO: Westview Press.

Roenthal, Uriel, Arjen Boin, and Louise Comfort, eds. 2001. *Managing Crises: Threat, Dilemmas, Opportunities*. Springfield, IL: Charles C. Thomas.

Rosenau, James N. 2003. *Distant Proximities: Dynamics beyond Globalization*. Princeton, NJ: Princeton University Press.

Rosenbloom, David H. 2000. *Building a Legislative-Centered Public Administration.* Tuscaloosa: University of Alabama Press.

Rosenzweig, Paul. 2003. "Securing Freedom and the Nation: Collecting Intelligence under the Law," Testimony before the U.S. House of Representatives Permanent Select Committee on Intelligence, Regarding Securing Freedom and the Nation: Collecting Intelligence Under the Law, April 9. Available at www.heritage.org/Research/HomelandDefense/TST040903.cfm.

Rubin, Claire B. 2004. "Major Terrorist Events in the U.S. and Their Outcomes." *Journal of Homeland Security and Emergency Management* 1 (Issue 1).

S. Report No. 107–351, H. Report No. 107–792. 2003. *Joint Inquiry into Intelligence Community Activities before and after the Terrorist Attacks of September 11, 2001: Report of the U.S. Senate Select Committee on Intelligence and U.S. House Permanent Select Committee on Intelligence.* 107th Congress, 2d Session. Washington, DC: U.S. Government Printing Office.

Salamon, Lester. 1981. "Rethinking Public Management: Third Party Government and the Changing Forms of Government Action." *Public Policy* 29 (Summer): 255–75.

Schmandt, Henry J., and John C. Bollens. 1982. *Metropolis: Its People, Politics, and Economics.* New York: HarperCollins.

Schulfofer, Stephen J. 2002. *The Enemy Within: Intelligence Gathering, Law Enforcement and Civil Liberties.* New York: Century Foundation.

Senate Committee on Governmental Affairs. 2003. *State and Local Officials: Still Kept in the Dark about Homeland Security.* Minority Report. Washington, DC: U.S. Government Printing Office, August. http://govt-aff.senate.gov/_files/sprt10833min_hs_statelocal.pdf.

Singer, P.W. 2003. *Corporate Warriors: The Rise of the Privatized Military Industry.* Ithaca, NY: Cornell University Press.

Smith, David G. 2002. *Entitlement Politics.* New York: Aldine de Gruyter.

Sparrow, Malcolm K. 2000. *The Regulatory Craft.* Washington, DC: Brookings Institution Press, 255–78.

Squassoni, Sharon. 2004. *Globalizing Cooperative Threat Reduction: A Survey of Options.* Washington, DC: Congressional Research Service.

Stern, Gary M., and Morton Halperin. 1994. *The U.S. Constitution and the Power to Go to War: Historical and Current Perspectives.* Westport, CT: Greenwood Press.

Stern, Jessica. 2003. *Terror in the Name of God.* New York: ECCO.

Steuerle, C. Eugene. 1998. "Government's Changing Capacity to Respond," In *The Government We Deserve,* eds. C. Eugene Steuerle, Edward M. Gramhich, Hugh Heclo, and Demetra Smith Nightingale. Washington, DC: The Urban Institute Press.

Stevens, Paul Shott. 2002. *U.S. Armed Forces and Homeland Defense: The Legal Framework.* Washington, DC: Center for Strategic and International Studies.

Stillman, Richard J. II. 1991. *Preface to Public Administration.* New York: St. Martin's Press.

Suleiman, Ezra N. 2003. *Dismantling Democratic States.* Princeton, NJ: Princeton University Press.

Technology and Privacy Advisory Committee. 2004. *Privacy in the Fight against Terrorism.* Washington, DC: Department of Defense.

Theoharis, Athan G. 1998. *A Culture of Secrecy.* Lawrence: University Press of Kansas.

U.S. Department of Justice (DOJ)—Office of Legislative Affairs. 2002. "Responses to Questions Posed to the Attorney General on U.S.A. Patriot Act Implementation, July 26, 2002." Available at www.house.gov/judiciary/patriotresponses101702.pdf.

U.S. Department of Justice—Office of the Inspector General. 2003a. *The Federal Bureau of Investigation's Efforts to Improve the Sharing of Intelligence and Other Information.* Washington, DC: U.S. Department of Justice.

————. 2003b. *The September 11 Detainees: A Review of the Treatment of Aliens Held on Immigration Charges in Connection with the Investigation of the September 11 Attacks.* Washington, DC: U.S. Department of Justice.

U. S. General Accounting Office (GAO). 2003. *Freedom of Information Act: Agency Views on Changes Resulting from New Administration Policy.* Washington, DC: GAO, September.

U.S. House of Representatives, Committee on the Judiciary, Subcommittee on the Constitution. 2003. "Anti-Terrorism Investigations and the Fourth Amendment after September 11: Where and When Can the Government Go to Prevent Terrorist Attacks?" May 20. Available at www.house.gov/judiciary/news051903.htm.

U.S. Senate Committee on the Judiciary. 2002. "The U.S.A. Patriot Act in Practice: Shedding Light on the FISA Process." September 10. Available at http://judiciary.senate.gov/hearing.cfm?id=398.

Waldo, Dwight. 1948. *The Administrative State.* New York: Ronald.

Watson, Bruce, ed. 1990. *United States Intelligence: An Encyclopedia.* New York: Garland.

Waugh, William. 1999. *Living with Hazards, Dealing with Disasters.* Armonk, NY: M.E. Sharpe.

Weich, Ronald. 2001. *Upsetting Checks and Balances.* New York: American Civil Liberties Union.

Wermuth, Michael A. 2004. *Empowering State and Local Emergency Preparedness: Recommendations of the Advisory Panel to Assess Domestic Response Capabilities for Terrorism Involving Weapons of Mass Destruction.* Santa Monica, CA: RAND.

The White House. 2002. "Status of Detainees at Guantanamo." Press Release, February 7.

Wilson, J. Brent. 1994. "The United States' Response to International Terrorism." In *The Deadly Sin of Terrorism: Its Effect on Democracy and Civil Liberty in Six Countries,* ed. David A. Charters. Westport, CT: Greenwood Press.

Part 2

Organizing for More Effective Government

3

Creating the Department of Homeland Security

An Old Approach to a New Problem

Frederick M. Kaiser

On November 25, 2002, the president signed into law the largest governmental reorganization since the creation of the Department of Defense in 1947. The creation of the Department of Homeland Security (DHS) was not an inevitable development. Indeed, after September 11 the president had experimented with alternative approaches that involved coordination of the relevant agencies' activities rather than an attempt to combine agencies into a new cabinet department.

The terrorist attacks of September 11, 2001—commonly referred to as 9/11 because of the date and emergency situation—resulted in one of the most devastating events in U.S. history and the deadliest terrorist assault on American soil. The loss of lives of noncombatants (nearly 3,000) is unequaled in U.S. history; and damage to property, industries, and other victims from the concerted attacks reached as high as $36 billion (Feinberg 2004; Ruben 2004; Clodfelter 1992; Dudziak 2004).[1] The crisis resulted in unprecedented statutory authority to combat terrorism (e.g., the U.S.A. Patriot Act), substantial funding for immediate assistance,[2] and new organizational arrangements.

The need to improve interagency coordination was one of the first priorities after 9/11. It was the principal reason for creating an Office of Homeland Security (OHS) and a Council on Homeland Security initially and the department later on, with the ultimate goal of strengthening the federal government's capability to combat terrorism (U.S. National Commission 2004).[3] The devastating attacks revealed serious defects in this respect. These were especially visible in intelligence gathering and analysis; information sharing, principally between intelligence providers and domestic consumers; preventive measures to reduce or stave off (potential) attacks; and response capabilities among federal units and between them and first responders at the state and local level.

Enhanced coordination has been perceived as a key component to improvement in all of these areas. The OHS, the first major organizational change in the aftermath of 9/11, was established to "coordinate the executive branch's efforts to detect, protect against, respond to, and recover from terrorist attacks within the United States" (Bush 2001b). The DHS—intended to provide a single, unified structure for combating terrorism—was deemed a necessity by the House Homeland Security Committee, which reported the final bill creating the department. The panel wrote that the new establishment was essential to meeting the new "imperative requiring the dozens of agencies charged with various aspects of homeland protection to work together" (U.S. House Committee on Homeland Security 2002, 64).[4] President Bush similarly emphasized the need to "end a great deal of duplication and overlapping responsibilities," by, for instance, providing "a coordinated effort to safeguard our transportation systems and to secure the border" (Bush 2002).

The focus on coordination among the agencies provides a view of major organizational developments in the aftermath of a crisis—here, at an unprecedented level in domestic matters—and a framework to analyze these changes, their causes, and their consequences. These include transformations in program and policy priorities as well as the rationales, differences, conflicts, and (uncertain) impacts surrounding changes to governmental organization and management. In so doing, this examination develops propositions that tie into matters of fundamental interest to public administration and political science, including:

- A substantial range of organizational and procedural options are available for the contemporary U.S. government to meet new or heightened demands and transformed priorities; these alternative structures include creating entirely new agencies, modifying existing ones, and/ or adding new coordinative mechanisms; within each of these possibilities is a wide range of choices.
- Rivalry exists among executive and congressional offices over a number of matters: which specific agencies, functions, duties, and jurisdictions would be transferred; what new entities would be created; what the jurisdictions and powers would be; and what effects would befall the former parent agency and its continuing missions because of the loss of personnel, resources, and internal units.
- The acceptance, modification, or rejection of possible changes are a response to and have implications for political power among competing

institutions, including Congress and the presidency, individual agencies and their officials, as well as organizations inside and outside government (e.g., employee unions, lobbyists, interest groups).

- Conflict and disputes erupt between the executive branch and the legislature over organizational arrangements, because of their implications for oversight and accountability as well as control over public policy and government agencies.
- Competition is evident between two distinct orientations for restructuring government: (1) integrating functions and activities through a consolidation or merger of agencies and (2) enhancing cooperation among agencies through coordinative mechanisms; underlying this dichotomy are different interpretations about the need for different types and degrees of change as well as their effect on policy implementation, of both the new priority mission (i.e., antiterrorism) and the preexisting ones.
- Differences between formal organizational arrangements and parallel (reinforcing or rival) informal structures have an impact on and implications for implementing programs and policies.
- Significant difficulties arise over accurately and reliably measuring the effect of organizational and structural arrangements on policy implementation, especially in calculating effectiveness in preventing and deterring terrorism; results here might be misleading indicators of success (e.g., no attacks on government buildings) or failure (e.g., assaults on them), because of the intrusion of other variables.
- A complete picture of change of such magnitude needs to incorporate other frames of reference besides organizational developments: whether there are sufficient resources; adequate numbers of personnel with appropriate expertise, skills, and training; activist leadership; additional necessary powers; and competent management (a product of people, structure, and systems).

Organizational Developments

Office, Council, and Department

The most significant organizational developments in homeland security have been the creation of the Office of Homeland Security, along with a companion council in 2001 (Bush 2001b), and the Department of Homeland Security the next year (Homeland Security Act of 2002), making it the fifteenth cabinet department. In addition, a plethora of related transformations have affected much of the national government. Although the changes are not of the magnitude or innovative character of those in national security following World War II, homeland security crosses a broad range of policies and programs and affects many agencies. Indeed, most departments and agencies are affected to some degree, either directly (via merger into the new department) or indirectly (via coordinative arrangements), because of their continued role in homeland security. The impact is widespread, in part because "homeland security" is a vague and extremely broad term that is being used for the first time as an organizing concept for the government. The now-defunct Office of Homeland Security revealed this breadth in its working definition: "Homeland security is a concerted national effort to prevent terrorist attacks within the United States, reduce America's vulnerability to combat terrorism, and minimize the damage and recover from attacks that do occur" (Office of Homeland Security 2002; Relyea 2002).

The Department of Homeland Security along with its coordinative capacity reflects this expanse. It combines all or parts of twenty-two separate departments and agencies, ranging from the old (U.S. Customs Service, 1789) to the new (Transportation Security Administration, 2001) and from those with narrow responsibilities and jurisdictions (Plum Island Disease Center, USDA) to those with broad ones (e.g., Customs Service, Coast Guard, and Secret Service). The units have varying degrees of autonomy as well as different specific missions, responsibilities, heritages, cultures, and organizational characteristics. Illustrative of these differences—disparities in some cases—are the U.S. Secret Service and the Immigration and Naturalization Service (INS). The Secret Service was transferred to Homeland Security, after a lifetime in Treasury, intact—that is, with all of its powers, responsibilities, and resources—and is to be "maintained as a distinct entity within the Department" (Kaiser 1988; Homeland Security Act of 2002).[5] The INS, by contrast, was subdivided. Part remained in Justice, while part (enforcement) moved to Homeland Security; there, immigration enforcement is combined with other units involved with border and transportation security and is subject to additional and different departmental controls and oversight than it had previously (Homeland Security Act of 2002).

In addition to the twenty-two agencies merged into the DHS, more than one hundred others—from the Agriculture Department (USDA) and the Central Intelligence Agency (CIA) to the Federal Bureau of Investigation (FBI) and the U.S. Postal Service (USPS)—have responsibilities and jurisdiction in homeland security. Some are substantial and critical, such as CIA and FBI intelligence services, while others are marginal and compartmentalized, such as the Federal Motor Carrier Safety Administration checks on trucks arriving from Mexico and Canada.

Coordinative Mechanisms

Consequently, even though much responsibility for the heightened mission is now consolidated in the DHS, a substantial amount of coordination is required between it and other governmental organizations. The resulting structures either replace or build onto preexisting arrangements, such as the office and initial council on homeland security. Recognizing the reality of numerous separate organizations performing a shared responsibility, the DHS's authorizing legislation (and the predecessor executive directives) set up coordinative mechanisms and grant specific coordinative responsibilities and powers to the department.

At least eight different types of coordinative devices are evident among the various organizational arrangements in homeland security following 9/11.[6] The categories and examples of these are as follows.

Councils Consisting of the President, Who Is Chairman, and Other High-Ranking Officials

The Homeland Security Council—chaired by the president with the vice president and specified department and agency heads as members—was initially established by executive order (E.O. 13228) and subsequently replaced by public law (Sections 901–06, Homeland Security Act of 2002), when the companion Department of Homeland Security was constructed. The statutory version reduces the council's immediate membership from its earlier incarnation (to the president, vice president, and heads of the departments of Defense, Homeland Security, and Justice) but allows for the president to designate other individuals. Such a high-level entity provides for coordination both instrumentally and symbolically. It demonstrates the highest level of commitment, because it involves the president directly and immediately. The council setting, moreover, gives power to the secretary of the DHS over his equals (other cabinet heads) and, before, to the director of the OHS over his "superiors" (cabinet heads). Note that only two other similar devices exist, the National Security Council and the USA Freedom Council, the former created by statute and the latter by executive order.

Committees of Department and Agency Heads and Other High-Ranking Officials

These include the principal committees of the Homeland Security Council as well as the President's Critical Infrastructure Protection Board (E.O. 13231 of October 16, 2001, by President Bush), which was established only eight days after the office and council on homeland security. This effort built on an earlier initiative—the Critical Infrastructure Coordination Group—in the Clinton administration (Presidential Decision Directive 63).

Specially Created Coordinating Offices

The now defunct Office of Homeland Security (E.O. 13228) was a prominent example of this type. In this case, the office was a construct of the presidency. This permitted the president to determine its responsibilities, jurisdiction, authority, budget, and, most important, power inside and outside government. Congress played virtually no role in the building or operation of the OHS; indeed, when a congressional panel wanted its head to testify formally on the full homeland security budget, the office and the White House rejected the invitation.[7] In sum, the presidency designed, constructed, and maintained the office structure; specified whom it would house; determined the area it would occupy; and kept competitors from encroaching on its domain. Similar offices, designed primarily for coordination rather than policy execution themselves, exist in only a few other policy areas, e.g., the Office of National Drug Control Policy and the USA Freedom Corps.

Specified Agency Heads and Other Officers with Qualified Authority to Call Upon Other Agencies and Departments for Assistance

The Director of the Secret Service, now a part of Homeland Security, has this power for its assigned protective duties as well as for security at special events of national significance (such as the presidential nominating conventions) and for national electronic crimes task forces. Various DHS officers and the secretary, in whom are vested all functions of all officers and organizations within the department, are authorized to perform duties associated with information sharing, operating the terrorist alert or warning system, and heading various other homeland security matters that involve other federal agencies. As a related example, the Director of Central Intelligence (DCI) is empowered to task other units in the intelligence community, which could assist in intelligence collection and analysis for homeland security. The DCI also plays a lead role in the new Terrorist Threat Integration Center, a multiagency center involving the CIA, FBI, DHS, and NSA.

Subcabinet Boards, Committees, and Councils

The homeland security council deputies committees illustrate this type of coordinative mechanism.

Task Forces and Partnerships

The Department of Homeland Security has authority, either new or gained from transferred agencies, to set up interagency partnerships and joint operational task forces. The former Federal Emergency Management Administration and the Secret Service, both transferred to the DHS, have extensive experience in many task forces. The legislation creating the department, moreover, sets up specific task forces and calls for interagency cooperation in several fields. Among these are: coordination with entities in the Justice Department, an Office for National Capital Region Cooperation, and a Joint Interagency Homeland Security Task Force.

Transfers of Personnel, Resources, or Units among Agencies

The DHS has authority to request personnel to be detailed to it from other agencies; the law specifies the CIA, FBI, National Security Agency, National Imagery and Mapping Agency, Defense Intelligence Agency, State Department, and "any other agency of the Federal Government that the President considers appropriate" (Homeland Security Act of 2002). The inverse of this may also occur, in selective circumstances. The U.S. Coast Guard, a "distinct entity" in the Department of Homeland Security, may still be transferred to the U.S. Navy in times of war or when the president directs, an extreme rarity in the past (Homeland Security Act of 2002).

Transfers or Sharing of Authority between and among Agencies

Cross-training and cross-designation of personnel as well as shared authority between DHS and other agencies exist on a limited basis; this can occur by virtue of its own authority, working arrangements with other agencies (often through memoranda of understanding), and, if needed, special deputation of department personnel by the U.S. Marshals Service.

Concluding Observations

A number of findings and conclusions emerge from this brief overview of interagency coordination in homeland security, the rationale for the metamorphosis, and its main causes and effects (Lewis 2003; Stanton and Ginsberg 2002). The most obvious is that organizational arrangements—beginning with a new office and ending with a new department and a multiplicity of coordinative mechanisms—have been transformed markedly since 9/11. Indeed, this set of establishments could well be the most far-reaching among domestic civilian agencies and second only to the national security restructuring after World War II.

The specific outcome was not a foregone conclusion. In fact, a large number of varied options for change were available for homeland security. These included: a coordinative office and council, as originally set up; a full department with or without a council; a circumscribed agency (e.g., in border security) with or without a council; and a variety of interagency coordinative devices operating alone or in conjunction with a new agency, department, or office. These options also offer different choices among the entities to be transferred to a new department or agency and to be under its coordinative jurisdiction. Despite the extent of these changes, further adjustments and adaptations are likely to continue—especially in the coordinative arrangements—as demands and priorities change, as new missions compete with former ones, as different leadership takes over, as levels of resources and expertise rise or fall, and as existing relationships become unnecessary or inadequate. The organizations, structures, and capabilities are still evolving.[8]

A difference of opinion arose about the (possible or potential) success of the initial arrangements—centering on the Office of Homeland Security— and about its continuity and stability in the future.[9] On the one hand, the new office and its director had prominence and political power, at least initially, through informal arrangements and relationships. Most important was the close working relationship with the White House, and particularly the president; the director and the office also benefited from the high visibility accompanying the president's announcement before a joint session of Congress and a national television audience.[10] This personalized arrangement, however, possessed the seeds of its own destruction. It could not grow over the long term, because political conditions and climate would inevitably change, for instance, when either of the principals left office, when the president focused on other obligations and interests, when the director's competitors asserted themselves, or when the director desired independent powers and increased resources, to be more effective on his own in combating terrorism. On the other hand, formalizing jurisdiction and authority over homeland security in statute—through a new department, council, and other interagency coordinative mechanisms—would help to provide stability over the long haul and it would enhance the powers and resources of the new offices and officers. Consequently, the search for long-term replacements, especially a new department or agency, arose in Congress and in outside organizations, even while the president instituted the Office of Homeland Security.[11] This union of agencies, initially rejected by the Bush administration, was later embraced fully by it and led to the establishment of the Department of Homeland Security, a revised council, and new or modified coordinative devices.

The different organizational arrangements have different implications for political power and control. In creating the office and council in 2001, the president shared virtually nothing of their organization, operations, and management with Congress. He determined their membership, leadership, budget, responsibilities, jurisdiction, authority, activities, operations, and real power. Reflective of this independence from Congress, the director of the office refused to testify before the Senate Appropriations Committee about antiterrorism funding.

Congress's involvement through legislation would change all this. The Bush administration's eventual sponsorship of a cabinet department came to dominate the agenda, both in general and in specifics; the president's proposal led the deliberations and largely determined the final product. Nonetheless, a transformation of this magnitude requires legislation. This allows Congress to influence critical developments and eventually, if not immediately, curtail the presidentially dominated process. This situation gives Congress opportunities to influence a number of important matters. Most significant was whether a new agency with consolidated jurisdiction and substantial powers and resources (as recommended by a commission headed by two former senators, a Democrat and a Republican) would prevail over a coordinative office (as recommended by a commission headed by a state governor, political ally of the president, and national Republican Party leader at the time). Congress contributed to the choice by developing plans to construct a full department, which was the approach eventually adopted by the White House. Legislation opens other doors for Congress to influence an agency's characteristics, in future remodeling if not in the initial design (when the president was the chief architect). These structural determinations include: the agencies to be moved, their degree of autonomy and continued responsibility for preexisting missions, the infrastructure of the new department, coordinative devices and requirements, funding levels and resources, controls over expenditures, the top offices and their occupants, their obligations to report to and testify before Congress, and audit and investigative requirements imposed on the department.[12]

Department status elevates the head of the operation and encourages a high degree of independence from the White House, causing the organization to become more a creature of Congress. The chief executive officer is a cabinet member directing a full department with substantial powers and separate funding, instead of being a presidential appointee with limited resources, authority, and discretion. Department status creates confirmed positions for the head and other top leadership; gives the organization and its officers specific public policy responsibilities and reporting requirements to Congress; and assures their attendance before congressional panels, for appropriations, authorizations, future legislation, and confirmation of officials as well as for oversight. In addition, the secretary and other department officials are given organizational support and protection. These—along with new and different affiliations, loyalties, and personal relationships within the department and with outside entities—separate them from the White House, while attaching them more frequently, if not more closely, to Capitol Hill.

All in all, the organizational transformations—a new department and interagency coordinative devices—reflect more than new policy priorities in response to a crisis. They also reflect old forms of political competition in response to rival sources of power, including the president and Congress as well as governmental organizations and private-sector stakeholders.

Notes

1. The 2,976 deaths were the highest ever of noncombatants on U.S. soil; this tragedy occurred when hijacked commercial airplanes were crashed into the World Trade Center in New York, the Pentagon in Washington, and a field in Pennsylvania. Only several battles of the Civil War exceeded this total, with 4,032 at Antietam and 7,058 at Gettysburg; and these involved American combatants on both sides of the battles. The attack on Pearl Harbor by Imperial Japan in 1941 led to 2,403 U.S. deaths (2,335 military personnel and 68 civilians). The economic impact of 9/11, which cannot be calculated precisely, reached $33 billion to $36 billion, by some estimates. A month later, deadly anthrax was sent through the U.S. mail to media outlets and the U.S. Congress, killing or afflicting some of those who came into contact with the poison.

2. The initial total of $55 billion consisted of $40 billion for emergency supplemental aid (P.L. 107-38) and $15 billion for airline industry aid (P.L. 107-42).

3. Interagency and intergovernmental coordination exists at four levels: among the units within an agency or department; between them and other federal agencies; between them and state and local governments as well as private sector participants; and between them and foreign governments directly.

4. U.S. House Committee on Homeland Security, H. Rept. 107-609(I) (2002), p. 64. President Bush used similar language in his statement when signing H.R. 5005, the Homeland Security Act of 2002, 107th Congress (P.L. 107-296), *Weekly Compilation of Presidential Documents,* vol. 38, Nov. 25, 2002, p. 2091 (p. 2 of statement).

5. Interestingly, the Secret Service was established at the time of the greatest challenge to domestic security, the Civil War, when in 1865 it was set up to halt massive counterfeiting operations. The service's protective assignments for the president (and eventually others), moreover, began in the mid-1890s, in response to immediate threats against President Grover Cleveland and his family. In the aftermath of the assassination of William McKinley in 1901, the third president murdered in a thirty-six-year period, protection was regularized; it was coordinated by the president's secretary through an interagency task force consisting of the Secret Service, the Post Office Department, the Department of War at ceremonial occasions and at other times when needed, the Washington Metropolitan Police, and other state and local law enforcement units where protected persons traveled.

6. There appear to be no systematic surveys or typologies of interagency coordinative devices. Existing studies tend to identify only certain ones, often in passing, or cover only a single type, with much of the analysis covering the state and local levels. The eight categories offered here do not necessarily compose a definitive listing. Nonetheless, this

list recognizes a wide range and diversity of types, each with its own characteristics, level and status, extent of operation, and potential.

7. The two views of the director's position are in stark contrast. The administration portrayed him as an adviser, an assistant to the president, and a member of the president's staff, whose being compelled to testify could undermine the separation of powers. By comparison, those calling for his appearance before the panel viewed him also to be an operational officer with influence over agency budgets and policy development and implementation. (For the committee's position, see Robert C. Byrd, chairman, Senate Committee on Appropriations, and Ted Stevens, ranking minority member of the committee, letter to Tom Ridge, special assistant to the president for Homeland Security, March 4, 2002, and letter to the president, March 15, 2002. For the administration's position, see Tom Ridge, assistant to the president for Homeland Security, letter to Honorable Robert C. Byrd, March 25, 2002; and President George W. Bush, "Press Conference by the President," March 13, 2002, available on the White House Web site [http://www.whitehouse.gov].)

8. Recently, Andrew Card, the White House chief of staff, suggested that the homeland security effort is "maturing. It's probably kind of in the teen-age [stage] right now. Some of the teen-agers are a little obstreperous, and some are not. And some are really sucking up to do a good job, and others are hoping they can sleep until 10 o'clock in the morning" (Simendinger 2004, 11).

9. See especially the different proposals from the Gilmore Commission, which advanced coordinative devices along the lines that the Bush administration initially adopted, versus those from the Hart-Rudman Commission, which advocated a new agency consolidating relevant organizations.

10. In announcing the creation of the OHS and its first director, former governor of Pennsylvania and former member of Congress Tom Ridge, President Bush referred to him as a "trusted friend." The president also emphasized that the director would hold a "Cabinet-level position," a rarity for the head of an office who is not confirmed by the Senate, "reporting directly to me" (Bush 2001a).

11. In fact, proposals for major changes in the field predated 9/11 and subsequent developments. In addition to the recommendations of the Gilmore Commission and the Hart-Rudman Commission, legislators sponsored bills that would have created a new agency or full department. These, in turn, reflected concerns for improvement and coordination similar to those that had existed in subfields, especially border control and intelligence sharing, for a long while. The border control initiatives, for instance, date to the Taft presidency and have continued through virtually every subsequent administration, from the executive, legislature, public commissions, and private organizations. The most far-reaching plan—to merge Coast Guard, Customs, and Immigration into the same department or into a new agency—however, did not reach fruition until now. (In 1930, however, a Hoover administration proposal passed the House but was not acted upon by the Senate.) For a survey of border management plans—which were usually designed to make combating illegal immigration or illicit drug/alcohol trafficking more effective or to make operations more efficient—see U.S. Senate Committee on Governmental Affairs 1988; Kaiser 1999; GAO 1993.

12. This last feature would occur, for instance, through a statutory office of inspector general and the Government Accountability Office, checks that do not normally apply to entities in the Executive Office of the President.

References

Bush, George W. 2001a. "Address before a Joint Session of Congress of the United States: Response to Terrorist Attacks of September 11." *Weekly Compilation of Presidential Documents* 37 (September): 1347–51.

————. 2001b. "Executive Order 13228," sec. 3. Issued October 8.

————. 2002. "Remarks on Signing the Homeland Security Act of 2002." *Weekly Compilation of Presidential Documents* 38 (December 2): 2091.

Clodfelter, Michael. 1992. *Warfare and Armed Conflict: A Statistical Reference, 1618–1991*. New York: McFarland and Co.

Dudziak, Mary. 2004. *September 11 in History: A Watershed Moment?* Durham, NC: Duke University Press.

Feinberg, Kenneth. 2004. Master of September 11th Victims Fund. Statement, U.S. Department of Justice, Washington, DC, January.

The Homeland Security Act of 2002. 2002. H.R. 5005, 107th Congress, P.L. 107-296, November.

Kaiser, Frederick M. 1988. "Origins of Secret Service Protection of the President: Personal, Interagency, and Institutional Conflict." *Presidential Studies Quarterly* 18 (Winter), 101–28.

————. 1999. *Reorganization Proposals for U.S. Border Management Agencies.* Washington, DC: Congressional Research Service.

Lewis, David E. 2003. *Presidents and the Politics of Agency Design: Political Insulation in the United States Government Bureaucracy.* Palo Alto, CA: Stanford University Press.

Office of Homeland Security. 2002. *National Strategy for Homeland Security.* Washington, DC: Office of Homeland Security, July. Available at www.whitehouse.gov/homeland/book/. Accessed May 14, 2006.

Relyea, Harold C. 2002. "Homeland Security and Information." *Government Information Quarterly* 19 (2002): 213–23.

Rubin, Claire. 2004. "Major Terrorist Events in the U.S. and Their Outcomes." *Journal of Homeland Security and Emergency Management* (1):1, article 2.

Simendinger, Alexis. 2004. "The Buzz: On the Record." Interview in *Government Executive* 36 (June): 11.

Stanton, Thomas H., and Benjamin Ginsberg. 2002. *Making Government Manageable: Executive Organization and Management in the Twenty-First Century.* Baltimore, MD: Johns Hopkins University Press.

U.S. Government Accountability Office. 1993. *Customs Service and INS: Dual Management Structure for Border Inspections Should Be Ended.* Washington, DC: General Accounting Office.

U.S. House Committee on Homeland Security. 2002. House Report 107-609(I), 64.

U.S. National Commission on Terrorist Attacks upon the United States. 2004. *The 9/11 Commission Report: Final Report,* Executive Summary. Washington, DC: U.S. Government Printing Office, 215–54, 383–428.

U.S. Senate Committee on Governmental Affairs. 1988. *Border Management Reorganization.* Washington, DC: Government Printing Office.

4

An Undersecretary for Management

Its Potential in the Department of Homeland Security

Alan L. Dean and Dwight Ink

At the time it was submitted to Congress, the structure of President Bush's proposed Department of Homeland Security (DHS) was criticized heavily. Many believed the number of functions assembled from twenty-two agencies was too large to meld together into a coherent organization that could take the quick action required for responding to future attacks. There were too many program management approaches, incompatible field organizations, and divergent information and communication systems that could not interact.[1] But there was an important exception to the objections raised by the critics.

Not well publicized was the widespread support that knowledgeable observers gave to the innovative provision in the DHS proposal for an undersecretary for management (USM). It embodied the broadest scope ever specified by law for a management official in a federal department. The office was viewed as a badly needed attempt to establish a center for comprehensive management leadership—one with the potential to overcome a serious deficiency of most current executive departments, namely, the dispersion of responsibility for management functions among numerous second- and third-tier officials. Only by creating a post at the undersecretary level with this broad scope of authority could a DHS secretary hope to shape this extraordinarily complex department into an organization that could operate effectively under stress.

To appreciate fully the challenge the DHS faces in establishing an effective USM, and how important that role can be, it is helpful to first examine past attempts to provide major agencies with a focal point for the coordination and direction of those offices and functions that affect *how* the organization functions, as opposed to *what* it is expected to do. This chapter will, therefore, describe earlier efforts to provide agency heads with a senior aide possessing the rank and scope of responsibilities needed to provide effective leadership in management matters.

As the Executive Branch has grown in size and complexity, legislation and executive directives[2] have compelled federal agencies to improve or institute numerous management systems. Early steps included merit appointments (1883), the executive budget (1921), and pay classification (1923). Since then, numerous laws and regulations have accumulated for the purpose of improving accounting systems, procurement and contracting, and a variety of support services.

Most departmental secretaries have been chiefly concerned with the time-consuming matters of policy, program implementation, relationships with the White House and Congress, and "care and feeding" of interest groups and public affairs. They often give little personal attention to matters of organization or internal management. Some deputy secretaries, that is, the number-two officials, have given attention to internal administrative needs or problems, but their efforts rarely have ensured consistent direction and coordination of numerous, interrelated management systems. More often they have focused on specific problems without addressing underlying causes or long-term solutions.

The U.S. comptroller general has proposed a version of the chief operating officer (COO) as a way of providing a focal point for management (GAO 2004, 2002), but this concept has its shortcomings. The office of COO would seem to blur the line between who is directing department operations and who is providing leadership in developing the mechanisms through which the operations can be directed. In general, it appears that the COO concept is too varied and unclear to rely upon for management leadership in a department. No departmental position today meets the need for management leadership on which a secretary can rely.

The capacity of departments to address management issues effectively has had a difficult and uneven history.

The Chief Clerk Emerges

An early development in the provision of leadership for administrative management functions at the departmental level was the emergence of the position of "chief clerk" in some agencies.[3] These officials were almost always veteran career civil servants who thoroughly understood how their departments functioned and had substantial institutional memories. Their specific titles, duties, and influence varied considerably from department to department.

An example of the classical chief clerk was provided by the War Department in the years before and during World War II. As the department's senior civil servant concerned with internal administration, he[4] oversaw numerous management functions that affected the Office of the Secretary or primarily concerned the department's civilian employees. He had direct responsibility for personnel policies and systems, and the director of the Office of Civilian Personnel reported to him. Since many categories of headquarters and field personnel and financial actions required individual approval or confirmation by the chief clerk, the office was viewed as more concerned with process than substance.

Enter the Hoover Commission

The years immediately following World War II saw a surge of interest in the organization, management, and efficiency of federal agencies. One major product of this concern was the 1948 establishment of the "Hoover Commission,"a bipartisan group of twelve presidential and congressional appointees chaired by former president Herbert Hoover that was created to review the organization of the executive branch.

Among its broad range of recommendations was one calling for the creation of an administrative assistant secretary in each department.[5] The commission report went on to suggest that length of tenure was desirable and, therefore, these management-oriented officials should be appointed from, and remain in, the career service. The commission recommendations were well received, and, very quickly, statutory assistant secretaries for administration (ASAs) were established in most of the executive departments.

Assistant Secretaries for Administration in Action

From 1949 to 1969, the ASAs played an important and constructive role in most executive departments. They provided the expertise and continuity sought by the Hoover Commission, and they provided a high-ranking official capable of overseeing most or all the departmental offices concerned with internal administration. Their informal organization, the Executive Officers' Group, met regularly to exchange ideas and improve interagency cooperation. It was often consulted by the leadership of the Bureau of the Budget.

During the Kennedy administration and the beginning of that of Johnson, a more activist domestic role for government led to the need for a broader management concept as programs multiplied and the task of implementing them became more complex. Yet an increasing number of ASAs were coming to be viewed as too preoccupied with administrative regulations, focusing

on limiting what program managers could do rather than on finding legitimate approaches to administrative management that would help accomplish
program objectives. Most were outside the mainstream of program development and management.

As one step to correct this weakness, the ASA appointments in the new
departments of HUD and transportation in the mid-1960s, while still appointed by the secretaries, also required formal approval by the president. In
addition to administrative management functions[6] both were given a strong
role in designing and monitoring program management structures and systems. They provided leadership in decentralizing program and administrative management and in designing coordinating arrangements in Washington
and the field offices. Joint administrative/program review teams were established to assess the effectiveness of new programs a few months after being
launched. Crosscutting teams were utilized in assessing program delivery
operations and their impact upon state and local assistance recipients.

This evolution of departmental management leadership took an important
step backward when the Nixon administration began replacing career ASAs
with political appointees, forcing some of the best career leadership out of
office. Several of the political replacements performed well. But too many
entered these positions with little knowledge of how government works and
too little understanding of the fundamental values that are basic to public service in a democratic society. Most took too long to fully grasp the many activities for which they were responsible, and did not provide the continuity that
the Hoover Commission had sought, frequently departing for higher-paying
private sector positions just as they were becoming fully on top of their jobs.

Fragmentation of Administrative Management Functions

The decline of the career ASA concept was shortly followed by a series of
statutes that made it impossible for any ASA (career or noncareer) to become
the key figure in internal management, as they had been in the DOT, HUD,
and several other departments.

The first such statute was the Inspector General Act of 1978, which had a
greater weakening impact on the role of ASAs than most people realize.
Despite some positive features of the Inspector General (IG) role, the transfer of audit functions from the ASAs to the IGs contributed to an unfortunate
departmental shift from emphasizing the prevention of abuse and poor management to investigating the problems after they occurred. The ASAs were
robbed of one of their most important management tools. Further, the statutory
language was interpreted by some as shifting management leadership to the
inspectors general. The Chief Financial Officers Act of 1990 further weakened

the remnants of ASA leadership capacity, as did later legislation establishing separate chief information and human capital officers (Wamsley 2004).

Emergence of the Undersecretary for Management (USM) Concept

It had become evident that there was no way to revive the career ASA position as contemplated by the Hoover Commission. But there clearly remained a need for a management official of higher rank than assistant secretary, and it was unlikely that such a senior officer could be given career status. The most promising way of again providing departments with an effective focus of leadership in management matters was to create a new post of under-secretary rank whose incumbent could provide department-wide administrative and program management leadership on behalf of the secretary.

The first faltering step toward an undersecretary for management had occurred by accident early in the Nixon administration. The ASA post in the Department of Health, Education and Welfare (HEW) became vacant and an effort was made to install a noncareer applicant with no experience in federal agency management. The ploy succeeded only when the White House persuaded the then Civil Service Commission to authorize a "rare bird" appointment. As the name suggests, rare birds were supposed to be individuals with extraordinary qualifications for hard-to-fill career positions. The new ASA's qualifications in no way met the criteria for a rare bird appointment.

The Bureau of the Budget (BOB) assistant director for management immediately informed the HEW secretary that his action was unacceptable. But recognizing that it was not politically feasible to remove the new appointee, he urged the secretary to establish an undersecretary for management position that oversaw the ASA and other management positions. It was a noncareer position that did not survive the tenure of the first, and only, incumbent, and provided only limited useful background for the more careful development of the concept as part of Nixon's ambitious departmental reorganization plans. When a later HEW secretary was pressured into accepting another ASA of marginal capabilities, he obtained the detail of a management-oriented OMB official who was designated management adviser to the secretary and served as executive director of a new Departmental Management Council chaired by the undersecretary.[7] This also was an interim arrangement, which was abandoned by the next secretary.

Both of these devices were utilized in HEW because the secretaries involved, and their undersecretaries, felt the need for a single staff member qualified to provide leadership in departmental management matters. But both were short-lived.

Nixon's Departmental Reorganization Program

The first major effort to create the USM position in each department was sponsored, ironically, by President Nixon, who had done so much to get rid of the career ASAs. It occurred even before the fragmentation of departmental management we have outlined.

In January 1972 President Nixon included in his State of the Union message recommendations for a massive restructuring of the domestic executive departments. The proposals called for the abolition of seven departments as well as several independent agencies, and the regrouping of their programs in four new, carefully designed departments. The structures of the proposed departments drew heavily from models developed earlier by the Department of Transportation (DOT) and Housing and Urban Development (HUD). A new and noteworthy feature of the draft bills submitted by the president in March 1972 was the provision, in each department, of an undersecretary for management.[8]

The appropriate congressional committees promptly conducted hearings on what was now known as "The President's Departmental Reorganization Program" and there was an encouraging degree of acceptance of the recommended departments of Community Development and Natural Resources. The undersecretary for management concept was welcomed by the key congressional committees and would have been included in any final legislation.

Unfortunately, President Nixon abandoned most attempts at departmental reform when he sought reelection, and the first serious attempt to provide for USMs came to naught.

The Academy and the Undersecretary for Management

Many Fellows of the National Academy of Public Administration, and especially those who have been deeply involved in matters related to the internal management of federal agencies, have endorsed the need for departmental USMs, and the merits of the concept have been supported by the Academy's Standing Panel on Executive Organization and Management and an ad hoc Academy committee concerned with the organization of homeland security programs.

Individual Academy panel reports have urged that departments seek legislation providing for USMs. An example is provided by the 1994 panel report *Renewing HUD* (NAPA 1994, 241). The project panel concluded that HUD should "develop legislation that would provide continuity of leadership by establishing an undersecretary for management and requiring that the individual in this position be appointed by the president and subject to Senate confirmation with qualifications to manage a large public organization set forth in the law." The recommendation also urged that a career staff be provided to support the work of the undersecretary.

The panel members were of the view that, in the absence of the proposed undersecretary position, the department would lack a dependable point of leadership with the rank, qualifications, and scope of authority needed to successfully implement the many actions needed to revitalize HUD.

Neither the president nor the HUD secretary has pursued the Academy panel's recommendation, and the department has made little progress in achieving a comprehensive reform of its management.

By the beginning of the George W. Bush administration, no department secretary had, and none could restore, a strong post with an incumbent who could provide leadership in the broad range of management organization and systems required for carrying out their program missions.

Moving the USM Concept into Practice

After decades of both progress and setbacks in efforts to provide departments with a focal point for management leadership, the Bush administration and the Congress took the step of establishing the first legislatively based undersecretary for management in the new DHS. This USM is having to break much new ground because there are no comparable positions in any of the domestic departments.[9]

The range of matters that the secretary is expected to deal with through the USM is shown in Appendix 4.1. It is the broadest ever specified by law for an internal management official. The creation of a post of such potential scope at the undersecretary level can greatly enhance the capacity of a DHS secretary to carry out the vital mission of homeland security. At the same time, if poorly managed and weakly supported, it will fail, and it may be many years before another attempt is made to fill the institutional management gap that exists in our federal departments.

Having been provided with an undersecretary for management by its authorizing statute, how is the DHS putting the office into practice? Thus far, the department has been very reluctant to provide to the authors information that is usually available about the steps taken to establish a new office and its initial goals. In the absence of such information, this chapter can at least discuss several factors that are likely to be especially critical as the DHS strives to advance this office to the level of management leadership contemplated by the president and Congress.

1. Strength of the Office

The broad USM legislative mandate, and its rank above that of an assistant secretary, should give the USM greater weight in exercising the departmental leadership role contemplated by the legislation than that enjoyed by incumbents of earlier more limited offices. However, this will not automatically occur. Much will depend on the breadth of experience and the leadership qualities of the incumbent. If appointments are made from outside government, it is essential that the person have prior government experience in senior managerial capacities. This is not a place for on-the-job training or political payoffs.

Every effort also should be made to select individuals prepared to serve as long as conditions permit, including service through changes in secretaries should a new secretary so desire. A fixed term would rarely help continuity through changes in administrations, however, as it is vital that a USM have the full confidence of the secretary being served. There should be a senior position under the USM occupied by a career person who could serve as acting USM during presidential transitions, providing some continuity of leadership. At this point, there is no such provision.

In fact, the leadership positions within the USM are filled by too many political appointees and not enough career appointees. With respect to fighting terrorism overseas, there is recognition of the value of depending on professional career military leaders who serve under a small number of political policy leaders in Washington. Why should professional career leadership be any less critical for protecting our homeland against terrorism? It is essential that the management of homeland security not be politicized. One of the principal purposes of the Senior Executive Service was to develop senior career executives that could be utilized in important leadership roles such as those needed in the USM. The current political/career leadership arrangement in the DHS must be changed.

Equally important to the USM's success will be the support given the USM by the DHS secretary, the OMB, and congressional oversight committees. Not surprisingly, there are indications that some of the administrative staff brought in from different agencies have sought to use their prior association with members and committees of Congress to limit the leadership role of the undersecretary. These pressures need to be countered soon or they will become a permanent fact of life that limits the potential of the USM. The OMB is supportive of the undersecretary concept, but it appears that congressional support and understanding of the undersecretary concept are mixed. At the same time, congressional support does depend in part on the level of information and cooperation offered by the USM and other department leaders.

2. Overcoming Fragmentation

The detailed legislative listing of the management functions that the secretary is to carry out through the USM is very helpful in making clear the breadth of leadership expected from the USM. Care should be taken to delegate them all at the outset. If some are withheld or delegated elsewhere in the beginning, it will be difficult later to draw them into the purview of the USM.

One of the great virtues of the USM concept is the opportunity to reduce, if not eliminate, the problems of the growing trend to fragment administrative functions as has been discussed. This fragmentation tends to compartmentalize different elements of management, often creates problems for program managers, and precludes a secretary from having one person to whom he or she can look for management information or to lead presidential or secretarial management initiatives. The various USM functions are all interrelated to some degree, each having an impact on one another. Every effort should be made from the outset to integrate them into a cohesive and comprehensive approach to management that is all inclusive.

It seems that much of the design of the complicated DHS field office structure is being led from outside the undersecretary's organization, although she is involved personally. If true, that is a bad precedent. First, in the establishment of a new agency or department, the structure and operating systems (whose designs are led by the USM) are interwoven in certain respects and their development should proceed in concert. A structure that is designed for only a limited field role, for example, could not properly support programs whose missions and program delivery systems require a strong field operation, and delegations of authority would exceed the capacity of the field offices to exercise those delegations responsibly (Ink and Dean 2004).

Second, designing the headquarters structure in one part of the department while designing the field structure elsewhere makes no sense. The two are integral parts of the whole and must be regarded as such. Although the legislative provision for designing the field organization is separate from the USM, we see no impediment to the USM's being assigned this responsibility by the secretary.

It is also important that in equipping the inspector general (IG) to carry out his or her responsibilities, the role of that office not be developed at the expense of the USM's leadership on management matters. This happened earlier when the establishment of the IGs removed the audit function from the ASAs, weakened the ASA management analysis capability, and diluted the ASAs' management leadership role.

3. Broader Use of Audit Function

Statutory inclusion of an audit function under the new USM is a more significant development than is generally realized. The inspectors general statutes have appropriately included an audit capability among the inspector general functions, but audit should not be confined exclusively to the IG office. Removing this important tool of management from the control of a secretary or agency head has had the effect of reducing their ability to move swiftly to identify and respond to weaknesses in departmental practices or to address an emerging scandal before it has escalated into the public domain. As noted above, the earlier transfer of total responsibility for auditing to the IGs has at times had the unfortunate effect of shifting departmental emphasis from prevention of abuse to that of later investigating a scandal that might have been avoided. The DHS statute will enable the department to emphasize the use of auditors in preventing abuse and poor management as well as to continue to conduct independent investigations through the IG.

4. Strengthening Management Analysis

The DHS statutory language also makes clear that the undersecretary will be responsible for the often-neglected management analysis function. This tool was once used far more extensively than today in cutting red tape and in designing processes that improved the effectiveness of programs in carrying out their missions. An effective analysis unit can help the new department break down the walls of its component organizations through designing organizations and operating systems that cut though organizational barriers.

It is encouraging to note the extent to which crosscutting task forces are being used in building the department. However, there also needs to be an institutional core for continuity and certain in-depth analyses that take more time than organizations can afford to detail to task forces. Further, such a unit can provide specialized management expertise not otherwise available.

5. Program Management

The task of consolidating differing administrative systems inherited from the agencies from which DHS was formed, and/or establishing compatibility among them, presents an unprecedented challenge.[10] It is so time consuming that the USM will have difficulty giving adequate attention to assisting program leaders in developing effective program delivery systems. Yet this role of providing leadership to the management dimension of designing new program processes and improving existing ones is one in which the USM concept should gain particular strength over the more limited capacity of most earlier ASAs.

This office is in a good position to ensure that administrative processes, such as personnel and procurement, do not drift apart from program managers. Over the years, this degree of separation has been a constant danger, resulting in administrative management's tending to become overly burdened with process and the administrative specialists becoming technicians rather than managers. It has contributed to program managers' looking upon administrative people as those who tell them what they cannot do rather than what they can do within the bounds of good management. Administrative management and program management approaches should be developed and maintained as two integral parts of a whole, a key role envisaged for the USM.

6. Monitoring

The USM should be charged by the secretary with the major ongoing responsibility for identifying deficiencies in the department's organization and management systems and the designing of measures to bring about improvements. In a department as complex and untested as the DHS there will be an unusually large number of problems to resolve during its formative years, with exciting opportunities for innovative improvements in how the department functions. For example, it has great potential for innovation in both internal and external coordination of diverse entities in Washington and the field.

The statute provides the USM with ample tools to monitor how well the departmental structures and systems are working. Its statutory role in tracking performance measures should ensure that management is integrated as an important element of measuring program performance to the fullest extent possible. This USM role is not to be confused with the separate role of the IG to bring an independent perspective to the search for abuse and other problems. Although these two activities are independent from each other, they should develop a constructive working arrangement in which they share information and one complements the other.

7. Department Culture

Every organization develops its own internal culture, as Michael Maccoby discusses in chapter 9, an informal characteristic that has a considerable impact on the effectiveness with which it functions. Because DHS depends so heavily on internal and external communication and coordinated planning and action, it must develop a culture that is multifaceted yet cohesive; one that can plan carefully yet act quickly; one in which information flows easily and rapidly yet that can safeguard critical information with care; and one that takes pride in itself yet does not guard turf at the expense of collaboration or the sharing of credit for success.

Developing this type of departmental environment will be a key element of the secretary's leadership, and the deputy secretary can also play an important role, but the USM will be their principal aide in bringing it about. The undersecretary has a broad range of tools to help shape the approach employees apply to their work. The USM design of personnel, information, and other administrative systems, in combination with the internal organization structures, can do much to break down internal barriers in their day-to-day activities. The USM can foster innovative, yet largely informal, means of communication among the department entities, especially between headquarters and field. Through this work, and the continued work of crosscutting task forces, this office can do much to block the evolution of organizational stovepipes and parochial concepts that undermine efforts to develop teamwork. On behalf of the secretary, it can establish both formal and informal incentives throughout the department for improvement and recognition of performance that advance a positive internal culture.

The authors hope the DHS establishment of an undersecretary for management will lead to its replication in other departments that struggle with fragmented management approaches led by individuals with highly varied levels of capability. The extent to which the USM position realizes its full potential in the DHS, and proves to be a valuable innovation in practice, will greatly affect the likelihood of that happening. It is time for federal departments and independent agencies to develop a different structure for management leadership that can better help advance our increasingly complex governmental missions. The authors believe the undersecretary for management under highly qualified leadership best meets that need.

Notes

1. In addition to the congressional debates, skepticism was expressed by a number of those in the field of public administration, including certain of our colleagues in the National Academy of Public Administration.

2. Especially executive orders and OMB circulars.

3. The term *clerk* once included far higher levels of civil servants than now occupy positions with that title.

4. In those days, the top career positions were still virtually all male.

5. The specific language included, "there should generally be an administrative assistant secretary who might be appointed solely for administrative duties of a housekeeping and management nature and who would give continuity in top management." (Hoover Commission Report, 26)

6. The career ASAs in HUD and the DOT were responsible for human resources, financial management, audit, budget, management analysis, support services, and investigations in the case of the DOT. This range of administrative functions soon disappeared from the portfolio of ASAs.

7. This council concerned itself with areas such as decentralization, field organization, the role of regional directors, Federal Regional Councils, and headquarters organization.

8. In the proposed Department of Community Development, the title was undersecretary for organization and management systems, but the intended functions were the same.

9. The State Department does have an undersecretary for management who is described as the "principal management official of the department," and who is listed as responsible for the direction and control of all budgetary, administrative, and personnel policies of the department. There is no mention of any role in program management that an effective USM should play.

10. The DHS approach is commendable for establishing a department-wide framework of administrative concepts and basic regulations within which the departmental components will have some degree of flexibility with respect to the processes of implementation.

References

General Accounting Office (GAO). 2002. *Highlights of a GAO Roundtable: The Chief Operating Officer Concept: A Potential Strategy to Address Federal Governance Challenges.* Washington, DC: GAO, October 4.

———. 2004. *The Chief Operating Officer Concept and Its Potential Use as a Strategy to Improve Management at the Department of Homeland Security.* Washington, DC: GAO.

Hoover Commission, 1949. *The Hoover Commission Report on Organization of the Executive Branch of Government* New York: McGraw-Hill Book Company, Inc.

Ink, Dwight, and Alan L. Dean. 2004. "Modernizing Federal Field Operations." In *Making Government Manageable*, ed, Thomas H. Stanton and Benjamin Ginsberg. Baltimore, MD: Johns Hopkins University Press.

National Academy of Public Administration. 1994. *Renewing HUD.* Washington, DC: National Academy of Public Administration (July), 241.

Wamsley, Barbara. 2004. "Technocracies: Can They Bell the Cat?" In *Making Government Manageable*, ed. Thomas H. Stanton and Benjamin Ginsberg. Baltimore, MD: Johns Hopkins University Press.

Appendix 4.1

The DHS statute sets forth a number of management responsibilities of the secretary that are to be acted on by the USM. These include:

1. the budget, appropriations, expenditures of funds, accounting, and finance;
2. procurement;
3. human resources and personnel;
4. information technology and communications systems;
5. facilities, property, equipment, and other material resources;
6. security for personnel, information technology and communications systems, facilities, property, equipment, and other material resources;
7. identification and tracking of performance measures relating to the responsibilities of the department;
8. grants and other assistance management programs;
9. the transition and reorganization process, to assure an efficient and orderly transfer of functions and personnel to the department, including the development of a transition plan;
10. the conduct of internal audits and management analysis of the program activities of the department;
11. any other management duties that the secretary may designate.

5

The Need for an Office of Federal Management

Now More than Ever

Ronald C. Moe

It is now the third decade of a debate over whether or not the Office of Management and Budget (OMB) is doing an effective job of managing the executive branch in the president's interest. The two sides in this debate have well-developed positions and strong partisans.

One side argues, and they remain dominant in the political sense, that the OMB was correct to integrate the budget and management elements in their organization into budget-dominated teams. In 1994, when the final consolidation took place and the "management side" of the OMB effectively ceased to exist, then OMB director Leon Panetta stated: "Critics of these recommendations [in the 'OMB 2000 Review'] may say the effort to 'integrate' management and budget will end in merely bigger budget divisions, whose management responsibilities will be driven out by daily fire-fighting over budget issues. . . . We believe this criticism is based on a false premise that 'management' and 'budget' issues can be thought of separately" (Panetta 1994; U.S. OMB 1994; Tomkin 1998; Dean, Ink, and Seidman 1994).[1]

Supporters of a budget-dominated OMB argue that to consider management issues apart from the budget is to ensure that these issues will not be addressed in an effective manner. After all, it is the budget process that gives the management issues and personnel "political clout." They point to the "President's Management Agenda" of the Bush administration as proof that management issues can be addressed within an admittedly budget-dominated OMB. In short, they argue that there is no need for change in the current institution or its priorities. Management is thriving.

The opposing side in this debate rejects the fundamental premise that "management" and "budget" issues are inherently inseparable. They begin their analysis of the current state of the OMB from the opposite premise:

119

namely, that "management" and "budget" are distinctive in their characteristics and cultures and that management, properly defined in this context to mean institutional capacity building, will inevitably suffer when it is incorporated into a budget-based decision process. Budgeting is necessarily and properly a tool for control, not for capacity building. No creative management idea, in their view, has ever emerged from the budget process.

Critics of the current budget-dominated OMB further contend that top-level institutional management is neglected and misdirected under the current organizational arrangement and that the only way for management to receive the attention it deserves and requires is for the present OMB to be reorganized into two separate and equal agencies within the Executive Office of the President (EOP): an Office of Federal Budget (OFB) and an Office of Federal Management (OFM).

Representative Stephen Horn, recently chairman of the House Subcommittee on Government Management, Information and Technology, as early as 1995 summed up the arguments for change:

> The capacity available to the President in the Office of Management and Budget (OMB) has steadily declined and now barely exists. Federal management organization, oversight authority, and general influence have been consistently overridden by recurring budget crises and budget cycle demands, despite conscientious intentions to give 'Budget' and 'Management' equal voice within OMB. . . .
>
> Management of the Federal Government should be a presidential priority. . . . To enhance the President's management capability, Congress should establish in the EOP a top-level management and organization oversight office (Office of Management) headed by an administrator who has direct access to the President. (U.S. House Committee on Government Reform 1995, 5, 8)

The arguments favoring the integrated OMB against the arguments favoring separate institutional units both reporting to the president have been heard now since the early 1980s.[2] This author is a partisan in the debate, believing that the evidence is persuasive that the experiment in organizationally meshing management and budget in the OMB has failed (R. Moe 1991, 1999). This chapter contends that only a separate Office of Federal Management can address the challenging issues confronting the executive branch in a comprehensive manner, one that views management from a presidential perspective. There will be a brief discussion of the concept of management, properly defined, and how this larger issue affects one's view of the sub-debate over a proposed OFM. An extended discussion follows on how an OFM might be organized and what functions it would perform. And finally, the debate over the future of central management in the executive branch is considered within the broader context of the worldwide movement toward disaggregating government and its impact on the democratic theory of governance.

Decline of Management at the OMB

In 1970, the Bureau of the Budget was reorganized and renamed as the Office of Management and Budget (OMB) to reflect what was intended to be an increased emphasis on management (Reorganization Plan 1970; Berman 1979). In one of the ironies of administrative history, the decline of management oversight within the executive branch began at the very moment that it received its symbolic equality with the budget responsibilities of the president. Prior to 1970, the top leadership of the Bureau of the Budget had been largely drawn from the career civil service, a cadre that took "neutral competence" seriously as its ideal (Heclo 1975). The mission of the agency had been to protect the institutional interests of the presidency, not the immediate political interests of the incumbent president. The latter was the responsibility of the White House staff.

Beginning in 1970, however, several trends influenced the practices of the OMB, trends that resulted in a much-debilitated OMB and hence a weakened presidency. The first trend was the politicization of the OMB;[3] second was the policy of disinvestment in the management infrastructure of the executive branch, a policy that included the management of the OMB (Bowsher 1988; Comptroller General 1989); and third was the contemporary thrust of the so-called new public management (NPM) (Kettl 2002) to include the "reinventing government" exercise of the 1990s and to weaken central management oversight of the executive branch in favor of the devolution of authorities and the disaggregation of government generally.[4]

Although staff numbers are necessarily a crude measurement, the loss of personnel on the "management side" of the OMB has been impressive. In 1970, 224 employees were on the management side of the OMB. This number was considered minimal at the time. By 1980, when President Jimmy Carter left office, the number had fallen to 111. The Reagan administration's concentration on budget cutting and regulatory review further reduced the management staff to only 47 (Riso 1989), compared at the time to 8,500 at the staff level of agency inspectors general. Finally, the Clinton administration, mistrustful of careerists in the OMB and willingly dependent upon a non-statutory, noninstitutional, and temporary National Performance Review (NPR) staff operating out of the vice president's office, decided to put the few remaining persons on the management side of the OMB out of their misery. Under the guise of the previously mentioned OMB reorganization of 1994 (OMB 2000 Review), they simply eliminated most of the positions and integrated the remainder into the budget side of the agency (OMB 1994; Light 2002). Five Resource Management Offices (RMOs) structured along budgetary, functional lines were put in charge of comprehensive management issues. Insofar as designated management functions remained in the OMB, they were located in much-reduced statutory elements of the agency, such as the Office of Federal Procurement Policy (OFPP) and the Office of Information and Regulatory Analysis (OIRA) (Tomkin 1998, 21).

The Bush administration has continued to adhere to the NPR philosophy and rhetoric of the Clinton administration, one element being a reaffirmation of a budget-dominated OMB. No appointment to the position of deputy director for management was forthcoming during the administration's first year and there were three short-term appointees in the next two years, showing how difficult it is to attract quality people to a position without critical authorities or resources.[5] The President's Management Agenda (U.S. OMB 2001) provides the basic thrust for the administration but also is simply a continuation of the philosophy that government and business are alike and that government should be managed according to private-sector corporate practices.

Critics of the current OMB and the integration of management issues and personnel into the budgetary process argue that management values and issues can be addressed properly only if management is institutionally separate from the budget. The absence in the executive office of an agency with institutional responsibilities is costly, not only in management and financial terms, but in political terms as well. After making the case that the president's institutional interests require attention, Paul Light of Brookings drew this conclusion on the proposal for an OFM:

> Some, once including this author, believe the answer [to the institutional decline of the OMB] is in rebuilding the old Division of Administrative Management, the notion being that the budget is the crucial lever for enforcing whatever management reforms a President might pursue. Far better to leave the M in OMB than to have it ignored entirely. Others, including senior members of NAPA [National Academy of Public Administration], have argued for the creation of an entirely new Office of Federal Management (OFM), the argument being that budget will always crowd out management. Far better to have M ignored on its own than completely submerged by budget. After waiting for three decades for OMB to begin the rebuilding, it appears that advocates of a separate office operating elsewhere in the Executive Office of the President have the winning argument. (Light 1997, 228; NAPA 1992)

The integration of budget and management responsibilities in one agency necessarily results in the subordination of management interests. The distinctions between the budgetary and management cultures are genuine. The budgetary culture necessarily and properly has a short-term, control perspective. The management culture, on the other hand, though not innocent of political interests and values, is a culture that tends to operate with a longer-term perspective and seeks to maximize the capacity of institutions to perform their statutory missions. The problem within the current OMB is not one of intentions or incompetence, but one of two incompatible missions being forced upon one agency.

General Management Laws: The Source of "Political Clout"

It is asserted with regularity by supporters of the present budget-dominated OMB that executive branch management would be weakened irreparably if separated from the budget process because it is only the budget that gives management the necessary clout. This assertion assumes that management, properly defined in a private corporate context, is a set of top-down processes and controls. Typically, the statement is made that agencies respond only to budgetary rewards and threats and little else. Management in this scenario is conceived as a series of centrally designed and directed management initiatives each geared to increasing measurable performance at the agency level.

The problem with this approach to management is twofold: first the OMB definition of management is too narrow and sterile, ignoring the richness of management when it is considered as institutional capacity building. And second, and somewhat counterintuitively, this narrow budgetary approach weakens the capacity of the incumbent president and the institutional presidency generally, to meet its responsibilities to have politically accountable management of the administrative structure.

In point of fact, the president can provide effective management leadership apart from the budget through the creative use of general management laws. It is in the writing and administering of general management laws, in cooperation with Congress, that the president acquires "clout" in the management of government. The budget is only one tool, albeit essential, in the managerial toolbox of the president.

The term "general management law," as used here, refers to those cross-cutting laws of general applicability regulating the activities, procedures, and administration of all agencies[6] of the federal government (Brass 2004a, 2004b). General management laws are intended to provide appropriate uniformity and standardization for government organization and governance processes. Uniformity and standardization by themselves, however, are not the objective of general management laws. Such an objective would stultify government since "one size does not fit all." What these laws do reflect, therefore, are the conceptual and legal agreements between the branches respecting the management of the executive branch. In functional terms, general management laws are statements of presumption guiding governmental behavior; that is, certain doctrinal provisions reflected in legal language stand until and unless an exemption is permitted. Exemptions may be assigned by a general statute to a category of agency (e.g., independent regulatory commissions), or they may be present in provisions of the agency's enabling statute. Exemptions from general management laws may be made mandatory or discretionary.

General management laws come in various guises and may be extensive in their coverage and impact—as is the case with the Administrative Procedure, Budget and Accounting, Ethics in Government, and Freedom of Information acts—or they may be of relatively low visibility (although visibility is not necessarily able to be equated with importance), such as the Federal Advisory Committee Act and the User Fee Act of 1951. In recent years, two somewhat contradictory trends have been evident. First, many new general management laws have been enacted (e.g., Inspector General Act; Chief Financial Officers Act), each supported and justified on its supporters' definition of a problem, but often with what some observers believe to be little consideration of its probable impact upon other related general management laws. Second, increasingly agencies and interest groups have been successful in gaining exemptions from the coverage of these acts, especially exemptions in the fields of personnel, compensation, and intra-governmental regulations.[7]

One purpose of these general management laws, and of the host of additional similar acts, is to shift the focus of deliberation and decision making to the general rather than the exceptional. The politics of general applicability is a politics through which the president, central management agencies, and Congress have the authority and leverage to keep the natural centrifugal forces of administrative practices within accountable limits. That is, the laws and regulations apply to all agencies, with the applicants for exemption carrying the burden of proof. The politics of exceptionality, on the other hand, occur when there are not present applicable general management laws or when those that exist have been permitted to atrophy or, conversely, become cumbersome or obsolete through extraneous amendments or technology.

In the arena of exceptional politics, the management of each agency tends to be viewed sui generis and is the sum of exceptional circumstances as interest groups, agency leadership, and congressional committees (the famed "iron triangles" of political science literature) are able to pursue their own agendas for policy making and administration.[8] The logical end result of an executive branch functioning under a culture of exceptional politics and administration is an executive that is disaggregated (not to be confused with decentralized) and largely unaccountable to the president, or to the Congress as a whole, for its activities. We are closer to this logical end of exceptional politics than is generally appreciated even by otherwise sophisticated observers of the governmental scene (R. Moe 2001).

Responsibility for the drafting and updating of management laws would, presumably, be a major responsibility of an OFM. The political clout associated with this responsibility should not be underestimated. An OFM would be a major player in setting the "rules of the game" for agencies and would constitute an institutional source of expertise and memory in service to the president. Thus, an OFM consisting of experienced generalists who have spent much of their career in the executive branch management could be a cadre of strength for both the presidency and to a lesser, but still critical, extent the Congress.

Entrepreneurs versus Constitutionalists: What Is the Purpose of Government Management?

The debate over whether or not there is need for a new, separate Office of Federal Management takes place within a larger debate over what the purpose is of management in the governmental sector. Although suggesting that there are simply two "camps" on this issue may be criticized as overly simplistic, it nonetheless is a useful analytic method to highlight the fundamental issues at stake. For these purposes, label the two opposing sides as "entrepreneurs" and "constitutionalists."

Although the Carter and Reagan administrations were not subtle in their populist distrust of government, and felt little need to posit a comprehensive administrative theory upon which to base their actions, the Clinton administration (1993–2001) decided to achieve similar ends with a new strategy.[9] They would "reinvent government" toward the end of making it both smaller and more concerned with "performance."[10] A bit of historical background is useful at this point.

Beginning in the immediate post–World War II period, several strands of economic literature emerged arguing a case for the superiority of markets over governmentally planned and managed economies, then dominant throughout the world. One strand consciously assumed the mantle of "public choice theory." At its heart, public choice theory rests on the premise that political as well as economic behavior is based on rational, self-serving maximization of material income or the satisfaction derived therefrom.[11]

The political impact of this premise has been extraordinary. By the mid-1980s, it had swept many nations, including the United States, to varying degrees and contributed its share to the collapse of the communist world and to centralized government planning and management generally. Planned economies fell from favor. Free-market advocates pushed a variety of related concepts internationally, many with profound implications for government management (Friedman 1962).[12] A new public management (NPM) model emerged in the early 1990s and rapidly gained international currency through its dissemination, if not uncritical support, by the Organization for Economic Cooperation and Development (OECD) (OECD 1995). The underlying premise of the NPM is that the governmental and private sectors are alike in their essentials and subject to the same generic management principles. Promoters of NPM ("entrepreneurs") rely on literature, propositions, and practices that strive for convergence of the governmental and private sectors (Bozeman 1987; O'Toole 1997; Eggers and Goldsmith 2003).[13] The acceptance of the convergence model of public management worldwide was both rapid and in some instances disruptive (Kettl 2000; Peters and Pierre 1998).

The American variation on the new public management was the "reinventing government" exercise, led principally by Vice President Al Gore. The reinventors largely rejected the language of public choice, however, preferring instead that of business schools (Gore 1997).[14] Reinventors accepted the underlying premise that the government and private sectors are fundamentally alike and subject to most of the same economically derived behavioral norms. In the private sector the principal, if not exclusive, objective is results, and this principle, in their view, should be applied to the governmental sector as well. Thus, the first principle of the 1993 National Performance Review (NPR) report reads: "Effective entrepreneurial governments cast aside red tape, shifting from systems in which people are accountable for following rules to systems in which they are accountable for achieving results" (U.S. NPR 1993, 6–7).[15]

This shift toward results over legal process as the primary value in government management is a statement about political power as well as administrative management. Vice President Gore indicated as much in 1993 when he stated: "CEOs—from the White House to agency heads—must ensure that everyone understands that power will never flow through the old channels again" (U.S. NPR 1993, 68). The NPR vision was to break down the barriers between the sectors and create a society of government/private partnerships. The partnerships, ideally, would be largely autonomous bodies run by managers under contract to meet negotiated performance standards. The entrepreneurs argue that managers should be deregulated, given freedom from alleged congressional "micro-management" (Kettl 1994, 309),[16] and subject to less supervision by the president and his central managerial agencies. Since the goal is greater managerial autonomy, there is relatively little interest in organization per se, or in the legal theories that encourage political accountability for agencies and officers.

Critics (constitutionalists) challenged the fundamental philosophical basis of the entrepreneurial management paradigm, arguing, among other things, that it tends to subvert the Constitution and is antidemocratic in thrust, if not intention.[17] Constitutionalists view the government and private sectors as distinct in character, with the distinctions founded in legal theory. The distinguishing characteristic of governmental management, contrasted to private-sector management, is that government actions must have their basis in public law, not in the financial interests of private entrepreneurs or in the fiduciary concerns of corporate managers. The frequently criticized hierarchical structure found in the executive branch is designed more to ensure accountability for managerial action than to control employees. In this view, the value of accountability to political leadership and the importance of due process in decision making trumps the premium placed on performance and results. However, it is less a question of pursuing one value at the expense of the other than it is a matter of precedence in the event of conflict.

According to the constitutionalists, the fundamental purpose of governmental management is to implement the laws passed by Congress, laws that may be wise or less wise, not necessarily to maximize performance (however it is defined and measured) or to satisfy "customers" (Terry 2002). Although political accountability and effective performance are generally compatible objectives, when these values come into conflict, the democratic values of legal process and political accountability take precedence over the unquestioned entrepreneurial values of efficiency and results.

Institutional capacity building, the principal managerial strategy of constitutionalists, is best understood as the intentional and planned enhancement of executive management, broadly interpreted, to achieve their statutory mission. This enhancement occurs through a creative combination of general management laws, personnel policies and practices, organizational culture, managerial leadership, and a balance between managerial initiative and conformity to presidential and central management agency policies. The quality of the general management laws and their supporting documents in large measure determines the quality of government management broadly defined. Poorly conceived and written laws cannot necessarily be overcome by well-intentioned and creative management leadership.

This debate between the entrepreneurs and constitutionalists is critical in determining the likelihood that one will favorably or critically consider the proposed Office of Federal Management. Entrepreneurs emphasize the values of agency autonomy and competition, the blending of the sectors, and the transferability of private sector practices to government tasks; and they are generally hostile toward government activity, structure, and personnel (Cullen and Cushman 2000). Institutional capacity building and political account-ability are not part of the mind-set or rhetoric of entrepreneurs, except occa-sionally when considering the armed forces and domestic security. The likelihood that entrepreneurs will look kindly upon an OFM, whose avowed intent is to bring the executive branch under more energetic presidential and central management leadership, is not high.

Constitutionalists, on the other hand, accept as their starting point the existence and applicability of legal theory (Newland 1997; Gilmour and Jensen 1998). Legal theory, with its testable propositions and precedents, permits a high degree of explanatory power, transparency, and predictability. It pro-vides for political accountability within the system. Constitutionalists tend to see these values placed at risk under the entrepreneurial style of manage-ment. They see capacity and accountability problems increasing as the gov-ernment is forced to rely ever more heavily upon third parties (often contractors, as Dan Guttman observes in chapter 10) for the delivery of ser-vices and even, in some instance, the making of policies (Cooper 2003; Goldstein 1992). They see problems constitutionally with such proposals and practices as, for example, the contracting out to private firms by the Internal Revenue Service for the collection of delinquent taxes (Phinney 2003, 6). They see the government in an advanced state of disaggregation with little presidential and central agency leadership to counter this trend. Not surprisingly, constitutionalists tend to believe a new and separate OFM is necessary to bring stability, accountability, and, in their terms, creativity to the task of government management.

The Proposed Office of Federal Management

This author, as noted, is a partisan for the constitutional approach to govern-ment management. The arguments made in favor of the NPM and entrepreneurialism do not pass, ultimately, the long-term test of competent and accountable government sector governance. Entrepreneurs function with-out solid theory and are forced to argue ad hoc solutions and "flavor of the month" nostrums to complex management issues. They seek to exert their leadership outside the executive branch's hierarchical legal framework and accept business-style epigrams ("Effective, entrepreneurial governments cast aside red tape . . .") as a substitute for theory.[18]

The following description and analysis of the proposed OFM starts from the premise that the arguments of the constitutionalists are persuasive as to the proper objectives of governmental management. It also accepts two other critical premises: (1) that the president and Congress are constitutionally intended to be comanagers of the executive branch and (2) that the president is the "chief executive officer" of the operations of the executive branch and that to meet this responsibility he or she must have strong central management agencies for support.

What would an OFM look like? An OFM might have six directorates each headed by an associate director. The six directorates (there could be more or fewer) could have the following general areas of responsibility: (1) government organization and management, (2) financial management, (3) human resources management, (4) information technology management, (5) asset and productivity management, and (6) regulatory policy and intergovernmental relations. The functions assigned each directorate and the authority to reorganize and reassign responsibilities would rest with the OFM director.

In summary form, a listing of functions to be performed by the OFM would include but not be limited to the following:

- a. organizational design and management oversight
- b. central legislative review and advice
- c. information technology policy
- d. statistical policy
- e. financial systems management
- f. regulatory review and clearance
- g. procurement, contracting policy, and privatization
- h. ethics oversight
- i. government corporations and enterprises
- j. real and personal property management
- k. advisory committee management
- l. federalism and intergovernmental relations
- m. productivity enhancement and program evaluation practices
- n. capital and asset investment management
- o. printing, reproduction policies, and Web site management
- p. inspectors general
- q. Freedom of Information Act and Privacy Act administration

Each of these functions is characterized by one or more general management laws plus a series of supporting executive orders and directives. The functions would be distributed among the six directorates to ensure reasonable internal compatibility and consistency. However, existing functions could be shifted from one directorate to another to reflect changing priorities and skill requirements. Also, the directorates may be reorganized from time to time as a consequence of new national needs and emergencies.

Since limitation of space precludes extensive discussion of all the proposed directorates and the various functions assigned to each, it is useful to focus on one directorate and its functions in order to obtain an appreciation for the subtleties and potential for an OFM responsible to the president and protective of his interests. In chapter 4, Alan L. Dean and Dwight Ink present case studies of substantial presidential accomplishments that similarly illustrate the importance of such an office. The first directorate, Government Organization and Management, is selected for analysis here in part because it is this directorate that will be largely responsible for whatever success an OFM ultimately has in support of the institutional presidency.

The Government Organization and Management Directorate (GOMD) will be the office of generalists whose mandate is government-wide and ranges across the other directorates. They will be responsible for providing the president and White House with the "big picture" of the management challenges facing the president and will be able to offer recommendations at the highest level of generality backed up by experience. Thus, all proposals for new or reorganized departments, agencies, or other entities of government, for instance, should be reviewed by the OFM with options being presented to the president for approval.

Organizational design, after all, is an art form with both managerial and political consequences, as Fred Kaiser shows in chapter 3. It makes a difference where a function is assigned within the executive branch. All departments and agencies are not equal in their commitment to a president's priorities or their capacity to transform a legislative mandate into a practical program. Agencies have different cultures, as Michael Maccoby shows in chapter 9 and the leadership of the new DHS is finding out, and these cultures must be understood, appreciated, and dealt with in a sympathetic and creative manner. Central management must have as its principal objective department and agency capacity building to accomplish statutory purposes.

Many elements of organizational design make a difference in management practices. Thus, an agency headed by a single administrator tends to have a very different character from an agency headed by a board or plural executives. How an agency or program is financed also makes a difference. Should the agency be fully reliant on appropriated funds or should it be financially self-sufficient through revenues generated for services rendered? If the latter, is a government corporation the best option to consider? What about the workforce and executive profile? Should a new or reorganized agency have essentially an in-house workforce of governmental officers, or should the agency be reliant on a third-party workforce of contractors? These types of questions, explored by Tom Stanton in chapter 1, all are interrelated and with consequences and need the attention of the best minds that are available both within and outside the government.[19]

The reality is that most management issues, unlike most budgetary issues, do not have high political saliency. The divisions of opinion rarely follow partisan lines. There are no inherently Republican or Democratic principles for structuring a regional infrastructure or for creating a government corporation. Issue differences are much more likely to surface over competing ways to finance programs or institutions. Studies covering many years and many administrations suggest the need for some continuity in executive branch management within the larger context of politically accountable officials (National Commission on the Public Service 1989).[20] All management should not have to start anew with each change in partisan administration.

Among the "products" of this directorate would be sets of workable templates to apply to organizational design and to management practices. Thus, with respect to government corporations, organizational location, governance structures, funding systems, personnel requirements, and the like would be conceptually defined with criteria and standards applicable government-wide, as is partially the case today with the Government Corporation Control Act (31 U.S.C. 9101 et seq.). Exceptions to such criteria are permitted, and may even be encouraged, but the presumption would remain that all governmental functions should reside within the executive branch and that political accountability to the president and Congress is the highest value. Illustrative of this general proposition would be the requirement that no government agency or corporation could create a subsidiary agency or corporation without the express affirmative approval of Congress and that this provision would be enforced. Today, increasingly, agencies and corporations are creating subordinate organizations, both governmental and private, on their own authority.[21] It would be this directorate that would be responsible for policing this practice and protecting the integrity of the federal government and public law against those political interests that benefit from a particularist interpretation of the law.

Central management, as it has evolved since 1970, has taken on a "stovepipe" or "silo" appearance. That is, a number of subfields of management now have their own general management law, statutory office or oversight council, funding, and personnel systems. Although the specific laws and organizations have been praised on occasion by the affected professional fields, critics see these arrangements as fragmented fiefdoms operating with considerable autonomy and little concern with how their activities relate to the whole.

Today the inspectors general constitute a major element of executive management but function with considerable managerial autonomy. They have their own general management law (the Inspector General Act of 1978); their own council, the President's Council on Integrity and Efficiency (PCIE); and considerable leeway in personnel matters. The financial officers in the various departments and agencies have their own law (Chief Financial Officers Act of 1990) and a Chief Financial Officers Council. The procurement community goes one step further with its own statutory office in the OMB, the Office of Federal Procurement Policy (OFPP). The program evaluators looked around, saw their protected colleagues, sought their own "full employment act," and succeeded in passing the Government Performance and Results Act (GPRA), thereby insuring considerable access to well-positioned federal jobs as well as the contracting sector. There is also a Chief Information Officers Council and a Chief Human Capital Officers Council. All the professional fraternities one by one were able to set up their own policy and managerial stovepipes (Wamsley 2004).

The point to recognize is that management in the executive branch today is highly fragmented in several ways. There are vertical lines of management patterned along professional lines. There are more agency-specific management laws than previously. And, as Dan Guttman recounts in chapter 10 with respect to government outsourcing, there is increasing reliance on third-party management systems as the core government itself diminishes in size.[22] A major purpose, although it is not likely to be articulated as such, of an OFM would be to counter these disaggregating forces at work and to strengthen the institutional presidency in reasserting its constitutional responsibilities.

It is reasonable to assume that the total personnel necessary for an OFM would be approximately 350 persons, some to be transferred from the existing OMB; some to be transferred from other agencies, such as the Office of Personnel Management (OPM); and still others to be appointed to new positions. The short-term political Program Associate Directors (PAD), so notable, controversial, and arguably necessary for the budgetary process, would not be necessary in an OFM. The working presumption would be that the directorates would be headed by Senior Executive Service (SES) appointees, although the OFM Director would have flexibility in appointments through use of the "excepted appointments" process, where special talents and political sensitivity may be needed.

Two Case Studies: Homeland Security and Asset Management

Two brief case studies illustrate the costs incurred upon the institutional presidency and the political system generally when the OMB no longer has the will or capacity to play the lead role in organizational management issues.

The first concerns one of the largest and most dramatic issues facing the country, homeland security, and the second a lesser, but still important problem, asset management by the federal government.

Homeland Security

When the nation was attacked by terrorists on September 11, 2001, citizens expected the government to respond rapidly and in a coordinated manner. It was evident that the existing rationale for organizing departments, agencies, and programs was no longer appropriate for the new challenges and that changes would be forthcoming. As Frederick Kaiser documents in chapter 3, the two options available to the president and Congress appeared to be (1) to keep the existing structure of government largely in place, relying on strong coordinative units and changed missions for agencies, or (2) to create a single department to which agencies and programs would be transferred. In either case, the president would be expected to take the lead or have a plan ready to place before Congress and the public.

Initially, the White House leaned toward option one, creating an Office of Homeland Security (OHS) and a Homeland Security Council (HSC) within the Executive Office of the President.[23] Governor Tom Ridge of Pennsylvania was appointed assistant to the president to direct the OHS. The rationale offered for this organizational choice was that rather than spend the time and effort to incorporate all the various domestic security agencies and programs into one unit, presumably a department, it was more critical that coordination be implemented from above. Ridge argued that his close proximity and easy access to the president gave him the authority and "clout" he needed to do the job.

Within months the opposing view, that all or most homeland security functions should be located in one department, gained congressional support and threatened to become a political issue in the sense that coordination by a presidential assistant, no matter how serious or well executed, did not equal in perception the commitment to be found in the creation of a new executive department.[24] By April 2002, President George W. Bush changed his mind. He decided to propose the creation of the Department of Homeland Security. The decision was more than simply a political gesture, however; he had found that the coordinative approach for such a large undertaking was insufficient and a strong, hierarchical structure was needed to ensure that decisions were made and enforced down the chain of command. The White House submitted its proposal for a Department of Homeland Security on June 24, 2002. As Harold Relyea noted, "The proposal, however, had its shortcomings. These resulted, at least partly, from the inexperience of its principal drafters: none of the four had previously prepared legislation for a new department and only one of them, if only briefly, had headed such an entity. Furthermore, the proposal had been developed somewhat hastily and in strict secrecy. Available reorganization expertise was not utilized; input and support from the agencies and professional constituencies directly affected was not sought" (Relyea 2003, 617).

The point to note is that the decision was made to create the department first and then enter the difficult planning process afterward. The OMB's role in this White House insiders' exercise was through the participation of OMB director Mitch Daniels. As for the OMB itself, its role was largely limited to extensive rewriting of budget scenarios based on organizational options. There is no recorded evidence of OMB participation in developing options on management capacity issues, although the OMB did play a significant role in designing the new department's Undersecretary for Management, described by Alan Dean and Dwight Ink in chapter 4. Any number of unnecessary controversies later arose because the departmental proposal and its addendums did not follow generally accepted norms of organizational management and ignored constitutional and long-standing comity practices with Congress. For instance, the president's bill provided for an unprecedented number of key positions to be presidentially appointed without Senate confirmation, a proposal guaranteed to encounter stiff opposition. The president also sought authority for reorganizations and reallocations of functions within the department without having to come to Congress for approval. Most of the questionable elements of the act would never have appeared if there had been a professionally competent staff resource available to design the technicalities of the departmental proposal in the first place. The White House was essentially "winging it" for what is generally agreed to be the largest executive reorganization in history, a reorganization that was still only partially complete several years later.[25]

It is difficult not to conclude that if an OFM had been in existence, it would have begun on September 12, 2001, to develop the organizational and management issues and options available to the president and other executive decision makers on how best to organize to meet this new national challenge. Having institutional memory of other reorganization challenges and what complex issues are involved in bringing together, in this instance, twenty-two separate agencies, would have put the White House ahead of the management curve rather than behind. Furthermore, the absence of an OFM as lead player in this exercise means that there will not be one agency where the "lessons learned" can be kept, studied, and integrated into contemporary administrative doctrine to serve any future similar eventuality.

Asset Management

The second brief case study involves the seemingly mundane, yet crucial, field of federal asset management. The federal government currently holds or manages a vast volume of assets including real, personal, and fleet properties; financial assets to include direct loans; and military hardware. Assessments of how well these assets are being managed are hard to come by and where available tend to be agency and functional specific. The scope of the problem has interested Congress and as of this writing a bill has been introduced, the Federal Property Asset Management Reform Act (H.R. 2548; 108th Congress), that, if enacted, would constitute another general management act. Two questions arise: Who, if anyone, is currently responsible for government-wide asset management policy? and Where might an OFM fit into the management of assets?

Thomas Stanton recently published a report on federal asset management generally in the executive branch (Stanton 2003b). He noted at the outset the critical and inherent differences between asset management in the private and governmental sectors and the special difficulties facing executive agencies due to statutory constraints, budget scoring practices, and long-term disinvestment practices that weaken the management of assets.

A number of short case studies are reported as "successful" efforts by particular agencies (e.g., U.S. Coast Guard; Resolution Trust Corporation) to manage their assets within the existing federal system and its rules. The individual agency initiatives (e.g., portfolio strategies) in this field are all informative and do suggest ways and means for other agencies to follow their example. Like most case studies, however, the sum of the parts is not cumulative and thus adds little to our theory or to comprehensive oversight and management. You will look in vain for a critical role being played by OMB today even though the monies involved are substantial.[26]

More specifically, the disposal of surplus federal property provides evidence of the weakness of approaching management from an entrepreneurial or agency-specific basis. Once again, it is Thomas Stanton who provides us with a set of case studies of asset sales (Stanton 2003a; Hinkle 1999).[27] The case studies address the question: How can the federal government obtain good value for the assets it sells? The four cases cited by Stanton each involved an end to the federal interest in the sold assets. This was a full divestiture, meaning, in part, that the assets were no longer governed by public law, but by private law. Problems are much more likely to be encountered when the government wishes to sell an asset but also wishes to retain some interest in the sold assets. This has been the case in what some believe to be an abortive attempt at privatization, the sale of the United States Enrichment Corporation (Guttman 2001).

Although each of the case studies provided its own lessons on how best to dispose of assets, they involved little central direction and assistance; success tended to be by muddling through. Asset disposal provides a classic case of where there was once a central capacity in the OMB to assist agencies, especially small agencies, that had to dispose of assets and where this OMB capacity has ceased to exist.

The government formerly possessed an institutional focus for knowledge about asset sales. This was the Credit and Cash Management branch, a small staff of seven people that provided support to federal credit agencies on a variety of management issues, including loan asset sales, and that reported to the deputy director for management of the Office of Management and Budget. The branch helped several agencies—HUD, the Veterans Administration, the Department of Agriculture, and the Department of Education—to conduct asset sales in the late 1980s.

The OMB abolished the office in 1995. A single person, the senior adviser for credit and cash management, continued to provide an institutional focus for agencies seeking support in enhancing their credit management practices. In 1996, he was able to help enact the Debt Collection Improvements Act, which encouraged agencies to conduct asset sales and also revised the budget rules to allow them to pay for the expenses of a sale out of the proceeds. Also, working with the Financial Management Service of the Treasury Department, he was instrumental in obtaining contractor support to assist the Small Business Administration (SBA) in developing and implementing the strategic planning process for its asset sales program in the late 1990s. It is at the beginning, when an agency views asset sales as foreign and potentially threatening, that such external support is most needed. The senior adviser for credit and case management retired some years ago and the position has gone unfilled at the OMB (Stanton 2003a, 43).[28]

This tale of managerial disinvestment and its negative implications for administrating the world's most complex institution is repeated over and over again. Here, Stanton does offer a modest institutional proposal for restoring this lost capacity for asset disposal management. "A small office within the federal government, possibly reporting to the OMB deputy director for management or else located in the Financial Management Service of the Treasury Department, would be helpful in supporting today's loose network of government officials and private contractors who are experienced in asset sales. That office would have the responsibility for maintaining touch with government agencies and the private sector and could provide an institutional source of information about design and implementation of an effective assets sales program" (Stanton 2003a, 43). The creation of a "small office within the federal government" is hardly a proposal to stir the soul. And is this not another bit of management fragmentation? Why not draw the appropriate conclusion from the evidence? For thirty years management, properly defined as institutional capacity building, has been intentionally downgraded within the OMB portfolio of responsibilities. Only a new and separate OFM, reporting directly to the president, provides any likelihood that management issues and organizational disaggregation will be addressed in a systematic and continuous manner.

Governmental Disaggregation: A Challenge to Democratic Governance

Thus far, discussion of the current OMB and the proposed OFM has centered on issues of domestic managerial practices and institutional theory. This is a proper and understandable approach. There is another dimension, however, to this discussion, or debate, that needs to be recognized. The new public management movement generally and recent management initiatives in the United States in particular have promoted, intentionally or otherwise, institutional disaggregation. Disaggregation is different from decentralization. Government administration in the United States is typically through legal delegation of authority. That is, Congress passes a law and assigns authority for its implementation to the president or department head. Then the president or department head delegates this authority to subordinates to actually administer the program. Delegation of authority permits decentralization. With decentralization, top officials remain accountable to Congress for the administration of the program. Delegation also permits re-delegation, thus affording both clear lines of accountability and administrative flexibility. Disaggregation, however, is of a different character.

Disaggregation in the executive branch has taken several forms: legal, organizational, financial, and personnel. More laws today contain the phrase "notwithstanding any other law to the contrary," than was the case thirty years ago. This phrase in a law is an invitation to agency-centered mischief, as whatever wording follows constitutes an exemption from executive branch doctrine and central management oversight. Organizationally, agencies such as the Social Security Administration and the National Archives have been split away from departments and assigned independent agency status. More agencies are being given full or partial control over their funding systems and revenues. Separate personnel and compensation systems are proliferating. These actions collectively are manifestations of how the executive branch is disaggregating and how accountability is being attenuated.

Disaggregation is particularly noticeable when a hybrid entity is created with attributes of both the governmental and the private sectors.[29] The most publicized of such hybrid entities are the government-sponsored enterprises Fannie Mae and Freddie Mac.[30] These large financial institutions straddle the sectors. They were chartered by Congress, yet are owned by private investors. There is no explicit guarantee in law for Fannie's and Freddie's liabilities. Correct or not, the market nonetheless considers the trillions of dollars of liabilities incurred by these government-sponsored enterprises (GSEs) to be contingent or potential liabilities of the federal government because of their federal charters. There is a general presumption that the federal government would not let these GSEs fail. Under the law, unlike other privately owned companies, they may not be placed into bankruptcy. To whom are GSEs accountable? GSE management is not primarily accountable to the federal government, nor to borrowers, but to the corporation's shareholders. Investors come first, followed closely by management's interests.[31]

There are today literally hundreds of entities functioning as hybrids in the netherworld of the quasi government. They range from the aforementioned GSEs through federally funded research and development centers (FFRDCs) such as the Institute for Defense Analysis; adjunct organizations under the control or direct supervision of an agency (e.g., National Pork Board and the Department of Agriculture; Securities Investor Protection Corporation and the Securities and Exchange Commission); nonprofit organizations affiliated with departments and agencies (e.g., National Park Foundation); venture capital funds (e.g., Russia Partners; CIA's In-Q-Tel company); and a host of other types of organizations difficult to categorize or, in some instances, to even find (Koppell 1999). One instance of this life in the quasi government is worth noting further. As part of Vice President Gore's "reinvention" exercise, a substantial downsizing of the civil service was ordered. Office of Personnel Management (OPM) director James King decided to "think outside the box" and came up with the idea to create a private corporation (an ESOP, employee stock-ownership plan) to privatize the work of seven hundred employees of the targeted Federal Investigations Division. The OPM decided to move on its own initiative without specific statutory authority.[32] The corporation was incorporated under the laws of the state of Delaware, a choice of venue known for its minimal reporting requirements. Under the incorporation papers, Philip Harper, a former security industry official, was the sole employee who owned the sole share.

The corporation began its existence in August 1996, at which time seven hundred former Office of Federal Investigations employees were separated from the government and became private employees and owners. In April 1997 it was reported:

[The] 700 employee-shareholders own about 91 percent of a company valued at $28.2 million. Harper and the other 11 company officers who together put up an initial seven-figure investment, hold the remaining shares. Under the terms of its corporate charter, USIS is governed by a nine-member board of directors. The board's five "inside" members include Harper and two others elected by employees; the three of them in turn nominate the two remaining members. However, as with most private companies, the board's role is limited. It does not run USIS—that's Harper's job, along with his immediate staff—instead concerning itself strictly with "ownership issues" like oversight. For example, it ensures that company resources are allocated in the best interests of employee shareholders, and it also approves key strategic decisions. Of course, such issues are made easy when you begin a business with the federal government as a guaranteed customer. (Sanders and Thompson 1997, 52)

The OPM awarded the U.S. Investigations Services (USIS) a noncompetitive three-year contract under a "public interest" exemption in federal contracting law (Barr 1996). From here on the financial story becomes and remains murky. Deep in a cave in the Pennsylvania mountains is where OPM kept its top-secret personnel security records. Here is where USIS operates. Exactly which assets were transferred to USIS is not clear but whatever they are, they were deemed to be worth $28 million. The inadequacy of this figure became immediately apparent as the Carlyle Group soon was able to purchase a substantial block of shares. The Carlyle Group is self-described as "one of the world's largest private equity firms, with more than $16 billion under management."[33] The Carlyle partners and owners are a bipartisan list consisting primarily of former political appointees and prominent foreign investors. The bulk of their investments are in businesses that are heavily reliant upon government contracts.[34] Their purchase of shares in USIS was wise, timely, and fortuitous because the now-private corporation underwent an incredible surge in business. In 1999 alone, the share value increased 702 percent.[35] Starting with 700 employees in 1996, the firm had by the end of 2002 some 5,600 employees with over 2,500 field investigators and 1,100 independent contract investigators. USIS has purchased a number of related companies.

In January 2003, most of the original ESOP employees sold their shares to another venture capital firm, Welsh, Carson, Anderson and Stowe, for a reported $545 million (Barr 2003). It is worth speculating as to what will happen to all the records and investigations if USIS owners, which are now principally the Carlyle Group and Welsh, Carson, Anderson and Stowe, decide to sell to another venture capital group.

The point of raising the USIS story is to illustrate what happens when there is no central management agency minding the store for the president and the people. The Clinton administration hailed the creation of USIS in 1996 as an example of the entrepreneurial spirit they were bringing to government. Leaving aside legitimate constitutional concerns about turning vital security records over to a private, for-profit corporation (is USIS covered by the Privacy Act?), who was protecting the interests of the American citizens while the original transaction was being consummated? Why were the assets listed at only $28 million when, as was immediately evident, they were many times higher? The one thing that we can say with assurance about this affair is that the OMB was nowhere to be found. Federal budget officials would not touch this issue and, if they had, would not have had the foggiest notion of what to do.

This growth in the quasi government poses many problems for our political institutions. To whom are these entities accountable and what laws govern their behavior? The executive branch of the United States was unique among the world's governments for its unity of character and coverage of general management laws. There were exceptions to the integrated executive branch concept, to be sure, such as the Smithsonian Institution, but by and large Congress and the president joined in keeping the natural pressures for disaggregation at bay. Whatever restraint there might have been under the traditional, or constitutionalist, model of government management, however, has been lost now that the entrepreneurial management model is ascendant. Coupled with the retreat by recent presidents from their managerial responsibilities and the intentional weakening of central management agencies, the natural forces of disaggregation are forging ahead largely unchecked.

For American critics of the trend toward administrative disaggregation, it is scant comfort to know that most developed countries are further down this road than the United States. In Great Britain, the term "quango" is used to refer to hybrid organizations living partially in the governmental and partially in the private sectors.[36] There are over 1,000 quangos in Great Britain, each seeking to maximize its "performance" (however performance may be defined) and political autonomy. Most OECD countries are finding, to their chagrin, that the road to disaggregation, paved by good intentions, leads to less political accountability, less coordination in addressing national problems, and, somewhat counterintuitively, often less flexibility. An interesting side note to the emergence of the quasi government abroad has been an increase in corruption and scandals. Although the data are partial, the OECD nonetheless estimates that hybrid organizations (technically nongovernment agencies) now receive 50 percent of the public expenditures among its European members and in some instances over 75 percent (OECD 2002).

Under the entrepreneurial vision of the future, society will consist principally of government/private partnerships based on pragmatic application of performance-oriented objectives. Skeptics of this vision see something very different emerging: a society where the centrality of public law unwisely is being displaced by business axioms. The focus of management, once the citizen, is now the "customer." Departmental integration as the norm is replaced by organizational dispersion, with managers institutionally insulated from political accountability. In the entrepreneurial paradigm, critics believe the protective wall between government and the private sectors is being breached, not merely for managerial convenience, but as a philosophy of governance.

The underlying concern regarding this process of disaggregation of government agencies and expansion of the quasi government is its impact upon democratic governance. Democratic governance assumes that the ultimate authority ought to reside with the people through their elected representatives in the legislature. At some point, all activities of a governmental nature must have their basis in public law, not in the particularistic and private interests of nongovernmental organizations. In many respects, however, the worldwide new public management movement is required to follow these democratic governance principles in the breach rather than the observance. By its nature, a disaggregated public sector with heavy reliance on hybrid organizations and other third-party arrangements is less democratic than a government of core departments and agencies. Entrepreneurial government may have its virtues, but democratic accountability is not one of them.

Conclusion

The past thirty years have been an era of populist insurgency against government generally. For many, government was the problem (and it often was) not the solution and thus arguments that the purpose of government management was to increase the capacity of agencies to perform their missions tended to fall on unreceptive ears. Management was first viewed in the 1970s as essentially a control mechanism tied to the budget. Cut back the budget and you cut back government. In the 1990s, however, the reinventing government exercise attempted at once to continue the antigovernment rhetoric while tying management to an entrepreneurial, private-sector management model. The reinventors believed you could have effective central management without central managers. Management is about changing cultures, they argued, not political accountability and capacity building. Thus, the 1990s saw executive management by non-statutory, noninstitutional, ad hoc bodies, such as the sometime President's Management Council. With the absence of a management arm at the OMB, disaggregation in its several forms set in. One consequence of the World Trade Center bombing in 2001, as James Carroll describes in chapter 2, was to jolt the political system back to reality and the requirement for presidential leadership, central management capacity, and a competent, if not necessarily larger, government.

The need for a separate OFM reporting directly to the president is greater today than even ten or twenty years ago. The core departments and agencies are in many instances "hollow," with an overreliance upon third parties to perform both operational and management responsibilities. There are both too many general management laws and directives and too many exceptions permitted to these laws. The contract state and the burgeoning quasi government are legitimate causes for concern about the state of our democratic governance. The OMB, with its current budget-dominated philosophy and diminished organization, is simply not equipped to perform the tasks required of it. The president and Congress must face up to the daunting task of rebuilding the nation's central management capabilities.

Former chair of the House Committee on Government Reform William Clinger summed up the current management challenges facing the president and the road to a solution best when he stated:

> In my years in Congress I witnessed the erosion of presidential authority, interest, and capacity in management with dismay. Every year, the interests of the President were weakly promoted as issue area after issue area was ignored by the Executive Office. Major crises, such as today's concern about the future of Medicare organization and administration, are being left to the vagaries of the subcommittee politics. . . . The truth is that the President has little in-house capabilities to frame and provide answers to organizational management issues. He is forced by the vacuum in management capacity and knowledge to become a defensive and reactive player. . . . Presidents nonetheless are going to be held responsible for how well the Medicare program works (whichever variation is adopted) without having much ability to shape the administrative issues in advance. . . .
>
> My experience has taught me repeatedly that the 30 years experiment of placing the President's responsibility for the budget and for executive management both in one agency has been a failure. This failure, I believe, is endemic to the situation and cannot be addressed and relieved without an institutional separation [of budget and management] within the Executive Office of the President. (Clinger 2001)

There is no more complex social organization in the world than the federal government. Its responsibilities are enormous and the demands upon it are insatiable. Although it may be fashionable today, even among those who consider themselves to be scholars of the institutional presidency, to caution that the government is essentially unmanageable and that presidents would be wise to stay clear of management problems as much as possible, this argument is false. Presidents really do not have a choice. They are hired by the people of the United States to manage their government.

The irony is that good management tends to be good politics as well. From a practical political perspective, little harms a president more than the perception that somehow he isn't managing the store. People will forgive much in presidents, including strong policy differences, but they do not forgive managerial incompetence.

Competent government is not some romantic objective blithely uttered. It is, quite simply, a necessity if the United States is to remain a serious player on the international scene. Presidents must be as much committed to competent government domestically as they are to competency in matters of international security. But it is difficult to envision a long-term commitment to a competent executive branch without an essentially nonpartisan Office of Federal Management dedicated to executive capacity building and protection of the institutional presidency. An OFM will not, by itself, be sufficient for competent federal management, but it is a necessary first step.

Notes

1. Tomkin's book supports the 1994 reorganization of the OMB.

2. The first statement of support for a separate Office of Federal Management (OFM) is found in NAPA 1983, 11–13. In 1986, Senator William Roth, then chair of the Senate Governmental Affairs Committee, introduced and held hearings on a bill that would, among other things, heave created a separate OFM within the Executive Office of the President, see U.S. Senate Committee on Governmental Affairs 1986; U.S. House Committee on Government Reform 1999.

3. Terry M. Moe states: "The Office of Management and Budget has been thoroughly politicized, both through appointments and its active involvement in distinctly political policymaking and lobbying processes" (1985, 235). Moe further argues that politicization of the OMB was both inevitable ("the logic of institutional development") and probably desirable given what he considers to be the disparity between public expectations of the president and his capacity to achieve desired policy results. Generally speaking, T. Moe is representative of the school that argues that the institutional presidency is strong (including the OMB) and dominant over Congress, which "has shown itself quite incapable of institutional coherence and political leadership—the president has increasingly been held responsible for designing, proposing, legislating, administering, and modifying public policy, that is, for governing" (T. Moe 1985, 239). An opposing view suggesting a pattern of congressional strength vis-à-vis the presidency is offered in Gilmour and Halley 1994; and Rosenbloom 2000.

4. On the disaggregation of government, see R. Moe 2004.

5. "The difficult part is finding somebody as good as we want," said OMB director Mitch Daniels, "who feels able to undergo what [the position] does" (Blair 2001, 3).

6. The term "agency" of the United States is critical to understanding how the federal government is organized and managed. Agency is a term and concept defined and employed generically to refer to all executive branch entities. The precise nomenclature used to designate an entity has no bearing upon its legal status. Thus, the Department of the Treasury, the Peace Corps, the Federal Bureau of Investigation, the Office of the Comptroller of the Currency, the Agency for International Development, the Pension Benefit Guaranty Corporation, and the Tennessee Valley Authority are all agencies of the United States. In Title 5 of the U.S. Code, it is indicated that the entire code applies to all agencies of the United States. This is critical because it means that all laws and relevant regulations apply to all agencies unless specifically exempted as a category of organization or exempted in the enabling legislation of the agency. There are presently many exemptions to this generalization, but those seeking exemption have been forced to accept the burden of proof to overcome the presumption of general applicability.

7. The loss of central management capacity and accountability is typified by the case of the Federal Aviation Administration (FAA). On April 1, 1996, the FAA was exempted from provisions of Title 5 that apply to personnel management except for specific provisions of law (e.g., Section 2301[b], relating to whistleblower protection) and was required to create its own personnel and compensation systems (Section 347; P.L. 104-50). Similarly, most of the provisions of the Federal acquisitions law (e.g., Federal Acquisition Streamlining Act: P.L. 103-355) were no longer applicable to the FAA. With respect to the personnel exemptions, the FAA later determined that they had been made too broad and a number of provisions of Title V were restored to cover the FAA.

Although at first blush FAA's exemption from most provisions of Title V would suggest that the agency has greater administrative flexibility than other agencies, it should also be recognized that in the absence of general management law standards, the agency must create its own "general management laws" and defend them against suits. Affected parties are much more likely to address Congress than the OPM or the OMB for redress on policies and practices they find unacceptable. It is an invitation to the much-decried congressional micromanagement. What recent experience suggests is that when management shifts to agreements between departmental and agency heads and congressional committees, and increasingly this means appropriations committees as was the case with the FAA, the president and the OPM tend to become non-players.

In the 108th Congress, the Department of Defense was seeking major exemptions from Title V so that it could "reorganize" its personnel system to fit its needs as it, not the OMB, defined them (Schwemle 2003).

8. In an assessment written after the close of the reinventing government exercise, James R. Thompson concluded that the net result of the "reforms" undertaken by the Clinton/Gore administration actually weakened the president and his central management agencies and unexpectedly and unintentionally strengthened Congress (Thompson 2001).

9. Beginning with President Jimmy Carter and continuing at least through President Bill Clinton, the thrust of executive reorganization, or "reform," changed from seeking ways and means to strengthen the government's capacity to meet its statutory requirements to seeking ways and means to de-construct the state and generally lessen the president's management role. Peri Arnold concludes that when executive reorganization is "no longer focused on the long-term project of developing executive governance, reform gains a populist accent and becomes a means through which 'outsider' Presidents manage hostility to government" (Arnold 1995, 407).

10. The term "reinventing government" came from David Osborne and Ted Gaebler's (1992) widely read account, *Reinventing Government: How the Entrepreneurial Spirit is Transforming the Public Sector* (Osborne and Gaebler 1992). This book strongly influenced

Vice President Al Gore. For a critical review of the reinventing government exercise, consult Norris 2000.

11. "Public choice can be defined as the economic study of nonmarket decision making, or simply the application of economics to political science. The subject matter of public choice is the same as that of political science: The theory of the state, voting rules, voting behavior, party politics, the bureaucracy and so on. The methodology of public choice is that of economics, however, the basic behavioral postulate of public choice, as for economics, is that man is an egoistic, rational, utility maximizer" (Mueller 1979, 1). See also Stretton and Orchard 1994. For an early American variation on this bureaucratic utility maximizer theme, see Downs 1967.

12. "The market vision has become the popular alternative conceptualization of the state and government. This view conceptualizes traditional public bureaucracies more as instruments of personal aggrandizement by civil servants than as instruments for unselfish service delivery to the public. It also conceptualizes public sector agencies as facing the same managerial and service delivery tasks as do organizations in the private sector and, therefore, as being amenable to the same techniques for managing them" (Peters 2001, 48).

13. Anne Laurent writes approvingly of the convergence trend in management: "Unbeknownst to most American taxpayers and to many federal employees, the government is growing its own businesses. Entrepreneurial outposts are taking root inside federal agencies in the fertile soil of management reform, new purchasing rules, downsizing, and performance pressure. Government's business people are shaking off the shackles of limited congressional appropriations and staving off job threats using money they earn selling services within their own and other agencies" (Laurent 2000, 7).

14. For a critique of the premises underlying the reinventing exercise, see R. Moe 1994.

15. "If you want better management, untie the managers' hands and let them manage. Hold them accountable for results—not for following silly rules" (Osborne 1996, 8).

16. Donald F. Kettl noted: "First, 'reinventing government' seeks the transfer of power from the legislative to the executive branch . . . Almost all of what the NPR recommends, in fact, requires that Congress give up power" (Kettl 1994, 309).

17. For further discussion of the implications of the New Public Management to democratic values, see R. Moe 2004; Rohr 2002.

18. Entrepreneurs assume they function from firm theory and that statements like "effective, entrepreneurial governments cast aside red tape, shifting from systems in which people are accountable for following rules to systems in which they are accountable for achieving results" have theoretical content. This statement is not, however, theoretical (that is, a proposition subject to disproof); rather it is a hortatory declaration, a call to right action. For instance, is being opposed to red tape (however that term is defined) really a theoretical principle on which to organize the administration of government? Or is the existence of red tape (presumably a metaphor for unnecessary regulations) actually a symptom of some more fundamental and unexamined theoretical problem? No one argues for "red tape" in principle, but when red tape is defined as regulations, there are many defenders depending on the specific regulation under discussion. By and large, entrepreneurs abjure theory, with its requirements of precision, predictability, replicability, and acceptance of disproof, preferring instead the enlightenment of success indicators, such as customer polling ("We will measure success by customer satisfaction"). For a discussion of what constitutes theory, see Popper 1959.

19. Thomas H. Stanton in chapter 1 provides a conceptually sound and well-documented case for the necessity to think in institutional terms when addressing the problems facing government today. "The events of September 11 have brought into sharp focus the

limitations on the federal government's ability to design effective organizations and working relationships with other partners, whether in the private sector or among state and local governments. Many years ago, the Executive Office of the President (EOP) included an Office of Management and Organization (earlier a part of the Administrative Management Division), housed first in the Bureau of the Budget and then in the new Office of Management and Budget (OMB), with responsibility for enhancing the management and organization of government organizations and programs. . . . Today, the capacity of such an office could help to address homeland security issues."

The author, while building a persuasive case on the current deficiencies in institutional thinking and management, simply concludes that such capacity must be restored but does not provide a specific institutional proposal as a remedy.

20. The National Commission on the Public Service was chaired by Paul A. Volcker, retired chair of the Federal Reserve Board. This 1989 commission is generally referred to as Volcker I. A second commission, referred to as Volcker II, issued a report in 2002 (see National Commission on the Public Service 2002). Both reports called for a substantial reduction in the number of political appointees and improvements in the Senior Executive Service.

21. Illustrative of agencies creating subordinate organizations, both governmental and private, on their own authority is the case of the Federal Communications Commission's (FCC) creation, through a third party, of the Schools and Libraries Corporation and the Rural Health Care Corporation as private corporations under the laws of Delaware to administer certain functions of the universal service programs for schools and libraries and rural health care providers. The General Accounting Office was asked by Senator Ted Stevens to determine whether the FCC had exceeded its authority in creating said corporations. The comptroller general concluded: "The Commission exceeded its authority when it directed the National Exchange Carriers Association, Inc. (NECA) to create the Schools and Libraries Corporation and the Rural Health Care Corporation. The Government Corporation Control Act specifies that '[a]n agency may establish or acquire a corporation to act as an agency only by or under a law of the United States specifically authorizing the action' (31 U.S.C. 9102). The entities act as agents of the Commission and, therefore, could only be created pursuant to specific statutory authority. Because the Commission has not been provided such authority, creation of the two corporations violated the Government Corporation Control Act" (General Accounting Office, 1998). No action was forthcoming as a result of this opinion by the comptroller general.

22. For an insightful discussion of the problems associated with determining the size of the core federal government as distinguished from what Paul Light refers to as "the shadow government," see Light 1999.

23. *Federal Register* 66 (October 10, 2001): 51812–17.

24. Governor Ridge had also become involved in a political controversy over his refusal to testify before congressional committees because of his status as a presidential assistant rather than a departmental or agency head (Mitchell 2002).

25. The decision of where to locate the headquarters of the Department of Homeland Security was not determined through preliminary planning; rather, it took over two years to finally conclude that the headquarters had to be in the District of Columbia (Hsu 2004).

26. To solve the problems of asset management Stanton proposes the formation of one or more working groups of agencies involved in asset sales. These working groups would encourage the exchange of information and experiences. The former Federal Credit Policy Working Group is cited as a model. But the weakness of the working group approach to management is also noted by Stanton. "The Federal Credit Policy Working Group has now largely dissolved as a means of promoting interagency development of improved practices. Also, except for its administration of debt management services, the Financial

Management Service (FMS in Treasury) has lost interest in supporting the improvements in practice by federal credit agencies. Yet, the experience of the federal credit agencies provides a valuable model for making progress on asset management issues." (Stanton 2003b, 35). One must reasonably question just how useful the interagency working group approach is compared with, say, a permanent unit with institutional support in an OFM.

The history of interagency committees as coordinating bodies is generally one of failures. The reason for this is basic: The power to coordinate does not normally carry with it the authority to issue binding orders. Management is based first on legal authority and then on skills of leadership and mutual interest among the members. If interagency committees are assigned appropriate tasks within their competence, they can be useful. But more often than not this is not forthcoming and their life expectancy can be short. As Harold Seidman graphically notes: "Interagency committees are the crabgrass in the garden of governmental institutions. Nobody wants them, but everyone has one" (Seidman 1998, 147).

27. The four case studies were: (1) sale of the Elk Hills oil field by the U.S. Department of Energy; (2) sale of loans and property by the Resolution Trust Corporation after the savings and loan debacle; (3) loan asset sales by the Small Business Administration; and (4) excess property sales by the Defense Reutilization and Management Service. See also Hinkle 1999, 246–48.

28. A unit in the OFM handling asset management and disposal might also be assigned the responsibility for overseeing the more general field of "privatization," an issue area with a mixed record.

29. For a more extended discussion of hybrid organizations constituting the quasi-government, see R. Moe 2001.

30. Fannie Mae is the Federal National Mortgage Association and Freddie Mac is the Federal Home Loan Mortgage Corporation. There is today a substantial body of literature on GSEs. See Stanton 2002. See also Wallison and Ely 2000; Stanton and Moe 2002.

31. Edward A. Fox, then president of Sallie Mae (Student Loan Marketing Association), told a Senate oversight subcommittee in 1982: "We are a private corporation and as such, with stockholders and bondholders, we have a fiduciary responsibility to those individuals. . . . We are not charged with subsidizing the guaranteed student loan program or subsidizing the students" (U.S. Senate Committee on Labor and Human Resources 1982, 135).

32. The OPM acted to create the U.S. Investigations Service (USIS) without explicit statutory authority. The corporation's Web page in 2001 stated: "On July 8, 1996, USIS was formed on the initiation of the President and Congress as an employee-owned company. USIS is steeped in the tradition of providing high-quality, timely investigative services to its customers" (www.usis.com/history/history/html, 2001 [USIS, n.d.]. The USIS, unlike the former ComSat or current American Red Cross, has no federal charter. The premise appeared to be that the OPM had the authority to do what it thought necessary or salutary in this instance, unless it received instructions to the contrary from Congress. "With respect to contracting with an ESOP trustee to establish an ESOP corporation, we determined that no statute prohibited OPM from contracting for these services and that expending funds to enter into such a contract was a necessary expense pursuant to applicable fiscal law authority. . . . Therefore, OPM's decision to contract with an ESOP does not require legislation" (U.S. House Committee on Government Reform, Subcommittee on Civil Service, 1995, 54).

This view by OPM as to its rights to establish a private corporation on its own authority is mistaken. The most fundamental distinction between public and private law jurisprudence lies in the realm of presumptions. In the governmental sector, the presumption is that the actions of an agency (in this case OPM) must have their basis in public law.

Silence in law is not permission to act. In the private sector, on the other hand, the reverse presumption holds sway. That is, private persons may act as they please unless there is a law prohibiting their actions.

33. www.thecarlylegroup.com (2003)

34. The Carlyle Group is a highly successful private equity investment firm with very prominent personages as full and limited partners. For a highly critical, yet informative, account of the Carlyle Group, to include its involvement with USIS, see Broidy 2003.

35. http://www.USIS.com (2003).

36. In Great Britain, and some other countries, the terms "quango" and "quago" are employed to refer to hybrid entities. A quango is essentially a private organization that is assigned some, or many, of the attributes normally associated with the governmental sector. A quago, on the other hand, is essentially a government organization that is assigned some, or many, of the attributes normally associated with the private sector. Under this schema, for instance, the Red Cross would be a quango while the Legal Services Corporation would, arguably, be a quago. For a general discussion of quangos and their implications for governance in the United Kingdom, see Flinders and Smith 1998.

References

Arnold, Peri. 1995. "Reform's Changing Role." *Public Administration Review* 55 (September/October): 407.

Barr, Stephen. 1996. "OPM, in a First, Acts to Convert an Operation into Private Firm." *Washington Post* (April 14): A4.

———. 2003. "For Once-Federal Background Investigators, Privatization Leads to Its Own Kind of Check." *Washington Post* (April 24): B2.

Berman, Larry. 1979. *The Office of Management and Budget.* Princeton, NJ: Princeton University Press.

Bingman, Charles F. 1992. *Two Presidents: The Bureau of the Budget and the Division of Administrative Management, 1939–1952.* Washington, DC: National Academy of Public Administration.

Blair, Bridgette. 2001. "OMB Pursues Reforms Despite Vacancy in Key Post: Search Is on for 'Spectacular Candidate.'" *Federal Times* (July 30): 3.

Bowsher, Charles A. 1988. "The Emerging Crisis: The Disinvestment of Government." Webb Lecture by the Comptroller General of the United States, National Academy of Public Administration, Dec. 2.

Bozeman, Barry. 1987. *All Organizations Are Public.* San Francisco, CA: Jossey-Bass.

Brass, Clinton T. 2004a. *General Management Laws: A Compendium.* Washington, DC: Congressional Research Service.

———. 2004b. *General Management Laws: Major Themes and Management Policy Objectives.* Washington, DC: Congressional Research Service.

Broidy, Dan. 2003. *The Iron Triangle: Inside the Secret World of the Carlyle Group.* New York: John Wiley.

Clinger, William. 2001. Letter to Vice President Richard B. Cheney proposing the establishment of an Office of Federal Management within the Executive Office of the President, July 24. Memorandum on file with author.

Cooper, Philip J. 2003. *Governing by Contract.* Washington, DC: CQ Press.

Cullen, Ronald B., and Donald P. Cushman. 2000. *Transitions to Competitive Government: Speed, Consensus, and Performance.* Albany: State University of New York Press.

Dean, Alan, Dwight Ink, and Harold Seidman. 1994. "OMB's 'M' Fading Away." *Government Executive* 25 (June): 62–64.

Downs, Anthony. 1967. *Inside Bureaucracy*. Boston, MA: Little Brown.

Eggers, William D., and Stephen Goldsmith. 2003. "Networked Government." *Government Executive* (June): 28–33.

Flinders, Matthew, and Martin Smith, eds. 1998. *Quangos, Accountability and Reform: The Politics of Quasi Government*. London: Macmillan.

Friedman, Milton. *Capitalism and Freedom*. Chicago, IL: University of Chicago Press.

General Accounting Office. 1989. *Managing the Government: Revised Approach Could Improve OMB's Effectiveness (GAO Management Review)*. Washington, DC: General Accounting Office.

———. 1998. *Letter to the Honorable Ted Stevens, United States Senate*. B-278820. February 10. Washington, DC. General Accounting Office.

Gilmour, Robert S., and Alexis A. Halley, eds. 1994. *Who Makes Public Policy? The Struggle for Control between Congress and the Executive*. Chatham, NJ: Chatham House Publishers.

Gilmour, Robert S., and Laura S. Jensen. 1998. "Reinventing Government Accountability: Public Functions, Privatization, and the Meaning of 'State Action.'" *Public Administration Review* 58 (May/June): 247–57.

Goldstein, Mark L. 1992. *America's Hollow Government*. Homewood, IL: BusinessOneIrwin.

Gore, Al. 1997. *Businesslike Government: Lessons Learned from America's Best Companies*. Washington, DC: National Performance Review.

Guttman, Daniel J. 2001. "The United States Enrichment Corporation: A Failing Privatisation." *Asian Journal of Public Administration* 23 (December): 247–72.

Heclo, Hugh. 1975. "OMB and the Presidency—The Problem of Neutral Competence." *The Public Interest* 38 (Winter): 80–95.

Hinkle, F. Jerome. 1999. "Selling Elk Hills—The Political Economy of Disinvestment." *Asian Journal of Public Administration* 21 (December): 246–48.

Hsu, Spencer. 2004. "Homeland Security to Remain in District: Called Victory for City Economy." *Washington Post* (June 17): B1.

Kettl, Donald F. 1994. "Beyond the Rhetoric of Reinvention: Driving Themes of the Clinton Administration's Management Reforms." *Governance* 7 (July): 309.

———. 2000. *The Global Public Management Revolution: A Report on the Transformation of Governance*. Washington, DC: Brookings Institution.

———. 2002. *Transformation of Governance: Public Administration for the Twenty-First Century*. Baltimore, MD: Johns Hopkins University Press.

Koppell, Jonathan G.S. 1999. "The Challenge of Administration by Regulation: Preliminary Findings Regarding the U.S. Government Venture Capital Funds." *Journal of Public Administration Research and Theory* 9: 644–66.

Laurent, Anne. 2000. *Entrepreneurial Government: Bureaucrats as Businesspeople*. Washington, DC: PricewaterhouseCoopers Endowment, 7.

Letter from the Comptroller General to Senator Ted Stevens. 1998. B-278820. February 10.

Light, Paul C. 1997. *The Tides of Reform: Making Government Work, 1945–1995*. New Haven, CT: Yale University Press, 228.

———. 1999. *The True Size of Government*. Washington, DC: Brookings Institution.

———. 2002. "The Incredible Shrinking Budget Office." *Government Executive* 43 (January): 66.

Mitchell, Alison. 2002. "Congressional Hearings: Letter to Ridge Is Latest Jab in Fight over Balance of Powers." *New York Times* (March 5): A8.

Moe, Ronald C. 1991. "The HUD Scandal and the Case for an Office of Federal Management." *Public Administration Review* 51 (July/August): 298–307.

————. 1994. "The 'Reinventing Government' Exercise: Misinterpreting the Problem, Misjudging the Consequences." *Public Administration Review* 54 (March/April): 111–22.

————. 1999. "At Risk: The President's Role as Chief Manager." In *The Managerial Presidency,* ed. James P. Pfiffner, 2d ed., 265–86. College Station: Texas A&M University Press.

————. 2001. "The Emerging Federal Quasi Government: Issues of Management and Accountability." *Public Administration Review* 61 (May/June): 290–312.

————. 2003. *Administrative Renewal: Reorganization Commissions in the 20th Century.* Lanham, MD: University Press of America.

————. 2004. "Governance Principles: The Neglected Basis of Federal Management." In *Making Government Manageable: Executive Organization and Management in the 21st Century,* eds. Thomas H. Stanton and Benjamin Ginsberg. Baltimore, MD: Johns Hopkins Press, 21–39.

Moe, Terry M. 1985. "The Politicized Presidency." In *The New Direction in American Politics,* eds. John E. Chubb and Paul E. Peterson. Washington, DC: Brookings Institution, 235–71.

Mueller, Dennis. 1979. *Bureaucracy and Representative Government.* Chicago, IL: Aldine Press, 1.

National Academy of Public Administration (NAPA). 1983. *Revitalizing Federal Management: Managers and Their Overburdened Systems.* Washington, DC: National Academy of Public Administration, 11–13.

National Academy of Public Administration. 1992. *Two Presidents: The Bureau of the Budget and the Division of Administrative Management, 1939-1952.* Occasional paper by Charles F. Bingman, Washington, DC: National Academy of Public Administration.

National Commission on the Public Service. 1989. *Rebuilding the Public Service.* Washington, DC: National Commission on the Public Service.

————. 2002. *Urgent Business for America: Revitalizing the Federal Government for the 21st Century.* Washington, DC: National Commission on the Public Service.

Newland, Chester A. 1997. "Faithful Execution of the Laws, Rule of Law, and Autonomy of Public Administration." In *Handbook of Public Law and Administration,* eds. Phillip Cooper and Chester A. Newland. San Francisco, CA: Jossey-Bass, 5–25.

Norris, Michael E. 2000. *Reinventing the Administrative State.* Lanham MD: University Press of America.

O'Toole, L.J. 1997. "The Implications for Democracy in a Networked Bureaucratic World." *Journal of Public Administration Research and Theory* 7 (July): 443–60.

Organization for Economic Cooperation and Development (OECD). 1995. *Governance in Transition: Public Management Reforms in OECD Countries.* Paris: OECD.

————. 2002. *Distributed Public Governance: Agencies, Authorities, and Other Government Bodies.* Paris: OECD, 16.

Osborne, David. 1996. "Bureaucracy Unbound." *Washington Post Magazine* (October 13): 8.

Osborne, David, and Ted Gaebler. 1992. *Reinventing Government: How the Entrepreneurial Spirit Is Transforming the Public Sector.* Reading, MA: Addison-Wesley.

Panetta, Leon. 1994. "Executive Memo: OMB Management Merger." *Government Executive* 26 (April): 8.

Peters, B. Guy. 2001. *The Future of Governing.* 2d ed. Lawrence: University Press of Kansas, 48.

Peters, B. Guy, and John Pierre. 1998. "Governance without Government? Rethinking Public Administration." *Journal of Public Administration Research and Theory* 8 (April): 223–43.

Phinney, David. 2003. "Contractors Could Collect Delinquent Taxes: Bill Would Let IRS Hire Private Firm." *Federal Times* (August 18): 6.

Popper, Karl. 1959. *The Logic of Scientific Discovery.* New York: Basic Books.

Relyea, Harold C. 2003. "Organizing for Homeland Security." *Presidential Studies Quarterly* 33 (September): 617.

Reorganization Plan No. 2 of 1970 (5 U.S.C. App.).

Riso, Gerald. 1989. "The New OMB: In Search of a Management Role." *Government Executive* 21 (April): 59.

Rohr, John. 2002. *Civil Servants and Their Constitutions.* Lawrence: University Press of Kansas.

Rosenbloom, David H. 2000. *Building a Legislative-Centered Public Administration: Congress and the Administrative State, 1946–1999.* Tuscaloosa: University of Alabama Press.

Sanders, Ronald P., and James Thompson. 1997. "Reinventing Government: Live Long and Prosper." *Government Executive* (April): 52.

Schwemle, Barbara. 2003. *Civil Service Reform: Analysis of the National Defense Authorization Act for FY2004.* Washington, DC: Congressional Research Service.

Seidman, Harold. 1998. *Politics, Position, and Power.* 5th ed. New York: Oxford University Press, 147.

Stanton, Thomas H. 2002. *Government-Sponsored Enterprises: Mercantilist Companies in the Modern World.* Washington, DC: AEI Press.

———. 2003a. "Lessons Learned: Obtaining Value from Federal Asset Sales." *Public Budgeting and Finance* 43 (Spring): 22–44.

———. 2003b. *Understanding Federal Asset Management: An Agenda for Reform.* Washington, DC: IBM Center for the Business of Government.

Stanton, Thomas H., and Ronald C. Moe. 2002. "Government Corporations and Government-Sponsored Enterprises." In *The Tools of Government,* ed. Lester M. Salomon. New York: Oxford University Press, 81–116.

Stretton, Hugh, and Lionel Orchard. 1994. *Public Goods, Public Enterprise, Public Choice: Theoretical Foundations of the Contemporary Attack on Government.* New York: St. Martin's Press.

Terry, Larry D. 2002. *Leadership in Public Bureaucracies: The Administrator as Conservator.* 2d ed. Armonk, NY: M.E. Sharpe.

Thompson, James R. 2001. "The Clinton Reforms and the Administrative Ascendancy of Congress." *American Review of Public Administration* 31 (September): 249–72.

Tomkin, Shelley Lynne. 1998. *Inside OMB: Politics and Process in the President's Budget Office.* Armonk, NY: M.E. Sharpe.

U.S. House of Representatives, Committee on Government Reform and Oversight, Subcommittee on Civil Service. 1995. *Outsourcing of OPM's Investigations Program,* Hearing, 104th Cong., 1st Session. Washington, DC: Government Printing Office, 54.

U.S. House of Representatives, Committee on Government Reform and Oversight, Subcommittee on Government Management, Information and Technology. 1995. *Making Government Work: Fulfilling the Mandate for Change,* H. Rept. 104-435, 104th Cong., 1st Session. Washington, DC: U.S. Government Printing Office, 5, 8.

———. 1999. *Creating an Office of Management,* Hearings, 105th Cong., 2d Session. Washington, DC: U.S. Government Printing Office.

U.S. Investigate Services. n.d. *Our History.* Available at www.usis.com-history.htm. Accessed May 14, 2006.

U.S. National Performance Review (NPR). 1993. *From Red Tape to Results: Creating a Government that Works Better and Costs Less.* Washington, DC: U.S. Government Printing Office.

U.S. Office of Management and Budget (OMB). 1994. "Making OMB More Effective in Serving the Presidency: Changes in OMB as a Result of the OMB 2000 Review." OMB Memorandum No. 94-16. Washington, DC, March 1.

———. 2001. *The President's Management Agenda—FY2002.* Washington, DC: Office of Management and Budget, August.

U.S. Senate, Committee on Governmental Affairs. 1986. *Federal Management Reorganization, Cost Control and Loan Accounting Reform,* Hearings, 99th Cong., 2d Session. Washington, DC: U.S. Government Printing Office.

U.S. Senate, Committee on Labor and Human Resources, Subcommittee on Education, Arts, and Humanities. 1982. *Oversight of Student Loan Marketing Association (Sallie Mae),* Hearings, 102nd Cong., 2d Session. Washington, DC: U.S. Government Printing Office, 135.

Wallison, Peter J., and Bert Ely. 2000. *Nationalizing Mortgage Risk: The Growth of Fannie Mae and Freddie Mac.* Washington, DC: AEI Press.

Wamsley, Barbara S. 2004. "Technocracies: Can They Bell the Cat?" In *Making Government Manageable,* eds. Thomas H. Stanton and Benjamin Ginsberg, 204–28. Baltimore, MD: Johns Hopkins University Press.

Part 3

Managing for More Effective Government

6

Observations on Organization and Management

Murray Comarow

Making Reorganization Work

When political leadership changes, or if government agencies are not accomplishing their missions, there is sure to be a spate of reorganization initiatives. These may range from government-wide restructuring to interagency or intra-agency consolidations or divisions of functions. If the past is prologue, these efforts are likely to be ad hoc in character, with mixed results. This chapter challenges reorganizers, including those studying the recommendations of the 9/11 Commission, to ponder some guidelines that underlie soundly conceived reorganization plans, and that may give pause to hasty action.

Principles

The literature on organization theory, bolstered by practical experience, reveals the following principles:

- Organization is policy; structural changes signal changes in priorities;
- Organization is not an end in itself; it can only provide an environment that promotes good performance;
- Organization informs managers and employees of their responsibilities and their relationships to each other;
- Form follows function; organizations must adapt as federal missions change or are transformed by technology or new externalities.

The literature also analyzes the pros and cons of various structures ("hierarchical" versus "organic," for example), and has much to say about the overblown "span of control" concept, distinctions between line and staff, and so forth. The core principle, on which most practitioners and organizational theorists agree, however, is that an enterprise should be organized in a way best calculated to achieve its purpose, its goals. This requires that those goals be clear and consistent, unlike those for the Agency for International Development or the old Atomic Energy Commission (AEC). In the latter case, AEC's mission to promote the use of nuclear energy conflicted with and sometimes overrode its safety mission.

The canon, however, pays little attention to the knee-jerk reorganization decisions often made by newly elected or appointed leaders, from the Congress and the president on down. The conviction that abolishing a department will save money seems to be an article of faith. In fact, it may do nothing of the kind. Abolishing a department and scattering its component programs among other agencies may have the opposite effect. Another article of faith: Placing the function in the White House guarantees better presidential oversight and will empower the executive in charge. There is little substance to this view; location is not empowerment.

President Reagan, true to his antigovernment campaign promise, proposed to abolish the departments of Energy and Education. His assertion that eliminating the Department of Energy would save $250 million in three years was disproved by the General Accounting Office (now the Government Accountability Office) in 1982.

Also without foundation is another assumption, that centralizing a number of functions under one executive will promote efficiency and performance. That notion of "reorganization by coagulation" is in the forefront of current efforts to reorganize our intelligence and antiterrorist agencies. It has a certain conceptual appeal but needs far more than that. Read on.

Multiple Agency Reorganization

In dealing with reorganization to defeat the terrorist threat, policymakers should keep these observations in mind:

1. No structural arrangement can reconcile all interests or resolve all conflicts; nevertheless, there is no substitute for organizing according to purpose, logical assignment of functions, and establishment of centers of accountability.
2. Opposing interests should be drawn together at the right levels of government, so that the vast majority of conflicts can be resolved below the level of the Executive Office of the President.
3. The objectives of the agencies involved must be plainly set out and must respond to a distinct and enduring public need.

4. There must be some assurance that the functions to be grouped under one head not only belong together, but that collectively they can be managed efficiently.

5. The agencies should be so structured that a high order of public interest is served in making policy rather than narrower advocacy positions.

With respect to observation number four above, consider the options facing Congress in reorganizing our intelligence capabilities. A super-director will need legal authority to run the show, including a substantial say in who gets the money and who gets hired (and fired) in senior positions. That authority is essential, but not sufficient. He or she will need many high-level, experienced deputies, assistants, and experts. They are all in short supply. To take them from the CIA, FBI, Homeland Security, or Defense would weaken those critical entities. These observations are valid regardless of whether the super-director is housed in the Executive Office of the President or elsewhere. Perhaps the best we can do organizationally to screen and cohere the flood of domestic and foreign data and human intelligence is to establish the 9/11 Commission's proposed "National Counterterrorism Center" and ensure that intelligence analysts are effectively insulated from political or "groupthink" pressures.

I was once asked to testify before a Senate committee on terminating the Department of Commerce. I said that that may be a sound idea in the abstract, but the rationale must rest on more specific and well-reasoned grounds. Where would each function go? What result might be expected? The devil is in the details.

The Challenge to Reorganizers

What's the Hurry?

You've been briefed, but the fact is, you don't really know. In the case of Congress, so many committees and staffers have been briefed by so many officials that a clear vision of the optimum choice will be hard to find. If you reorganize now, you'll be relying heavily on advice from those with axes to grind. If you wait, it will be more your baby, a product of your better understanding. And you will have had a chance during this period to assess the competence of your advisers.

Reorganization Usually Impedes Performance

Even the soundest reorganization can slow down the agencies in the short run—and sometimes much longer. The Environmental Protection Agency took years to get going. The same was true of the Department of Defense, established by the National Security Acts of 1947 and 1949, until it was reorganized in 1958, and even then.

Personal relationships—the "invisible network" on which all enterprises depend—are strained or broken by reorganization. Does this mean that it's always bad to reorganize? Not for a minute. It means that you should go slowly until you are persuaded that structure is the root cause of the performance, rather than management or external causality, and that the long-term benefits you hope to get exceed the costs.

Why, Exactly, Do You Want to Reorganize?

- "*To get control.*" Wrong. Nobody really "controls" a large institution—the word has virtually disappeared from the management lexicon. In addition to the military services, the secretary of defense has jurisdiction over sixteen agencies, two universities, and a college. No secretary of defense would say he or she "controls" these entities. The job is infinitely more complex. Hiring a bevy of special assistants is a particularly bad idea. It won't give you "control" but it will generate tension and hostility as the staff's authority is eroded.
- "*To get rid of John Doe.*" Wrong again. John can be reassigned or fired. (It is a myth that government managers can't be pushed out, but that is another topic.) Conversely, it's just as bad to set up an activity tailored to one individual's talents. Any reorganization should be based on careful analysis and need, not targeted, as is often the case, to deal with one or a few individuals. When that person leaves, you will probably reorganize again. And again. . . .
- "*To shake up the bureaucracy.*" At a National Academy of Public Administration meeting, a top functionary of President Clinton's "Reinventing Government" effort vigorously defended this point of view. But a leader's job is to motivate: This is largely achieved, if at all, by mutual trust and by recognizing good work. Only slackers, incompetents, and functionaries who espouse such nonsense should be singled out for "shaking up."
- "*We're not fully meeting our objectives.*" Why not? If you're sure that the underlying reason is structural misalignment, go for it. But if the failure to reach the agency's goals is due to other factors, reorganization may well make matters worse.

How an Agency Head Should Reorganize

You've studied the situation, sorted out the root causes of your difficulties, identified a promising approach, and sounded out the cognizant congressional committees and affected groups. Most important, you've defined what the reorganization expects to achieve and you're ready to invest the political capital to make it happen. It looks like reorganizing is the right move.

- *Hire a consultant?* Maybe, if you can identify a good one who can work with an in-house group. Consultants have the outsider's advantage of objectivity and, hopefully, relevant prior experience. Watch out, however, for their tendency to recommend boilerplate fixes, or, at the other extreme, radical changes to demonstrate "outside-the-box" creativity. Make sure you get the individuals or team named in the firm's proposal. Top names in proposals to secure the contract often mysteriously disappear. Alternatives to a consultant include an in-house team, individuals borrowed from other agencies, retired executives, or some combinations of these.
- *Announce your decision to reorganize.* It will upset your staff, but (1) you can't keep it a secret and (2) when it leaks, in ways you may not like, your people will be doubly upset.
- *Invite employee input.* This will permit opposition to form, but that will happen in any event. Asking staffers and the often-neglected field personnel to comment can have three positive outcomes:
  - You may get some valuable ideas
  - Your rationale may gain converts or abate opposition
  - At the very least, you will deprive in-house critics of an irrefutable argument, i.e., "The so-and-sos never even asked us, and if they had. . . ."
- *Is it lawful?* Ensure that the relevant laws, including reduction-in-force and veterans' preference statutes, are obeyed. As the Postal Service once belatedly discovered in the case of veterans, calling a reduction in force a reorganization doesn't make it one in the eyes of the court. If there's any doubt about legality, get an opinion from the Department of Justice or eminent outside counsel.
- *How will it affect women and minorities?* Irrespective of court decisions, anticipate the reaction and explain your position in human terms. Don't wait until racism and sexism charges force you to play catch-up.

Be Reasonable in Your Expectations

A strong enterprise needs effective people who share its institutional goals. It needs adequate resources and sensible procedures. And it needs good organization. Structural reform will not offset lack of resources, poor management, or weak political support from the White House or interest groups. Good people can make a poor organization work up to a point; incompetents can drag down the best-organized agency. Sound organization increases the chances that the agency's goals will be reached, no small thing. Ask yourself:

- Do the functions belong together?
- Will the programs serve the public interest, rather than specific clients?
- Have opposing yet complementary interests been drawn together at the right levels?
- Are specific individuals accountable for reaching specific objectives?

There is no perfect arrangement that will mediate among all interests, much less resolve all conflicts. Admit mistakes ungrudgingly, and make adjustments as required.

The physician's ethic is germane, "First do no harm." Reorganizations come at a price. Be sure that future benefits outweigh the costs, i.e., that the revised structure, in time, is more likely to achieve your objectives or enhance your ability to manage.

Executive Development

Government cannot do its best for the nation unless government people are encouraged to give their best to the nation and see a fair chance of recompense and promotion. Unbelievable Fact: There is no true Federal Executive Development Program. Most agencies act as if Executive Development means Taking Courses.

Training can be worthwhile, but not as the primary tool. Managers are made by letting them manage, mistakes and all. Courses may enrich the experience if well designed and relevant. Fifty years ago, Peter F. Drucker wrote in *The Practice of Management,* "[M]anagement cannot make rational and responsible decisions unless it selects, develops and tests the men who will have to follow them through—the managers of tomorrow." It is time the federal government listened.

The Office of Management and Budget should take this on, but should not, Heaven help us, lay a giant Executive Development cookie cutter on government. The needs of agencies differ enormously. The OMB should help each agency to work out the program best for it. Agency leaders who develop successful programs could, under OMB guidance, work with other agencies as mentors. The job is easy to describe, extremely difficult to execute.

Give everyone a shot. Identify people who are smart, who have commitment, who work well with others. (Keep an eye open for late bloomers.)

Give them increasing and diverse responsibilities. Evaluate them, working with, not against or over, line managers. Stretch them over time. Run the whole operation from your top office. The result should be higher overall quality—a rare value in modern life.

Leadership

It comes with the title only for a little while, and then it must be earned. The greatest government or industry leaders intuit the Talmudic dictum to "treat a man—not as he is—but as you would wish him to be." Such leaders:

- Share responsibility with their managers;
- Do not rely on formal communications systems; they go among the troops and listen hard;
- Are scrupulously fair, have integrity, and avoid the appearance of conflict of interest or favoritism;
- Where possible, establish mutually agreed-upon goals, not objectives imposed without consultation;
- Insist that their managers act like managers by wiping out unnecessary functions, controlling costs, and removing marginal or incompetent people; and
- Care about their employees as people and visibly show that they care.

Management Style in a Time Frame

A six-month crash program is not organized like a long-term or permanent operation. Sprinters make lousy marathon runners and vice versa. You need different management styles.

- *The Sprint:* intense, challenging, creative, consuming, high risk.
- *The Marathon:* build relationships, trust, keep developing talent, prudent risks.

The Situation of Senior Bureaucrats

Their bosses are political appointees who are not big fans of bureaucrats, and are likely to be gone in less than two years. Some appointees are well qualified, and may bring new and welcome insights. Others are unqualified. Both types have this in common: they will be measured by their bosses on a political scale.

In the private sector, a CEO or CFO will be primarily valued based on shareholders' satisfaction. Consulting firms, law firms, and accounting firms track and reward partners' and associates' billings. Political appointees, how-ever, score by supporting the administration's political agenda, sometimes shortchanging the agency's mission. This dynamic is intensified by the appointee's sense of impermanence. The appointee must work fast to attract the eye of political superiors, another type of "sprint." Career executives run marathons. Michael Maccoby analyzes other cultural differences between appointees and career officials in chapter 9.

Presidents Demean Public Servants

President Carter successfully played the anti-Washington card in his 1976 campaign and during his term, declaring in 1978, "Now my biggest prob-lems are inflation and dealing with the horrible federal bureaucracy. And the one that's been the most frustrating, I think, is the bureaucracy." Since the president is the bureaucrats' boss, Carter's bleat was really a confession that he lacked the skill, or the will, to manage his employees.

President Reagan took the Carter ploy to a higher, or perhaps lower, level. In his first inaugural address, he proclaimed that "Government is not the solution to our problem. Government is our problem." Taking the words at their face value, that's an astonishing and feckless stance, but much of the public ate it up, and the pundits scarcely winced. Reagan succeeded in distancing himself from the "bureaucrats" as if he had no constitutional responsibility for their performance in conducting the busi-ness of government.

Under President Clinton, Vice President Gore's much-touted Partner-ship for Reinventing Government initiatives congratulated themselves on getting 385,000 workers off the federal payroll, at a cost of $5 billion for buyouts. They offered no reliable count of how many were replaced by consultants and contractors, much less an analysis of the differences in cost or quality of work.

A Break with Tradition

It was not always thus. During World War II, government organizations, with strong private-sector support, provided our armed forces with the material that drove us to victory. Subsequently, corruption and mismanagement by elected and appointed politicians generated a demand for neutral profession-als, working within a merit-based career federal service. In his campaign, President Eisenhower pledged to reform the famously corrupt Internal Rev-enue Service. He did just that, replacing every political appointee except the commissioner with a career public servant.

Contempt for government and for "bureaucrats," trumpeted by presidents, candidates, and politicians of both parties, has seeped into the public consciousness and has become embedded in our culture. The consequences are grave, but they have remained largely unexamined, even by prestigious organizations such as my own National Academy of Public Administration.

To do the people's business was once regarded as a calling. Today it is often perceived as a sinecure, or worse. A society that devalues its public servants screens out the people it needs most.

Trust Is the Indispensable Lubricant

Granted the occasional sullen bureaucrat who drags his or her feet or conspires to undermine a program, the vast majority of career executives want to be trusted, to be part of the action, to have their voices heard in making policy, and to have a respected role in implementing it.

Henry L. Stimson, secretary of war during World War II, said, "The only way to make a man trustworthy is to trust him, and the surest way to make him untrustworthy is to distrust him and show your distrust." That is the secret of motivating federal executives, a secret so obvious that it has been lost upon most of our political leaders.

Alienating federal careerists has consequences:

- They tend to act out the very role in which they are cast by their political superiors, a classic case of self-fulfilling prophecy.
- They tend to look to their peers, or to specific segments of their constituencies, for approval and recognition, rather than to their bosses.

In ways that can't be measured, this hurts the nation pervasively and profoundly.

The Defensive Crouch

Business executives are expected to take risks. It is taken for granted that some initiatives will fail. They are judged on performance and the bottom line. Government executives are scrutinized by the Congress, the Government Accountability Office, presidentially appointed inspectors general, the print and electronic media, and especially the often-contentious special interests they serve or regulate. Spending taxpayers' money in a program that may not succeed takes guts. If it fails, you will be criticized, count on it. Your successes will be brushed aside. That is why many career executives work in a "defensive crouch."

Congress Contributes to Inefficiency

On August 8, 2004, the *New York Times* reported that since January 2003, Department of Homeland Security officials "testified before 300 Congressional hearings and held 2,000 briefings for members of Congress or their staffs . . . an average of 4 hearings and 25 briefings a week." No fewer than 88 committees and subcommittees were involved. The drain upon executive energy was enormous. Congress, impatient with inefficiency in the executive branch, thus contributes to inefficient management. One committee in each house should be established.

Loyalty

You surely see yourself as a loyal person. To whom or what are you loyal? To your boss, your conscience, the public, the law, or perhaps to a "Higher Authority"? Your agency head instructs you to award a sole-source contract in violation of lawful procurement rules. Doing so would demonstrate your loyalty to him or her, but not to the public. If you are a lawyer, it would also violate your oath as an officer of the court. You must decline to sign, and take the consequences. Surprisingly, this may actually turn out to be to your advantage.

A much more difficult case would involve a policy decision that your chief has the right to make, but that you believe is dead wrong and not in the public interest. Do you "go along to get along," as the legendary Sam Rayburn remarked? Do you quietly resign? Do you blow the whistle, as a matter of loyalty to your own conscience and to the public interest?

Whistleblowers

They are our heroes, the darlings of pack journalists, and some deservedly so. Brave men and women have indeed put their careers and their futures on the line and have exposed corruption and waste, and some have paid dearly. All honor to them.

And then there are others, those with axes to grind, whose aim may be to harass a superior or competitor. Others are so committed to a point of view that they see a different course of action as outrageous. And still others are just wrong, or fail to see that choices are often made among imperfect alternatives.

Take Risks

If you think of a hot idea to improve some aspect of the agency's work, you may be told:

- We tried that ten years ago and it didn't work.
- It can't be done because we don't have the money; or the unions would raise hell.
- Let's study it and give you a report in six months.

Don't fall for these excuses. Forge ahead.

A Personal Note

I have been a government executive. I practiced private law (still do). I was a partner in a major consulting firm. I taught in a law school and in a school of public administration. I am grateful to this blessed nation for these opportunities; all were challenging and fulfilling in various ways. My deepest satisfactions, however, derived from government service. To be part of an effort to improve some aspects of our national life is a gift beyond measure.

Do not be deterred by uninformed or negative blather. Go for it—it might work for you, too.

7

Managing Change that Makes a Difference

Dwight Ink

Since the shocking events of 9/11, the Washington management community has engaged in extensive debate regarding the daunting task the new Department of Homeland Security (DHS) faces in meeting its difficult mission. The unprecedented complexity involved in building this new department has renewed interest in presidential management initiatives to structure and operate departments and agencies more effectively. In developing new approaches, it is a mistake to neglect past experience that can be of great help when adapted to new circumstances.

No prior departmental structure offers a blueprint for how the DHS or other new departments should be structured and operated (Dean 2004). Circumstances are continually changing. Further, past management reforms have not had a high success rate with respect to achieving changes that have truly made a difference. Enormous effort, and much rhetoric, has been devoted to so-called reforms that have produced scattered examples of improvement but little has happened of a magnitude that can be seen by the public as having made a difference. Some have taken us backward. Yet mixed in with these disappointing experiences have been important presidential initiatives from time to time that did bring about important changes. These successes often benefited in a major way from giving high priority to certain basic management strategies that have enduring value. Future crises such as those that may face the DHS will require the type of quick action that could profit most from adapting basic management strategies that have been proven to bring about change that makes a difference.

This chapter focuses on selected management strategies that have been of special help to presidential initiatives over four decades in achieving changes that made a significant difference, changes that were thought unrealistically bold by most people at the time. At first glance, these strategies seem rather commonplace. So they are if applied in a business-as-usual manner. But in the

166

cases cited, they were applied in uncommon, some would say extreme, ways that made a huge difference in successfully meeting the intended objectives. The fact that not all program outcomes met with universal approval does not detract from the value of these strategies to a variety of presidents who were seeking change. When executed by experienced people, they should be equally adaptable to help future administrations meet especially difficult challenges.

Four of these strategies merit special attention:

1. The first strategy was that of moving bold reforms rapidly, including the value of a presidency's utilizing the transition in a way that permits beginning implementation quickly after inauguration. This is in sharp contrast with the usual approach of spending the first year to eighteen months, the period in which conditions are most favorable for action, setting goals and merely planning implementation.
2. The second was that by emphasizing fundamental concepts of good management, officials were able to take greater-than-usual risks and develop highly innovative approaches that were tailored to each circumstance rather than relying on models or conventional wisdom that limit creativity.
3. Third was to take bold steps with respect to openness and outreach throughout the course of an initiative. The resultant saving of time, the forging of trust, and the lowering of opposition pay big dividends.
4. Fourth was an unusually close working relationship between the career and political leadership in each case, and the mutual respect they held for each other. The relationship seemed to the participants much like a partnership.

The balance of this chapter illustrates how these strategies have been applied in selected presidential initiatives through the years in ways that truly made a difference.

Disaster Recovery

On Good Friday of 1964, Alaska was struck by the most severe earthquake ever recorded on the mainland of our continent. Registering over 9.2 on the Richter scale with an agonizing duration of nearly four minutes, it caused an area that was equal in size to Virginia, Maryland, New Jersey and Connecticut combined to either rise or sink permanently by five feet or more. The majority of Alaskans lived in this area. Many water and sewer systems were broken beyond repair; all harbors for fishing boats—the heart of Alaskan economic life—in this huge area were made inoperable; key transportation systems were knocked out; and thousands of homes and businesses were destroyed or severely damaged. In order to prevent most Alaskans from scrambling to the lower forty-eight states, public utilities and harbors had to be back in operation before the early fall freezes halted the rebuilding. Rampant inflation also had to be prevented and new types of recovery financing and new approaches to earthquake insurance for businesses and homeowners had to be developed. These required that several pieces of urgently needed legislation to be pushed quickly through a busy Congress in which the Senate was paralyzed in a lengthy civil rights filibuster.[1]

Unfortunately, no engineer could be found who believed that the extensive studies required to determine where it was safe to rebuild, followed by design and construction of new buildings, could all be accomplished within the short Alaskan construction season. The task was further complicated by the fact that for the first time this country decided to move beyond the policy of simply restoring facilities to what they had been before the disaster. Rather, they were to be rebuilt to new, modern standards and redesigned in a way that would enhance the economic development of Alaska, whose finances were precarious in those pre-oil days.[2]

Unlike hurricane recoveries, most of this critical work could not begin until massive soil tests could determine where it was safe to rebuild. Further complicating the task was the fact that testing had to await the lengthy trucking and barging of drill rigs from the lower forty-eight states, creating an almost intolerable delay in view of the short time available for rebuilding.

Yet only four months after the quake, it was clear that something had happened that was enabling these enormous challenges to be met. Recovery was succeeding beyond the hopes of the most optimistic. The *Anchorage Times,* highly skeptical at first, printed an editorial entitled "Government at its Best" in which the paper lauded the "remarkable performance" of the career leadership assigned to the task.[3] Alaskans did not need to go south as winter approached.

This remarkable recovery effort under President Johnson changed our approach to later disaster recoveries, and laid the foundation for much of the New Federalism programs of President Nixon, which had an impact on virtually every community in the nation.

In addition to the strong determination of the Alaskan people, several management strategies were critical to achieving this unexpected success.

Rapid Action

Machinery that responds to disasters has to go into action very quickly. Unfortunately, two days after the Alaskan earthquake of March 27, 1964, it became clear that the existing organizational arrangements at the national, state, and local levels were not equipped to handle a disaster of this magnitude and complexity. Johnson moved quickly and only five days after the disaster he had established a totally unprecedented structure involving both the executive and the legislative branches—an innovative arrangement that would ordinarily be viewed as much too controversial and time consuming to design and install.[4] Government typically agonizes for months in organizing structures far less complex and precedent setting than this.

Extremely tight construction schedules were soon established, despite warnings that past experience indicated they would be impossible to meet.[5] In the case of roads and utility lines such as water and sewer distribution systems, contractors were initially shocked to find that the time allotted was frequently only 10 percent of what experience had shown to be a typical period for design and construction once the location had been determined. Federal agencies were told to rely heavily on incentive contracting, including substantial reduction or total loss of fee for failing to meet target dates. On-site monitoring was intensive. Using streamlined management approaches and around-the-clock shifts, this new machinery led to the establishment of peacetime records in reconstruction even though this was the most complicated natural disaster recovery in our history.

Without this unusually rapid pace, Alaskans would have suffered a physical and economic crisis arguably beyond that experienced by any state since the Civil War. Much of the state would have been abandoned by fall, faced with a long and uncertain road to recovery.

Innovative Design

A major reason no engineer thought at the time that Alaskan reconstruction could progress sufficiently during the short construction season to prevent most residents from abandoning the state was because their mind-set was based on conventional management practices used in prior rebuilding. Within a few days, it became clear that relying on past approaches would fail miserably. President Johnson moved in an entirely different direction.

First, in an unprecedented move, Johnson reconstituted most of his cabinet as the Federal Reconstruction and Development Planning Commission for Alaska, chaired by a powerful senator, Clinton Anderson.[6] No such organizational arrangement has ever been used before or since. Because a senator is not supposed to give direct orders to departments and agencies, Johnson appointed a senior career official from the Atomic Energy Commission as executive director of the commission. He reported jointly to Anderson and Johnson. Although not unique, joint reporting is not something most of us usually recommend. Four congressional staff members were assigned to the executive director and served under his direction. Their role as an integral part of his staff enabled them to keep key congressional members fully informed as well as alerting the executive director to potential problems with the Hill in time to avoid them.

This novel legislative-executive branch linkage eliminated misunderstandings between the two branches and reduced the time for passing legislation to a small fraction of the usual period. With one exception, the bills were passed within a few weeks of being drafted, in sharp contrast to the typical legislative process. It also gave tremendous leverage both to the commission chair in policy formulation and to its executive director in operational decision making, critical ingredients to dealing with emergencies having great urgency.

Also without precedent, tacit approval of both the president and congressional leadership was given to waive any procedures that agencies and the executive director thought jeopardized their ability to meet important deadlines. Public hearings, for example, were often dispensed with because of the time they consume. This remarkable level of flexibility illustrates the capacity of our government to innovate quickly when necessary.

Further, because virtually every federal agency and every Alaskan state and local department was involved in the recovery effort,[7] the usual fragmented management working relationships among the three levels of government were replaced by a common planning and implementation mode of operation that had never been tried before so far as the author is aware. It is interesting to note that the highly complex coordination activities moved smoothly[8] without issuing any procedures. One exception was a unique reporting system through which field personnel informed simultaneously all levels within the state and federal governments of progress and problems.

Urgency demanded simplicity. None of the interagency coordinating groups were given authority as a group, relying instead on the agency authority residing with the agency members and the support of the executive director and the Bureau of the Budget (BOB) management staff. Most of these unique organization and management measures so crucial to success were fully operational less than two weeks after the earthquake.

Without this highly innovative streamlining of federal organization and processes that were established so quickly, the president's effort would have failed, working great hardship on the Alaskan people and threatening the short-term economic viability of the state. One can also imagine the political embarrassment Lyndon Johnson would have suffered.

Openness and Outreach

The executive director divided his time between Washington and Alaska, first spending roughly ten days in Washington working on emergency legislation and policy issues and consulting with Anderson and members of the commission. He then devoted about the same number of days to time in Alaska, flying by plane from one devastated community to another, reminiscent of the circuit riding of the itinerant preacher in pioneer days. In addition to several key members of his staff, the Alaskan Field Committee members representing the key federal agencies were on board the flights, as were several Alaskan state officials. At each stop, the group would meet around a large table together with the local officials, generally in a high school gymnasium that could accommodate residents. Business and church leaders were active participants, as was the public.

At the first round of such meetings, there was an explanation of what types of federal assistance might be available, and under what conditions. The discussion then proceeded to develop an initial list of reconstruction projects, such as water and sewers, harbors, housing, schools, and transportation. Ballpark cost estimates were included, recognizing that all would have to be modified. The possibility of special Small Business Administration (SBA) and Federal Housing Administration (FHA) loan arrangements was included, as were appeals for restraint needed to avoid wage and price escalation.[9]

Assignment of most lead responsibilities among agencies of the three governments were made at these initial meetings, and preliminary timetables were established. Every citizen had an opportunity to speak briefly. There were no federal plans, no state plans, just community plans that integrated all three levels of government into common goals and plans. Despite strong steps by the chair to limit the length of comments, these meetings lasted most of the night and sometimes into the morning.

On the executive director's next visit to Alaska, similar meetings were again held, in which the timetables were made firm and budgets set. Again, every meeting was public, and citizens could raise their objections and make their suggestions. There was enough citizen participation to give the public a good understanding of what was possible and what was not. The executive director also spent considerable time inspecting each of the scores of rebuilding projects, talking with the residents or businesses in the damaged neighborhoods. This open approach enabled all the stakeholders to see the decision making firsthand and participate in the process.

In Washington the attorney general of Alaska had an office next to that of the executive director, and participated in all the staff meetings as well as those of the commission. The GAO had free access to all of the commission records. No formal requests were required. Visiting officials from Alaska were also accorded free access to any records except memos from the executive director to Anderson or Johnson regarding personnel.[10]

Since all elements of the communities were engaged in the planning, most people developed a sense of ownership in their community projects and worked hard to help them succeed.[11] Further, virtually no time had to be diverted from the frantic pace of rebuilding to explain and defend policies and decisions. The press was there to see developments as they unfolded, enabling the reporters to file highly accurate accounts. Too often, leaders believe that urgency prevents such extreme openness and extensive outreach. Alaska presents a vivid example of how this strategy can save considerable time in the long run. In fact, it is very unlikely that the effort could have succeeded with the typical level of limited openness and stakeholder participation. It would seem that the DHS might profit from a careful review of the unusually streamlined operational techniques used in Alaska.

Political-Career Partnerships

Within the extremely broad presidential mandate to save Alaska, the career executive director and his staff were free to use whatever management approaches they thought necessary without having to get approval from the political leadership. As mentioned above, this extended to suspending Bureau of the Budget or agency procedures believed to be jeopardizing the recovery goals, a remarkable example of confidence by political leadership of both branches in the integrity and judgment of the career service. This vote of confidence, in turn, gave the career leaders a huge incentive to use that operational freedom responsibly and judiciously.

Members of the Federal Field Committee were the highest-level persons from each federal agency located in Alaska. All were in the career service. Soon they were delegated agency authority far beyond what they had been provided heretofore. Their stellar performance in these enhanced roles was often a great surprise to their respective headquarters. Had the career leaders been required to seek approval from political levels in Washington for reconstruction decisions within budgets and policies approved by Washington, it is very doubtful that the recovery could have succeeded.

Of critical importance to Johnson's success was the fact that the sweeping management and engineering changes were designed and implemented by highly experienced professional people who could move far more rapidly than could have outside leadership brought in from the private sector.

Later, large quantities of oil were found and extracted in northern Alaska, making a huge difference in the economic health of the state. Since this help was not available in 1964, the management strategies outlined above were a lifesaver to Alaska.

New Federalism

Toward the end of the Johnson administration, it had become apparent that the well-intentioned Great Society programs were so centralized, and so laden with red tape, that most were falling far short of serving the public in ways that were intended. Building on the Alaskan experience and several earlier pilot projects initiated by the BOB, a major streamlining of the federal system of state and local grants was begun immediately after President Nixon was inaugurated.

Because virtually every domestic field was involved, it was widely predicted that strong opposition from a great range of special interest groups would sink this initiative before it could get off the ground.[12] Fear that the proposed streamlining would be simply a cover for Nixon to weaken assistance programs initiated by Democrats was widespread. Yet the BOB-led effort, through its new Office of Executive Management (OEM), overcame this opposition and moved forward with considerable speed in producing highly positive results. (In chapter 5, Ronald Moe argues for the restoration of an office with this capacity in the Executive Office of the President.) The resulting increase in federal responsiveness to local problems was welcomed by hundreds of communities from coast to coast. It drew bipartisan support from Congress as the members saw that the streamlining of management strengthened, rather than weakened, the effectiveness of programs they supported.

Rapid Action

Only a few days after his inauguration, Nixon forwarded to Congress a request to renew reorganization plan authority for the president, an authority he used effectively during his first term.[13] Two months after inauguration he issued two orders focusing on departmental management. The first one directed six departments and two independent agencies to decentralize, streamline assistance to states and communities, and improve interagency coordination under a program already developed by BOB management staff and ready to begin.[14] The other directed five departments and independent agencies to adopt standard regional boundaries and standard regional cities for all programs requiring interagency or intergovernmental coordination. Nixon was not simply announcing an intent to establish boundaries and select cities in the future; the cities and boundaries had been selected and were specified.[15]

Progress reports from the departments on actions taken, not merely progress on developing plans to take action at some unknown point in the future, were due to BOB on May 1, 1969. Just four months after Nixon had taken office, the director of the Office of Executive Management met with the president to provide a progress report on actions taken by the various departments.[16] This remarkable speed with which Nixon's management agenda got under way was one of the keys to his first-term success regarding governmental management initiatives.

Innovative Design

In seeking to overcome the service delivery problems of the highly centralized, procedurally burdened, federal assistance programs of the Great Society era, Nixon surprisingly drew on several pilot operations conducted near the end of the prior Democratic administration, even though it was his intent to adopt a management strategy that was the opposite of that used in the Great Society. He planned a massive decentralization. His conservative Republican supporters were surprised and worried, however, by his intent to rely much more heavily on local governments than on states in overhauling the delivery system, despite the consensus that local leadership was heavily tilted Democratic.

Nixon quickly proceeded to perform major surgery on the way in which most of these hundreds of assistance programs were administered. Agencies were given great freedom to pursue innovative techniques, but within two broad guidelines. First was to avoid tinkering with the existing system wherever possible. Rather, the departmental teams were to start with a look at what was truly necessary and rebuild from scratch. Second was to look at the needs from the perspective of the communities and their citizens, rather than from the perspective of Washington staff. Programs were authorized by Congress to serve the people, not Washington, a basic Nixon premise.

This strategy was far bolder than the traditional approach of limited incremental intergovernmental management improvements, often and typically limited to only one type of grant at a time. Under OEM leadership, grant processes for nearly four hundred domestic programs were reviewed from their initial application to final approval,[17] as was the approach of the departments to oversight. Not everyone followed the basic guidelines, and some processes were simply not susceptible to major change, but the majority of grants systems were redesigned, some dramatically streamlined.[18] Before-and-after performances were then recorded and audited to ensure that claims of success were verified independently before making them public, a rarely used government-wide approach that enhanced public credibility.

The new standard regions, each with their regional councils, were designed to expedite grant administration and bring more of the decision making nearer the grantees. Similar regional moves had been considered earlier by both Eisenhower and Johnson, but each had decided such a sweeping change was too drastic to have a realistic chance of success.

The OEM established a group of "council watchers" to ensure that the regional councils served as expediters rather than evolving as another level of government, a move that Congress had rejected earlier as giving the BOB too much power over operations of departments and agencies. However, in this case the BOB quickly developed strong bipartisan support from Congress in pursuing this new vigorous leadership role, in contrast to the more typical congressional attitude of believing that the BOB/OMB exercises too much power over the departments.

These actions were packaged as the Federal Assistance Review (FAR), and became core components of Nixon's New Federalism, which later also encompassed revenue sharing.

FAR succeeded in slashing the time and effort all three levels of government had to devote to managing federal assistance to state and local governments. Administrative costs had been typically absorbing 30 percent to 40 percent of the funds Congress provided for these programs.[19] But cost savings were only part of the change. Federal responses were far quicker and had greater credibility because most of them came from federal field people who understood the local issues better than officials in Washington. Further, local leaders generally knew who in a field office could be held accountable for decisions as contrasted with those grantee decisions that earlier had been caught up in the slow-moving, cumbersome Washington decision-making process that typically involved many offices in ways that defied accountability. Public access improved greatly.

The results of the streamlining accomplished by the departments through FAR were very visible in communities throughout the country, including many of the disadvantaged neighborhoods that had been the seedbeds for the burnings and violence of the 1960s. On occasion the seven major public interest state and local groups forwarded joint letters commending the BOB/OMB on FAR. Proceeding along the traditional management improvement path would have produced virtually none of those changes that could have been seen by local communities as making a difference to them.

Outreach

During Nixon's presidential transition, even before inauguration, a series of informal discussions took place among the executive directors of the Big Seven public interest groups (also known as the PIGs) and several career people from HUD and the BOB. Immediately after inauguration, consultations with these groups intensified, supplemented by meetings with key individual state and local leaders around the nation including Dick Lugar, the innovative mayor of Indianapolis, and Ronald Reagan, governor of California.

Within two weeks after inauguration, the OEM director met jointly with the chair and ranking minority member of the House and Senate committees concerned with government organization and intergovernmental affairs, an area in which Senator Edmund Muskie was providing very strong leadership. With the support of Bryce Harlow and Bill Timmons in the White House, the OEM followed a pattern of first securing White House agreement in principle to a new initiative, followed within days by consultations on the Hill with both majority and minority members and staffs. The OEM was then able to refine the White House–approved initiatives in ways that preserved the president's objectives while revising language that otherwise would bar congressional action on the Hill. In the process of these consultations, members of Congress experienced enough participation to share a sense of ownership in the final program. This resulted in a stronger bipartisan desire to help the initiatives succeed than one generally finds. The GAO was kept currently informed, and the comptroller general, Elmer Staats, often made valuable suggestions on management system reforms.[20]

Draft BOB circulars to implement new legislation or executive orders were developed with agency involvement and then circulated widely before appearing in the Federal Register, but with short deadlines for response. Close consultations on grant reform with the leadership of the Big Seven as a group continued during the first six months of the Nixon presidency and continued less frequently thereafter.[21] These consultations were supplemented by OEM visits to inner-city neighborhoods and other communities having the most difficulty in coping with state and federal red tape. This produced informal information channels in each area that ranged from power brokers down to former gang members who provided information about neighborhood conditions not otherwise available.

By producing diverse information flows from across the nation, this federal-local teamwork enabled the OEM to quickly gather data in several weeks that would have otherwise taken months. These facts, and the early support of state and local leaders, gave the White House confidence in moving quickly with the executive orders prepared by the OEM for launching the presidential initiatives to streamline the federal assistance programs.

Political-Career Partnerships

For an administration not thought to be friendly to the career service, it is interesting to note that the leadership for the Federal Assistance Review (FAR) was entrusted to the career service. The president relied on the BOB career management staff (OEM) for leading the design and implementation of the whole program. This included developing and delivering congressional testimony and addressing national conferences of governors and mayors. Particularly important was the support of the career deputy BOB director, Phillip "Sam" Hughes. The interagency steering group was composed primarily of career assistant secretaries.

Similarly, most department heads looked to career leaders, especially their assistant secretaries of administration for management leadership in their departments. The same was true of major field offices that tended to be headed by career people. Toward the end of Nixon's first term, however, a number of assistant secretaries and field office heads were replaced by political appointees, a practice that accelerated during his second term and that of President Carter.[22]

During Nixon's first term, many White House staff worked closely with the OEM in removing political obstacles for the whole management agenda of the president, especially John Ehrlichman, Patrick Moynihan, Bill Timmons, Arthur Burns, and Peter Flanigan. The career OEM director participated in the daily 7:30 a.m. meetings of the White House staff, unusual access for a career person. Until the 1972 presidential campaign, the BOB/OMB career staff and the political leadership of the Nixon administration functioned as a team, a productive arrangement that collapsed with the election.

Each of the foregoing strategies that contributed so heavily to Nixon's first-term management success were sharply reversed as the 1972 presidential campaign progressed and the ill-fated second term began. The author believes this reversal was an important factor in the more secretive and manipulative White House environment that produced Watergate and the infamous Plumbers Group activities.[23]

Civil Service Reform

Beginning with the 1883 Pendleton Act, our government gradually replaced the corrupt patronage system of personnel management with one based on merit. Unfortunately, the system accumulated more and more procedures over the years until it became too cumbersome and rigid to serve the needs of management. At the same time, actions by the Nixon White House staff and some members of Congress showed that the system no longer gave effective protection against the political undermining of the merit concept.

President Carter called for a comprehensive review and reform of the system, resulting in the 1978 Civil Service Reform Act. This reform provided a balanced approach that emphasized decentralization and simplification of the system to permit the managers to manage, but also built into the law stronger safeguards against abuse of increased flexibilities.

It brought about the largest set of changes since the system was begun in 1883. They included the establishment of the Office of Personnel Management (OPM), the Merit System Protection Board, and the Special Counsel to replace the Civil Service Commission (CSC); the Federal Labor Relations Authority (FLRA); and the Senior Executive Service (SES). The reform also initiated a government-wide linkage of pay and performance, authorized pilot projects to try innovative practices not authorized by the personnel sections of Title 5 of the United States Code, and called for major decentralization and simplification of personnel actions "to permit managers to manage." An important set of Merit Principles and Prohibited Practices were embedded in government-wide legislation for the first time as safeguards against renewed onslaughts against the merit concept for public service.

After twenty-five years of experience, including a rather disappointing quality of implementation, it is now time to build upon that important reform. New laws are now extending the flexibilities and simplification envisioned in 1978, as well as authorizing new approaches. One can argue that the Carter reform assumed a management capability beyond that actually possessed at the time by OPM and most agencies, especially in linking pay to performance, but it certainly did produce changes that began to free up agency managers to manage while also strengthening legal safeguards against abuse.

Rapid Action

Carter's civil service reform had some difficulty competing for attention the first several months, as the appointment of the executive director and eight of the nine task forces was not completed until early July.[24] It then moved on a very fast track. By the end of November a broad range of 125 specific recommendations was forwarded to Scotty Campbell, the chair of the Civil Service Commission; the OMB; and the president. As a result of the unconventional approach followed by Scotty Campbell and supported strongly by the OMB, the most comprehensive set of federal personnel recommendations ever proposed were developed within a few months, and many pages of resultant legislation were submitted by Carter to Congress early in its next session. Most of it passed in October, less than two years after his inauguration.[25]

One seldom finds government-wide management reforms of this complexity that fare so well in Congress. Had Campbell permitted the more customary slower pace for government-wide reforms, it is highly probable that the lost momentum would have led to the fading of congressional interest and support, leaving the reform package vulnerable to erosion of content.

Innovative Design

First, Campbell and the president decided to embark on a comprehensive review of the federal personnel system, something that had never been done in the nearly one hundred years since the beginning of the federal government's merit system. The boldness of this strategy presented a potential for a much greater change than earlier, more limited steps. At the same time, because it was unprecedented in scope, the chances for failure, and the political risk to Carter, were substantial.

Second, in planning this major reform of the civil service, President Carter rejected the conventional wisdom that said the only way to bring innovation and new ideas to the table is to appoint some type of presidential commission composed of people with stature from business and academia, as well as several nationally recognized former top government political individuals. The most successful such effort by an outside group had been chaired by a former president, Herbert Hoover, but Hoover did rely heavily on former government personnel, both political and career. By 1977, however, career people were thought to be resistant to change and incapable of thinking outside the box. Presumably, this was just the opposite of the leadership most people wanted for the formidable task of bringing about significant change.

Campbell, however, thought otherwise. As described in the next section on political-career partnerships, he looked to the career leadership to play the principal role in designing this presidential reform.

A third major innovation involved the policy framework. Earlier approaches to improving the system dealt with specific problems from either the management perspective that sought more supervisory flexibility or those striving to protect employee rights and the integrity of the public service from political abuse. This endless series of limited "fixes" tended to result in steps to increase management control that then kept being countered by new procedures to protect against abuse of these flexibilities. The whole system began to drown in red tape, yet the disastrous 1972–73 period demonstrated that the protective measures were not strong enough to guard against major political assaults. The Civil Service Reform Act, in contrast to earlier piecemeal steps, sought to address the problem on a much broader basis with a perspective not primarily from the viewpoint of either management or the employee, but from that of the public. "The staff recommendations in this report are based on the premise that jobs and programs in the Federal Government belong to neither the employees nor to managers. They belong to the people."[26]

Finally, this reform initiative rejected the overused opinion survey as the principal research tool. Conventional approaches focused only upon the specific elements of the system drawing the most complaints, and then revised along the lines suggested by the opinions that had been gathered. This had resulted in piecemeal changes that typically made little visible difference.

Instead, the Carter approach relied on facts more than opinion. Task force research looked at total processes in depth. For example, it flowcharted each step that had actually taken place in a number of personnel actions among different agencies, rather than looking at only the much smaller number of steps reflected in the formal procedures. It was found that actual practices were frequently very different from those the opinion surveys indicated, as well as quite different from what the manuals prescribed. The biggest barrier to removing or demoting unproductive employees, it turned out, was not legislation, which had usually received the blame, but poor management. Scotty Campbell's team had the philosophy that if one does not fully understand what causes a management failure, it is unlikely that the recommended solution will improve anything.

Political-Career Partnerships

Having been dean of Syracuse University's Maxwell School of Citizenship and Public Affairs, and a professor of political science, Scotty Campbell knew that many career men and women were among those most anxious to rid the departments of the excessive regulations and procedures that made it so difficult to make government work effectively. It was the career people who experienced firsthand how excessive red tape bound their hands in carrying out their missions. The federal personnel system was one of the most rigid and process-dominated elements of government operation.

Scotty also believed that because career leadership knew so well the territory that needed reform, they could hit the ground running and drastically cut the time needed to develop a meaningful design for reform. Timing was critical because major legislative proposals have the best chance of success when developed early in a new administration. He also believed their recommendations would likely be more practical than those coming from outsiders who would be less knowledgeable about what was workable and what could best pass Congress.

As a result, a former senior career official was named executive director. Career men and women composed the leaders and members of all but one of the nine task forces serving under him. Relationships between these career people and the political leadership were outstanding, and under Campbell's skillful guidance, this gave the participants the feeling that they were engaged in a true partnership. Reflecting this close-knit cooperation, the report that Campbell forwarded to President Carter and the Congress was written by the career leadership without change by the CSC, the OMB, or the White House. At no time had political appointees in the CSC, the OMB, or the White House pressured the career task forces or the executive director with respect to any of the final 125 recommendations.[27] As Campbell had anticipated, this unusually strong career role was reassuring to the Congress, helping to counter concerns about the reform expressed by some employees who thought the provisions too drastic.

Openness and Outreach

Great emphasis was placed on extensive outreach by the CSC commissioners and the project staff during every stage of development; a special task force position was established to develop an open/outreach strategy. At the outset, meetings were convened with various interest groups to explain the nature of the presidential project and its unusual breadth.[28] Thereafter, other stakeholder meetings were held, and the nine task forces were encouraged to communicate with those outside the project.

Staff of the key House and Senate committees were invited to sit in the staff meetings of the executive director, and a senior GAO staff member was also free to sit in these meetings as well as those run almost continuously by the task forces, who were all assembled in one huge room with an open space arrangement.[29]

About three months after the task forces were formed, a press conference was held at which Campbell and the executive director distributed draft option papers from each one.[30] These papers reviewed the major issues being addressed, together with options for change in each case. The papers were also sent out to hundreds of organizations and individuals with a short deadline for comment. Each task force then developed recommendations for action, taking into account the comments received. Another press conference was held, and these action papers were distributed to well over a thousand recipients. They were circulated directly to several levels within federal departments and agencies in order to better assure that reactions were not limited to the views of top departmental officials.

Public hearings were held in several locations involving over 5,000 participants. Four months after being formed, each task force developed its final recommendations and submitted them to the executive director, who based his own recommendations heavily on the task force reports, which were also published.

Not everyone agreed with these recommended actions, but no one could be surprised by them or could say they had no chance to be heard. Further, the design teams knew the potential criticism in advance of the final report and were able to reduce some of the objections in the final drafting. This extensive exposure meant that neither the White House nor the congressional sponsors were caught off guard by any unexpected issues or attacks.

Agency Closure

The Office of Economic Opportunity was established by President Kennedy as a temporary agency to develop innovative approaches that might address the special problems of disadvantaged communities and families. After a period, those innovations that worked were to be woven into the activities of the established departments, after which the agency was to be terminated. Nixon had tried to end its existence through a highly confrontational approach and had failed. In fact, conventional wisdom had come to hold that an independent agency simply could not be abolished. Yet in 1981, President Reagan made a new attempt to eliminate the antipoverty agency, now called the Community Services Administration (CSA). Reagan was also expected to fail, and in the process provide a rallying point for critics to campaign against his administration as being indifferent to the plight of the poor. Marches and protests were expected, as well as hostile congressional hearings and a highly negative media.

This time the outcome was remarkably different from the Nixon failure. Despite strong opposition to the policy of closure, there were no protest marches and no negative editorials or congressional hearings regarding the way in which the agency was closed. Further, instead of sabotaging the closure and undermining the president and agency head, most CSA career men and women worked hard to make the closure successful, despite the fact that virtually every one of them was opposed to the policy of closure.

Rapid Action

The independent agency did close precisely on schedule, an action unprecedented at the time. By moving very rapidly, it was possible to close the agency by the end of the fiscal year, just eight months after inauguration and only seven weeks after Congress agreed. A slower pace in managing the closure would have required extending funding into the next year, not only increasing the cost but also placing the closure in jeopardy.

Innovative Design

When President Reagan stated in 1981 his intention to abolish the CSA, a quick review turned up no example of a peacetime independent agency with a nationwide constituency having been abolished since the Supreme Court declared the National Recovery Act (NRA) unconstitutional.[31] There was virtually no experience upon which to build.

Conventional wisdom regarding downsizing was ignored by the new CSA leadership, and numerous political pressures to repeat the failed confrontational approach of the early 1970s were rejected.

At the time Reagan took office, employees slated for losing their jobs through agency downsizing had been typically regarded as people who were (a) too despondent to be very productive and (b) in need of spending most of their time hunting for new employment rather than being required to carry their normal workload. As a result, they were edged outside the mainstream of activity, leading to their feeling that they were rejects. Their self-esteem dropped, reducing the self-confidence needed for marketing themselves in another organization, and the agency lost productivity.

In the case of the CSA, a number of ultraconservative Republicans were uneasy about the appointment of a career director, who would likely be too sympathetic toward the employees and lack the backbone to close the agency. To lessen this risk, pressure was brought by them to bring in a cadre of "believers" to control the closure. They also pressured the director to distance himself as much as possible from the career leadership, whom they regarded as strong anti-Reagan Democrats poised to sabotage the closure at every turn. The director thought this assessment of their political affiliation was probably correct. But, contrary to the conservatives' distrust of these men and women, the director, with support from Ed Meese, counselor to the president, as well as the OMB leadership, gambled that most of them would be willing to respond to the presidential decision to close the agency in a responsible manner, provided it was done in a professional way that showed respect for people even if they disagreed strongly with the closure policy.

The work faced by CSA employees was doubly burdensome because they were given a two-track assignment during the period prior to the point that Congress voted to permit closure by October 1, only seven weeks away.[32] The first track was to continue effective execution of the antipoverty programs as required by law; the second was the distasteful track of planning for closure should Congress so decide. Instead of being given a lighter load and shoved aside, they were asked to do double duty for the government in addition to their job hunt. The great majority of employees responded remarkably well to these difficult circumstances, some taking considerable pride in their ability to perform well under great stress. One incentive was their being reminded that their ability to find new jobs would be influenced by how they performed in their last CSA assignment.

Openness and Outreach

Reagan's CSA director spent much of his time working with groups who were strongly opposed to the 1981 closure. As mentioned above, the CSA leadership involved the career men and women extensively in planning and executing the closure, rather than the more common approach of setting them aside. The director also visited numerous community action agencies, natural enemies of the closure. Against the advice of Republican Party activists, the director accepted an invitation to speak at the national conference of community action agencies, which was expected to be a volatile forum for venting anger over Reagan's closure plans. Surprisingly, his speech was well received by the supposedly hostile audience. Although he probably persuaded not a single attendee to favor closure, his willingness to meet with them and express respect for their views despite his policy disagreement was disarming to those poised for protest.

The director appealed to leading congressional opponents, such as Senator Ted Kennedy (D-Mass), to help him conduct the closure in a manner that would cause the least possible pain to those involved in the CSA programs. In fact, he kept in close contact by phone with John Sweeney, who was leading the opposition. Each alerted the other to major steps they were about to take. Despite total disagreement on the policy of closure, they came to respect each other, each never criticizing the other personally.[33]

This CSA involvement of stakeholders that opposed the closure helps explain the fact that the expected use of the closure as an emotional centerpiece for marches and rallies attacking the director and the Reagan administration did not materialize. Opposing statements centered on the policy issues, as they should have, rather than attacks on unsavory motivations or allegations of improper actions that could provide juicy fodder for negative media publicity of the type that is often especially damaging to a president.

The unusual emphasis on openness that accompanied the CSA outreach is illustrated by the invitation to the GAO to come in early and closely observe the closure as it began. Rather than requiring a written request from the GAO for documents it wished to examine, the common practice at the time, the director instituted a simple library arrangement whereby a GAO representative could check out any document he or she wished to look at by simply leaving a slip recording what documents were taken, when, and by whom. In return, the GAO alerted the director immediately to any problems it saw emerging, enabling the director to take quick corrective action rather than waiting for the GAO draft report, when the problems would have grown more serious.[34]

Political-Career Partnerships

As mentioned above, Reagan took the unusual step of assigning the politically volatile task of closing the agency to a longtime career person, thereby sending a signal that the action was to be managed in a professional, rather than a political, manner, despite the political stakes involved. Instead of the government's bringing in a cadre of "loyal" political people to manage the closure and edging the CSA career leaders aside, as the director had been urged to do, the CSA people that the director inherited were given leadership assignments extending to chairing interagency and intergovernmental task forces involved in the closure.

These leadership opportunities helped preserve morale, and placed a number of employees in a better position to find new work after closure. The director was warned against bringing the CSA regional field directors to Washington, where they could lobby Congress and the press to block the closure. Instead, they were convened in headquarters several times for progress reviews, and they engaged in one or two phone conferences each week. Their strong leadership was a key factor in the closure. No evidence of undermining activities by the field personnel ever came to the attention of the director. When one afternoon the director found that political "advisers" had been imposed on each regional director to ensure they followed the party line, the advisers were removed immediately. The president of the local union, understandably a dedicated opponent of the closure, was nonetheless named to the CSA closure steering group, adding to the chagrin of many of Reagan's most conservative supporters. His participation was of great value. Everything legally possible was done to facilitate CSA employees' finding other employment, and considerable unpaid outside help was drawn upon, since funds could not then be used for this purpose.

In keeping with the political-career partnership approach, the director never had a meeting alone with the political appointees or a meeting from which political appointees were excluded. Each group had an essential interdependent role.

The decision to manage the closure in a way that reflected confidence in the professionalism of most CSA employees played a major role in reducing expected opposition and negative publicity.[35] It also enabled the Reagan administration to draw upon the valuable knowledge and energy of these employees during the challenging task of closure. It also saved President Reagan from a major political battle. Sadly, the sacrifice of these employees, who worked so hard to close the agency they loved and bring their own jobs to a close, was never recognized by the Reagan White House.

Nuclear Cleanup

Although not a major presidential initiative, an important current adaptation of the foregoing management strategies can be found within the much-maligned nuclear weapons cleanup program. It is the story of one element of the program, that of Rocky Flats in Colorado.[36]

For years, few government programs were in such disrepute as that of addressing the problem of cleaning up radioactive facilities no longer needed for our nuclear weapons deterrent. Because there was uncertainty as to whether there might be a future need to revive some of those nuclear operations, they were inexcusably left in limbo without adequate attention to maintenance of the safety standards required as buildings and machinery aged. As it became clear that they would not be needed, the estimated time and cost needed to clean up and close the facilities were too discouraging to generate meaningful plans. The program was rudderless and drifting.

Rocky Flats, north of Denver, was one of the major targets of this criticism. Adjacent communities became increasingly concerned about the state of affairs. These legitimate concerns were increased by the abysmal failure of the Department of Energy (DOE) to share unclassified safety information with them. Secrecy always gives rise to rumors, and the negative speculation escalated community protests well above what would have otherwise existed. An exasperated Congress established the independent Defense Nuclear Facilities Safety Board to help ensure the safety of these unused weapons facilities.

In 1995 the projected cleanup of the Rocky Flats facilities was estimated to stretch out as long as sixty or seventy years before the area could be used for other purposes that would benefit the community.[37] Costs were then estimated as high as nearly $37 billion,[38] though there was so much uncertainty about how the cleanup would be done that these were more "guestimates" than estimates. No one really knew.

The completion actually occurred at the end of 2005, rather than 2055 or 2065. DOE estimates the total cost at about $7 billion, as compared to the earlier $37 billion. This drastic reduction is in sharp contrast with most cost and schedule estimates that typically increase with time. Community safety concerns have also been greatly reduced. What has contributed to this remarkable project reform?

One major factor has been an adaptation of the management strategies discussed in the foregoing cases.

Rapid Action

With the congressional pressure, and the DOE change in cleanup leadership, the whole approach to timing changed radically. Instead of a passive approach that seemed to regard the problem as nearly insoluble, the new leadership decided that cleanup was doable if a clear goal of closure was established and significant contractor incentives were provided to achieve those goals as well as imposing credible contractor penalties for failure to do so. In addition to reducing the period in which communities remained deeply concerned about safety, it was thought that the best way to reduce costs to an acceptable level was to sharply reduce the time required to reach closure. At the same time, this collapsing of the timetable could not be permitted to compromise safety. By focusing so heavily on outcomes, in this case the mission of a rapid, but safe, closure, rather than continuing to be preoccupied with inputs and outputs that made virtually no progress toward the ultimate goal, the pace had to be increased dramatically. This required a drastic turnaround in management strategies.

Innovative Design

The change from the traditional maintenance and operation type of contract used in DOE facilities to a highly incentivized fee approach required a fundamental shift in contract management from one of managing the contractor to one of managing the contract. This was a highly significant innovation for the weapons facilities that demonstrated great courage on the part of the DOE and its prime contractor, particularly in view of the uniquely sensitive role of nuclear safety. The impressive Rocky Flats cost savings could not have been achieved without these and other basic innovations.[39]

Openness and Outreach

The Rocky Flats facility was once the center of public criticism, with the DOE suffering from an image of secrecy and mystery that robbed it of any credibility regarding community radiological safety. The reverse became true at Rocky Flats under new DOE and contractor leadership. Community groups that once attacked the Rocky Flats office now praise it for candor and accessibility.[40] This transformation came about as the result of extensive open meetings with the public, sharing of an enormous amount of data, and quickly advising communities of emerging problems, as opposed to the DOE past practice of discussing problems reluctantly and only after being pressed for some period of time. Community groups have participated actively in discussions regarding potential impact outside the facilities of safety issues. Congressional committees have been kept far better informed. Together with the impressive progress toward closure, this strategy has replaced congressional displeasure with support.

Political-Career Partnerships

The vision of a Rocky Flats transformation was initiated by a DOE assistant secretary in Washington and a career manager of Rocky Flats in the mid-1990s. However, it was a successor manager, a career nuclear physicist from Savannah River Operations Office, Jessie Roberson, who was largely responsible for bringing about the dramatic changes at Rocky Flats. She later became assistant secretary for Environmental Management (EM), where, as a political appointee, she oversaw the whole departmental cleanup effort. Strong support came from Robert Card, DOE undersecretary, who had headed the Rocky Flats contractor organization during the days that Roberson headed the DOE field office.

EM is a highly professional organization, combining new approaches with some of the earlier managerial techniques employed by the legendary Admiral Hyman Rickover, father of the nuclear navy, who built one of the most skilled engineering teams ever assembled. The Rocky Flats career SES experience gave Roberson great credibility with the EM employees in her political appointee role as an assistant secretary. One does not see among EM personnel the usual "us and them" view of political versus career public servants.[41]

General Observations

Since none of the precise circumstances that gave rise to the foregoing presidential initiatives will ever be replicated in the future, one might ask why bother with these vignettes of management history?

The author believes there is considerable significance in the fact that, although these initiatives were spread over four decades, and were addressing very different challenges, the management strategies singled out for discussion in this chapter were applied in ways that made major contributions to each. Because of their enduring value, it would seem that much greater attention to these strategies could have substantially improved the Planning, Programming and Budgeting System (PPBS), the Grace Commission, Reinventing Government, and the Bush Management Agenda.

Considerable time has been spent on nonproductive goals of inventing new basic concepts such as the ill-advised efforts to remake government like a business. This led, for example, to the change in emphasis from serving the public to serving the customer, forgetting that private employment and public service grow out of different bodies of law and have a number of fundamental differences. It has led to an emphasis on efficiency that is dollar dominated over the more important government goal of effectiveness that includes efficiency but gives higher priority to achieving the agency mission. Business practices were not used in most of the work of government employees as they pursued the strategies discussed in this chapter. In fact, they would have been highly counterproductive in the important openness and outreach strategies. However, the management practices of the private enterprise were of immense value by virtue of extensive use of contractors in the Alaska and Rocky Flats cases. This was fundamentally different from the application of business practices to work that is inherently governmental.

In the view of the author, most of our reinvention efforts in recent years would have had a greater impact had they been directed more heavily toward developing innovative ways of adapting proven concepts and strategies to new challenges. Innovative utilization of rapidly changing technology, an important tool of effective outreach and openness, is an area in which both the Gore and the Bush programs deserve credit for having done just that. But many other areas have been neglected. Internal departmental communication systems, for example, have declined in important ways. As Dan Guttman observes in chapter 10, despite the push for outsourcing and incentive contracts, we have not seen the actions necessary to increase the contract management capacity that is woefully inadequate in most departments. Increasing the credibility of competitive sourcing and employee incentive awards has had very little success. Departmental structures and operations are often done on an ad hoc basis with insufficient attention, for example, to accountability or to headquarters/field roles and relationships. Intergovernmental and interagency management have been given scant attention.

Rapid Action

Although a fast start is an almost universal goal of incoming administrations, they generally fail to do so, especially in the field of management reforms. The planning phase of ambitious initiatives, such as Clinton's Reinventing Government or the Bush Management Agenda, usually dominates the first year of a presidential term if not longer. At times, government-wide action of significance may not begin until the third year, when it is far more difficult to mobilize for broad reforms and too late to institutionalize major changes before the next election. In addition, delays increase costs and weaken support. Why did the Nixon, Carter, and Reagan initiatives we have discussed move so rapidly? Effective use of proven management strategies is one of the principal reasons.

One example was the quick development of a political-career partnership, mentioned below, in which experienced career men and women were drawn upon for top leadership roles for the design and implementation of each initiative.[42] These people knew the problems far better than outsiders, and required far less time getting started than those brought in from outside to design the changes. Further, their experience provided them with a good feel for what type of, and how much, radical change was doable. At times, limited agency capabilities require the phasing in of radical change, but it must be done carefully in a way that does not lose momentum. Finally, this strong career involvement in designing the reform reduced many of the alarming rumors about negative impacts, and resulted in a better understanding of the reform by large numbers of career implementers, thereby enabling them to move the action forward more rapidly.

The cases discussed here suggest that congressional oversight committees tend to have greater confidence in the ability of career men and women to design workable reforms than in new political appointees, and are less likely to delay presidential plans while probing for hidden political agendas of an incoming administration. Also, the lengthy confirmation process means that waiting for most of the new political team to be in place inevitably delays transforming broad policy objectives into specific plans and proposals.

Three of these initiatives also benefited heavily from having utilized the presidential transition period effectively in planning management initiatives that could be launched quickly after inauguration. Too often management issues are pushed aside because most transitions are somewhat chaotic, and the new team has difficulty focusing effectively on even the most vital policy issues, much less management.[43] Despite pronouncements to the contrary, management is given low priority, something that most presidents-elect and their aides believe can be added after the important policy issues are addressed and the new administration gets its feet on the ground.[44] As a result, management loses out in transitions, increasing the difficulty of matching the rhetoric about "bringing government closer to the people" and "making it work better at less cost."

Another problem, as Ronald Moe points out in chapter 5, is the fact that presidents no longer have an institutionalized change agent, such as the former management staff of the BOB and the early OMB, to provide government-wide leadership and agency support in helping a new president to move out quickly. This was the crucial factor in launching Nixon's New Federalism. BOB management staff also provided critical support that helped ensure the surprising success of the Alaskan recovery. Although much reduced in capacity, OMB management staff still provided important support for Carter's later civil service reform. But by the time the CSA closure occurred, the OMB management staff was able to offer very little help.[45] The remaining fragments of the OMB staff that had been experienced in addressing structural and crosscutting management issues on behalf of the president were abolished later as a part of the Reinventing Government movement. Few are aware of the seriousness of this loss.

In addition to this lack of central leadership capacity, few departments and agencies have an effective focal point for management leadership, as these functions have been splintered and the senior career leadership reduced in stature and effectiveness. Many have been replaced with political appointees, who are not only often delayed by the appointment process but they are rarely sufficiently informed on governmental operations to provide leadership for a quick start at the gate. When they do get ready, they are anxious to go and not much interested in building bridges from old systems to the new. Neither are many of them skilled at institutionalizing advances that do emerge. Combined with the disappearance of OMB management assistance capacity, the weakening of departmental management leadership has greatly handicapped recent presidents in launching new reforms effectively. A very promising development, however, has been the Bush inclusion of an undersecretary for management in the DHS, as is discussed in chapter 4.

Political-Career Partnerships

Sharply contradicting the conventional wisdom about career people allegedly resisting change and lacking innovation, in each of the cases covered in this chapter we saw that the political leadership relied on career leadership to an unusual extent in developing a practical partnership. Within this framework, the political leadership always set the broad policy and retained its ability to withdraw delegated authorities, should that become necessary. Career leadership roles (a) enabled each initiative to be launched quickly and at less cost, as noted above; (b) resulted in approaches that were highly innovative, yet practical; (c) helped both congressional committees and those at lower levels in the bureaucracy to better understand what the president was seeking to achieve, and (d) decreased potential opposition.

These advantages should cause future White Houses to consider utilizing career men and women in stronger leadership roles for the design and execution of new presidential initiatives than is typically the case. The Grace Commission was particularly deficient in this respect, contributing heavily to its failure.

As an example, the Department of Homeland Security should rely more heavily on career field office leadership in responding to terrorist threats and attacks.[46] It is an area in which a nonpartisan, professional approach is essential, just as it is in most law enforcement and military organizations. To do so, however, the DHS will have to increase attention to field training, delegations of authority, coordination, and communication systems (Ink and Dean

2004, chapter 8). More rigorous testing of the interagency and intergovern-mental planning and operations is required. We seem to have learned little from our earlier successes.

It also should be stressed that the effectiveness of career men and women depends heavily on good political leadership. Political appointees that come into office after campaigning against the "bureaucracy" whom they distrust and keep at arms length will not be well accepted by the career employees on whom they must rely for implementing the president's agenda. The White House and department heads must understand that those appointees who respect career employees, and understand their value, are able to develop a highly productive partnership that is crucial to the success of presidential initiatives. This critical aspect of good government is given low priority in most of the presidential nominations and congressional confirmations.

Without effective career and political leadership, and a sense of partner-ship between the two, efforts to apply the foregoing management strategies would have failed in every initiative discussed in this chapter.

Innovative Design

Basic management strategies have been invaluable for successful presiden-tial initiatives, but none of those described in this chapter used detailed mod-els drawn from prior reform efforts. Neither did any of them seek to pattern their management after business practices, although each one engaged skilled managers to administer contracts and grants that did utilize the contributions of the private sector. It was recognized that all major presidential initiatives for change occur under conditions, and with objectives, that are somewhat different from what has gone before. Therefore, trying to fit their manage-ment design into some existing model was viewed as unduly limiting and likely to work against innovation. Instead, each initiative was approached de novo to a considerable degree.

This strategy might appear to involve an unacceptable level of risk. But instead, the author believes it illustrates the principle that the more highly qualified the managers, the better grounded in basic concepts of manage-ment, and the more the implementing operations can be shielded from politi-cal interference, the more innovative and free of procedural constraints one can afford to be. The DHS would seem to be an ideal candidate for applying this principle.

Even though it is doubtful that anyone would again recommend respond-ing to a crisis by setting up a cabinet commission chaired by a senator, as Johnson did in addressing the Alaskan disaster, his radical version of "think-ing outside the box" saved Alaska from a near-fatal crisis. There may be future crises in which it will be prudent to institute some other highly unusual linkage between the executive and legislative branches for a short period. The Alaskan experience should provide a degree of encouragement in seeking bold management solutions often required to meet major crises, including some the DHS may face.

Openness and Outreach

The degrees of outreach and openness we find in the development of most management reforms range from the extensive efforts described in the foregoing cases to virtually nonexistent. The Grace Commission outreach was one dimensional, thereby limiting its credibility and usefulness. Reinventing Government (NPR) performed very unevenly in this respect. It is true that considerable outreach to certain elements of various departments occurred during the NPR planning phase. Yet many of the special reinvention teams were poorly linked with the bulk of a department's workforce, and some of the most experienced and innovative career leaders were prohibited from even talking with the teams. A better planned and executed outreach would have led to better results. The Bush Management Agenda has done better in some respects, but the isolation of the DHS architects has been severely criticized, and rightfully so. These reform efforts all failed to utilize the extensive outreach that served so well those initiatives discussed in this chapter.

An especially important outreach component of the initiatives covered in this chapter has been the close working relationship with key committees of Congress and the openness and level of consultation with which the executive branch dealt with them. This emphasis on transparency in the case of Nixon's grant reforms was particularly striking in view of the later veil of secrecy for which much of his presidency is remembered.

Experience has shown that a heavy investment of effort in working with Congress saves time, usually reduces the extent to which Congress changes presidential management initiatives, and results in a more supportive congressional attitude toward the success of these initiatives. The view that consulting with Congress, and freely sharing information, restricts the action of a president and weakens the office of the president runs counter to the experience of the initiatives covered in this chapter. In fact, it has often been the failure of an administration to work with Congress that has resulted in a weakening of the presidency.[47] An understanding of the wisdom of working closely with Congress has been missing in recent years, a mistake often followed by a later congressional reluctance to work with the president when he ultimately did seek cooperation.

There is a fear that exposing early drafts to outside comment, and exposing the architects to external scrutiny, will generate an unnecessary amount of opposition too early, producing an unacceptable amount of delay. However, the unusually high degree of openness practiced in the foregoing presidential initiatives produced the opposite results.

Extensive outreach efforts and unusual levels of openness in these initiatives produced a greater diversity of good ideas on which to base the designs. They also instilled greater confidence in the integrity of the process and reduced the level of opposition. Contrary to conventional wisdom, they also saved considerable time in the long run. Finally, they led to some sense of ownership of the initiative among most stakeholders, thereby increasing their incentive to help it succeed.[48]

It must be remembered, however, that ambitious outreach steps, as with any strong emphasis on team approaches, require the maintenance of accountability, and the managerial capacity to reach decisions and take action on a timely basis regardless of divergence of views.

Conclusion

Finally, a review should be made of other management strategies that have played key roles over an extended period of time in enabling presidential initiatives to produce changes of significance. That review should take note of the ways in which these key strategies are mutually reinforcing. It should also look at the extent to which the success of these strategies depended upon effective political leadership as well as the development and utilization of highly skilled career leaders. The author believes that these cases would support the view that when executed effectively, a number of management strategies have demonstrated their enduring value in meeting public needs under changing circumstances. Instead of dismissing as dated those strategies that have been found effective in the past, we need to adapt them for use in future initiatives so presidents can move ahead more rapidly and more successfully with priority initiatives.

Notes

1. The bitter Senate debate culminated in the landmark Civil Rights Act of 1964.

2. Among other things, this required quick enactment of several pieces of legislation in the midst of a major Senate civil rights filibuster.

3. *Anchorage Daily News*, August 10, 1964. On October 12, Alaska governor William A. Eagan sent an equally laudatory letter, referring to the "successful culmination of the responsibility which was placed in the trust" of the commission staff.

4. The Federal Reconstruction and Development Planning Commission for Alaska was established by Executive Order 1110 on April 2 and chaired by Senator Clinton Anderson. It is described later.

5. The *Anchorage Times* August 10 editorial noted that these tight time schedules "became even tighter under the staff's constant prodding and watchful eye."

6. Initially, the commission was composed of the departments of Agriculture, Commerce, Defense, the Interior, HEW, Labor, and the Treasury. Later, the State Department was involved. Independent agency members were the Atomic Energy Commission, Federal Aviation Agency, Bureau of the Budget, Federal Power Commission, Housing and Home Finance Agency, General Services Administration, Federal Deposit Insurance Corporation, Federal Home Loan Bank Board, Federal Reserve System, Office of Emergency Planning, Small Business Administration, and Veterans Administration.

7. In addition, Canada, Norway, and the Soviet Union were also involved.

8. In his October 12 letter, Governor Eagan expressed the view that the "Federal, State and local levels were coordinated ... in a way, I am certain, has never been accomplished before in the history of American disasters."

9. Usual approaches for avoiding inflation through wage and price controls were much too complex and took too long to establish. Instead the Agricultural Research Office coordinated an alert system that depended on a successful volunteer system, reinforced by considerable jawboning by the executive director.

10. However, the executive director was startled to learn that Johnson had released to the press his first progress report to Anderson and the president, a report that was quite candid regarding both progress and problems in each community.

11. Not everyone agreed with the decisions, but their opportunity to voice their objections in public minimized opposition.

12. The OEM director was called before a House Appropriation Committee informal session to urge the administration to drop the whole initiative before Congress killed it, a position the committee dropped by the end of the session.

13. On January 30, 1969, Nixon sent a special message to Congress requesting "New Authority to Reorganize the Executive Branch."

14. March 17, 1969.

15. Issued the same date, this sweeping order directly affected every senator, governor, and hundreds of mayors and members of the House of Representatives, many of whom were irate as they descended on the BOB management staff to argue for different boundaries and cities. Their demands were resisted except that the number of regions was increased from eight to ten.

16. Memorandum for the president, "Priority Management Improvement Projects Led by the Office of Executive Management," May 21, 1969, outlined subjects to be covered in an Oval Office meeting with Nixon.

17. The number of programs varies with how they were defined.

18. The processes were reformed but the program content was left unchanged, an important distinction that soon disarmed the initial critics.

19. Local governments later complained, however, that state red tape was beginning to replace portions of the procedural quagmire eliminated by the federal government.

20. Close congressional consultation explains a major reason all seven plans Nixon submitted under the presidential reorganization authority during his first term were permitted to go into effect. This policy of consultation was one of several positive strategies Nixon sharply reversed at the outset of his ill-fated second term.

21. These discussions were true consultations in advance of decisions, in contrast to many so-called consultations that consist largely of informing groups of decisions already reached.

22. In the view of the author, this politicizing of key management positions contributed heavily to the later gradual erosion of the New Federalism gains.

23. The reversal of the successful first-term strategy of working closely with Congress, combined with the rapid replacement of openness with secrecy, were also the direct causes of Nixon's failure to get congressional approval of his proposed departments of Community Development and Natural Resources.

24. The initial delay did not seem significant at the time, but later, the lost months exacted a price by reducing the period available for implementation before the next election and a change in OPM leadership.

25. Signed into law by Carter on October 13, 1978.

26. Final Staff Report of the Executive Director, Vol. 1, p. vii, The President's Personnel Management Project, 1977.

27. At one point Campbell alerted the executive director that the White House might be quite concerned about his draft recommendation to replace presidential orders with legislation as a framework for labor relations. At the same time, he stressed that he merely wanted the director to be aware of a possible White House reaction, and the executive director should feel free to recommend what he thought best. He did, and the FLRA was one result.

28. During an early meeting with all the federal union leaders, surprisingly little interest was exhibited by the participants. Finally one leader explained that the plans were too grandiose to be taken seriously, a union view that changed radically in subsequent months as it became clear that the presidential project was for real.

29. Committee staff seldom took advantage of this invitation, but it enhanced the credibility of the process and gave congressional staff assurance that they could keep their members informed to whatever extent desired.

30. The compensation task force was formed later than the others and developed on a separate track. Some of the labor relations decisions also came later.

31. Peacetime agencies had been combined, renamed, and reduced in size and scope, but no closures were discovered since World War II. Whether or not this OMB review was accurate, no information concerning how such closures might have been managed was available.

32. The congressional vote was to provide no funds for CSA beyond September 30, the end of the fiscal year.

33. Credit for this unusual communication linkage goes to John Sweeney, who initiated it.

34. Today, it is the policy of the GAO to provide management with an early alert to possible problems, a practice that has benefited both the GAO and the agencies.

35. Congressional enthusiasm for active opposition to closure was also somewhat reduced as information emerged regarding the depth to which the agency's award of contracts and grants had become politicized prior to the Reagan administration. No career person, for example, was permitted to even make recommendations regarding the award of large grants and contracts. Judgments on the comparative merits of these proposals were closely limited to political appointees who did not wish to be burdened with career views that might not be politically advantageous.

36. These strategies are being applied at most of the cleanup sites, but at the time of this writing, it was the only one sufficiently near completion to assess its success with confidence.

37. The DOE Baseline Environmental Management Review for 1995 contained a rough estimate of cleanup activities possibly continuing until nearly 2060.

38. Ibid.

39. It should be stressed that had this drastic shift to incentive contracting been attempted in the absence of skilled DOE managers with extremely competent staff, the result could have easily been a disaster. Incentive contracting that is managed by inexperienced federal personnel does not work. As Dan Guttman discusses in chapter 10, government as a whole faces a major problem today because its outsourcing and its heavy reliance upon contractors has badly outpaced its in-house capability to manage those contracts. No one knows what this might have cost the public in terms of tax dollars, delays, and outcomes.

40. A few concerns remain among some, but the numbers are small and the contrast with earlier days is remarkable.

41. EM has only three political positions, the assistant secretary and two advisers.

42. This was key to the early success of Nixon's New Federalism, yet it ran counter to the general pattern of the Nixon presidency with the passage of time.

43. The difficulty of integrating management with policy initiatives during transition planning was exacerbated in the case of George W. Bush because much of his transition planning was delayed by the Florida controversy.

44. Carter's transition under the leadership of Jack Watson did give some attention to management, particularly the civil service reform. Reagan's transition, at the initiative of Ed Harper, included a small three-person unit that dealt exclusively with management issues, including the question of closing the antipoverty agency, another case covered in this chapter. Later transitions have given little recognition to the importance of effectively managing the implementation of their new initiatives, despite the degree to which effective implementation will have much to do with the success or failure of a president.

45. The deputy OMB director, Ed Harper, provided strong policy support, but the absence of OMB management staff handicapped the CSA director, who found little management capacity in the CSA.

46. A notable exception is the Coast Guard, which does rely on professional career leadership.

47. Nixon's failed effort to close the Office of Economic Opportunity by withholding its funds was one of several such efforts that led to the Impoundment Control (Title X of the Congressional Control Act of 1974). That statute prevented the president from impounding money in instances where it would lapse if not spent. The Nixon second-term effort to misuse presidential power by circumventing Congress on departmental reorganizations also boomeranged.

48. Clearly, there are circumstances that do not lend themselves to the degree of transparency practiced in these cases. National security is an obvious example. But it is the position of the author that in most instances, outreach and openness are far too constrained, as in designing the Department of Homeland Security, or are not properly managed, as in the case of Johnson's Great Society programs, with the result that timetables are unduly stretched, overhead costs rise, and outcomes are disappointing. Even in the area of national security, there are many examples of problems exacerbated by failure to utilize the degree of outreach and openness that was possible.

References

Anchorage Daily News. 1964. Editorial, August 10.

Dean, Alan L. 2004. "Organization and Management of Federal Departments," In *Making Government Manageable*, eds. Thomas H. Stanton and Benjamin Ginsberg, chapter 7.

Ink, Dwight, and Alan L. Dean. 2004. "Modernizing Federal Field Operations." In *Making Government Manageable*, eds. Thomas H. Stanton and Benjamin Ginsberg, chapter 8.

Memorandum for the President, "Priority Management Improvement Projects Led by the Office of Executive Management" May 21, 1969, outlined subjects to be covered in an Oval Office meeting with Nixon. (See Footnote 17.)

The President's Personnel Management Project. 1977. "Final Staff Report of the Executive Director" 1: vii. (See Footnote 27.)

8

Developments in the Federal Performance Management Movement

Balancing Conflicting Values in GPRA and PART

Beryl A. Radin

It is hard to find any aspect of U.S. society today that does not focus on issues related to performance. Pick up any daily newspaper and one is likely to find some discussion and consideration about the way that institutions of our society are able to perform according to expectations. The daily press is especially concerned about performance in the public sector. This concern focuses on all levels of government (federal, state, and local) and cuts across many policy sectors. Perhaps the most frequent treatment of performance in the press highlights education and public expectations that children in public schools will perform more effectively than they had in the past. But this anxiety moves beyond education; it includes health, environment, welfare, foreign policy, national security, and a range of other public sector areas. It also is found in the for-profit private sector as well as the nonprofit sector. It is not an exaggeration to characterize concern about performance as ubiquitous.

It is difficult to argue against a widespread concern about performance, particularly in the public sector. Citizens who pay taxes want their tax contributions to be used effectively. Elected officials facing shrinking budgets want to be sure that they can defend the allocations of funds that they make every year in the annual budget process. Non-public organizations have found that their boards of directors increasingly scrutinize the way that they allocate their funds and ask questions about the performance of those allocations and the performance of the top executives.

Although the focus on performance is appealing, it is also misleading. Much that is done in the name of accountability actually interferes with the responsibilities of individuals to carry out public work and accomplish what they have been asked to do. The criteria that have been developed often do not help resolve the conflicting values that are found within U.S. society. Instead, they further polarize the multiple perspectives on issues, increase the fragmentation in the system, and redirect the focus of the work.

Despite the use of the same vocabulary and seemingly similar agendas, those who are concerned about performance operate within quite different contexts. Although individuals use the same words, the meanings that they give to these terms are not always the same. One reason is that there is not merely a single motivation for concern about performance. At least three agendas are at play:

- *A negative agenda:* This agenda seeks to eliminate programs and often blames those running the programs for problems. In the public sector it blames the bureaucrat for problems and tries to cut back on responsibilities of government.
- *A neutral agenda:* This focuses on a concern about change. Individuals with this agenda argue that what worked in the past does not always make sense in the current or future environment.
- *A positive agenda:* Advocates of this approach believe that performance information will allow them to make a case for their programs and respond effectively with data to those to whom they are accountable.

Performance in the Federal Government

During the past decade, the concern about performance has taken many different forms. Performance information has been touted both as a basis for future decision making and as a mechanism to evaluate ongoing performance. It is the basis for a federal law, the Government Performance and Results Act (GPRA), enacted in 1993 and implemented several years later with interest by both the Congress and the Executive Branch. It is also the basis for a process undertaken in the federal Office of Management and Budget (OMB) during the Bush administration called the Program Assessment Rating Tool (PART), which attempts to link Executive Branch budget and program recommendations to the performance of specific federal programs.

Because the concern about performance is so pervasive, it takes on the form of a movement. It moves beyond specific initiatives in a few areas to reflect a general consideration in the society at large. It has become part of the language and words such as "outcomes," "performance measurement," and "achievement" roll off the tongues of a wide range of citizens. It may not be an overstatement to say that "performance" has joined motherhood and apple pie as one of the truisms of the contemporary U.S. culture. Who would want to say that they are against performance assessment?

It is the argument of this chapter that both GPRA and PART—like a number of earlier federal management reform efforts—do not fit easily into the institutional structures, functions, and political realities of the U.S. system. That system is designed to include multiple values and players, but both recent reform efforts focus almost entirely on efficiency values, and PART, especially, focuses only on the executive branch.[1]

Despite the array of management reform efforts over the years, couched in different guises and forms, few attempts to deal with management have resulted in much significant change. This is not to deny that achievements have emerged from the efforts, but they are modest and usually limited to the concerns of program managers. They do not often meet the expectations of the government-wide actors.

GPRA and PART repeat the tendency of architects of management reform to focus on what have turned out to be fairly ineffective approaches. The time and energy that have been expended in this process have created significant opportunity costs within the federal government. Many of these reforms have been based on outside experience, borrowing ideas from the private sector or local government, and from the experience of nations with parliamentary systems or smaller and more homogeneous populations. Too often these reforms evoke a compliance mentality and cynicism among the individuals in the bureaucracy who are expected to change. In fact, some have identified a malady called "reform fatigue" that has set in.

More importantly, this chapter emphasizes the major weakness of GPRA and PART. It is a prime example of the difficulty of dealing with federal management as a government-wide strategy and set of generic activities and requirements. The public administration community has focused on a set of institutions and processes that do not touch the core of the nation's decision-making processes. They operate largely as rhetorical entities without the ability to influence substantive policy and budgetary processes. The rhetoric emerges from the executive branch through those concerned about management in the OMB, from the legislative branch through the government reform and affairs committees of the two houses of Congress, and from organizations such as the National Academy of Public Administration.

GPRA: The Original and Driving Force of the Federal Performance Effort

The Government Performance and Results Act (GPRA) is the legislative requirement passed by Congress in 1993 that requires all federal agencies to develop strategic plans, annual performance plans, and performance reports. These are implemented within the constraints and realities of the annual budget process. All of these requirements are supposed to elicit a focus on the outcomes that have been achieved with the use of federal resources and to justify funding requests in terms of both promised and actual outcomes.

On its face, GPRA seems quite straightforward—indeed, almost innocuous. It clearly follows the tradition of past reform efforts within the federal government. In a report on the historical antecedents of the performance budgeting movement, the General Accounting Office concluded that GPRA "can be seen as melding the best features of its predecessors. . . . Nonetheless, many of the challenges which confronted earlier efforts remain unresolved and will likely affect early GPRA implementation efforts" (GAO 1997, 7).

At the same time, there are differences between GPRA and earlier efforts. Its enactment as legislation (rather than as executive orders) includes a role for Congress that is unusual in government reform efforts. In addition, GPRA's inclusion of pilot projects and providing a number of years for start-up are an unusual way for reform to be implemented. Most programs are enacted and expected to be carried out in less than a year. Although GPRA was enacted in 1993, its real requirements did not take effect until 1997. This four-year period was expected to provide time for agencies to prepare their submissions. However, many agencies did not use that time and waited until the 1997 date approached to think about the process (Radin 2000).

A number of assumptions embedded in GPRA have made it difficult to implement (Radin 2000). First, it assumes that a single piece of information will be able to meet the complex decision-making needs of both the executive and the legislative branches. Second, the focus on outcome performance measures (and the avoidance of process and output measures) denigrates the role of the federal government in many program areas. Third, it assumes that it is possible to directly link planning, management, and budgeting processes through performance information. Fourth, it assumes that it is possible to avoid partisan political conflicts and the differences in policy constructs between programs (programs that range from efforts that are delivered directly by the federal government to those that are hands-off block grants to others, particularly state and local governments). And fifth, the imposition of performance measures establishes a set of expectations and processes that, according to a number of observers, moved agencies to emphasize more centralized relationships than were anticipated.

PART: The Current Federal Executive Branch Performance Effort

Most presidential administrations, including the George W. Bush administration, seek to put their own imprint on management reform efforts.

Although some believed that the passage of GPRA in 1993 established an approach to management reform that both involved the Congress and the White House and was bipartisan, the current administration has created its own approach to performance management within the executive branch. This approach is implemented by the Office of Management and Budget alongside the GPRA requirements.

This effort is called the Program Assessment Rating Tool (PART) and is viewed as a part of the Bush management agenda—the effort to integrate the budget and performance assessments. It is described as including four purposes: (1) to measure and diagnose program performance; (2) to evaluate programs in a systematic, consistent, and transparent manner; (3) to inform agency and OMB decisions for management, legislative or regulatory improvements, and budget decisions; and (4) to focus program improvements and measure progress compared with prior year ratings (OMB 2004a).

PART started as a small-scale effort and reported information on 67 programs as a part of the FY 2003 presidential budget. Following that, it expanded to include 20 percent of federal programs within the FY 2004 budget document (231 programs). It was anticipated that the analytic process would further expand to include 20 percent more federal programs for the FY 2005 budget. By early 2006, OMB listed almost 800 program assessments on its new website, www.expectmore.gov. Some changes were made in the requirements but the general format remained fairly consistent. Unlike GPRA, which focuses on agencies and departments, the PART analysis focuses on specific programs. The OMB budget examiner for each program plays the major role in evaluating the assessments.

Each program included in the special PART volume of the budget documents was rated along four dimensions: program purpose and design (weight 20 percent); strategic planning (weight 10 percent); program management (weight 20 percent); and program results (weight 50 percent). Questionnaires were available to agencies (but completed by the OMB budget examiners) that were theoretically fine tuned to respond to the program type; thus different questionnaires were given for competitive grant programs; block/formula grant programs; regulatory-based programs; capital assets and service acquisition programs; credit programs; direct federal programs; and research and development programs. Five categories of ratings were used: effective, moderately effective, adequate, results not demonstrated, and ineffective. Of the programs included in the FY 2005 budget document, 11 percent of the programs were rated effective, 26 percent moderately effective, 21 percent adequate, 5 percent ineffective, and 37 percent results not demonstrated (OMB 2004b). In the FY 2007 budget document, 15 percent of the programs were rated effective, 29 percent moderately effective, 28 percent adequate, 4 percent ineffective, and 24 percent results not demonstrated (OMB 2006).

The patterns of rating programs are not clear regarding the FY 2004 process, largely because of variability among the OMB budget examiners, as was pointed out by the GAO in its assessment of the process (GAO 2004). Moreover, the rating process seemed to pay little if any attention to equity issues. Rather, ratings emphasized issues dealing with efficiency values. The OMB has noted that every program should have an efficiency measure or be in the process of developing one. There is no discussion of equity in the instructions (OMB 2004b). The over-300-page document that was issued as a part of the federal budget does not give attention to protected groups (such as specific racial, ethnic, or women's groups) within the society. In addition, there appears to be a pattern of rating block grant programs as "results not demonstrated."

The Two Performance Efforts: Similarities and Differences

The rhetoric of performance was a predominant language of the public sector at the end of the twentieth and beginning of the twenty-first centuries. This rhetorical style employs a vocabulary that highlights outcomes rather than inputs, processes, or even outputs. It focuses on the benefits derived from the use of public-sector funds and seeks to establish a framework that moves away from traditional incremental decision making, in which budgets are created largely on the basis of past allocation patterns. It has been used to counter the public's disillusion with government as well as the government bashing that has been employed by political figures at all points on the political spectrum. Although the concern about performance is pervasive, it is not expressed consistently; it takes many different forms and attaches to efforts at all levels of government.

A number of aspects of the U.S. institutional setting have an impact on the implementation of reform efforts such as GPRA and PART. These include the institutional conflict between the legislative and executive branches; the fragmentation of responsibilities within the legislative branch; intergovernmental relationships; tension between the OMB and departments and agencies; and differentiated responsibilities and roles inside agencies and departments.

*Institutional Conflict between the Legislative and
Executive Branches*

Because GPRA established a shared set of expectations for both the legislative and executive branches, this reform effort directly collides with the institutional design of separation of powers. PART does not deal with that conflict at all since it essentially ignores the role of Congress. The U.S. institutional structure rarely provides the means for a smooth path from one institutional setting to another. The system of shared powers within the national political setting creates tensions and frequently leads to conflict between the two ends of Pennsylvania Avenue. The U.S. system assumes a complex society with very diverse players with multiple and often conflicting agendas.

GPRA calls for the development of information (in the form of strategic plans, performance plans, and performance reports) that will be used by these very different institutions with diverse cultures and responsibilities. The literature on the stages of the policy process provides strong evidence of different perspectives that are at play when a policy issue moves from the policy adoption stage to the policy implementation stage. These differences are directly linked to the different perspectives that flow from the very different institutional settings. Although these differences are often a source of frustration (when a policy or program does not emerge from implementation activities in a form that meets the original expectations of the policy adopters), they can lead to more useful accountability relationships and are also a source of creativity and new ideas.

GPRA did establish a formal set of shared responsibilities between the two branches of government with a few words in the legislation that called for the involvement of Congress in the strategic plan development.

The Fragmentation of Responsibilities within the Legislative Branch

Although there is a tendency to speak of Congress as if it operates as a unified, monolithic institution, the fragmentation in the structure of the legislative branch does not allow it to speak with a single voice. It is difficult to expect a body with a combined membership of 535 individuals to operate in lockstep, particularly in a country where political party discipline is usually quite weak.

The differentiation between the roles of the authorizing and appropriations committees is perhaps the most formal expression of the reality of multiple voices. Despite the increased role of the appropriations committees over the past decades, the authorizing committees often look at programs and policies in different ways (including reauthorizing and oversight responsibilities) than do the appropriators.

GPRA was constructed with close linkages to the budget process and PART focused only on the Executive Branch budget process. In at least a few instances, agency and department officials have actually pleaded with Hill appropriations staffers to use GPRA performances plans in their decision-making process but have had very little success in that setting.[2]

Some appropriations committee staff do believe that GPRA may eventually provide them information that they can use to minimize the power of interest groups, which do not tend to discuss the effectiveness of programs they are supporting. There is little indication that Congress is using the PART information; this is not surprising since the OMB did not consider the congressional perspective on the programs.

A few examples exist of the use of GPRA submissions, and the concept of performance measures has been included in legislation that has emerged from several authorizing subcommittees. But GPRA's concentration on performance outcomes—to the exclusion of processes and outputs—is not always welcomed by the appropriating committees. As one individual put it, although GPRA wants to move beyond counting beans, in many programs Congress wants to count beans and focus on the processes of implementation.

Intergovernmental Relationships

Besides the horizontal separation of powers defined by the separate branches of government, the U.S. system is designed to minimize the power lodged in the national government. There has been constant debate over the appropriate role of the federal government since the beginning of the nation. Although this discussion often takes place in the context of specific policies and programs, it is also a part of the overall rhetoric about the role of government. During the past decade, increasing attention has been paid to the devolution of responsibilities for the implementation of programs that are partially or mainly funded with federal dollars. Fewer and fewer federal domestic programs are entirely implemented by federal staff. Instead, responsibility for making allocation decisions and actually delivering services has been delegated to state and local governments or to other third parties (often nonprofit organizations) (Beam and Conlan 2002).[3]

Both GPRA and PART move against this tide. The PART process does include a separate analytical matrix for block grants, but there is little indication that the approach to block grants is really different from other program designs. In fact, the rating of block grants as "results not demonstrated" in the 2004 budget process does not give attention to the limited ability of the federal government to require states and localities to report specific information about program implementation. Many block grants were created to minimize or eliminate the role of the federal government and, instead, to give significant amounts of discretion to state or local governments. Efforts to hold federal government agencies accountable for the way that programs are implemented assume that these agencies have legitimate authority to enforce the requirements that are included in performance measures. The imposition of federal performance requirements is viewed as an attempt by the federal government to take away the discretion that was designed within the program. In some cases, the federal agencies have worked closely with their partners to devise a set of performance measures that are mutually agreed upon. More often, however, these partners—especially states—have worked to protect their discretion in programs that are politically sensitive such as Medicaid and Temporary Assistance for Needy Families (TANF).

Third-party perspectives thus create a major problem in the performance context of determining which party defines the outcomes that are expected. States that already have performance measurement systems in place also do not want to shift to a national system if their current activities provide them with useful information. In this sense, if performance information is taken seriously, it can lead to centralization and an increase in the federal role.

Tension between the OMB and Departments and Agencies

Historically, as Ronald Moe documents in chapter 5, federal government-wide management reform has been centered in the management staff of the Office of Management and Budget,[4] reflecting the effort from the White House to approach management issues from the perspective of the government as a whole. Although the management side of the OMB was effectively eliminated (or at least drastically reduced) after the reorganization of the agency early in the first Clinton term, there continues to be a small staff within the OMB that was given the lead responsibility for GPRA. PART relies on budget examiners to evaluate program information from the agencies. The relationship between performance information and the budget process provides the OMB, at least theoretically, with an opportunity to make tradeoffs across programs and organizational units and to deal with management issues as an aggregate.

The OMB's niche in the process is built around the budget process—a process that has always involved a set of tensions between the Executive Office of the President and individual departments and agencies. The budget process provides limited opportunities for the discussion of specific aspects of programs and policies. The shorthand discussion of numbers is not conducive to capturing the detailed nuances of program operations. It tends to accentuate questions of efficiency—using limited resources—rather than issues related to program effectiveness or equity concerns. In addition, the OMB itself is actually quite decentralized. Budget examiners within the OMB possess both budgetary and management responsibilities for a specific set of programs and have significant autonomy to deal with agencies. As a result, some OMB staff gave serious attention to the GPRA submissions while others dealt with them only in a broad brush fashion. As noted earlier, budget examiners play the crucial role in assessing PART submissions and vary considerably in the way they have applied the requirements. Some OMB staffers describe the agency as the preeminent government agency that already uses performance information in the process of developing the budget. In that sense, the view that GPRA started the government's interest in performance actually demeans what longtime OMB staffers view as the longer history of their contributions.

Differentiated Responsibilities and Roles Inside Agencies and Departments

Several institutional tensions are at play within agencies and departments that affect the GPRA implementation effort. Although the legislation links GPRA requirements to the budget process, some agencies and departments have chosen to give responsibility for the development of the strategic plan, performance plans, and performance reports to their offices responsible for planning (and sometimes evaluation). Although some of these offices are involved in the budget process, more often they operate separately from the budget staffs. As a result, the development of the documents—although they are usually attached to the budget itself—is a separate and parallel process.

In addition, whether found in the planning staffs or the budget staffs, GPRA and PART implementation may be located in decentralized program units or in centralized offices that are located in the Office of the Secretary. At least some departmental performance documents do not reflect significant input from program staff and are instead the work of centralized planning or budget offices. The PART submissions continue this process but have moved the process up the departmental hierarchy, often to the cabinet secretary level.

Both GPRA and PART inherited the structural tension between short-term political appointees and long-term career staff discussed by Murray Comarow in chapter 6. Although political appointees may be committed to the concept of performance accountability, they have limited opportunities to integrate the process into standard operating procedures. From the perspective of the long-term career staff, as long as the process is viewed in compliance terms (largely satisfying the Congress and the OMB), it can have only limited influence on an agency's culture and decision processes.

Can Performance Deal with Multiple Functions?

It is not surprising that the multiple functions included within the performance umbrella—planning, budgeting, and management—are constructed around the diverse institutional settings and reflect the fragmentation of the U.S. system. Although both GPRA and PART seek to deal with these three functions as an aggregate, each of the functions is a complex entity that contains its own conflicting approaches as well as conflict between functions.

The tendency to paper over the differences among functions is a problem that is experienced beyond U.S. borders. An Organization for Economic Cooperation and Development (OECD) report warns about speaking of financial management and performance management as though they are homogeneous activities:

> In reality, financial management and performance management systems tend to develop separately as parallel systems that may or may not (or only to varying degrees) be harmonious or even compatible. Similarly, they may or may not be appropriately aligned (individually or collectively) to achieve the objectives of an effective resource management system. . . . In some systems it may not be clear whether processes are attached to performance management or financial management systems (e.g., target setting, control systems). (Pollitt 1999, 11)

Diverse Functions of Budgeting

Much of the performance rhetoric speaks of the budget process as if it were a simple, well-defined set of activities that produces rational allocation patterns. This approach not only removes issues of values and political choices from the process but also ignores the multiple functions of budgeting. Allen Schick has detailed three very different functions of the budget process: *strategic planning* (deciding on objectives, resources required to attain the objectives, and policies that govern the objectives); *management control* (assuring that resources are obtained and used effectively and efficiently); and *operational control* (assuring that specific tasks are carried out effectively and efficiently) (Schick 1997, 221). Schick notes that these three approaches rarely receive equal attention in the operation of budget systems. In fact, he notes that they "have tended to be competing processes in budgeting with no neat division of functions among the various participants."

In addition, there are at least two distinct stages within the budget process: budget execution and budget creation. Separate staff offices within agencies tend to have responsibility for each of these stages and each kind of office approaches its responsibilities with different mind-sets and skills. Budget execution is usually the purview of accountants and auditors while budget creation is more closely linked to policy and political agendas. The performance rhetoric has tended to treat the two stages as if they were a single entity, ignoring the different dynamics between them.

Diverse Functions of Planning

The performance approach to planning follows a similar simplistic path. It ignores the reality that little precision attaches to the term "planning," which can describe a wide variety of approaches to the definition of goals, explication of needs, determination of resources, and establishment of priorities and objectives.

One study of planning found six distinct types of planning in use in a single federal agency: *rational-comprehensive planning* (an attempt to lay out a universe that pictures a future state of affairs, based on gathering of information); *strategic planning* (an attempt to match organizational competencies with threats and opportunities from the environment); *management control planning* (an attempt to lay out goals and means in understanding and improving organizational operations); *sectoral planning* (planning limited to a particular sector or problem area or a focused subset of a sector or problem area); *advocacy planning* (planning that begins with premises or program goals that are set outside the program system); and *compliance planning* (planning that focuses on the steps followed to comply with requirements) (Radin et al. 1981, 20).

Each of these approaches to planning contains its own set of dynamics and approaches. Each also leads to different emphases and results. Yet the performance rhetoric involving planning tends to ignore these differences and fails to acknowledge the entanglements that emerge from the planning complexity. In at least one federal agency the officials charged with GPRA implementation found the GPRA planning process too broad based and cumbersome to make strategic policy decisions.

Diverse Approaches to Management

Improvement of service delivery and the internal management of the federal government were among the various purposes of the GPRA legislation. In this functional area—as in the other two functions—little attention was paid to the multiple actors and agendas at play in the process of managing federal programs.

Concerns about management and responsibilities for improving existing systems are found at every level of the federal establishment from the White

House to the specialist at the program level. The imprecision of the performance rhetoric makes it difficult to know which level of management activity is meant to be emphasized. One can identify at least four levels of management that are affected by these activities: executive control, centralized department control, decentralized agency control, and program management. Each level has its own set of interests and responsibilities involving management. Most are responding to external demands for management and performance information rather than information that can be used as routine feedback to improve program management.

Executive Control

This level of management emphasizes the role of the Executive Office of the President, particularly the OMB. It attempts to overcome the fragmentation of both policy and budgetary responsibilities and, instead, to look at federal agencies as subunits of the same large system.

Centralized Department Control

This level of management emphasizes the responsibilities of the cabinet secretaries and holds them accountable for the detailed management of the agencies found under their umbrella. It tends to ignore the legal and political autonomy of the agencies inside the department.[5]

Decentralized Agency Control

This approach to management focuses on the role of the agencies—the subunits within departments—and holds them responsible for management responsibilities.

Program Management

This final level of management highlights the details of implementation. Rarely would this information focus on program outcomes; rather, it would emphasize output and process data that fits into the authority and standard operating procedures of the program staff.

Policy Design and Politics

The one-size-fits-all, government-wide approach to management reform that is illustrated by both GPRA and PART does not fit easily into the reality of policy design and politics. Like its predecessors, GPRA does not exhibit a conceptual sensitivity to the very eclectic and diverse array of program and policy forms that make up the federal government's portfolio. James Q. Wilson has characterized the differences in that portfolio by examining the different types of political environments that surround agencies as well as the differences between the mechanisms that have been used to structure the federal role (Wilson 1989). Through its use of different analytical matrices, PART does give lip service to different policy designs; however, it does not appear that these actually lead to different evaluations of programs.

Another perspective on the differences in policy design was described by the GAO in a report on *Balancing Flexibility and Accountability: Grant Program Design in Education and Other Areas* (Westin 1998). That report highlighted the vast differences among federal grant programs, noting that: "These differences reflect three critical design features: whether the national objectives involved are performance-related or fiscal; whether the grant funds a distinct 'program' or contributes to the stream of funds supporting state and local activities, and whether it supports a single activity or diverse activities."

Where Are We Now?

 A number of observations can be made about the current state of federal performance activities.

The relationship between the PART requirements and the GPRA requirements is not clear and is often confusing to program officials. Some of this confusion stems from a difference in approach: GPRA focuses on agencies while PART focuses on programs. But even the GPRA involvement of Congress has evoked a very limited impact on legislative decision making. The GAO has noted that PART was not well integrated with GPRA and described the process as one of tension (GAO 2004, 27).

The PART effort focuses only on the president's budget and is thus limited to an executive branch perspective. Agency officials have found themselves caught in a PART assessment that moves in a direction that is very different from what they know they can expect in the congressional appropriations process.

The assessment of program purpose and design by OMB staff has been viewed by some critics as an attempt to preempt the role of the Congress. Legislation is often constructed for a range of political reasons that may not be clear or relevant to OMB budget examiners. Although some critics believe that it is not appropriate for the OMB to second-guess Congress in terms of assessment of program purpose and design, PART gives the OMB such authority. The congressional interest in GPRA has been largely through the government reform committees and not the authorizing and appropriating committees.

Both GPRA and PART are described as value-free enterprises that "simply" rate achievement of program goals. Program goals often include several purposes and multiple values. The PART effort appears to focus only on the achievement of efficiency goals. There is little in the process that highlights program effectiveness and basically nothing that assesses the achievement of equity goals within programs. This is similar to the GPRA experience. In many instances, there is a subtle but significant overlay of ideology that has had an impact on the ratings.

Program assessments do not acknowledge the difficulty of collecting performance data in program areas that involve block grants to states. Although PART did employ a questionnaire that was meant to capture the problems involved in block grants, the assessment process does not reflect the special problems involved in this program area. Many of the block grant programs were found to have "results not demonstrated" and there was little acknowledgment that federal agencies have limited authority to require data from state agencies charged with implementation of these programs. There was a similar problem with GPRA when federal agencies defined performance measures for states and localities.

In order to satisfy both GPRA and PART requirements, agencies would need to collect new data; however, agencies are constrained both by the mandates of the Paperwork Reduction Act and by budget limitations. A number of agencies would like to be able to collect data on the achievement of program outcomes. However, they are limited in doing so because of requirements that they reduce the number of data elements. This was a problem in the GPRA implementation and it continues with PART.

The autonomy of OMB budget examiners has created a highly variable pattern of dealing with PART. Similar types of programs may be rated differently if they are within the purview of different examiners. There is a high degree of discretion that is found within the implementation process. The GAO noted that "OMB staff were not fully consistent in interpreting the guidance for complex PART questions and in defining acceptable measures" (GAO 2004, 6).

It is not at all clear how the OMB used the PART ratings. Some programs received positive ratings but budget reductions. Others received lower ratings but budget increases. Little information exists that allows agencies to understand how the data are used.

Conclusion

Both GPRA and PART represent attempts to devise federal management reform through a government-wide strategy and a set of generic activities and requirements. Although such a reform approach is not new, its past record is not positive (Downs and Larkey 1986). Overall, neither GPRA nor PART has significantly influenced either substantive policy or budgetary processes. Rather, they have bred a sense of cynicism and compliance among federal managers. Their emphasis on efficiency values has driven out a concern about other values that are important within the U.S. political system.

Although it is commendable to be concerned about the performance of federal agencies, there is little to suggest that the approach intrinsic to these efforts has actually improved performance.

Notes

1. A similar argument was made in a January 2004 Government Accountability Office report (GAO 2004).

2. This observation came from various presentations made by agency officials at meetings attended by the author on performance management.

3. For a description of different grant program designs, see Beam and Conlan 2002.

4. Other staff in the OMB and the agencies have also been involved in the process.

5. For an alternative approach see Radin 2002 and 2004.

References

Beam, David R., and Timothy J. Conlan. 2002. "Grants." In *The Tools of Government: A Guide to the New Governance,* ed. Lester M. Salamon. New York: Oxford University Press.

Downs, George W., and Patrick D. Larkey. 1986. *The Search for Government Efficiency: From Hubris to Helplessness.* Philadelphia, PA: Temple University Press.

General Accounting Office (GAO). 1997. *Performance Budgeting: Past Initiatives Offer Insights for GPRA Implementation.* GAO/AIMD-97-46, March. Washington, DC: U.S. General Accounting Office, 7.

Government Accountability Office (GAO). 2004. *Performance Budgeting: Observations on the Use of OMB's Program Assessment Rating Tool for the Fiscal Year 2004 Budget.* GAO-04-174. Washington, DC: U.S. Government Accountability Office.

Office of Management and Budget (OMB). 2004a. "Performance and Management Assessments." *Budget of the United States Government.* Washington, DC: Office of Management and Budget.

———. 2004b. "PART Frequently Asked Questions." No. 27. Available at www. whitehouse.gov/omb/part/2004_faq.html. Accessed May 14, 2006.

———. 2006. "Expectmore.gov: Expect Federal Programs to Perform Well, and Better Every Year" Available at www.whitehouse.gov/omb/expectmore/about.html. Accessed May 14, 2006.

Pollitt, Christopher. 1999. "Integrating Financial Management and Performance Management." Public Management Service, Public Management Committee, PUMA/SBO 99 (July), 11.

Radin, Beryl A. 2000. "The Government Performance and Results Act (GPRA) and the Tradition of Federal Management Reform: Square Pegs in Round Holes?" *Journal of Public Administration Research and Theory* (January), 111–35.

———. 2002. *The Accountable Juggler.* Washington, DC: CQ Press.

———. 2004. "The Cabinet Officer as Juggler: The Accountability World of the Secretary of Health and Human Services." In *Making Government Manageable,* eds. Thomas H. Stanton and Benjamin Ginsberg, chapter 4. Baltimore, MD: Johns Hopkins University Press.

Radin, Beryl A., Robert Agranoff, Edward Baumheier, and C. Gregory Buntz. 1981. "Evaluation of the Planning Requirements Reform Demonstration Project of the US Department of Health and Human Services, Volume I, Final Report." Washington, DC: USC Washington Public Affairs Center, 20.

Schick, Allen. 1997. "The Road to PPB: The Stages of Budget Reform." Reprinted in *Classics of Public Administration,* eds. Jay M. Shafritz and Albert C. Hyde, 4th ed. Fort Worth, TX: Harcourt Brace College Publishers, 221.

Westin, Susan S. 1998. "Testimony before the Education Task Force, Committee on the Budget, U.S. Senate." *Balancing Flexibility and Accountability: Grant Program Design in Education and Other Areas.* Washington, DC: U.S. General Accounting Office, February 11.

Wilson, James Q. 1989. *Bureaucracy: What Government Agencies Do and Why They Do It.* New York: Basic Books.

Part 4

Addressing Critical Issues

9

The Many Cultures of Government

Michael Maccoby

Integrating twenty-two disparate agencies into the Department of Homeland Security is a major management challenge. Typically, government managers address the task of integration in terms of the levers they most control: structure, processes, performance measurements, and incentives. This approach, although essential, is usually insufficient to create the kind of cooperation required for effectiveness. Left out are the cultural factors, the values and norms that most determine behavior in an organization. As an anthropologist and psychoanalyst who has been a management consultant to leaders in both government and industry, I have found that by understanding both organizational culture and the role of personality at work, leaders become better able to achieve their goals, especially when they need to integrate different cultures.

Anthropology teaches us to view cultures both diachronically, in terms of their history, and synchronically, in terms of their adaptation to their environment. A culture may include behavior norms that were adapted to an environment of the past but subsequently have become embedded in rituals, practices, and a shared sense of identity that resist change. When companies or government try to integrate different organizations, people may be unaware of the cultural values that distort communication or cause conflict.

I have worked with different kinds of cultural conflict in the private sector, as can be seen in the example in the text box, and also with government organizations. At one of the national laboratories connected to the Department of Energy (DOE), it was difficult to get the scientists and engineers to focus on the same priorities. The engineers wanted to solve problems while the scientists wanted to do more cutting-edge research, especially if that led to publishable work that furthered their careers. At the World Bank, when staff was challenged to address the alleviation of poverty rather than to focus on infrastructural projects, this called for the different knowledge sectors to

Box 9.1

Here is one example of the need to overcome cross-cultural differences, taken from my experience consulting to business. In 1988, ABB, a large electrical engineering company, was formed by integrating ASEA, a Swedish company, with Brown Boveri, a Swiss company. ABB also had sizable organizations in Germany and the United States. Right away, there were serious communications problems, and ABB management asked me to investigate. I found that although the formal organization—structure, processes, measurements, and rewards—was the same in all countries, the informal organizations or cultures were different. And these differences could be understood in terms of diachronic and synchronic analysis. Swedish management culture emphasized consensus. Managers spent time at offsite retreats, sometimes with their families, to develop close bonds that reduced friction. Furthermore, the Swedes had a tradition of selling products to third-world countries. This meant producing products that were relatively simple to service. It also meant that the Swedes tended to tell their customers what they needed to buy. In contrast, the Germans mainly produced products for internal customers, highly trained electrical engineers who demanded sophisticated products and a guarantee that there would be no outages in the national electrical grid. In Germany, the customer was king. For the Swedes, especially those selling their products in the Middle East, the king might be the customer. The Germans were critical of Swedish management by consensus, accusing the Swedes of lacking integrity because they went along with decisions without sufficient analysis. German managers disapproved of offsite socializing with colleagues, since they believed friendships interfered with objectivity. They believed that good decisions would result from a clash of viewpoints based on solid evidence; however, once the boss made a decision, it was essential to fall in line. The Swiss were different from both. They were used to developing costly customized engineering solutions for different cantons. Management decisions always involved a great deal of time for discussion and buy-in. Sometimes, this led to reversing an agreement they had made with the Swedes or the Germans, which provoked accusations of bad faith. The problem had to do with the relationship among the Swiss managers; all of them served in the army reserve. A subordinate at work might be a manager's commanding officer in the army; it was obviously better for all managers to respect each other's views. The U.S. organization was different from all of these. It was based mainly on mass production of products for a large

(continued)

Box 9.1 *(continued)*

national market, with a traditional hierarchical bureaucracy. More than the others, its success depended on competing on the basis of cost as well as quality. Decisions were made by technical experts and there was little discussion about them. By understanding and respecting these differences in culture, ABB managers avoided confusion, conflict, and the distrust they had experienced. The differences might still cause problems, but managers were better able to resolve them.

---

work together. But each group had a different agenda and different ways of thinking. For example, the health group wanted to fund hospitals, while the economists argued that funds invested in nutrition and clean water would save more lives than hospitals, which would be used mostly by the middle class. I was asked to facilitate a meeting between economists and anthropologists. The anthropologists saw economists as detached number crunchers who never got close to real people. The economists saw the anthropologists as fuzzy-minded softies who overgeneralized from their experiences in a few villages. To use its considerable knowledge more effectively, the bank would have to integrate the anthropologist's micro understanding of how to improve the way people live and work together with the economist's macro analysis of investment alternatives.

Different Cultures of Government and Business

Some in the field of public administration have looked to business in two ways: as a model for organization and as a partner through contracting out work. Ronald Moe in chapter 5 and Dan Guttman in chapter 10 analyze these respective tendencies. However, both as a model and as a partner there are significant cultural differences between government and business organizations. Although managers in both are continually challenged to improve both effectiveness and efficiency, government is constrained by the requirement of carrying out and enforcing laws. In contrast, business is focused on providing value to customers and financial return to owners within the framework of law.

There is another difference. When government looks to business as a model, it may not choose the right business model. Businesses continually change their structures and systems to adapt to a changing business environment and new production technologies. Some of the most advanced companies, such as General Electric (GE) and International Business Machines (IBM), have been transforming their work from just producing and selling products to offering products wrapped in services, technology combined with business solutions. This has called for changes in organization, skills, and leadership. Many businesses have struggled to combine the different organizational cultures of production, research and development (R&D), and solutions. Their divisional silos, that is, functional and product organizations, resist change. Change from a production to a solutions mode requires breaking the silos, developing cross-functional capability and the ability for the organization to share what they have learned. It also requires changing the measurements and incentives that reinforce bureaucracy so that managers gain incentive to collaborate across organizational boundaries. As Thomas Stanton suggests in the introduction, much of government is organized in a bureaucratic industrial model of production, rather than as an organization better adapted to collaborating across boundaries and producing customized solutions.

Another fundamental difference between business and government is rooted in the two different cultures, with different value systems, that must collaborate to do the work of the federal government. These are the cultures of political leaders and the civil service. Murray Comarow provides a view of these two cultures in chapter 6. To be sure, managers at Homeland Security, and those in other departments, may have to deal with many subcultures. The Coast Guard, Federal Emergency Management Agency (FEMA), and Secret Service all have strong organizational cultures with their own norms and traditions. For example, when it was an independent agency, before its incorporation into the Department of Homeland Security, FEMA was relatively small, close knit and fast acting, different from typically slow-moving bureaucracies that take their time analyzing information. The Coast Guard has a tradition of saving people in trouble, as well as protecting the coastlines of the United States. Military and policing services as well as the Foreign Service create a stronger sense of identity and loyalty than do most civil service organizations. And a strong sense of identity, including mythologizing past achievements, can become a powerful resistance to change.

Defining Organizational Culture

There is no generally accepted definition of organizational culture, even though the term is commonly used in business and government. Even cultural anthropologists debate about the best definition of culture. In common discourse, it means "the way we do things around here." More specifically, organizational culture includes the values that determine the norms, attitudes, and behaviors that are long lasting in an organization and socialized into new hires.

A useful way to conceptualize organizational culture is a variation of the 7S model. This model includes the hard Ss of *strategy, structure,* and *systems* (measurements and processes) together with the soft Ss of management *style, skills, shared values,* and *staffs.*[1] I have substituted *social character* for staffs as a way of introducing the different values, emotional attitudes, and sense of identity that employees bring with them to the organization. Social character and skills can cover the intent of the staff S to indicate the different types of people needed to implement an organizational strategy. The value of this model is twofold. First, it allows us to operationalize and to a certain degree measure the elements of an organizational culture. Second, it is systemic, meaning that it describes elements of an organization that interact and that should be evaluated in terms of how well they support the organizational strategies and mission. For example, the performance evaluation systems should be used to reinforce those behaviors that further organizational goals. This model also highlights the importance of understanding the social character of employees as a means to engage them in embracing the shared values essential to carrying out a common organizational strategy. This framework also helps to differentiate the two major cultures of government: (1) elected officials and political appointees and (2) the civil service.

Using the 7S model, here is how these two cultures differ. Political culture in the federal government is shaped by the need to satisfy the White House and its political constituency. The key values shared by political appointees are responsiveness and loyalty to the president. Ideology is important to the political constituencies that support the president and therefore appointees may be selected in part because they express and further a particular political ideology. Rewards to appointees come from good press, presidential approval, and ultimately the voting public. The management style of political appointees tends to be inspirational and at times dictatorial. This is due to both a social character focus on short-term success and also the fact that most appointees don't expect to be around a long time so they want to cut through red tape and get results quickly. This causes them to push the civil servants for fast action. But the civil servants may not share this urgency and may even believe that the commands are legally questionable. Appointees tend to display skills of deal making, negotiation, and rhetoric. In order to succeed, they need to negotiate with the White House, especially OMB; with Congress; and with contractors. In their attempts to motivate the civil service, they tend to depend on their powers of persuasion, as well as on the levels of power they control. The social character of people attracted to the risks and rewards of politics might be that of the gamesman, focused on the strategy

Figure 9.1 **The 7S Model**

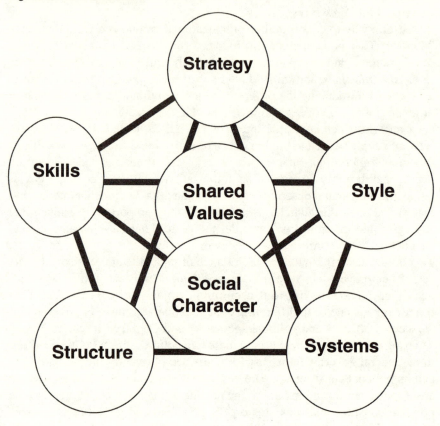

Source: Adapted from Peters and Waterman 2004.

and tactics of winning the political game; the jungle fighter focused on gaining personal power and destroying enemies; or the narcissistic visionary who is motivated to change the world.[2]

In contrast, civil service culture has a long-range focus, and the shared values of civil servants are program efficiency and employment security. Civil servants take pride in the efficient and effective implementation of programs that comply with laws. The relationships civil servants have with legislators, especially those who head committees that oversee their work, are as much or more important to them than their relations with the political appointees who flash by. Strong congressional players who have oversight of civil service functions often protect programs and civil servants from the executive

Table 9.1

The Political and Civil Service Cultures of Government

	Political culture	Civil service culture
Shared values	Political responsiveness Loyalty	Program efficiency Employment security
Strategy	Short-term agenda White House relationships Ideology based	Long-range focus Congressional relationships Rules and regulations based
Structure	Political partnership Networks for power	Bureaucratic hierarchy Networks for protection
Systems	Selection by politics Rewards by publicity and White House approval Votes, polls, and press evaluations	Selection by expertise Rewards by promotion, recognition, and obtaining resources Cost-benefit evaluation
Style	Inspirational-persuasive Confidential with inner team Cutting through red tape	Bureaucratic-legalistic Rule bound Managing red tape
Skills	Deal making Negotiation Rhetoric	Problem solving Technical competence Organizational knowledge and tactics
Social character	Gamesmen Jungle fighters Narcissistic visionaries	Experts Helpers Defenders

branch appointees. Although the political culture emphasizes cutting corners to get fast results, the civil service emphasizes rules and regulations that may block these political initiatives, or slow them down. Although the informal political structure is one of partnerships and alliances to gain power, the networks of the civil service are more for protection against arbitrary authority than to achieve results. The civil service style is bureaucratic and rule bound, going by the book. The skills rewarded are those of problem solving and technical and organizational competence. Rewards are promotion, recognition, and increased ability to obtain and employ resources. The social character of the civil service is dominated by experts but also includes people who find their main satisfaction in helping others. And there is a significant minority who are motivated by defending the public from those who threaten them or who undermine the law.[3]

A generation ago, my colleagues and I studied the social character of auditors in the Department of Commerce. We found differences in the social character of experts, helpers, and defenders. The experts, including three-fourths of the auditors, most valued doing the job efficiently, following the rules, and making sure that others also followed them. Experts were also differentiated according to their intellectual orientation. Those auditor-experts who were detail minded approached their work as monitors checking that everything was in order, while those who were systems minded analyzed the systems they were auditing to determine whether they were effective means of implementing program intent. The helpers preferred a role where they could teach people to do things the right way. The detail minded focused on fixing mistakes; the systems minded gravitated to the role and identity of management consultants, helping their clients not only to evaluate their systems but also to improve or redesign them. In contrast to the other two types, the defenders found their satisfaction in catching wrongdoing. The detail minded saw themselves as detectives; the systems minded focused on uncovering and bringing to justice fraudulent activity, especially from contractors who they thought were defrauding the public. (One such auditor was called "audit man" by his colleagues.) By understanding the social character of the auditors, the assistant secretary in charge of administration was able to make sure the right people were put in jobs when they would be motivated as well as competent. For example, helpers were sent to audit certain minority-run businesses that were headed by people who made mistakes because of lack of training, not because of intent to defraud. However, where there were indications of criminality, experts or defenders were sent. These differences in social character were also found in IRS agents, who indicated on a questionnaire their preferred approach to work. Again most were experts, a few were defenders motivated to discover fraud, and some were helpers, who preferred roles where they could help their colleagues or respond to queries from taxpayers.

My more recent studies show a changing social character in the workplace, resulting from historical changes in family structure and the formation of personality in childhood. In contrast to the bureaucratic-hierarchical personality that fit the traditional government workplace, there is a new generation with a more interactive-democratic personality that bridles against the traditional bureaucracy. These employees are motivated by opportunities to develop their skills and work with clients and colleagues to solve problems. They want to participate in decisions about how they will carry out organizational strategy. Their personality fits the needs of organizations that use knowledge to customize solutions (Maccoby 2003).

Although the social character of the people who work in the Department of Homeland Security has not been studied, there is good reason to believe there would be a similar distribution of types to those government agencies and armed services we have studied.[4] With the differences in culture of the bureaucracies, services, and political appointees that have been brought together, management is faced with a major challenge. Furthermore, Homeland Security managers must integrate the work of private-sector contractors so that they effectively further the department's mission.

Integrating Homeland Security

How much of a common organizational culture does Homeland Security need? Is it really possible to make services like the Coast Guard mesh with typical federal bureaucracies? The answer, I believe, is that the goal should not be uniformity. That would describe a pure bureaucracy. The subcultures of Homeland Security are unlikely to shed the histories and sense of identity that provide pride and meaning for people. To attempt to blot out these identities would provoke resistance and undermine positive motivation for work. Rather, Homeland Security management should aim to develop effective collaboration between the different subcultures.

Effectiveness requires information flow and collaboration across boundaries. Indeed, a major reason for creating the department was past failure of such collaboration. The lessons from the companies most advanced in developing solutions capability is that collaboration across organizational boundaries is not achieved merely by changes in organizational structures and incentives, although these can sometimes be useful. At companies like IBM, GE, and Citicorp, "network leaders" are needed to facilitate collaboration. Their effectiveness depends on developing relationships of trust (Galbraith 2002).

In a federal department like Homeland Security, this role usually would have to be played by civil service managers. The political leaders would lack the longevity and relationships required to facilitate collaboration across boundaries. However, the networking role is best played by people whose social character fits, especially the interactive self-developers who are natural facilitators and networkers. The other types find this kind of role more difficult. Expert managers are most comfortable when they control their own shop. Helpers tend to work best supporting a boss or building organizational families. Managerial defenders organize like-minded followers into commando-type strike forces that push for autonomy.

Homeland Security managers are attempting to increase collaboration and are encountering resistance. In June 2004, at a meeting organized by

Avaya and Tapestry Networks, a group of business and technology managers joined chief information officers (CIOs) from Homeland Security and the military to address the challenge of improving effectiveness in protecting the nation. They agreed that differences in organizational culture presented the major challenge. One problem was communication among different organizations. The easy part was to install communication technology. The hard part was getting people to communicate in a timely way. Another problem was determining who was in charge when there was need for collaboration across organizational barriers. Here the political and civil service cultures clashed. The political and business leaders complained about civil service middle managers protecting their individual lines of organizational authority ("stovepipes"), undermining attempts at organizational transformation, and waiting things out with the attitude that "this too shall pass." The solution suggested by the meeting participants was more engagement by senior leaders, who should not just "delegate and walk away." However, they were vague about the content of this engagement.

Clearly, there is no simple solution to getting the many cultures of government to collaborate effectively. If there were one, we would all know it. However, in addressing the challenge, managers do not focus sufficiently on understanding the different cultures, even when they agree that organizational culture is a major, even the major, problem. How can understanding of these cultures be an aid to management?

First, as Murray Comarow contends in chapter 6 and Dwight Ink in chapter 7, political appointees and civil service managers need to respect and acknowledge the legitimate differences in their functions, cultures, and values. It is often the case that the civil servants devalue the political appointees as representatives of interest groups, not respectful of laws and not working for the best interests of the public. In turn, the political leaders view civil servants as dragging their feet, resisting the mandates given them by the electorate. In fact, political appointees ultimately report to a president who has been given a mandate for change. However, as long as Congress or the Supreme Court have not changed the laws, the civil service has the obligation and responsibility to implement them. Keep in mind that the founding fathers of this republic did not value efficiency of government above the protection of individual liberty. Checks and balances will inevitably limit the ability of the federal government to adopt the best practices of business.

However, increased cultural understanding between leaders of the two cultures—political and civil service—will significantly facilitate the business of government, especially when the mission of Homeland Security is made clear and civil servant managers are brought into the process of developing and implementing strategy. Although impatient political appointees may complain that this takes too much time, the alternative will be ineffectiveness. Covering all the 7Ss can help. Developing the soft Ss—shared values and interactive skills—turns out to be harder than designing the hard Ss of structure and systems, but they are also more important for the effectiveness of organizations like the Department of Homeland Security. This requires not only designing new leadership roles but also developing new leadership skills, and selecting people whose social character motivates them to build relationships of trust and facilitate participative decision making. It requires aligning measurements and rewards to support the strategy. In summary, it requires that managers go beyond complaining about organizational cultures and learn how to lead them to effective collaboration.[5]

Notes

1. This model was first popularized by Peters and Waterman 1982.
2. I described these social character types in Maccoby 1976 and 2003.
3. I described these government social character types in Maccoby 1995.
4. Besides Commerce and the IRS, these included managers in the State Department, the Peace Corps, and the Army Corps of Engineers. I have been aided in this research by Richard Margolies, Barbara Lenkerd, and Margaret Molinari.
5. I know of no study that describes how to integrate the complex government and private-sector cultures of Homeland Security. However, managers can find examples of techniques to facilitate collaboration in Hecksher et al. 2003.

References

Galbraith, Jay R. 2002. "Organizing to Deliver Solutions." *Organizational Dynamics* (May): 194–200.
Heckscher, Charles, Michael Maccoby, Rafael Ramirez, and Pierre-Eric Tixier. 2003. *Agents of Change Crossing the Post-Industrial Divide*. New York: Oxford University Press.
Maccoby, Michael. 1976. *The Gamesman, The New Corporate Leaders*. New York: Simon & Schuster.
———. 1995. *Why Work? Motivating the New Work Force*, 2d ed. Alexandria, VA: Miles River Press.
———. 2003. *The Productive Narcissist: The Promise and Peril of Visionary Leadership*. New York: Broadway Books.
Peters, Thomas J., and Robert H. Waterman Jr. 2004. *In Search of Excellence. Lessons from America's Best-Run Companies*. New York: Harper Business Essentials. Original edition, New York: Harper & Row, 1982.

10

Contracting—An American Way of Governance

Post-9/11 Constitutional Choices

Dan Guttman

In earlier ages, today's modern Western states relied on nongovernmental actors to perform core "governmental" activities under contractual arrangements—tax collection, public finance, war fighting, and building and maintaining empires (Corvisier 1979; De Soto 1989; Ferguson 1999; Kamen 2002; Mallett 1999; Petrie 1999; Schama 1989; Strayer 1970: Strouse 2000; Taylor 2001; Wild 2000).[1] In the global transformation from government to governance—the performance of public purposes by a mix of state, market, and civil society actors[2]—the United States is the pioneer in the renewed deployment of private contractors to perform the basic work of government.

At mid-twentieth century, U.S. reformers undertook to grow government through the use of contractors. Those present at the creation saw that they were engaging in reform of constitutional dimensions, that is, a reform that would alter basic structures of government. They recognized that this reform would challenge the "axiomatic" premise that officials should retain the capacity to supervise and evaluate the basic work of government, including that done by contractors. A half-century of reform yielded many successes—including the Manhattan and Apollo projects and victory in the Cold War.

At the same time, the challenge to the premise of official control remained unaddressed. To the contrary, bipartisan limits on the number of civil servants ("personnel ceilings") assured that as government grew, third parties would be increasingly needed to perform its basic work—planning, policy and rule drafting, managing the nation's nuclear weapons complex, serving as go-betweens in dealings with citizens and other governments, and managing the federal official and contractor workforce themselves.

As a consequence, the country has yet to debate and develop a coherent framework, both of law and of underlying cultural bedrock, for a world in which

230

the presumption that officials have the ability to account for the work of government may, by increasing official admission, no longer be valid. To punctuate the point, the evidence that the official workforce can no longer be presumed to have capacity to account has long gone well beyond anecdote; red flags counseling due diligence are omnipresent; they include high-level official admissions of systematic deficiency, years of Government Accountability Office (GAO) findings of agency-wide deficiencies, and continuing failures of third-party oversight in sensitive and showcased programs. Indeed, proponents of increased third-party reliance do not so much urge the adequacy of oversight as assert that better procurement management is needed. Government procurement law, for its part, accepts as a given that officials, not contractors, are in control, and that officials will have the skills and experience needed to supervise and evaluate the basic work of government. It does not address the difficult questions that present themselves when this premise does not obtain in fact. The renewed appreciation of the critical role of government since September 11 brings these questions to the fore.

What are the alternative frameworks for holding contractors, and other third parties who perform the work of government, to account in the age of governance? Three alternative visions or models now coexist.

First, governing law and policy enshrine what might be called the "presumption of regularity/rule of law/public law" vision. This vision presumes that officials have the capability to oversee and control government. Call this the "presumption of regularity," in keeping with long-standing legal tradition that officials may be presumed to act with the good faith, diligence, and competence expected of them.[3] Further, consistent with the Western Rule of Law tradition, this model envisions that officials should be subject to rules that define and limit government authority and protect against government abuse ("public law"). These rules need not apply to contractors because contractors will be accountable to officials, and because application of the rules to contractors would constrain the qualities for which they are valued and deter them from serving government.

Second, there is the "governance/accountability" vision. This vision reflects operative bipartisan political consensus that public purposes are best performed by mixes of state, market, and civil-society actors, that is, "governance." This vision does not focus on who is doing the public's work, but on fostering "accountability" for that work. "Accountability," begins a recent Kennedy school compendium on "market-based governance," "underpins civilization" (Donahue and Nye 2002, 1). In the world of governance, accountability is to be provided by (1) modern management and social science techniques, which will align public and third-party interests (e.g., by the structuring of contract performance standards and incentives); (2) the use of competition (political stakeholders and the business competitors of contractors) to supplement the diminished official workforce in policing government and its contractors; and (3) transparency as an aid to the first two means. Although not forsaking the premise that officials must be able to account for all government work, governance proponents suggest that the civil-service workforce must be transformed into a workforce that functions substantially, or even primarily, to manage third parties.

Third, there is the "muddling through/common law" vision (best called a model, because it is implicit in developments, and not the subject of express advocacy). In the absence of coherent congressional and executive oversight, this model has, by default, become the primary means by which new rules of law are set to govern contractors and other third parties who perform the basic work of government. This model accepts that rules of public law should apply to those who perform public tasks, and applies them on a piecemeal basis to nongovernmental actors who perform the public's work. This model has a heritage both in Anglo-American legal tradition, which, as in the case of public utilities regulation, has long applied public obligations to private entities who perform public purposes, and in public procurement law itself, which may be seen as an effort to meld the unique concerns of sovereignty to the law generally applicable to contracts between private actors.

Each alternative has its strengths, but each is suboptimal. Time will tell whether the choice among visions (or some combination/alternative) will be, as the first of the Federalist Papers, *Federalist One,* put it, the product of reflection and choice or accident and force. At present, the window of opportunity for the former course—reflection and choice—is uniquely and surprisingly open. The revival of interest in government since September 11, concomitant concern for the official workforce's "human capital," debate over the Bush administration's proposal to put up to 850,000 (of about 2 million) civil-service jobs out for competition with contractors, and public awareness of the role of third parties in war fighting and nation building are strong stimuli to reflection. Despite all this, the third-party workforce that performs the basic work of government remains substantially invisible, not only to the public at large but often within government itself. If there is to be choice on the new framework, data, analysis, and reflection remain to be had.

In this context, this chapter discusses the constitutional alternatives available and how they came to emerge. It then identifies a research agenda that may help legislators, policymakers, regulators, and citizens sort through the alternatives. The chapter concludes with a series of questions of what might be called "cultural" dimensions that underlie today's constitutional choices.

Background: Where We Are and How We Got Here

Contracting Out as Reform of Constitutional Dimensions

The writings of the public servants, businessmen, and scholars present at the creation show that the post–World War II growth of the contract bureaucracy was the product of design, not bureaucratic happenstance. At the dawn of the Cold War, reformers believed that the harnessing of private enterprise to public purpose would serve two complementary purposes. First, the private sector would provide both technical expertise and powerful political support for increased federal commitment to national defense and public welfare tasks. Second, the private bureaucracy would countervail against the dead hand of the official bureaucracy and alleviate concern that a growing government meant a centralized Big Government. The officials, consultants, and scholars saw themselves as engaged in reforms of profound, even constitutional dimensions (Guttman 2000, 2003).

In his 1965 *The Scientific Estate,* public policy scholar Don Price, first dean of the Kennedy school, described the transformational import of the "fusion of economic and social power" and the "diffusion of sovereignty": "the general effect of this new system is clear; the fusion of economic and political power has been accompanied by the diffusion of sovereignty. This has destroyed the notion that the future growth of the functions and expenditures of governments . . . would necessarily take the form of a vast bureaucracy" (Price 1965, 75).

This basic and benign reconstitution of government, marveled John Corson, a New Deal civil servant who, at mid-century, opened the management consulting firm McKinsey's Washington office, took place with "little awareness." Corson began his 1971 book *Business in the Humane Society:* "There is little awareness of the extent to which traditional institutions, business, government, and universities and others, have been adapted and knit together in a politico-economic system which differs conspicuously from the conventional pattern of our past" (Corson 1971, iv).

Postwar contracting, Corson proclaimed, was a "new form of federalism" under which the federal government gets its work done by private enterprise.

It was left to President Eisenhower, in his farewell address, to provide another portrait of the implications of developments:

> The conjunction of an immense military establishment and a large arms industry is new in the American experience. The total influence, economic, political, and even spiritual, is felt in every city, every state house, every office of the Federal government. We recognize the imperative of this

development. Yet we must not fail to comprehend its implications. . . . In the councils of government, we must guard against the acquisition of unwarranted influence . . . by the military-industrial complex (Eisenhower 1961).

The reformers were aware that the "blurring of the boundaries between public and private" raised troubling questions about the constitutional premises of our government. Following President Eisenhower's warning, the concerns were incisively identified in a 1962 cabinet report to President Kennedy (U.S. House of Representatives 1962). The "Bell Report":

- declared that reliance on contractors and grantees has "blurred the traditional dividing line between the private and the public sectors of our nation";
- deemed it "axiomatic" that government officials (i.e., civil and special services and appointees) must do the work and have the competence required to account for all work of government; and
- warned that, unless corrective action were taken, there would be a brain drain of officials into the contractor workforce.

The Bell Report put its finger on the problem. In the short term, the use of contractors to respond to Cold War emergency made sense; over the longer term, the axiom of official control would be challenged unless corrective action were taken. The relation between the rules governing officials and those governing contractor employees provided incentive for official talent to migrate into the contractor workforce; why shouldn't experienced officials choose to work as contract and grant employees, where they would be free from official pay caps and the stringent constraints of official ethics rules, while continuing to perform important and interesting work?

The Bell Report backed away from answering the basic questions it raised. The new public/private mix, it found, was essential to Cold War programs, and "philosophical issues" needed to be deferred to a later date. Following the Bell Report, driven by the hydraulic force of personnel ceilings, third-party government grew without pause for philosophical review.

New Organizational Relationships: A Capsule Summary

Cold War agencies, the Atomic Energy Commission, Department of Defense, National Aeronautics and Space Administration (NASA), and U.S. Agency for International Development (USAID) provided the initial template for the deployment of contractors as a permanent workforce for the performance of central public tasks. Building on informal relationships established before

World War II and cemented by wartime contracts between and among government, industrial firms, and universities, these Cold War agencies shaped the building blocks that served as the Legos for future developments (Dan Guttman 2003).

- Under the "project management" model, famously exemplified by nuclear weapons complex "management and operating contractors" and Defense Department weapons project "systems managers" and "systems analysts," the government delegated public projects central to Cold War missions to contractors. Agencies created new contract institutions—"independent nonprofits" such as RAND and Aerospace—to manage contractor teams and advise on planning and spending.
- Under the "support service" model, agencies called on contractors to provide personnel on an "as-needed" basis to supplement the civil service in the daily work of government, be it planning, rule writing, dealing with citizens or other contractors, and/or clerical support.
- Under the "technical assistance" model, pioneered in Cold War foreign aid programs, contractors were called on to aid other governments (initially foreign, but then state and local) in social and economic development.

In the 1960s and 1970s these models were transferred from Cold War agencies to civilian agencies such as the departments of Transportation and Housing and Urban Development, the Office of Economic Opportunity, and the Environmental Protection Agency. The transfer was eased by the (pre-Vietnam) charisma of contractor-associated management techniques, but driven in any event by the force of personnel ceilings. As in the case of the Cold War agencies, the promoters of third-party government viewed third parties as purveyors of new management techniques, but also as tools in the politics of bureaucratic reform. The reformers claimed that social problems could be solved if "institutional obstacles" to change were overcome, for example, teacher unions that resisted local school reform (Guttman and Willner 1976).

The Age of Governance

In the 1980s and 1990s, the notion of smaller government gained popular support around the globe. Citizens, however, generally wanted no diminution in governmental functions. To address this inconsistency, new strategies for the reform took hold in the United States and elsewhere under the banner of terms such as "reinventing government," "public-private partnerships," "devolution," "privatization," and "deregulation," as Ronald Moe discusses in chapter 5. These strategies sought to make government more responsive and efficient by engaging nongovernment actors in its functions.

In the U.S. federal government, the new strategies were embraced with little regard for the fact that they had long been adopted. Thus, after identifying the "new" means to use nongovernment actors to deliver social services, Osborne and Gaebler, the authors of the highly influential book *Reinventing Government*, noted that "surprisingly" many of these innovations had already been deployed by the federal government (Osborne and Gaebler 1992, 30). Nonetheless, U.S. public agencies rushed to put old wine in new bottles. Programs that had long been operated through private contract were, following the Thatcher revolution, now said to be examples of "privatization." A 1997 General Accounting Office (GAO) review of "privatization" by state and local governments discovered that "contracting out" was the means for "privatization" in 78 percent of the cases surveyed, grants were employed in 8.4 percent of the cases, and vouchers in 4 percent. Remarkably, though not surprisingly, "asset sales" represented just 0.17 percent of cases (GAO 1997).

On taking office, the Clinton administration's government reinventors committed to reducing the civil-service workforce by 300,000. Reinventors acknowledged, even boasted, that their regimen would blur conventional boundaries between government and the private sector. *Reinventing Government* explains: "Those who still believe government and business should be separate tend to oppose these innovations. . . . But the world has changed too much to allow an outdated mindset to stifle us in this way. 'We would do well,' [public administration scholar] Harland Cleveland writes . . . 'to glory in the blurring of public and private and not try to draw a disappearing line in the water'" (Osborne and Gaebler 1992, 43).

The Bush administration's competitive outsourcing program, a component of the administration's management agenda, is the latest turn in the reform tradition (White House 2003). In November 2002, the White House affirmed its intent to put as many as 850,000 (out of 2 million) civil service jobs out for competition (Stevenson 2002). Proponents of competitive outsourcing explain that the intent is to expose the civil service to competition, and not to eliminate it. Even so, the administration's approach does not confront the actuality, by official admission, that the oversight capability of the civil service is too often inadequate to oversee the third-party workforce.

A Consequence of Contract Reform: The Presumption of Regularity Dispelled

The presumption of regularity—the "axiomatic" proposition expressed by the Bell Report that officials must have the capacity to evaluate and supervise all government work—can no longer be taken for granted.

In December 2002 Comptroller General David Walker told *Government Executive Online:* "I'm not confident that agencies have the ability to effectively manage cost, quality and performance in contracts" (Peckenpaugh 2002b). The GAO's high-risk list includes contracting at the departments of Defense, Energy, and Housing and Urban Development; NASA; and the IRS (GAO 2003c). In announcing her departure in September 2003, the head of the White House Office of Federal Procurement Policy told *Government Executive Online:* "There is still not a lot of oversight in some areas of our contracting system, and I think it will haunt us" (Peckenpaugh 2003). Lamentably, if further demonstration of how little regularity can be taken for granted were needed, in late 2005 her successor resigned as White House procurement policy chief coincident with his arrest as part of the Abramoff lobbying scandal (Smith and Schmidt 2005).

High-level affirmations of deficient oversight are coupled with continued indication of oversight deficiencies in agencies performing the government's most sensitive work. Public discovery of the profound reliance on contractors in Iraq for war fighting and nation building has even raised these concerns to the level of front-page news. For example:

The Department of Defense

Post–Cold War Department of Defense (DOD) downsizing came at the cost of a disproportionate reduction in the procurement oversight workforce (GAO 2002a). As the new millennium began, high-level DOD officials lacked rudimentary data on how DOD was spending its contract dollars, particularly the perhaps one hundred billion dollars being spent on "services." The department hired a contractor to perform a "spend analysis," and a further contractor to analyze the kinds of services DOD was buying and the market of providers (GAO 2003b; Defense Acquisition Excellence Council 2003).

The Department of the Army, for its part, has been well aware of the invisibility of its contractor workforce to high officials. In October 2002, the Department of the Army announced that the army would permit private contractors to compete for "non-core" positions held by 154,910 civilian workers (more than half of the civilian workforce) and 58,727 military personnel (Peckenpaugh 2002a). This announcement came on top of a wave of earlier army outsourcing. In a March 2002 memo to the Defense Department hierarchy, Army Secretary Thomas White explained:

> In the past eleven years, the Army has significantly reduced its civilian and military work force. These reductions were accomplished by an expanded reliance on contractor support without a comparable analysis of whether contractor support services should also be downsized. Currently, Army

planners and programmers lack visibility at the Departmental level into the labor and costs associated with the contractor workforce and of the organizations and missions supported by them. (White 2002)

In April 2002 the army told Congress that it lacked basic information about the sheer size of the contractor support service workforce, with its own estimates ranging from 100 to 600,000 (Brown 2002). Although Secretary White had called for needed data collection in 2002, by mid-2004 the effort had yet to begin (Peckenpaugh 2004).

The Nuclear Weapons Complex

Since its inception as the Manhattan Project, the nuclear weapons complex has been managed and operated by contractors (Hecker 1997; U.S. Senate 1980, 1989). In 1993 Secretary of Energy Hazel O'Leary told Congress that the 15,000 Department of Energy officials, whose primary function is the management of the nuclear weapons complex, lacked the capacity to manage a contractor workforce estimated to be well over 100,000 (U.S. House of Representatives 1993). In the mid-1990s promised reforms led to congressional inquiries regarding hundreds of millions, even billions, in actual or projected cost overruns (U.S. House of Representatives 2000). In March 2003, after a decade of contract reform, the GAO reported: "DOE has developed little objective information to demonstrate whether the reforms have improved results. . . . And the proportion of projects with significant cost increases and schedule delays was actually higher in 2001 than in 1996" (GAO 2003b).

Under Bush administration goals, about 10,000 official jobs would be eligible for competitive outsourcing (i.e., were not deemed "inherently governmental") (GAO 2002b). In 2001, the DOE reported that it had 14,700 employees (civil servants and officials), and over 100,000 contractor employees; 44 percent of the official workforce was over fifty years old and nearing retirement (Department of Energy 2001). In brief, an agency that could not manage its contractor workers with 15,000 officials was possibly going to be called on to manage them with perhaps thousands less.

Homeland Security: Organization and Mission

The new homeland security organization(s) are drawing on contractors for staffing and organizational design and for soup-to-nuts management of central missions.

In an award said to showcase the use of contractors to perform federal "HR" (human resource) functions, the new Transportation Security Agency

(TSA) employed a contractor to hire tens of thousands of airport baggage screeners. The contract costs escalated from $100 million to $740 million. In September 2003 the *Washington Post* catalogued the inquiries and litigation in the ongoing post mortem (Goo 2003; U.S. Senate 2003).

The Coast Guard is relying on a venture headed by Lockheed Martin and Northrop Grumman to develop a Coast Guard for the twenty-first century. The thirty-year "Integrated Deepwater" project is estimated to cost in the range of $17 billion. In March 2004 the General Accounting Office reported that, "[m]ore than a year and a half into the Deepwater contract, the key components needed to manage the program and oversee the system integrator's [Lockheed/Northrop team] performance have not been implemented" (GAO 2004a, 3).

Homeland Security: Contracting Out Big Brother

Homeland Security laws and programs are subject to considerable scrutiny by those concerned about civil liberties; there has been less scrutiny of the reality that these programs are often performed by contractors. For example, in late 2002 public controversy developed over the Department of Defense's "Total Information Awareness" program, a high-tech effort to mine and organize personal data. The controversy focused on government as Big Brother, generally neglecting the reality that the program was primarily performed by contractors, overseen by a skeleton official team (Mayle and Knott 2002). If the government were directly performing the work, citizens would have the protections from Big Brother provided by the constitution and other laws; it is by no means clear that these protections apply when the work is performed by third parties.

The role of contractors was highlighted when, in the summer of 2003, the press revealed that JetBlue had turned over data on passengers to a government contractor. JetBlue explained that all data in the contractor's possession had been destroyed and "no government agency had access to it" (Shenon 2003).

NASA

NASA, conceived as a response to the Cold War space race, has been fundamentally dependent on contractors since its birth (Mcdougall 1985). The congressional determination to rely fundamentally on contractors was analyzed (and approved) in *AFGE v. Webb* (1978), where civil servants who were subjected to reductions in force unsuccessfully challenged NASA's decision to contract out NASA's basic work. Faced with statutorily imposed personnel ceilings, the court found that NASA had no recourse but to call on support service contractors.

In its January 2003 report on high-risk areas, the GAO stated, "Much of NASA's success depends on the work of its contractors—on which it spends over $12 billion a year. Since 1990, we have identified NASA's contract management function as an area at high risk, principally because it has lacked accurate and reliable financial and management information on contract spending, and it has not placed enough emphasis on end results, product performance, and cost control" (GAO 2003c).

Following the Columbia tragedy, the *Washington Post* observed that "NASA may hire the astronauts," but "at the Johnson Space Center . . . the contractors are in charge of training the crew and drawing up flight plans. The contractors also dominate mission control, though the flight directors and the 'capcom' who talk to the crew in space are NASA employees" (Cha 2003). NASA shuttle official Linda Ham further limned NASA's contractor dependency, explaining that: "she had relied on an analysis by Boeing that indicated no threat to the mission from the impact of the foam. 'We must rely on our contractor work force who had the systems expertise to go off and do that analysis,' she told reporters last month. 'We don't have the tools to do that. We don't have the knowledge to do that or the background or expertise to do that kind of thing'" (Wald and Schwartz 2003).

War Fighting and Nation Building

Iraq and Afghanistan brought to the fore public recognition of the role of contractors on the battlefield and in nation building.

Public attention initially focused on the role of Halliburton in providing logistical support services in Iraq—under a support service arrangement called LOGCAP initially deployed in the Clinton era (Mayer 2004). By mid-2004, however, it was becoming clear that Halliburton was only the most visible tip of the iceberg. In addition to direct DOD contracts with large contractors such as Halliburton, official inquiry revealed that "supply schedule" contracts (contractors prequalified by the General Services Administration to offer services throughout government without further competition) were often being used as employment agencies to supplement the short-staffed military and civilian workforce in Iraq.

Official inquiry and press reports revealed that the department too often employed contractors under supply service contracts beyond the scope of the underlying contract authority. Thus contractor interrogators at the Abu Ghraib prison were hired under a supply schedule contract that was to provide for information technology (Department of Defense Inspector General 2004; GAO 2004b; Harris 2004a).[4]

Moreover, as the DOD's inspector general found on review of Coalition Provisional Authority contracts, contractors were essentially being used to buy a workforce that would be integrated into the official workforce, at odds with the general prohibition against contracting for personal services (Department of Defense Inspector General 2004). It also emerged that the deployment of contractor interrogators at Abu Ghraib prison was without due regard for the army's 2000 determination that intelligence activities, such as the interrogation conducted at the prison, are inherently governmental activities and/or too sensitive to contract out (Brinkley 2004; Center for Public Integrity 2004a).[5]

The reliance on contractors in nation building is not new. USAID's foreign aid programs have historically fundamentally depended on contractors. However, when Iraq nation building began, deficiencies evidenced in post–Cold War restructuring occurred.

The conduct of U.S. aid in Russia, the most critical effort of the immediate post–Cold War period, is an oft-told story. The "restructuring" led to the transfer of state assets to the "oligarchy" or "kleptocracy" (Hoffman 2002; Reddaway and Glinski 2001; Wedel 1998). USAID funding was substantially administered by the Harvard Institute for International Development, under a cooperative agreement. In 2000 the Department of Justice brought suit against Harvard (and individuals) to recover over $100 million for alleged misconduct and breach of contract (Associated Press 2000). In November 2002, the USAID inspector general recorded that "[s]ince 1997 several USAID sponsored task forces and focus groups reported that USAID's employees, managers, customers, and procurement officials believe that there are serious deficiencies within the procurement function" (Agency for International Development 2002, 10).

In May 2003 *Government Executive* reported, with regard to USAID oversight of its Iraq restructuring contracts: "there are only four contracting officers from AID in Iraq now, said Timothy Beans, the acting director of AID's Office of Procurement. In order to ensure that Bechtel and other firms are performing under the terms of their agreements, the agency plans to contract out oversight soon" (Harris 2003).

Similarly, in early 2004 the Coalition Provisional Authority called on teams of contractors to manage the work being done by the primary reconstruction contractors (and their subcontractors) (Harris 2004c). The full dimensions of reliance on contractors in nation building in Iraq, and the particulars of their oversight, will take time to fully gauge.

National Security–Related Privatization

The most significant privatization of the Clinton era similarly raised basic questions about the government's ability to execute and oversee national security/foreign policy contracting. The 1998 privatization of the U.S. Enrichment Corporation turned over to a privately owned company the tasks of ensuring continued economic operation of the nation's only nuclear fuel enrichment facilities and the administration of a key nonproliferation agreement with Russia. Prior to the privatization, independent experts, members of Congress, and others had pointed out that the government had not provided means to account for the public obligations should the privatized entity fail to perform, and that, because of likely conflicts between and among public and stockholder obligations, failure was likely. Shortly following the privatization, failures began to occur, and in 2000 both presidential candidates promised bailout assistance. In 2001 a federal court, upon review of the previously secret documentation underlying the privatization decision, found that the privatization was a "model" of how not to privatize. The continued performance of the public obligations transferred to the private corporation remains an open question (Guttman 2001; Hamilton 2000; Stiglitz 1998, 2002; Weinstock 2001).

The Internal Revenue Service

The IRS has been on the GAO high-risk list, in part, because of its inability to organize itself to perform the contractor-dependent activity modernization of datakeeping, at a projected cost of many billions of dollars. In October 2003, IRS commissioner Mark Everson conceded that the effort "has not been successful at all" because the IRS "management structure . . . is not adequate" to the task.

In response to inquiry about the IRS's controversial plan to contract out tax collection to debt-collection agencies, Mr. Everson "explained why he could not hire more staff tax collectors, 'Budget scoring rules make it impossible,' he said" (Johnson 2003).

Grants

The procurement system encompasses only a portion of federal use of contract-like agreements to perform the public's work (Salamon and Elliott 2002). Although "grants" are awarded under a differing body of law, they also are used to deploy nongovernmental actors to perform government work. In a summer 2001 white paper in support of the Bush administration's Faith-Based and Community Initiatives, the White House explained:

> The Federal Government . . . has little idea of the actual effect of the billions of social service dollars it spends directly or sends to State and local governments. . . .

Billions of Federal Dollars Spent, Little Evidence of Results

The Federal Government spends billions of dollars annually to assist needy families, individuals, and communities, often using the funds to support services provided by nongovernmental organizations. Although Federal program officials monitor nonprofit organizations, State and local governments, and other groups that receive the funds to ensure that they spend Federal money for designated purposes and without fraud, Federal officials have accumulated little evidence that the grants make a significant difference on the ground.

Routinized Granting Without Performance Monitoring

In some Federal discretionary programs, a small number of organizations perennially win large grants, even though there is little empirical evidence substantiating the success of their services. . . .

Moreover, virtually none of the programs has ever been subjected to a systematic evaluation of their performance that meets rigorous (or, in most cases, even rudimentary) evaluation research standards. (White House 2001)

Federally Funded Health Care

The administration of federally funded health care is the subject of enormous attention in its own right, but may also be viewed as part of the pattern of reliance on contractors (and other third parties). The U.S. health care system relies on third parties to oversee and administer Medicare, Medicaid, and other federally funded public health programs. Here, too, the GAO has recognized the administration of these programs to be high risk. Here, too, important questions of law and policy are raised as nongovernmental actors make decisions that affect patient choice of, and access to, health care.

Alternative Constitutional Visions

The presumption of regularity can no longer be taken for granted. What will replace it? Public procurement law presumes that officials are in control and does not, at least at present, contemplate circumstances where they are not. Thus procurement law, as presently constituted, does not provide a replacement. At present, three alternative visions or models coexist.

The "Presumption of Regularity/Public Law" Vision

The presumption of regularity/public law vision presumes that officials should be, and in fact are, possessed of the skills and experience needed to supervise and evaluate the work of government and contractors. This vision has two pillars. First, it is sustained by continued bipartisan declarations that officials must perform "inherently governmental" functions. Second, it is sustained by the Western "rule of law" tenet that officials must be subject to laws that define their authority and protect the public from government abuse ("public law").[6]

U.S. governmental bodies possess a long tradition of laws enacted to prevent abuse of power by government officials. These laws begin with the constitution, which defines and limits the conduct of officials, but not necessarily of third parties, even where they may act on the government's behalf. September 11 highlights the practical import of this distinction. Whether or not the Bill of Rights protects citizens against abuse by a homeland security personal data gatherer or baggage inspector may depend on whether the baggage checker or data gatherer is an official or a contract employee.

The official workforce is also governed by statutory provisions that are not applicable to third parties. The Freedom of Information Act (FOIA), by its terms, applies to "agency" records. Contractors, the courts have found, are not "agencies," even where it has been found and admitted that they perform decisional roles. For example, in *Public Citizen Health Research Group v. Dept of HEW* (1981), the court majority agreed that private medical review organizations created to review Medicaid/Medicare payments did indeed make public decisions. Nonetheless, it found that the application of the FOIA to them would be at odds with congressional intent to place the decisions in the hands of "independent medical organizations operated by practicing physicians, and not government agencies run by government employees."

Similarly, the work of officials is subject to a body of conflict-of-interest provisions, pay caps, and labor rules that do not apply to contractors (Guttman 2003).

The current role of "contractors on the battlefield" provides acute illustration of the implications of differing rules governing government and contractor employees (though the differences are with prime regard to rules governing soldiers, not civilian officials). Contract employees, the press reported, may avoid risky combat-zone work without fear that their absence will subject them to penalties under the Uniform Code of Military Justice (Bianco and Forest 2003; Campbell 2000). Similarly, the involvement of some contractor employees in alleged abuses at the Abu Ghraib prison provoked head scratching as to whether and when contractor employees could be held to account for the alleged misconduct (Groner 2004).[7] The differing sets of rules may work to contractor employee disadvantage as well as advantage. Whether and how the protections accorded by international law to state combatants apply to contractors is a matter of debate.

Where the presumption of regularity is valid, it makes good sense to limit the application of public laws to officials. Public laws need not apply to contractors because they can be presumed to be accountable to officials who are subject to such laws, and because the application of the rules to contractors might unduly constrain qualities for which they are valued and deter them from contracting with government.

But, on inspection, the presumption of regularity is questionable in law as well as fact. From the vantage of the constitution, the Supreme Court held in *Flagg Brothers v. Brooks* (1978), there are few "exclusively" governmental functions. If the law is the guide, the current "stopping point" for contracting out basic government work is the principle that only officials can perform "inherently governmental function." This principle is now codified by statute (the Federal Activities Inventory Reform (FAIR) Act of 1998) as well as Office of Management and Budget (OMB) circulars.

On further inspection, the concept of inherently governmental function embodied in current law and policy does not assure that government will retain the capacity needed to oversee the contractor workforce (Guttman 2004b).

First, as a consequence of decades of personnel ceilings, much inherently governmental work has already been contracted out. Second, much of the workforce needed to assure official oversight is not classified as inherently governmental, for example, the management and oversight of contractors. USAID will not simply outsource contract oversight in Iraq, as noted, but, through master contract awards to companies like Bechtel, turns over to prime contractors the job of awarding and managing tens, probably hundreds, of millions of dollars in the contracts to be overseen. Indeed, the General Services Administration's supply schedule contracts, discussed above in connection with Iraq contracting, provide for "off-the-shelf" use of contractors to manage the contract process, including A-76 competitive sourcing.

The discrepancy between the coverage of the "inherently governmental function" concept and the scope of "core" activities that must be performed if officials are to retain oversight capability is now well appreciated, but steps to address this discrepancy remain to be defined and taken.

Third, there appears to be nothing in OMB Circular A-76 to require that decisions to contract official jobs be preceded by review of the ability of remaining officials to account for further contracts. There is no assurance that remaining officials will have the experience and expertise needed to oversee contractors; to the contrary, the dual sets of rules governing contractors and officials provide incentive for capable officials to join the contract workforce.

In sum, the presumption of regularity/public law model may still be an ideal, and it continues to be asserted in law and policy. But the presumption is at odds with reality. The government's capacity to supervise and evaluate contractor work is too often lacking, and current law and policy do not, by their own terms, assure that remedial corrective action will be taken.

The "Governance/Accountability" Vision

The governance/accountability vision describes a future government whose work is performed by a mix of public, private, and civil society institutions. (This mix, as noted, is now conventionally referred to as "governance.") Proponents of the governance/accountability vision focus on the means needed to assure "accountability," rather than who it is that is doing the public's work. When measured by bipartisan policy, as expressed through decades of personnel ceilings, the Clinton-era Partnership for Reinventing Government, and Bush-era competitive outsourcing, this vision is the governing norm.

On inspection, the basic means of accountability put forth by governance proponents appear to be threefold:

- application of modern management and social science techniques (e.g., incentive contracting; principal agent theory) to craft contracts that ensure contractors will have appropriate incentives to perform;
- use of political stakeholders and the business competitors of contractors to supplement the diminished official workforce in ensuring the effectiveness of contract arrangements; and
- transparency as an aid to management techniques and nongovernmental watchdogs.

Each of these means is of obvious value, but none is a panacea, particularly where the official workforce lacks the capacity to supervise and evaluate contractor work.[8]

Social and Management Science Technique

The value of modern techniques and theories of public management is readily apparent, but limitations are apparent as well. For example, successful performance or incentive contracting depends on (1) a purchaser with the ability to specify performance; (2) the possibility of meaningful performance measures that can be identified, agreed upon, and implemented (3) the existence of resources to oversee and monitor performance; and (4) the practical ability to take action, including replacing the contractor, where performance is unsatisfactory. In the case of government activities for which performance measures are increasingly invoked, for example, programs where technological innovation and/or new approaches to seemingly intractable public problems are called for, one or more of these conditions may often be absent. This is more likely the case where, as now, official oversight capability is admitted to be suboptimal.

Incentive or performance contracting is not new. At the birth of the modern state, soldiers, tax farmers, and empire builders were rewarded in proportion to their achievement. This history confirms that incentives may work, but also provides ample cautionary tales. Pre-revolution French tax farmers were evidently well incentivized for their work, and quite good at collecting taxes, but did so to the political detriment of the old regime (Schama 1989). Similarly, the East India Company was well rewarded for its management of India, and rewarded itself to the periodic consternation of Parliament (Wild 2000). (Indeed, Edmund Burke waged a vigorous campaign against the company's corruption of politics in Britain, as well as its activities in India [Muller 2002]).

At the turn of the twentieth century, the birth of management science gave new lift to the notion that performance should be measured and incentives aligned. Today's use of performance measures in education follows a century after the attempt to apply them to the nation's schools during the progressive era (Callahan 1964). Still more recently, institutional economists and game, network, public choice, and principal-agent theorists have urged the importance of understanding institutions and the practical applications of this understanding (Coase 1988; Jensen 2000; North 1982; O. Williamson 1996).

Even so, real-world experiments demonstrate that modern technique remains imperfect, and can be terribly counterproductive when applied with lack of institutional understanding. Thus, as Peck and Scherer's classic study of DOD weapons contracting suggested, application of performance technique to government contracting is constrained by the inability to penalize poor performance without doing damage to the very market needed to sustain competition (Peck and Scherer 1962). More recently, a decade of Department of Energy performance-based contract reform did not tame the beast (GAO 2003b).

The point, of course, is not that incentives do not work or that they should not be used. Rather, incentives must be used with care and humility. The front pages provide too-frequent illustration of the ways in which performance goals and incentives designed by the best and most well-intentioned experts may yield unintended adverse consequences. Incentives can divert attention from other important goals, work too well on their own terms, or encourage distorted reporting.

For example, corporate governance scandals at Enron, Worldcom, and elsewhere may be best understood, John Cassidy explains, not as the unpredictable antics of a handful of crooked executives but as the tale of expert structured performance incentives, here stock options calculated to align management and shareholder interests, gone wrong (Cassidy 2002). Still more recently, the press revealed that application of performance measures to schools in Houston and New York stimulated the production of dropouts (Lewin and Medina 2003; *New York Times* 2003; Schemo 2003).

At the global level, ongoing retrospectives of governance practitioners on the consequences of reforms induced as conditions to multilateral funding report the discovery by governance experts that institutions are hard to understand and that public/private relations are difficult to engineer, particularly in other cultures (Easterly 2001; Guttman 2004a; Naim 1999; Nellis 2002; Stiglitz 2002; J. Williamson 2000; World Bank 2000; World Bank Group 2003).

Competition

The use of competitors and stakeholders to keep the system honest is not new. *Federalist Ten* famously explains that "factions" are with us to stay and should be made the best of. By the same token, Madison perceived competition as a necessary aid in structuring government, and not a substitute for it. Similarly, Adam Smith, author of the *The Theory of the Moral Sentiments* and of *The Wealth of Nations*, perceived self-interest to be a remarkable means of social ordering, but one that still required control in the public interest.

Today, the utility of contractors is associated with the notion that they bring competition and market forces to bear on government activities. This is true where commercial markets exist for government purchases, for example, the purchase of computer equipment, food, or maintenance services. However, where government is the primary, or predominant, purchaser of the services or goods at issue, the picture is less clear.

In their seminal analysis of weapons contracting, Peck and Scherer questioned the notion of the "market" as applied to government contracting (Peck and Scherer 1962). In important instances, most notably high-technology weapons but also social welfare services, if the government wants the benefits of a market it may have to create and maintain it. In the classic market, the failure of individual competitors is no cause for public concern. Where Boeing and Lockheed may be the only potential sources, there is tension between the principle of rewarding/penalizing poor performance and the need to assure continued availability of alternative providers. Disbarment or even suspension of a major contractor is rare (unless, perhaps, as in the case of an Enron or Arthur Andersen, the contractor manages to do itself in first) (Project on Government Oversight 2002).

Similarly, the invocation of competition as key to the benefits of contracting is often without regard to the realities of competition in the "government market," particularly where the item purchased is not a routine commercial staple. By statute, competition is the preferred means of contracting. In practice, competition is limited on basic counts. The means of limitation include: (1) socioeconomic preferences, which limit competition to members of a designated class such as small businesses; (2) provision for limitations of sources that must be solicited in many settings; (3) bundling of work into larger and/or longer contracts; (4) effective delegation of contracting determinations to contractors themselves, under the award of larger contracts with provisions for subcontracting; and (5) the limited number of providers for some key public goods and services. These limitations all have their justifications, but they are limitations nonetheless. As Professor Steven Schooner argues, 1990s efforts to streamline procurement highlight the tension between the drive to make contracting more businesslike and efficient and the existence of competitive oversight (Schooner 2001).

Perhaps most significantly, a recent study of $900 billion in Defense contracting shows that even where provisions for limiting competition are not invoked, in too many cases only one or two bidders show up to play. The evidence indicates that this is not only in the case of hardware buys where, as is well known, the numbers of competitors have been dwindling to two or three (Lockheed and Boeing) since Cold War heyday—but also in the area of service contracts, where reasons for limited competition appear more difficult to understand (Center for Public Integrity, 2004c).

Transparency

Transparency is a centerpiece of governance, but not of government contracting for the work of government. Within government itself, highest-level officials often lack basic data on their contractor workforce. Contractor-drafted documents may be passed on as official work product, leaving top officials in the dark as to the origin of the policy drafts immediately before them. Contractors work side by side with officials in official office space and attend and participate in official meetings, often with no clear signal to the uninitiated as to who is who (Daniel Guttman 1976, Dan Guttman 2003; U.S. Senate 1980 1989).

As to the press and public, contracting out is practically invisible. For example: (1) agency organization charts and telephone books do not include contractors, even where they work alongside officials in government buildings; (2) the public database of contracts lags behind real time, provides skimpy and often useless descriptions of the work being done, and does not include subcontracts that likely vastly outnumber prime contracts; (3) Freedom of Information Act requests are time consuming and the data provided is often substantially redacted (on claims to business secrecy); and (4) data on contractor performance, where it exists, is rarely publicly available.

Some suggest that third-party government can be rendered more transparent. Indeed, the rhetoric of governance insists on transparency of public activities. But, as courts construing the FOIA have found, there may be legitimate reasons for limiting transparency with regard to nongovernmental institutions, even when they perform the public's work. Transparency requirements must account for the effect of such requirements on the qualities for which these institutions are valued. Whether the values of openness and institutional integrity can be simultaneously honored is, as discussed below, a question that remains to be addressed.

Conclusion

Ultimately, governance proponents do not so much assume that official oversight capability is no longer relevant as declare that because it must exist it will exist. This declaration, often accompanied by acknowledgment, even hand-wringing, about diminished procurement oversight capacity, is followed by a declaration that officials must be transformed into good contract managers. However, save for promises of "better training" and "better incentives" there is little elaboration on precisely how this will be done. In 2002, the Commercial Activities Panel, mandated by congress to revisit the "A-76" policy and chaired by the comptroller general, dutifully reaffirmed the principle that officials must be able to account for the work of government, but did not specify steps to take where, in light of the evidence including the GAO's own continued findings, this principle cannot be assumed to govern (GAO 2002b; Peckenpaugh 2002b).

In sum, the "governance/accountability" model has great strengths. Nevertheless, it appears to presume that official oversight will remain sufficient for accountability mechanisms to work or that accountability mechanisms will obviate any deficiencies. Neither of these presumptions, on current evidence, is warranted.

The "Muddling Through/Common Law" Model

The "muddling through/common law" model operates, by default, to fill the void that remains amidst the failure of Congress and the Executive Branch to reformulate the "presumption of regularity/public law" model in the light of changed circumstances (Lindblom [1959] 1994). Under this model "public law" rules are selectively imposed on nongovernmental actors who perform public purposes.

The Anglo-American tradition provides highly relevant precedent for the translation of public obligations to private actors who perform public work. The most notable example, the Supreme Court's decision in *Munn v. Illinois* (1876), applied rules governing state-chartered monopolies to private "businesses affected with a public interest" (Freeman 2000, 2003; Daniel Guttman 2000, 2003). From another perspective, public contract law may be seen as an effort to sort out the extent to which the law of private contracts must be modified to reflect the role of the sovereign state as contracting party (Schwartz 1996, 1997).

In the absence of coherent oversight by Congress and the Executive Branch, the rules governing third-party performance of government work are, by default, being made on a case-by-case basis in which third parties themselves are often the driving force. The resulting rules may be essential but, because of the limited interests of the third parties who drive them, may not completely protect the public interest.

The rule-making process is illustrated in the application of conflict-of-interest and freedom-of-information laws to contractors. The organizational conflict-of-interest rules as applied to contractors emerged conceptually in the mid-twentieth century. When the military located the original Project RAND contract within the Douglas Aircraft Corporation, competing aerospace manufacturers complained that the arrangement was unfair. The fear was that RAND might recommend weapons projects on which Douglas, through its affiliation with RAND, would have the inside track. To resolve the conflict-of-interest concerns, the RAND contract was spun out of Douglas into a new nonprofit organization (Smith 1966). Following a similar episode in the management of the Intercontinental Ballistic Missile (ICBM) program (which resulted in the creation of Aerospace, another nonprofit, to manage the program), the organizational conflict-of-interest concept crystallized in the notion of the "hardware ban" in which "think" contractors could not be affiliated with hardware providers that might compete for the spending that flowed from their recommendations (Nieburg 1966).

As initially cast, an essential problem with the organizational conflict-of-interest concept was that it protected the interests of competing contractors but did little to protect the interests of the public at large. Indeed, as Don Price wrote in 1965, the "dog that didn't bark" was the failure of Congress to express concern at the interlocking directorates of aerospace contractors that governed the defense department's "independent" nonprofits (Price 1965). The notion that an independent "public interest" required protection (e.g., an interest above and beyond that of individual contractors or agencies) was a latecomer to organizational conflict-of-interest policy. It was not until the late 1970s that the "public interest" became a criterion for evaluating contractor conflicts of interest (Guttman 1978).

Even so, in contrast to the conflict rules governing officials, organizational conflict-of-interest rules do not require that contractors with conflicts be barred from employment. This lesser standard makes sense if it is assumed that officials, who themselves are conflict free, have the capacity to evaluate contractor work. But the latter assumption is no longer valid. Moreover, contractor disclosures are not available to the public (they are deemed business secrets under the FOIA). There appear to be virtually no public audits of the integrity of the review and disclosure process. One of the few such audits, conducted by Senator David Pryor in 1989, found that contractors did not turn straight corners in their disclosures, and that official reviewers did not act on information that showed conflicts to exist (*Energy Daily* 1990; Daniel Guttman 2003).

Similarly, the Freedom of Information Act, by its terms, applies to records of "agencies." Courts have repeatedly found that contractors were not agencies under the law—regardless of their role in decision making. In the late 1990s, outcry over lack of access to grantee-developed data underlying regulations led to amendment of the FOIA (the "Shelby Amendment") to provide for such access. Even so, the law required the amendment of an OMB circular applying to grants (A-110), which governs awards to universities and other nonprofits, but not to those primarily profit-making entities playing similar roles under contracts (Daniel Guttman 2003).

Finally, courts may play an increasingly important default role in the muddling-through model. In the absence of executive and congressional attention, it appears that courts may be receptive to arguments that challenge the presumption of regularity and, consistent with the common law tradition, may act to fashion new rules for emerging public/private mixes. Thus, although the Supreme Court in *Flagg Brothers* did not seize the opportunity to identify exclusively governmental functions, in *Lebron v. National Railroad Passengers Corporation* (1995) it declared a readiness to look behind formal labels applied by Congress in determining whether institutions are subject to constitutional provisions.

Lebron dealt with Amtrak's refusal to permit an artist to post his work in a station. Amtrak is a wholly owned government corporation under the Government Corporation Control Act, 31 U.S. Code section 9101(1)-(2)(A). In creating Amtrak, Congress took pains to free it from constraints otherwise applicable to agencies (e.g., federal procurement rules). Most directly, Congress declared that Amtrak "will not be an agency or establishment of the United States Government" (45 U.S. Code section 541).

Justice Antonin Scalia, for the Court majority, held that Amtrak was subject to the Constitution for purposes of the First Amendment claim made by the artist, notwithstanding the congressional declaration that Amtrak was not an "agency or establishment" of government. Congress, Justice Scalia explained, can dispose of Amtrak's status for matters within its control (e.g., procurement rules), but "it is not for Congress to make the final determination of Amtrak's status as a governmental entity for purposes of determining the constitutional rights of citizens affected by its actions." On review of the circumstances surrounding Amtrak's creation, the Court majority held that Amtrak "is an agency or instrumentality of the United States for the purposes of individual rights guaranteed against the Government by the Constitution." *Lebron* evinces the readiness of the Court to serve as active arbiter of "public" status for purposes of the Constitution, and to look behind corporate form in order to do so.

Similarly, in further cases, courts have indicated a readiness to apply private law to fashion a remedy that may hold contractors to account where existing public law does not provide for remedy. Thus, although courts have historically limited the rights of private citizens to seek court relief as third-party beneficiaries of government contracts (an opportunity available where contracts between private parties are involved), courts may be ready to provide this recourse, where public law, for example, the Administrative Procedure Act, does not provide a forum and where facts show remedy is needed (see the cases discussed in Daniel Guttman 2000, 2000a, 2003).

Similarly, although, since the famed demise of the "non-delegation" doctrine in the New Deal, courts have been hesitant to expressly invoke the doctrine as bar to Executive Branch action, there is evidence that courts may nonetheless step in where (sub)delegation to contractors denies citizens of processes or fairness that would obtain if work had been performed by officials. Thus, courts may provide that contractor decision-making roles should be predicated on procedural protections that would be available if officials performed the work (e.g., conflict of interest protection, review rights). Thus, even where courts conclude they have no authority to order a remedy, they may make findings of fact that provide bases for further action before executive agencies or Congress.

In short, although the non-delegation doctrine may be dead as a doctrine that focuses on institutional form, it may be in for revival as a doctrine that focuses on principles of fairness, with the institutional form as a variable; that is, decisions made by those outside the penumbra of public law may be presumed to require further scrutiny for fairness.

Nonetheless, although the role of courts will be of the essence if the muddling-through model continues to govern, the use of courts to decide constitutional principles of governance is not optimal. Most basically, courts decide only those matters presented to them in "cases or controversies"; the matters before courts for written decision depend in the first instance on the resources and interests of parties. Parties reasonably have interests in resolving their own cases, and, in general, in not developing larger issues of fact and policy. In some cases, of course, the disputes under review may be typical of the fact patterns that must be addressed by any new principle. In the case of government by third party, however, these fact patterns are both varied and still largely unexplored. Courts called on, by default, to decide basic principles of governance in this context may be asked to make decisions with less than the full deck needed to make them (Daniel Guttman 2000, 2003).

In sum, the three currently operative models all have their virtues, but all raise basic questions.

Choosing Among Visions: An Agenda for Research and Reflection

Because reliance on contractors to perform the basic work of government remains invisible in substantial respects, independent analyses of how and how well the system works are few and far between.[9] If there is to be informed choice among constitutional visions, there is ample room for further research and analysis to support this choice.

What Special Qualities Are Available from the Contract Bureaucracy?

Expertise

According to common lore, contractors provide the public with access to expertise unavailable within the official workforce. The truly unique expert needed on a "temporary or intermittent" basis may be employed as a special employee under Title 5 of the U.S. Code (which governs civil servants and other employees and officials). Nonetheless, the view is not myth. Contractors presently possess considerable expertise not available within the government, or, at least, within the programs for which the contractor is at work. However, unaddressed questions include (1) the extent to which this reality does not reflect the state of nature, but is an artifact of the determination to grow government through third parties, and (2) whether the country can make do with diminished official oversight capability by relying on networks of contractors for contractor oversight.

Much of the contractor workforce consists of those trained as officials in the first instance. Contractors purveying homeland security expertise tout former intelligence and law enforcement officials on their staff, just as aerospace firms have historically been prime employers of former military and defense officials. With the privatization of the federal Office of Personnel Management's investigation branch, discussed by Ronald Moe in chapter 5, federal personnel clearances are performed by those who trained to do them as officials. As auditing, human resources, and procurement management are increasingly contracted out, the same will also be the case for these further core government functions.

Moreover, an effect of personnel ceilings has been to assure that experts in newly created fields are trained and learn as contractors, rather than as civil servants. Cold War agencies played a famed role in the funding of cyber technologies, but the government's information technology workforce has, from the start, been substantially private (Ferris 2003).

Institutional Qualities

The notion that the qualities of government agencies, nonprofits, and profit-making institutions differ is commonplace, and a pillar of the governance perspective.

Indeed, the view that the institutional qualities of these organizations fundamentally differ has congressional and judicial imprimatur. Thus, as noted, in deciding whether the Freedom of Information Act should apply to nonprofit entities, even where they admittedly are making public decisions, courts have explained that Congress intended to protect the autonomy of these groups in order to assure that their qualities will not be constrained when they aid government (see Daniel Guttman 2003; and *Forsham v. Harris* [1980]; *Washington Research Project v. Department of Health, Education and Welfare* [1974]; *Public Citizen Health Research Group v. Department of Health, Education and Welfare* [1981]).

Similarly, in deciding whether private prison guards should have the benefit of immunity from suit that would be afforded a similarly situated official, Supreme Court Justice Stephen Breyer explained in *Richard v. Mcknight*:

> Petititioners [private contract prison guards] . . . overlook certain important differences [between government and contractor] that, from an immunity perspective, are critical. First, the most important special government immunity producing concern—unwarranted timidity—is less likely present, or at least is not special, when a private company subject to competitive market pressures operates a prison. Competitive pressures mean not only

that a firm whose guards are too aggressive will face damages that raise costs, thereby threatening its replacement, but also that a firm whose guards are too timid will face threats of replacement.

[M]arketplace pressures provide the private firm with strong incentives to avoid overly timid, inefficiently vigorous, unduly fearful, or 'non-arduous' employee job performance . . . To this extent, the employees before us resemble those of other private firms and differ from [other] government employees. (*Richard v. Mcknight,* 1997, 409–10)

Justice Breyer took pains to clarify that the difference between the private and public guards was not personal, but institutional: "This is not to say that government employees, in their efforts to act within constitutional limits, will always, or often, sacrifice the otherwise effective performance of their duties. Rather, . . . government employees typically act within a different system . . . often characterized by multidepartmental civil service rules that, while providing employee security, may limit the incentives or the ability of individual departments to reward, or punish individual employees" (*Richard v. Mcknight,* 1997, 410–11).

In short, it is an axiom of governance, which calls for reliance on a mix of institutions to perform public purposes, that institutions have differing qualities. Nonetheless, governance also encourages the restructuring of existing institutions, the creation of new ones, and the blurring of boundaries between and among public and private institutions. Governance proposes to do this by altering institutional incentives and by creating new institutions and new relationships among existing institutions.

Thus, governance reformers appear to be of several minds about institutional qualities, sometimes treating them as a binary phenomenon (either present or not), sometimes as a continuum (more or less present), and sometimes as a matter of engineering design, not nature.[10]

As to binary treatment, much contracting out and "privatization" proceeds as if the use of a nongovernmental entity is the only way to obtain "businesslike" qualities of innovation and efficiency. This perspective neglects a rich public administration tradition. In the United States, but also in many other countries, public agencies have long deployed corporate forms where business-type qualities are needed to perform the public's work (OECD 2002; Seidman 1997; Stanton and Moe 2002; Wettenhall and Thynne 2002; Wettenhall 2003).

The "privatization" of the U.S. Enrichment Corporation (USEC) illustrates the view of institutional qualities as on/off switches. That privatization, as noted, involved the transformation of a government-owned corporation into a private shareholder-owned corporation. Nobel economics laureate Joseph Stiglitz, who unsuccessfully opposed the "privatization" from within the Clinton administration, observed that the essential benefits of the corporate form were already available to USEC in its status as a government corporation. As Stiglitz explained at the time, the privatization essentially created a further set of conflicts between and among stockholder interests and USEC's commitment to fulfill national security and domestic security needs (Guttman 2001; Stiglitz 1998, 2002).

Conversely, governance encourages the blurring of boundaries between and among institutions. As the Bell Report asked four decades ago, "In what sense is a business corporation doing nearly 100 percent of its business with the Government engaged in 'free enterprise?'" (U.S. House of Representatives 1962). More recently, the Clinton and Bush administrations have urged that the civil service be rendered more businesslike. Indeed, a high-level consensus proclaims the civil service "dead"—yet leaves unresolved what will replace it (Zeller 2003).

The convergence of institutional qualities may be a desired end. Nonetheless, its pursuit suggests the need to reexamine presumptions about differing institutional qualities that underlie the deployment of third parties to perform the government's basic work.

Organizational Efficiencies

Governance proponents emphasize the failure of traditional "hierarchical" public agencies to obtain the benefits of networking, particularly as made possible by cybertechnologies (Eggers and Goldsmith 2003). Ongoing inquiries into the intelligence failures related to 9/11 and Iraq, and now the Katrina disaster of course, have punctuated the importance of coordination between and among federal, state, and local agencies.

On paper, the contractor bureaucracy might seem ideally suited to provide coordination and networking qualities and efficiencies. In contrast to officials, contractors may (1) work simultaneously for multiple agencies focused on a common problem and (2) work for multiple components within an agency—for example, under separate contracts with headquarters and field offices. Moreover, contractors may also simultaneously work for beneficiaries or objects of agency programs, such as localities or private corporations. For example, in regard to homeland security, a given contractor may (1) have on staff former officials from the many agencies now involved, (2) work on contract for many of these agencies, and (3) also work for relevant local, private, and multinational interests.

The role of third parties as providers of coordination and network capabilities requires examination. Two kinds of questions immediately present themselves.

First, are efficiencies that appear plausible on paper actually realized, and, if so, at what potential cost? For example, when a contractor works simultaneously for multiple agencies at work on a common problem (and is employed, in part, because of this factor), can the public assume that it will provide coordination/networking among them? On the other hand, potential for conflict of interest may run hand in hand with potential for congruence and synthesis of interests. This may be the case where, for example, a contractor works at the federal level in program design and/or evaluation and at the state and local levels in program implementation, or for agencies and nongovernmental entities regulated or served by the agency. Once again, if there is confidence in official capacity to check for conflict, the game may be worth the candle; if not, how will the potential for coordination efficiencies, that is, congruence of interests, be balanced against the potential for conflicts of interest?

Second, to what extent are efficiencies available only through use of third parties instead of official workforces? Are official organizational structures (and personnel rules) inherently less capable of taking advantage of network opportunities? Here, as discussed below, comparative cross-country study may be of particular value.

What Role Do Third Parties Serve in the Political Process?

Third parties have long been deployed for reasons that are political, as well as technical (i.e., obtaining efficiencies and expertise). Any choice between official and third-party workforces, therefore, needs also to consider the respects in which they differ on this dimension. These include (Guttman and Willner 1976, Daniel Guttman 2000, 2003):

- Contracting has been used as a bipartisan tool to grow government programs while pretending that Big Government itself is not growing.
- As a corollary, contractors have been said to provide a countervailing force to check and bring reason to the dead hand of bureaucracy.
- Contracting is used to build a constituency for programs, both through the use of contractors as tools in Executive Branch politics (as exemplified in the creation of RAND to help advance the cause of the Army Air Force within the military establishment), and before Congress and the public (as most famously and successfully illustrated in the determination that NASA would rely heavily on contractors in the competition with Russia).
- Contracting may be used as a tool in the politics of nations, as the Bush administration's declaration that countries not supporting the Iraq war would not be given reconstruction contracts illustrates (Jehl 2003).

Finally, of course, contracting may serve as a tool of traditional political patronage. The "Nixon Personnel Manual," unearthed by Congress during the Watergate hearings, mused:

> In 1966, Johnson offered legislation, which Congress passed, [that] required the Executive Branch . . . to reduce itself in size to the level of employment in fact existing in 1964. The cosmetic public theory . . . was that . . . a personnel ceiling for the Executive Branch would first cut, and then stabilize, Federal expenditures connected with personnel costs . . . What the Johnson Administration did after passage . . . was to see to it that "friendly" consulting firms began to spring up, founded and staffed by many former Johnson and Kennedy Administration employees. They then received fat contracts to perform functions previously performed within the Government by the federal employees. The commercial costs, naturally, exceeded the personnel costs they replaced. (U.S. Senate 1974)

In sum, the roles played by contracting in the political process include, but are by no means limited to, the traditional notion of patronage in the sense of choice of contractors based on party preference. The use of contractors to advance particular programs may well be bipartisan (e.g., in the sense of promoting a program like the early space program) or nonpartisan (in the sense of addressing conflicts within agencies that may not reflect party divisions), and may be to the benefit of the contractor business at large (by expanding the pie). In all these respects, the role of contractors may differ from that which could be played by a technically equivalent official workforce.

How, and How Well, Do the Means of Accountability Work?

As discussed, competition, management technique, and transparency are the key tools said to provide for accountability of the third-party workforce. Basic research on these means is in order, and there should be benefit from a comparative, that is, cross-country, perspective.

It appears that the U.S. experience is distinct in the extent of its reliance on private contractors to perform the government's work. In other countries similar work may be performed directly by the government or by corporate forms under government authority or ownership. This does not mean that other countries do not employ contractual relationships, and invoke the tools of accountability (competition, performance technique, and transparency) invoked in the United States. However, elsewhere the contract may be more frequently between public entities (e.g., ministry and agency or ministry and government corporation). Cross-country comparisons may yield a better understanding of what it takes to make accountability mechanisms and contracts work.

What Is the Scope of the Third-Party Universe that a Constitutional Vision Should Address?

As noted, work performed by nongovernmental actors under federal procurement statutes and rules may often be similar to that performed under grants or other third-party arrangements (Salomon and Elliott 2002). Governance calls for review of the premises of the distinctions that now exist.

For example, the logic of comparative institutional qualities initially supported distinct legal rules that apply to contracts, grants, and other contractual arrangements. Grants have historically gone to public or nonprofit entities. By the logic of institutional qualities, the requirements for alignment of such interests with the public interest differ from the requirements for profit-making entities (which have differing qualities and respond to differing incentives). Governance, however, calls into question the assumptions about institutional qualities.

Conclusion: How Will We Know If Muddling Through Is Not Good Enough?

The presumption that officials have the capacity to oversee and evaluate the work of government contractors is, by widespread admission and evidence, no longer secure. Whether a constitutional vision is affirmatively chosen, or the muddling-through model will govern by default, due diligence is in order on federal use of third parties to perform the basic work of government. At this late date, government itself, as well as the public at large, lacks basic information on the third-party workforce, and on the ability of officials to oversee that workforce. Moreover, as contracting out proceeds apace, there is no requirement that such information be developed and made available.

Most fundamentally, the shift from government to governance calls into question the potential of culture(s) to find means to account for state power when it is designedly diffused. Whether muddling through will be enough to account for new developments may ultimately depend on the adaptability of the basic cultural premises that governance draws on and challenges. A checklist of these cultural premises would include:

Rule of Law/Public Law

At the forefront, as contracting out in the United States illustrates, governance calls into question the future of the rule of law, in the sense of a body of public law that is applicable to define and limit those entrusted with public purposes.

Proponents of governance at home and abroad urge that "the rule of law" must go hand in hand with the creation of new mixes of public and private actors that will compose governance systems. But, as the contracting out of the federal government's work illustrates, there has been too little effort to develop a coherent body of rules of public law that will apply to nongovernmental actors who perform the public's work in the age of governance.

Will the public law tradition be adaptable and adapted to governance's use of nongovernmental actors perform the public's work? Will nongovernment actors be subject to some, or all, constitutional and statutory provisions that are applied to officials? Are new principles of law needed to govern nongovernment actors who perform governmental functions?

The Anglo-American legal tradition provides for the application of rules initially applied to state actors to private actors who come to perform public purposes. The public procurement law tradition, from the other direction, provides precedent for the melding of public law purposes to private law form. To the centuries-old bodies of public utility and contract law, Congress and the Executive Branch have added a framework of law—the concept of inherently governmental function and organizational conflict of interest—that also address the difficult problems attending the late-twentieth-century reliance on contractors. It may be, in sum, that the tools to govern contractors who perform the basic work of government are, in large measure, available; whether they are employed in a coherent fashion remains to be seen.

Rule of Social/Management Science

From another perspective, public law is not being rendered irrelevant but is evolving in keeping with the modern jurisprudential view that social and management science will replace tradition, legal precedent, and natural law as the basis for rules. As Oliver Wendell Holmes Jr. urged over a century ago, and his disciples urge today, the law should not depend on precedent established hundreds of years ago when better tools are available (Holmes 1897; Posner 1993).

Consistent with what might be called the jurisprudential perspective of "pragmatism," governance proponents urge that social and/or management science (plus new information technology) will permit the effective ordering of complex relationships among public and private institutions as never before. Where the Founding Fathers saw the understanding of human nature as the building block for a science of politics, governance proponents see institutional nature(s), with institutions read broadly to include formal and informal institutions and rules, as the building blocks of governance. Proponents of governance urge that modern management and social science will permit the design of new institutions and the ordering of relations among them as never before.

Indeed, mid-twentieth-century accomplishments such as the Manhattan, Apollo, and Cold War weapons programs provide powerful precedent for this view. In these cases, however, the government bought technology for its own direct use. Whether similarly successful designs will emerge to address outstanding social problems, homeland security, and nation building—where the users (or "customers" in the governance vernacular) of the goods and services at issue are not limited to the federal government—remains to be seen.

Institutional Nature(s) Up for Grabs

Governance's design to reorder old institutions and create new ones—to blur the boundaries—sets in motion the very institutions on whose qualities governance proponents would draw. How does the premise that institutions can be understood and used as building blocks fit with the design to modify institutional relationships in ways that likely affect their character?

Most basically, as the boundaries between official and private workforces further blur, do we risk losing the qualities most valued in both? How effectively can government constrain nongovernment actors (whether profit-making corporations, NGOs, universities, churches, or other entities) without diluting their valued qualities of autonomy and independence? By the same token, as government undertakes the fundamental restructuring of the civil service, with design to render it more businesslike, will the civil service lose the qualities that rendered it valuable?

These, and similar, questions, bear continued reflection as the country simultaneously engages in basic reform of the civil service and extended deployment of third parties.

The Future of the Public Service Ethos

The reordering of government induced by governance underscores the import of an ethos of public service while putting this ethos up for grabs. In the West the concept of the merit-based civil service is recent, a late-nineteenth-century development in Britain and the United States (Jenkins 1997; Skowronek 1984). Nonetheless, as now codified by law and embodied in over a century of experience, there is an assembled tradition of considerable value. How will this ethos evolve as public purposes are increasingly performed by nongovernmental actors?

As Justice Breyer, quoted above, explains, the issue is not simply whether individuals who work as officials or third parties are well intentioned and have the public interest at heart.

The ethical problems of political life, as Max Weber most famously pointed out, are often those of people who believe they are doing good (Weber 1946). As the Supreme Court explained in the classic exposition of the conflict-of-interest law applicable to officials, we must presume that those who perform the public work are honorable and good men and women (*United States v. Mississippi Valley Generating Company,* 1961, 549–50).

Professor Dennis E. Thompson, drawing on Weber, explains that where, as in modern government, decisions involve "many hands," ethical questions are particularly difficult (Thompson 1987). There is often a disconnect between (1) those legally responsible for a decision and (2) those who, because of superior knowledge or actual involvement, are effectively responsible. Governance, as exemplified by contracting out, seeks to address one of Weber's classic problems—the dead hand of bureaucracy—by "diffusing sovereignty" (as Don Price put it). In doing so, however, it brings more hands to bear on the decisions, exacerbating the problem of many hands.

Where decision making involves many hands, rules must not only locate authority but also be bedrocked in a realistic appraisal of the reality of decision making. In order for well-intentioned people to know where their ethical obligations lie, they must know (1) whether their role is truly only advisory, (2) whether they really are the decision makers, or (3) whether their role lies somewhere in between.

Under current law, we presume that officials bear responsibility for government decisions, while contractors play advisory or secondary decisional roles. If this presumption no longer reflects reality, ethical questions with practical consequences arise. When, for example, should a contractor who knows that the responsible official lacks the capacity to design, direct, or evaluate contractor work accept the work, on the premise that the official is in charge; when should the contractor insist on further official reflection, or even reject the work? In practice, answers to such questions may not require formal rules. But they will at least require wisdom gained from practical experience and the appreciation that official authority may not be commensurate with the resources needed to exercise that authority.[11]

In any event, at present there appears to be no express or coherent concept of public service to govern the nongovernmental workforce that performs the work of government. Perhaps the closest analogy are professional codes—from medicine, social science, law, and prior civil or military service—that individual members of the workforce may honor (Payton 2004). However, contract employees who do the work of government come from all professions and none. Moreover, professions themselves are undergoing transformations in their own right, as guilds are subjected to market forces.

Moreover, there is a basis for caution about the ready transferability of professional codes, even were the professions themselves not undergoing considerable institutional change. In its review of Cold War–era government-funded human radiation experiments, a presidential commission found that civilian medical researchers paid substantial attention to issues of the risks to which they were exposing citizens, but routinely violated the ethical principle that citizens should be informed of the risks to which they were being exposed. Private contract and grant researchers and research institutions lagged well behind military biomedical researchers and the military in the application of principles of "informed consent" (President's Advisory Committee on Human Radiation Experiments 1996).

Citizenship and Public Opinion

Finally, where will the citizen fit into a world characterized by governance by new mixes of public and private institutions where "bowling alone" and the "sidelining of citizens" is a matter of concern (Ginsberg and Crenson 2002)? Woodrow Wilson, in his seminal 1887 article on public administration, posited that public administration would be a science, that the "field of administration is a field of business," and that "administrative questions are not political questions" (Wilson 1887). Nonetheless, perhaps even so, he declared that "public opinion shall play the part of the authoritative critic."

Today, however, the public lacks basic information on its rapidly changing public service, and lacks the benefit of congressional and executive deliberation of alternatives that view the new public workforce as a whole that includes officials and third parties. In this context, the twenty-first-century U.S. public has sharp reason to assume for "governance" the role of authoritative critic that Wilson proposed the twentieth-century U.S. public assume for "public administration." There could be no better place for the public to start than to demand that needed information about the dimensions of change be made public and that public deliberation on the governance alternatives before the country begin.

Notes

1. Professor Strayer explains: "Precisely because in the pre-state era there can be no sharp distinction between public and private, any persisting institution may in time become part of the state structure though it was not originally intended to have this function. The Commonwealth of Massachusetts and the British Empire of India grew out of the institutions of private corporations" (Strayer 1970, 7–8).

Kamen (Kamen 2002, 288) considers the Spanish Empire in its heyday as a series of contractual arrangements, with the Genoese providing financing, continental Europe providing soldiers, and conquistadors providing riches:

> The Spanish monarchy from its inception was a vast entity in which non-Spaniards always had a crucial role. Like any great enterprise it was highly expensive to run. In times of peace, basic operations such as communications, trade and transport of supplies between the territories of the monarchy required a degree of efficiency that the central government could never guarantee, since it had no personnel who could carry out the task. Virtually all the important operations were therefore contracted out. (Strayer 1970, 7–8)

The conquistador expeditions were "private enterprises led by independent military contractors in pursuit of profit" (Taylor 2001, 57). Taylor explains: "Following French and Spanish precedent the [British] crown subcontracted colonization by issuing licenses and monopolies to private adventurers, who assumed the risks in speculative pursuit of profits" (Taylor 2001, 118).

Ferguson provides a pithy case study of nineteenth-century "privatization of diplomacy"—the Rothschilds' proposed resolution of the fabled nineteenth-century Schleswig-Holstein dispute. Each of the potential buyers of the disputed territory—Prussia, Russia, and Italy—was strapped for cash:

> To the Rothschilds, the answer seemed to be obvious; [Italy and Prussia] should privatize state assets, preferably railways, to buy Holstein and Venetia respectively [from Austria]. At the same time Austria's financial position was so precarious that even selling one or both of these territories was unlikely to balance the budget. Austria had already sold off most of her state railways, so privatization was not the answer; instead, the already privatized railway lines should seek tax breaks from the government as part of the price of financial assistance. This was the essence of [the Rothschild] vision in 1865: a complex of interdependent transactions designed to liquidate Austria's unsustainable Empire without the need for an economically disruptive war. (Ferguson 1999, 130–31)

2. In July 2002, the Brookings Institution, the oldest Washington think tank, renamed its governmental studies program the "governance" program, joining the World Bank, the UN, the Ford Foundation, and other elite institutions in embracing the term *governance.*

3. See, for example, *United States Postal Service v. Gregory,* 534 U.S. 1 (2001) ("Although the fairness of the Board's own procedure is not before us, we note that a presumption of regularity attaches to the actions of government agencies"); *Moffat v. United States,* 112 U.S. 24 (1884) ("The presumption as to the regularity of the proceedings which precede the issue of a patent of the United States for land, is founded upon the theory that every officer charged with supervising any part of them, and acting under the obligation of his oath, will do his duty, and is indulged as a protection against collateral attacks of third parties"); and *United States v. Chemical Foundation, Inc.,* 272 U.S. 1 (1926) ("The presumption of regularity supports the official acts of public officers and, in the absence of clear evidence to the contrary, courts presume that they have properly discharged their duties. . . . Under that presumption, it will be taken that [an official] acted upon knowledge of the material facts").

4. Indeed, when queried by the press about contracting beyond the scope of underlying supply service contract authority, contractor counsel indicated that the practice was not one that contractors themselves would police, in part, it appears, because there had been no effort by the government to penalize out-of-scope contracting:

> Contractors usually don't turn down government requests for their services, even if those requests are for work that falls slightly outside an agreement, said Claude P. Goddard, a government contracts attorney at Wickwire Gavin PC in McLean. Until the CACI case, there has not been a negative reaction to such practices, he said.

> "What I have seen is kind of a wink and a nod by GSA, sort of turning a blind eye," Goddard said. "So you'll see all sorts of things being ordered that you wouldn't think would fall within the scope of the products or services of the actual schedule that the company holds."
>
> Jacob B. Pankowski, a government contracting lawyer with Nixon Peabody LLP, said: "I don't know of any cases where a contractor has rejected an order on the basis that it's not within the scope of their government-wide order—nor would one expect them to. The gist of this threatened action [against CACI] is to require government contractors to become the policemen of government contracting officials' conduct." (McCarthy 2004)

In mid-2004, following continued disclosures of problems with Iraq and other supply service contracting, Department of Defense and General Services Administration officials declared a new "zero-tolerance" policy for violating acquisition law and policy (Harris 2004b).

5. The Army Field Manual on Contractors on the Battlefield was itself written by a DOD contractor (Center for Public Integrity 2004b).

6. Legal scholar Zhenming Wang of China provides a helpful perspective:

> Under the rule of law, the primary purpose of the legal system is to regulate and restrain the behavior of government officials. There must be laws regulating the authority of the government and its officials—political behavior must comply with legal rules. Moreover, these laws should clearly delineate the constitutional functions of the government. This understanding of the role of law is inconsistent with traditional Chinese legal thinking, in which the law is regarded as an instrument for rulers to govern the ruled. (Wang 2000)

7. In March 2004 the Department of Defense did propose a rule that would contractually apply the Geneva convention to defense contractors. As to the Uniform Code of Military Justice, however, the proposed rule stated only that the code would apply "where applicable," evidencing apparent internal disagreement as to when and whether the code is applicable to civilians (*Federal Register* 2004).

8. Of course, the Congress, courts, press, and public will continue to have oversight authority and interest. However, they have hitherto been able to rely on the premise that officials can be presumed to have capability to account to them for the work of government.

9. For example, save for the General Accounting Office's invaluable work, the studies relied on to demonstrate contractor efficiency are in the handful, and produced by entities that are themselves substantially dependent on federal contracts. Above and beyond lack of transparency, analytical difficulties and resource limitations have hampered research. In 1995 Congress heard testimony from the Office of Management and Budget and the General Accounting Office (GAO) on the policy that "commercial" activities be contracted out—a policy that had then been in effect for nearly four decades (U.S. House of Representatives 1995). The GAO testified: "During our long history of our work in this area, we have consistently found that evaluating the overall effectiveness of contracting out decisions and verifying the estimated cost savings reported by agencies is extremely difficult after the fact. As a result we cannot convincingly prove nor disprove that the results of federal agencies' contracting-out decisions have been beneficial and cost-effective" (U.S. House of Representatives 1995, 14).

Since 1995, the GAO has continued its work on A-76 efficiencies, and the Center for Naval Analysis, a federally created contract research center (among those sometimes termed "FFRDCs," or Federally Funded Research and Development Centers), has done substantial work on A-76.

10. Australian public management scholar Roger Wettenhall provides an analysis of the ways in which public/private mixes are talked about—as dichotomies (e.g., public, private), trichotomies (state, market, civil society) and spectra (Wettenhall 2003).

11. See Michael Oakeshott's classic formulation of "practical" learning (Oakeshott 1991).

References

Agency for International Development, Inspector General. 2002. "Audit of USAID's Workforce Planning for Procurement Officers." Audit Report Number 9-000-03-001P, November 12.

Associated Press. 2000. "Feds Sue Harvard for $120 Million over Russia Program." CNN.com (September 27). Available at http://archives.cnn.com/2000/US/09/27/harvard.russia.ap/index.html (accessed March 2006).

Bianco, Anthony, and Stephanie Anderson Forest. 2003. "Outsourcing War." *Business Week* (September 15).

Brinkley, Joel. 2004. "Army Bars Interrogation by Private Contractors," *New York Times* (June 12), A5.

Brown, Reginald (assistant secretary of the army [Manpower and Reserve Affairs]). 2002. Letter to the Hon. Ted Stevens, Ranking Member, Committee on Appropriations, Subcommittee on Defense, U.S. Senate, April 12.

Callahan, Raymond. 1964. *Education and the Cult of Efficiency: A Study of the Social Forces That Have Shaped the Administration of the Public Schools,* chapters 2–5. Chicago, IL: University of Chicago Press.

Campbell, Gordon. 2000. "Contractors on the Battlefield: The Ethics of Paying Civilians to Enter Harm's Way and Requiring Soldiers to Depend on Them." Prepared for presentation to the Joint Services Conference on Professional Ethics, Springfield, VA, January 27–28.

Cassidy, John. 2002. "The Greed Cycle: How Corporate America Went Out of Control." *The New Yorker* (September 23), 64–77.

Center for Public Integrity. 2004a. "Private Contractors." June 13. Available at www.publicintegrity.com/wow/report.aspx?aid=32.

———. 2004b. "Contractors Write the Rules." June 30. Available at www.publicintegrity .org/default.aspx

———. 2004c "Outsourcing the Pentagon." Available at www.publicintegrity.org/oil/

Cha, Ariana. 2003. "At NASA: Concerns on Contractors." *Washington Post* (February 17).

Coase, R.H. 1988. *The Market and the Firm*. Chicago, IL: University of Chicago Press.

Corson, John. 1971. *Business in the Humane Society.* New York: McGraw-Hill.

Corvisier, Andre. 1979. *Armies and Societies in Western Europe 1494–1789,* trans. Abigail T. Siddal. Bloomington: Indiana University Press.

De Soto, Hernando. 1989. *The Other Path: The Economic Answer to Terrorism.* New York: Basic Books.

Defense Acquisition Excellence Council. 2003. "Agenda." October 7. Available at www.acq.osd.mil/dpap_archive/daec/index.htm.

Department of Defense Inspector General. 2004. "Contracts Awarded for the Coalition Provisional Authority by Defense Contracting Command-Washington." D-2004-057 (March). Washington, DC: Department of Defense.

Department of Energy. 2001. "Workforce Analysis." Washington, DC: Department of Energy, July. http://www.ma.mbe.doe.gov/pol/WFAnal.pdf.

Donahue, John, and Joseph Nye. 2002. *Market-Based Governance.* Washington, DC: Brookings Institution Press.

Easterly, William. 2001. *The Elusive Quest for Growth: Economists' Adventures and Misadventures in the Tropics.* Cambridge: MIT Press.

Eggers, William D., and Steven Goldsmith. 2003. "Networked Government." *Government Executive* 15 (8; Supplement), 28–33.

Eisenhower, Dwight D. 1961. "Farewell Radio and Television Address to the American People." In *Papers of Dwight David Eisenhower,* eds. Louis Galambos and Daun Van Ee, paragraph 421. Baltimore, MD: Johns Hopkins University Press.

Energy Daily. 1990. "Contractors Lied on Conflict of Interest, Says DOE." March 27.

Ferguson, Niall. 1999. *The House of Rothschild: The World's Banker 1849–1999.* New York: Penguin.

Ferris, Nancy. 2003. "Give and Take." *Government Executive* 35 (8; Supplement).

Freeman, Jody. 2000. "Private Parties, Public Functions and the New Administrative Law." *Administrative Law Review* 52(3): 813–58.

———. 2003. "Extending Public Law Norms through Privatization." *Harvard Law Review* 116: 1285.

General Accounting Office (GAO). 1997. *Privatization: Lessons Learned by State and Local Governments,* GAO/CGD-97-48. Washington, DC: General Accounting Office.

———. 2002a. "Acquisition Workforce; DOD's Plans to Address Workforce Size and Structure Challenges," GAO-02-630 (April). Washington, DC: General Accounting Office.

———. 2002b. *Commercial Activities Panel Final Report: Improving the Sourcing Decisions of the Government,* GAO-02-847T. Washington, DC: General Accounting Office.

———. 2003a. "Best Practices: Improved Knowledge of DOD Service Contracts Could Reveal Big Savings," GAO-03-661 (June). Washington, DC: General Accounting Office.

———. 2003b. "Department of Energy: Status of Contract and Project Management Reforms," GAO-03-570T (March 20). Washington, DC: General Accounting Office.

———. 2003c. "High Risk Series: An Update," GAO-03-119 (January). Washington, DC: General Accounting Office.

———. 2004a. "Coast Guard's Deepwater Program Needs Increased Attention to Management and Contractor Oversight," GAO-04-389 (March). Washington, DC: General Accounting Office.

———. 2004b. "Contract Management: Contracting for Iraq Reconstruction and for Global Logistics Support," GAO-04-869T (June 15). Washington, DC: General Accounting Office.

Ginsberg, Benjamin, and Matthew A. Crenson. 2002. *Downsizing Democracy: How America Sidelined Its Citizens and Privatized Its Public.* Baltimore, MD: Johns Hopkins University Press.

Goo, Sara Kehaulani. 2003. "Airport Screeners' Hiring Under Scrutiny." *Washington Post* (September 12), E01.

Groner, Jonathan. 2004. "Untested Law Key in Iraq Abuse Scandal." *Legal Times* (May 11).

Guttman, Dan. 2000. "Nuclear Weapon." *Environmental Forum* (November–December): 18–33.

———. 2003. "Contracting United States Government Work: Organizational and Constitutional Models." *Public Organization Review: A Global Journal* 3(3): 281–99.

———. 2004a. "De gobierno a gobernanza: La nueva ideología de la rendición de cuentas, sus conflictos, sus defectos y sus características." In *Politica y Gestion Publica*, ed. Oscar Oszak. San Diego, CA: Fondo de Cultura Economica USA.

———. 2004b. "Inherently Governmental Functions: The Legacy of 20th Century Reform." In *Making Government Manageable: Executive Organization and Management in the 21st Century*, ed. Thomas H. Stanton and Benjamin Ginsberg. Baltimore, MD: Johns Hopkins University Press.

Guttman, Dan. 2004c. "The Shadow Pentagon." (September 29). Available at www.publicintegrity.org.

Guttman, Daniel. 1978. "Organizational Conflict of Interest and the Growth of Big Government." *Harvard Journal of Legislation* 15: 297.

———. 2000. "Public Purpose and Private Service: The Twentieth Century Culture of Contracting Out and the Evolving Law of Diffused Sovereignty." *Administrative Law Review* 52 (3).

———. 2001. "The United States Enrichment Corporation: A Failing Privatization." *Asian Journal of Public Administration* 23(2): 247–72.

———. 2003. "Privatisation, Public Purpose and Private Service." *OECD* (Organization for Economic Cooperation and Development) *Journal on Budgeting* 2(4): 89–160.

Guttman, Daniel, and Barry Willner. 1976. *The Shadow Government*. New York: Pantheon Books.

Hamilton, Martha. 2000. "Approaching Critical Mass." *Washington Post* (January 31).

Harris, Shane. 2003. "AID Plans to Contract Out Oversight of Iraq Contracts." *Government Executive Online* (May 20).

———. 2004a. "Army Requested Company's Interrogators for Iraq Prison." *Government Executive Online* (May 26).

———. 2004b. "Defense, GSA Officials Vow to Clean up Contracting." *Government Executive Online* (July 13).

———. 2004c. "Outsourcing Iraq." *Government Executive* 36 (July).

Hecker, Sigfried. 1997. "Nuclear Weapons Stewardship in the Post Cold War Era: Governance and Contractual Relationships." Attachment to S.S. Hecker Written Statement to Senate Committee on Energy and Natural Resources Hearing on "Governance of the Department of Energy Laboratories," June 24.

Hoffman, David. 2002. *The Oligarchs: Wealth and Power in the New Russia*. New York: PublicAffairs.

Holmes, Oliver Wendell, Jr. 1897. "The Path of the Law." *Harvard Law Review* 10: 457.

Jehl, Douglas. 2003. "A Region Inflamed: Pentagon Bars Three Nations from Iraq Bids." *New York Times* (December 10), A1.

Jenkins, Roy. 1997. *Gladstone: A Biography*. New York: Random House.

Jensen, Michael C. 2000. *A Theory of the Firm: Governance, Residual Claims and Organizational Forms*. Cambridge, MA: Harvard University Press.

Johnson, David Cay. 2003. "New I.R.S. Chief Plans to Focus on Enforcement." *New York Times* (October 16), C6.

Kamen, Henry. 2002. *How Spain Became an Empire*. London: Penguin.

Lewin, Tamar, and Jennifer Medina. 2003. "To Cut Failure Rate Schools Shed Students." *New York Times* (July 31), A1.

Lindblom, Charles. [1959] 1994. "The Science of Muddling Through." In *Public Policy: The Essential Readings*, eds. Stella Z. Theodolou and Matthew A. Cahn. New York: Prentice Hall. First published in *Public Administration Review* 19 (1959): 79–88.

Mallett, Michael. 1999. "Mercenaries." In *Medieval Warfare: A History*, ed. Maurice Keen. New York: Oxford University Press.

Mayer, Jane. 2004. "Contract Sport." *The New Yorker* (February 16 and 23).

Mayle, Adam, and David Knott. 2002. "Outsourcing Big Brother: Office of Total Information Awareness Relies on Private Sector to Track Americans." Available at Center
for Public Integrity Web site, www.publicintegrity.org/default.aspx.
McCarthy, Ellen. 2004. "Government Contractors Sometimes Stretch Their Deals." *Wash-
ington Post* (May 31).
McDougall, Walter A. 1985. *The Heavens and the Earth: A Political History of the Space
Age.* Baltimore, MD: Johns Hopkins University Press.
Moe, Ronald C. 2001. "The Emerging Federal Quasi Government: Issues of Management
and Accountability." *Public Administration Review* 61 (May/June).
Mote, E.W. 1999. *Imperial China: 900–1800.* Cambridge, MA: Harvard University Press.
Muller, Jerry Z. 2002. *The Mind and the Market: Capitalism and Its Critics.* New York:
Knopf.
Naim, Moses. 1999. "Fads and Fashion in Economic Reforms: Washington Consensus or
Washington Confusion?" Working Draft of Paper Prepared for IMF Conference on
Second Generation Reforms, October 26.
Nellis, John. 2002. "External Advisors and Privatization in Transition Economies." Cen-
ter for Global Development Working Paper 3.
New York Times. 2003. Editorial: "Houston's School Dropout Debacle." (July 21), A14.
Nieburg, H.L. 1966. *In the Name of Science.* Chicago, IL: Quadrangle.
North, Douglass C. 1982. *Structure and Change in Economic History.* New York: W.W.
Norton.
Oakeshott, Michael. 1991. "Rationalism in Politics." In *Rationalism in Politics and Other
Essays.* Indianapolis, IN: Liberty Press.
Office of Management and Budget. 2003. *Circular A-76 Revised.* May 29.
Organization for Economic Cooperation and Development (OECD). 2002. *Distributed
Public Governance: Agencies, Authorities and Other Government Bodies.*
Osborne, David, and Ted Gaebler. 1992. *Reinventing Government: How the Entrepre-
neurial Spirit Is Transforming the Public Sector.* New York: Penguin.
Payton, Sallyanne. 2004. "Professionalism as Third-Party Governance: The Function and
Dysfunction of Medicare." In *Making Government Manageable: Executive Organiza-
tion in the Twenty-First Century,* eds. Thomas H. Stanton and Benjamin Ginsberg.
Baltimore, MD: Johns Hopkins University Press.
Peck, Merton, and Frederick Scherer. 1962. *The Weapons Acquisition Process: An Eco-
nomic Analysis.* Boston, MA: Harvard University.
Peckenpaugh, Jason. 2002a. "Army Secretary Announces Massive Outsourcing Plan."
Government Executive Online (October 10).
———. 2002b. "Competition Target Stays the Same; A-76 Changes Could Transform
Outsourcing." *Government Executive Online* (December 3).
———. 2003. "OMB Outsourcing Chief to Step Down." *Government Executive Online*
(September 4).
———. 2004. "Army Contractor Count Stymied in Red Tape." *Government Executive
Online* (June 4).
Petrie, Donald A. 1999. *The Prize Game: Lawful Looting on the High Seas in the Days of
Fighting Sail.* Annapolis, MD: Naval Institute Press.
Posner, Richard A. 1993. *The Problems of Jurisprudence.* Cambridge, MA: Harvard Uni-
versity Press.
President's Advisory Committee on Human Radiation Experiments. 1996. *The Human
Radiation Experiments: Final Report of the President's Advisory Committee.* New
York: Oxford University Press.
Price, Don K. 1965. *The Scientific Estate.* Cambridge, MA: Belknap Press.

Project on Government Oversight. 2002. "Federal Contractor Oversight: Failure of the Suspension and Debarment System." Available at www.pogo.org/.

Reddaway, Peter, and Dmitri Glinski. 2001. *Tragedy of Russia's Reforms: Market Bolshevism against Democracy.* Washington, DC: U.S. Institute of Peace.

Salomon, Lester M., and Odus V. Elliott. 2002. *The Tools of Government: A Guide to the New Governance.* New York: Oxford University Press.

Schama, Simon. 1989. *Citizens: A Chronicle of the French Revolution.* New York: Alfred A. Knopf, 72–79.

Schemo, Diana Jean. 2003. "Questions on Data Cloud Luster of Houston Schools." *New York Times* (July 11): A1.

Schooner, Steven L. 2001. "Fear of Oversight: The Fundamental Failure of Businesslike Government." *American University Law Review* 50: 627.

Schwartz, Joshua. 1996. "Liability for Sovereign Acts: Congruence and Exceptionalism in Government Contracts Law." *George Washington Law Review* 64: 533.

———. 1997. *Cases and Materials for a Survey of Government Procurement Law.* Washington, DC: George Washington University.

Seidman, Harold. 1997. *Politics, Position and Power: The Dynamics of Federal Organization.* New York: Oxford University Press.

Shenon, Philip. 2003. "Airline Gave Defense Firm Passenger Files." *New York Times* (September 20), A1.

Skowronek, Stephen. 1984. *Building a New American State: The Expansion of National Administrative Capacities.* Cambridge: Cambridge University Press.

Smith, Bruce L.R. 1966. *The RAND Corporation: A Case Study of a Non-Profit Corporation.* Cambridge, MA Harvard University Press.

Smith, R Jeffrey and Susan Schmidt. 2005. "Bush Official Arrested in Corruption Probe." *Washington Post* (September 20), A01.

Stanton, Thomas H., and Ronald C. Moe. 2002. "Government Corporations and Government-Sponsored Enterprises." In *the Tools of Government,* ed. Lester M. Salomon. New York: Oxford University Press, 81–116.

Stevenson, Richard. 2002. "Government May Make Private Nearly Half of Its Civilian Jobs." *New York Times* (November 15), A1.

Stiglitz, Joseph. 1998. "This Privatization Proposal is Radioactive." *Wall Street Journal* (June 2), 1.

———. 2002. *Globalization and Its Discontents.* New York: W.W. Norton.

Strayer, Joseph. 1970. *On the Medieval Origins of the Modern State.* Princeton, NJ: Princeton University Press.

Strouse, Jean. 2000. *Morgan: American Financier.* New York: Random House.

Taylor, Alan S. 2001. *American Colonies.* New York: Penguin.

Thompson, Dennis E. 1987. *Political Ethics and Public Choice.* Cambridge, MA Harvard University Press.

U.S. House of Representatives. 1962. *Report to the President on Government Contracting for Research and Development* ("Bell Report"). Washington, DC: Executive Office of the President, Bureau of the Budget. Appears in Appendix 1 to Part 1, "Systems Development and Management," Hearings before the Committee on Government Operations, 87th Congress.

———. 1993. Testimony of the Hon. Hazel O'Leary, "DOE Management." Hearings before the Subcommittee on Oversight and Investigations of the House Committee on Energy and Commerce, 103rd Congress.

———. 1995. Statement of Nye Stevens, Director of Planning and Reporting, General Government Division, General Accounting Office, and John Koskinen, Deputy Director for Management, Office of Management and Budget, Hearing before the Subcommittee on Civil Service, Committee on Government Reform and Oversight, 104th Cong., 1st Session, March, 29.

———. 2000. "DOE's Fixed Price Cleanup Contracts: Why are Costs Still Out of Control?" Prepared Statement of Ms. Gary Jones, General Accounting Office, Hearings before the Subcommittee on Oversight and Investigations of the House Committee on Commerce, 106th Congress.

U.S. Senate. 1974. "Federal Political Personnel Manual." In *Presidential Campaign Activities of 1972,* Senate Resolution 60: Executive Session Hearings before the Senate Select Committee on Presidential Campaign Activities, 93rd Congress.

———. 1980. *Oversight of the Structure and Management of the Department of Energy.* Report by Staff of Senate Committee on Governmental Affairs, 96th Congress.

———. 1989. "Report to the Chairman of the Federal Services Subcommittee by the Majority Staff." In *Use of Consultants and Contractors by the Environmental Protection Agency and the Department of Energy,* Hearing before the Subcommittee on Federal Services, Post Office and the Civil Service of the Senate Committee on Governmental Affairs, 101st Congress.

———. 2003. Statement of the Hon. Kenneth Mead, Inspector General, Department of Transportation, before the Committee on Science, Commerce and Transportation, Subcommittee on Aviation, February 5.

Wald, Matthew, and John Schwartz. 2003. "Shuttle Inquiry Uncovers Flaws in Communication." *New York Times* (August 4).

Wang, Zhenming. 2000. "The Developing Rule of Law in China." *Harvard Asia Quarterly* IV (Autumn). Available at www.fas.harvard.edu/~asiactr/haq/200004/0004a007.htm.

Weber, Max. 1946. "Politics as a Vocation." In *From Max Weber: Essays in Sociology,* eds. H.H. Gerth and C. Wright Mills. New York: Oxford University Press.

Wedel, Janine. 1998. *Collision and Collusion: The Strange Case of Western Aid to Eastern Europe 1989–1998.* New York: St. Martin's Press.

Weinstock, Matthew. 2001. "Meltdown." *Government Executive* (February).

Wettenhall, Roger. 2003. "The Rhetoric and Reality of Public-Private Partnerships." *Public Organization Review: A Global Journal* 3(1): 77–107.

Wettenhall, Roger, and Ian Thynne. 2002. "Public Enterprise and Privatization in a New Century: Evolving Patterns of Governance and Public Management." *Public Finance and Management* 2(1): 1–24.

White, Thomas E. 2002. "Accounting for the Total Force: Contractor Workforce." Secretary of the Army's Memorandum for Under Secretary of Defense (Acquisition, Technology and Logistics) and Others. March 8.

White House. 2001. "Barriers: A Federal System Inhospitable to Faith-Based and Community Organizations." Available at www.whitehouse.gov.news/releases/2001/08/unlevelfield3.html

———. 2003. "The President's Management Agenda." http://www.whitehouse.gov.omb.budget/2002/mgmt/pdf.

Wild, Antony. 2000. *The East India Company: Trade and Conquest.* Lyons Press.

Williamson, John. 2000. "What Should the World Bank Think about the Washington Consensus?" *World Bank Observer* 15 (August).

Williamson, Oliver. 1996. *The Mechanisms of Governance.* New York: Oxford University Press.

Wilson, Woodrow. 1887. "The Study of Administration." Reprinted in *Political Science Quarterly* 56 (December).

World Bank. 2000. *Reforming Public Institutions and Strengthening Governance: A World Bank Strategy Report.* November.
World Bank Group. 2003. "Private Sector Development in the Electric Power Sector." July 21.
Zeller, Shawn. 2003. "Smashing the System." *Government Executive* 15(16) (November 15): 30–40.

11

Improving the Military Personnel System

Cindy Williams

The end of the Cold War brought dramatic changes for the U.S. armed forces. Rather than planning for major warfare in Europe, the military was faced with smaller regional wars and frequent deployments around the world. Three hundred thousand troops returned from Europe, and the size of the active force was reduced by about one-third.

The tragic events of September 11, 2001, led to additional changes. The roles of the Army and Air National Guard and the Army, Naval, Marine Corps, and Air Force Reserves in homeland security expanded dramatically, with tens of thousands of reservists standing duty at U.S. airports for a period of several months. For the first time in decades, the services conducted active, large-scale air defense within the continental United States. A new command was established to consolidate Department of Defense (DOD) operations related to homeland security.

In addition, the nation called upon the military for levels of offensive activity not seen since the Vietnam War. As of this writing, the U.S. military was involved in large and deadly operations in Iraq and Afghanistan that could continue for years. More than half the army's deployable active-duty units saw action during 2004. Even a brigade that normally stands guard in South Korea was sent to the Persian Gulf; another unit, designed to test the mettle of the rest of the army at the ground forces training range in Ft. Irwin, California, was instead sent to Iraq. By the end of 2005, the National Guard, initially meant to be a genuine reserve and called up only in case of a massive conventional war, was supplying nearly half of the U.S. troops sent to Iraq to keep the peace and quell the insurgency there.

These post-9/11 developments have revealed serious human resource problems in the armed forces. For example, all the services are short of people in key occupations, yet they have excess personnel in other occupations; during recent years, 40 percent of occupations in the U.S. armed forces were overstaffed, while another 30 percent were understaffed (CBO 2003b, 36). The services have attempted to entice people in overstaffed fields to switch occupations or leave active duty, but with little effect. The situation is so tough in the air force and the navy that both services want to convince some of their members to move to the army (which is hiring to increase its numbers)—despite deep cultural differences that can make it difficult for members brought up in one service to thrive in another (Trowbridge and Tice 2004).

In addition, although most members of the National Guard and the reserves earn more money when called to active duty than they do in their civilian jobs, about one-third of them earn less, and they are crying foul. Reservists' families also complain about discontinuities in benefits like health care and a lack of support and information. The strain is reflected in weakened morale, especially in the guard and reserves, where recruiting and retention have suffered (Ricks 2004; Josar2003; Moniz 2003a, 2003b; Rees 2004).

Another problem is the high cost of military pay and benefits. Excluding the added costs of operations in Iraq and Afghanistan, taxpayers devote nearly $140 billion annually to pay and benefits for military personnel, retirees, and veterans. The significance of that cost to taxpayers is obvious. Perhaps less obvious are the problems posed by the high cost of people for the military itself.

For example, some of the military's post-9/11 problems could be ameliorated by expanding the size of the active-duty army. In the spring of 2004, Secretary of Defense Donald Rumsfeld agreed to add 30,000 troops, but only for a period of four years. Indeed, the secretary has steadfastly refused to consider even a modest permanent expansion, citing the high cost of people (Svitak 2003). The 30,000 troops added on a temporary basis will cost some $2.5 billion annually in pay, benefits, and other support—nearly what the army was spending in the year 2005 to develop the Future Combat System, its premier new fighting capability (CBO 2003a; DOD 2004).

Perhaps more troubling, to avoid the high costs of people in uniform, the nation is turning increasingly to contractors to fill military roles. For many activities, outsourcing can be a healthy choice.[1] In fact, by relying more on contractors, the Department of Defense could reduce the number of specialists in uniform whose opportunities in the outside labor market strain the military pay system.[2] On the other hand, as the nation witnessed in Iraq, and as Dan Guttman analyzes in chapter 10, turning key jobs over to contractors can raise serious concerns, both on and off the battlefield (Singer 2001; Schwartz 2003; Wood 2003; Avant 2002). Such problems cannot be solved by adding money; in fact, increasing military pay and benefits can complicate the situation by making troops even more expensive relative to contractors.

The problems revealed during recent years might appear to stem from the increased military activity after 9/11. In fact, they were not so noticeable before the events of that day sparked the Bush administration's war on terrorism. They have their roots not in recent events, however, but instead in deep structural flaws in the personnel system the nation uses to manage its military people and reward them for their service and sacrifice. Solving these problems will require reforming the system of rewards to build an incentive structure that is more effective for the nation, for our service members, and for the military as an institution.

Since the United States ended the military draft in 1973, every member of the U.S. armed forces is a volunteer. Although intangible factors like patriotism or a chance for adventure are important draws for many who volunteer to serve, the military relies heavily on good pay, benefits, training, and career prospects—the tangible rewards for service—to maintain its competitive edge as an employer in U.S. labor markets. Military pay and benefits and the personnel policies that underpin them are crucial to attracting the right people to join the military, to stay as long as they are needed, and to do the best job they can in service to their country.

Some people suggest the military's human resource problems could be solved by bringing back the draft. From the point of view of the military and society, that would be a mistake.

For the military, shifting to an all-volunteer force was arguably the most important innovation since the Vietnam War—and a key enabler of the transformation in other aspects of military affairs that took place between Vietnam and the 1991 Gulf War. Ending the draft reduced disciplinary problems to a minimum, because every man and woman in uniform chose to join. With pay adjusted to attract large numbers of recruits of above-average cognitive aptitudes the all-volunteer system also enabled dramatic improvements in personnel quality. Indeed, every applicant for enlisted service has been required to take a battery of tests, including the Armed Forces Qualification Test, or AFQT, which measures cognitive aptitude in comparison with the aptitudes of a civilian comparison group. Since the mid-1980s, more than 60 percent of enlisted entrants have scored above the median of the civilian population.

At the same time, substantially longer periods of service under the all-volunteer system meant more time for training, a higher return on the military's investment in training, and lower turnover in the military workforce. Those advantages added up to a military workforce that was very well suited to exploit the high-technology equipment associated with the post-Vietnam transformation. Reinstituting conscription would reverse those advantages and could greatly complicate efforts to transform the military in the future.

Returning to the draft would pose grave problems for society as well. Even with a deployable army doubled in size, U.S. forces could not use more than a small fraction of the nation's men and women of military age. Proponents of a new draft say the inequities that plagued the system during the 1960s could be avoided through a lottery system. But a lottery, no matter how fairly run, cannot erase the fundamental inequities caused when some are forced to serve while most are not. The better solution by far is to correct the flaws in the personnel policies that underpin the volunteer system.

Problems brewing beneath the surface of the military personnel system may seem acceptable during peacetime. When lives and military outcomes are not immediately at stake, it may seem as if the nation can buy its way out of the worst problems. Alternatively, it may seem that the military can muddle through with a few half-hearted reforms, tweaking things here and there to accommodate the challenges of raising and maintaining a strong force, and adapting incrementally to changes in operations and technology as they come up. But in wartime, even modest setbacks in filling the ranks with the right people can ripple rapidly through the force and its leadership, increasing the risks to fielded troops and making it more difficult for them to achieve military aims.

As of this writing, the combination of a slow economy, high unemployment, patriotic spirit, stop-loss orders that forbid many soldiers to leave service even if they want to, and generous bonuses had kept active-duty recruiting and retention at the levels needed. Nevertheless, there were signs of weakness. If the economy heats up, making jobs in the private sector more plentiful and attractive, or if the information sector revives, drawing critical specialists away from the military when it most needs them, then military effectiveness could suffer badly. The nation can no longer afford to wait to reform the system, nor can it get by with disconnected bits and pieces of reform. Rather, to deal with today's realities and put in place the capacity to respond and adapt quickly to future strategic and economic changes, the nation needs a fundamental revision of military personnel policies.

This chapter examines flaws in seven key aspects of military personnel policy and recommends an integrated program of reforms to fix them.[3] The recommendations vary across a spectrum of time-urgency and difficulty; implementing them will require a combination of immediate action and sustained effort. For example, the services could act immediately to concentrate cash bonuses to attract and retain people in critical occupations in the active forces, or in strained units of the National Guard and the reserves. Similarly, Congress could act immediately to increase cash bonuses for occupations that are hard to fill, while slowing down the across-the-board raises that add to every member's pay. An Internet- and telephone-based assistance system for military families could be developed quickly.

On the other hand, some of the reforms proposed here—especially a move toward cafeteria benefits and broad changes to the officer career and retirement systems—are likely to meet with stiff resistance and will take years to implement. Nevertheless, those proposals are well worth pursuing for the long-term advantages they offer.

The chapter takes the point of view that getting the military personnel system right should be a key goal of executive organization and management in the United States. It begins with a brief review of the system in the context of public administration and a discussion of similarities and differences between the military workforce and workers in other public institutions. It then outlines specific problems in seven areas and recommends solutions for them. It ends with a brief wrap-up and some suggestions for overcoming the hurdles that stand in the way of change.

The Military Personnel System Is a Key Component of Executive Management

The U.S. military is the strongest security provider in the world. It owns more advanced equipment and is more capable of projecting power to any region on earth than any other military in the world. Because of its unique role in U.S. life and its unique power, it is sometimes easy to forget that it is also the largest employer in the United States, with some 1.4 million active-duty service members, 880,000 paid members of the guard and reserve, and 650,000 civilian workers.[4] In addition, the Department of Defense provides services to some 1.7 million men and women who retired from the military, typically after serving for twenty years or more.

In support of the uniformed men and women and retirees, the department runs the largest payroll system and the most ambitious personnel management and placement systems in the world. It manages one of the nation's largest health care systems. It owns the tenth-largest chain of grocery stores in the United States. It also runs its own school systems in the United States and abroad, and one of the most highly rated chains of child care centers in the nation.

Including benefits for veterans and retirees, the federal government devotes about $140 billion a year to military pay and benefits—about three times as much as it currently spends on homeland security. At that cost, military pay and benefits constitute one of the largest public enterprises in the United States.

As with other areas of public administration, military personnel policy lies at the nexus of three crucial sets of interests: those of the taxpayer, those of the individuals who serve in the military, and those of the military as an institution. Achieving a balance that works among the three sets of interests is never easy. Moreover, the Department of Defense faces challenges similar to those encountered by other public-sector employers: a vibrant U.S. labor market within which it must compete in the war for talent; the requirement to recruit, retain, and motivate capable people; the necessity of sorting the workforce so that good people move up to higher positions; and the responsibility of inducing them to move on when their services are no longer needed.

The military differs from other public-sector employers in crucial ways, however. Perhaps the most important and obvious is that its employees can be called upon to risk their lives, to manage violence, and to kill on behalf of the nation. They are also typically required to move frequently, sometimes to locations where their spouses find it difficult to get work or where children's schools do not meet their parents' quality standards. Those differences can have profound consequences for personnel management, especially because the military workforce is extremely young.

As a labor force, the military is distinguished by its youth. Nearly half of all active-duty enlisted personnel are under age twenty-five (compared with 15 percent under age twenty-five in the nation's civilian workforce). Fewer than 7 percent of them are over forty years of age. Managing such a youthful workforce brings unique challenges, especially where their families are concerned.

Moreover, in contrast to much of the federal workforce, the military is predominantly a "blue-collar" organization. Only 15 percent of active-duty military personnel are officers, who typically hold a four-year college degree. Most of the rest are in the enlisted force; they typically do not have college degrees, though increasingly they have some college experience. Unlike many blue-collar workers, however, military workers are not represented by unions.

Another feature that distinguishes the military from other public-sector employers is the extraordinary diversity of its occupations. In the wars in Afghanistan and Iraq beginning in 2001, special forces and infantry troops, tank and artillery crews, commanding officers from all the services, helicopter and fighter pilots, airplane and ship mechanics, computer-network specialists, communications experts, intelligence analysts, and foreign-language specialists fought together against the adversary. Cooks, stock clerks, purchasing officers, financial experts, doctors, lawyers, clergy, space system operators, unmanned aerial vehicle controllers, tanker and transport pilots, and information professionals supported them. Military jobs run the gamut from low technology to high technology, from operating or maintaining vehicles to directing their acquisition. The diversity poses a particular challenge for an employer with a strong tradition of preferring internal pay equity over competitiveness in the labor market—a challenge that grows as the compensation gap widens in the private sector between workers with high-technology skills and those without them.

Finally, the military is unique in the nation for the high level of support and respect it enjoys as an institution. For several decades, surveys have shown the military at the top of the list for citizen respect—well above any other federal institution. That support can make it difficult to make any changes to pay and benefits policies, especially if the changes appear to weaken or break the compact between society and those who serve.

Problems with Military Personnel Policies and Reform Recommendations

The Department of Defense has ambitious goals for transforming the way the U.S. military fights, in large part by exploiting information technologies to achieve information superiority. Transformed forces are meant to rely less on mass and more on information than today's military to achieve their lethality and survivability. They are also meant to be more agile and autonomous. Those attributes have important implications for military people, who increasingly must be versatile, savvy users of information systems and make critical decisions formerly held at higher echelons.

The military's outmoded pay and personnel policies stand in the way of its plans for transformation. Inflexible pay scales blunt the services' capacity to compete for people with technical skills or information savvy that bring top dollar in the private sector, or even to hold on to people with skills that are especially valued inside the military, without substantially overpaying those with less-valuable skills. Old-fashioned concepts of the enlisted recruit can make the military less attractive than it should be to young people who went straight to college or technical school after high school. The retirement system draws too many people whose skills do not grow with experience to stay longer than is useful, but induces others to leave when their technical skills or their contributions as leaders are at their peak. Officer personnel policies can make it difficult for technical specialists to have rewarding careers and for future leaders to accumulate the knowledge they require.

U.S. military pay and personnel policies are also out of step with the educational and career aspirations of U.S. youth, with changes in U.S. society, and with human resources practices in the private-sector firms against which all public employers must compete for talent. Absent a fundamental makeover of military personnel policies, people problems will subvert the services' transformation goals, and the costs will eat away at other aspects of U.S. military might.

The remainder of this section describes specific problems in seven over-lapping areas of military personnel policy and recommends solutions for them. The recommendations are largely cost neutral, that is, they will neither save nor add to government costs. Over the long term, however, they could help to avert the staffing crises that are sure to raise future costs well above today's if fundamental change is not undertaken. Transforming the policies related to military personnel in light of changing strategic, demographic, social, and labor realities is a crucial component of executive branch reform.

Military Cash Pay

With some notable exceptions, a service member's cash pay does not depend on his or her occupation. Rather, it is determined largely based upon rank, length of service, family status (whether he or she is married or has children), and location of work. The lack of variation in pay can make it difficult to reward individuals whose skills bring top dollar in the private sector or whose contributions inside the military are particularly critical without also, at great expense, increasing the pay of all service members. The situation may be an underlying cause of the problems that have surfaced recently for U.S. forces in Iraq as members of the special operations forces leave the service of their nation to take jobs with contractors who will pay them substantially more (Schmitt and Shanker 2004). If information specialists and other technical experts find military pay too low to compete with offers from the private sector, then the problem may well become a showstopper for military transformation.

Proponents of today's system argue that one-size-fits-all pay creates a sense of equity that leads to organizational solidarity. They also say that varying pay according to skill or performance could erode good order and discipline by putting more money in the pockets of subordinates than of their superiors. Existing bonus programs contradict those myths, however. For example, on a navy submarine, reenlistment bonuses can put thousands of dollars more per year in the pocket of a nuclear electronic technician than a mess specialist. Yet the two work in close quarters and face the same dangers, with no apparent lack of solidarity or discipline.

Concerns about internal pay equity and pay compression arise in private firms too. Nevertheless, the private sector typically pays competitive wages to valuable employees rather than risk having them hired away by other firms. As a result, there is much more variation in pay within private-sector firms than in the military (Asch, Hosek, and Martin 2002).

In the military, bonuses and special pay make for some pay separation across occupations. As currently used, however, such pay makes up only a tiny fraction of the total money the government spends on military people, and most of it is concentrated in a very few specialties, such as medicine, aviation, and navy nuclear specialties. It is noticeably absent for the information specialties at the heart of military transformation.[5] To reverse deep imbalances in staffing and clear the way for transformation, the nation must find a way to bring greater variability into military cash pay, allowing the services to pay individuals at levels that are more in keeping with their value inside as well as outside the military. In the near term, leaders should move to concentrate and improve bonuses in the critical, understaffed occupations. Over the longer term, they should work toward a new, more flexible pay structure that accounts for differences among occupations and skills (Cymrot and Hansen 2004).

The Military Retirement System and Up-or-Out Rules

The military retirement system, a defined-benefit plan that dates to the 1940s, in many ways resembles the pension schemes of state governments or large private firms of the mid-twentieth century. It stands in stark contrast to the flexible, portable, early-vesting systems of today's corporate and government worlds and would be illegal in a private firm today.

The military plan provides no pension for members who serve for fewer than twenty years. For those who stay on active duty for at least twenty years, it provides an immediate lifetime annuity that increases annually with the cost of living. The twenty-year "cliff vesting" attracts people who stay for more than a few years to continue in service for twenty years. Then, because the pension is immediate and generous, the system encourages them to leave within a few years (Asch and Warner 1996).

In addition to the carrot of retirement, the services have a stick they can use to force members to leave: "up-or-out" rules that require individuals to quit active duty if they are not promoted according to a fairly rigid schedule. Up-or-out rules permit the services to remove members not suited for higher-level positions and at the same time to manage the size of the cohort at each rank. Together with the retirement system, they work as a blunt tool for force management. Unfortunately, however, both the up-or-out rules and the retirement system are one size fits all, in the sense that members are induced to stay or leave without regard to their occupations.

The combined systems cause the military to keep many people after they should leave and to lose others just as their expertise becomes most useful. The military would be better off if some people, for example many infantry soldiers, would leave within twelve years, while others, for example nurses or scientists, would stay for much longer careers. Keeping a soldier when he or she is no longer needed can result in a force that is older than desired. It also raises the costs of the retirement system, a problem that is dramatically compounded by the recent expansion of retiree entitlements. On the other hand, when the military loses its experienced nurses after twenty years of service, it must backfill by recruiting and training more new nurses than it would otherwise need. A less-rigid retirement system with earlier vesting opportunities, coupled with up-or-out rules that vary by occupation, would give service members greater flexibility to shape their own careers and would improve the services' ability to shape the forces they need for the future. The following discussions of enlisted and officer career patterns include specific recommendations.

Recruitment, Training, and Career Patterns for the Enlisted Force

About 16 percent of active-duty service members are officers or warrant officers. The remaining 84 percent serve in the enlisted force. Traditionally, enlisted members joined the military directly out of high school, and most still do. But the educational aspirations of U.S. youth have changed since World War II, as an increasing share of U.S. high school graduates opt for college or technical school instead of entering the workforce right after graduating.

The way the services think about enlisted recruits has not changed much, however. Regardless of a recruit's level of education or technical proficiency, he or she still typically enters service at the lowest level of rank and pay. The military generally assumes that its recruits are blank slates, and runs its own schools to train welders, machinists, graphic designers, court reporters, and a host of other specialists. As a result, the services are hindered in competing for people already trained in valuable skills, and they waste money in providing training that is widely available in the private sector.

The nation needs to update the way it thinks about and rewards the enlisted force. Concepts of careers and training should be transformed by closing down the military schools that duplicate training already widely available in the private sector, and instead aggressively recruiting young people who are already trained in the needed skills. These changes could be carried out as part of the process of base closures and realignments that will be necessary during the coming decade. In addition, new, occupation-specific up-or-out rules should allow for longer careers for highly skilled individuals, whether or not they assume the leadership roles typically associated with higher rank. Retirement policies should allow for earlier vesting and greater portability and should vary by occupation.

Congress changed the rules for military retirement in 1986, but overturned the reforms as part of a major expansion of retiree entitlements during the late 1990s. One way to protect a new system from repeal would be to keep the current system for enlisted members who prefer it, or those whom the services wish to keep for twenty years or more. By adding a voluntary defined-contribution plan, with a generous government matching contribution available only to those who depart before twenty years on a schedule preferred by the government, the nation could revamp the incentive structure to keep the right people for the right amount of time, without harming the retirement prospects of members who prefer the current system (Cymrot and Hansen 2004).

Officer Career Patterns

Because the retirement system offers a generous and immediate pension after twenty years of service, most career officers depart when they are still in their early forties. But fitting all the jobs expected of an officer into such a short career can be an enormous challenge, and officers are often rushed from one position to the next without learning what they need to know (Tillson 2001; Lewis 2002; Trefry 2003). The Goldwater-Nichols Act of 1986 exacerbated the problem by requiring officers to serve for several years in joint positions in order to be considered for promotion to general or admiral. A fundamental overhaul of officer career patterns is in order.

In a transformed system, competitive up-or-out rules in the junior ranks, similar to today's, would be followed by stringent selection into the "career force" at the twelve- to fifteen-year point (depending upon service and occupation). The retirement system would be transformed to provide severance pay and a deferred annuity for those who do not make the career cut, or who choose to leave before they have completed a full career, but to induce those selected as career members to stay in the force for substantially longer careers than they would have today. Those who stay in the career force would be rewarded with increasingly challenging jobs and higher pay as they gain experience. The new model would allow career officers much more time in critical jobs, thus building the cadre of future leaders whose talents and skills will be the bedrock of future forces (Rostker 2004).

Pay and Benefits for the Guard and Reserve

The Army, Naval, Marine Corps, and Air Force Reserves are strictly federal entities, commanded through the Department of Defense. In contrast, the Army and Air National Guard perform both federal and state missions and are commanded by the governors of the states to which they belong, except when called up for federal missions. A governor can order the National Guard personnel under his or her command to state active-duty status for various operations, including natural disasters and civil disturbances.[6]

After the Cold War ended, the nation transformed the way it uses the guard and reserve. Rather than a genuine reserve, to be tapped only in major emergencies, the reserve components became a ready source of units and people for peacekeeping and humanitarian interventions. The events of September 11, 2001, ushered in another round of change. Today, the guard and reserve play key roles in homeland security, take over the stateside duties of deployed active forces, contribute to the occupation in Iraq, and more—and still conduct training for major combat operations. Antiquated personnel systems create inappropriate incentives and also make things difficult for reservists and their families.

For example, members earn more for a day of reserve training than they do for a day of active duty, making training time more financially attractive than active service. Also, bonuses and special pay, which could prop up recruiting and retention in hard-to-fill units and positions, are not widely used. Such improperly skewed and insufficient incentives stand in the way of a reserve force that today shoulders more than its share of the burden of deployment.

In addition, the structure of military benefits still presumes a reserve force that trains part-time and is mobilized only rarely. As a result, when called to active duty, members often encounter transitional problems and extra expenses related to benefits such as health care. Those problems are especially hard on the families of reservists; if not fixed, they have serious implications for future morale and retention.

The cold-war mentality also applies to the basic model of reserve service and training. Increasingly, the old model of one weekend per month and two weeks in the summer does not apply. Some reservists need more training time or will be on active service for longer periods; others require less. Yet rigid compensation structures make it difficult to reward people appropriately along a continuum of service.

The problems are compounded by a payroll system that cannot keep up with members' transitions between reserve and active duty, leaving some members with no paychecks or problem paychecks for months at a time. For example, in a 2004 case study of six Army National Guard units, the Government Accountability Office (GAO) found that 450 of 481 mobilized soldiers had "at least one pay problem associated with their mobilization" (Kutz 2004, 5). Such problems are rooted in obsolete payroll systems and flawed business management systems that affect other areas of defense operations as well (Kutz 2004, 14, 24). The Department of Defense is working to develop new payroll and business systems. Given the importance of the reserve component to ongoing operations, the urgency of modernization in this area cannot be overstated. In addition, the nation needs urgently to overhaul the structure of pay and benefits and the conditions of service for guard and reserve members.

One of the most important remedies is to reorient the pay system so as to reverse the skewed incentives of today's structure and reward more seamlessly a member's participation along a continuum of service. Those goals could be met by developing a new, two-part payment structure, with one part for participation (to be granted regardless of training or mobilization status) and a second part for each day of training or active duty. Members would be paid the same amount for an active-duty day as for a training day. Participation pay could vary depending upon occupational specialty or unit, to help achieve localized recruiting and retention goals. The reserves should also have new bonus programs and proficiency pays to attract people to hard-to-fill units and occupations.

Finally, the nation must find better ways to ease the transition to active service for the families of reservists, particularly in the area of health care. As of this writing, Congress is considering a proposal to extend the military's Tricare health care coverage to all reservists and their families, regardless of mobilization status. Doing so would cost billions of dollars a year, however. A far less expensive yet effective option is to allow those members who are called to active service to choose between covering their families through the military's Tricare health care program and having the government subsidize the cost of their existing health insurance (Gotz 2004).

In-Kind Pay and Benefits

For many members of the military, goods and services provided directly by the government constitute an important part of total compensation. In-kind support and benefits include military housing, health care, and subsidized groceries and child care. The Congressional Budget Office calculates that such noncash benefits account for more than half of the government's spending on military pay and benefits (CBO 2004).

The military's in-kind offerings recall the days of the garrison army, when goods and services were hard to find near military posts and most military people lived on the post. Now, concentrated as they are on large military installations and focused to a large extent on families, many in-kind benefits seem increasingly out of place with an expeditionary military in the modern world. In addition, they are generally inequitable to single members, reservists, and members who do not live on bases. Moreover, because they often involve government monopolies underwritten by subsidies and tax-free status, many are economically inefficient, costing taxpayers substantially more to provide than they are worth to the individuals who receive them. Transforming the military into a more agile, expeditionary, responsive force will require transforming this part of military compensation.

The most useful change would be to convert to cash as many in-kind benefits as possible. Installation-centered benefits like family housing, commissaries, and child care would be especially appropriate for such "cashing out." In addition, service members should be permitted to tailor their benefits to their individual needs through a new "cafeteria plan," similar to plans widely available in the private sector. To provide whatever in-kind offerings the Department of Defense keeps, the nation must make its government-owned and -operated businesses more cost effective and responsive to customers. One way to do that is to put them on a more even footing with private contractors, for example, by making them pay taxes like civilian firms, and to open their activities to private-sector competition (Murray 2004).

Family Support Services

Nearly 60 percent of all service members have families. The Department of Defense provides a wide array of goods and services to make military life attractive to families and to help them cope with the strains of military life. But the way the defense department delivers them today is out of step with today's realities. For example, although 70 percent of active-duty families and virtually all guard and reserve families live outside of military installations, most of the support offered to families is installation centered. Furthermore, although military operations are increasingly carried out by the services working jointly, the delivery of family support is still typically service specific. As a result, from the point of view of family members, help can seem disjointed and difficult to access. The problem is particularly acute for the families of reservists, who may live nowhere near a large military installation, or for whom the nearest base may belong to a different service.

The services also rely on old-fashioned means of communicating and providing support. Rather than making information widely available through the Internet or brochures, they often rely on word of mouth through a network of volunteers whose spouses serve together in a military unit. Yet, as in the rest of the United States, those spouses increasingly are not "stay-at-home moms" but are men and women with full-time jobs outside the home.

One of the most important problems faced by military families is that frequent moves can undermine career progression for military spouses. With more than half of military spouses in the civilian labor force or seeking work, spouses' careers are important both for military family income and for satisfaction with military life. In addition, military families are increasingly concerned about the safety and educational environments in the public schools of the communities to which the military moves them. Such problems can harm retention.

Military family support services are badly in need of a makeover. To improve coordination and reduce duplication, the multiple systems run independently by the individual services, i.e., service stovepipes, should be eliminated and replaced by a joint structure that provides family and community programs to all of the services. Support should be less centered on installations and volunteers. A modern "push" system for information and benefits would improve outreach to families; an Internet- and telephone-based employee assistance program could handle basic questions and provide referrals that today require the assistance of numerous volunteers and paid staff.

In addition, the DOD should make some money available to help the spouses of military members make progress in their careers despite the frequent moves and absences of the military member. New programs could include relocation payments to help defray the costs of finding a new job and reimbursement for education and professional licenses. Finally, the department should take concrete steps to improve the educational prospects of the children of military families, for example, by providing members with better information about local schools and instituting more interaction between military and school leadership (Raezer 2004).

Reforming Military Personnel Policies for the Future

In recent years, taxpayer costs for military people and retirees have risen at nearly three times the rate of inflation, but the added money has resulted in only marginal improvements for the military as an institution and for the individuals who serve. It is hardly surprising that today's pay and personnel policies do not work as well as they should in today's environment. Many of them were created more than fifty years ago; although in step with industrial practices of the 1940s, they have not kept up with fundamental strategic, social, economic, business, or labor realities.

Outdated policies get in the way as the services try to compete in today's labor market for the people they need. They get in the way of individuals who want more flexibility and satisfaction from their careers. Some of those individuals should become tomorrow's military leaders, and the consequences for future military outcomes could be grave if they become disaffected or depart. Unless things change in more fundamental ways, the services will find it increasingly difficult to attract and keep the people they need. This chapter offers a reassessment of military pay and personnel policies in light of the future that the military faces. It identifies a range of interconnected problems and recommends specific improvements.

During the past decade, a range of experts and commissions have criticized the nation's military personnel policies and recommended reform (Chu and White 2001; United States Commission on National Security/21st Century 2001). In vision statements, the military services embrace personnel policy reform as a key component of military transformation. Secretary of Defense Donald Rumsfeld and his civilian staff have called for reshaping incentive structures and altering military career patterns (Jeremiah 2001; Garamone 2003; Crawley 2004).[7] Yet few changes have been made, either because the seriousness of the situation has not been recognized or because institutional and political hurdles stand in the way. But the problems emerging from today's large deployments make the consequences too grave and immediate and the benefits of reform too important to put off any longer.

Reforming entrenched processes and traditions is not easy in any institution. For an institution as conservative as the military it is especially difficult. Pay and pay equity are emotionally sensitive issues for all Americans, making the prospect of change all the more daunting (Rosen 2004). Moreover, numerous powerful claimants have important stakes in the system: members and committees of Congress, civilian leaders in the Pentagon and the White House, military family and retiree associations, veterans organizations, and contracting firms that provide goods and services to military members and families, to name a few (Punaro 2004). In addition, military pay and benefits are often treated as a political football between warring parties or candidates for office.

As in other aspects of military transformation, a comprehensive program of policy experiments, simulations, and related activities would help to fine-tune reform plans and build support for them (Krepinevich 2002). In addition, a collaborative process similar to the one that cemented reforms and resulted in the Goldwater-Nichols Act of 1986 would help to develop a base of support among the stakeholders and push through changes in laws and regulations (Punaro 2004). Reforming the policies related to military pay, benefits, and careers will not be easy, but it will be possible. It will be a crucial component of executive management reform over the next several years.

Notes

The author is grateful to the Smith Richardson Foundation for its sponsorship of the project that led to this chapter, and to the Ford Foundation for supporting the initial work that led up to it.

1. For example, the private sector offers a competitive marketplace for facilities up-keep, accounting, jet engine repair, and pediatric medical care. During the 1990s, the

defense department outsourced some of those activities, and more could still be done. See Williams 2001.

2. Under a legislative proposal of Secretary of Defense Donald Rumsfeld, up to 320,000 military jobs would be turned over to civilians, leaving that many extra military slots for combat or national security jobs. See Lee 2003.

3. The ideas presented here are drawn from the edited volume *Filling the Ranks: Transforming the U.S. Military Personnel System* (Williams, ed. 2004), and from a project titled "Transforming the Rewards for Military Service," sponsored in 2002 through 2004 by the Smith Richardson Foundation (Williams 2004).

4. The DOD reserve components include the Army and Air National Guard and the Army, Naval, Marine Corps, and Air Force Reserves. Of the 1.2 million reservists, about 880,000 are in the Selected Reserve and paid to train or work. The remainder are in the Individual Ready Reserve. This article focuses on people in uniform; it does not examine policies related to defense civilians.

5. In the National Defense Authorization Act for Fiscal Year 2003, Congress authorized a new "critical skills retention bonus" that would allow the services to provide substantial new bonuses to members in critical areas. The new program could greatly improve pay flexibility, but the services have been slow to use it and Congress has been slow to appropriate the money to pay for it. See Abell 2003.

6. See www.arng.army.mil/About_Us.

7. www.defenselink.mil/news/Jul2003/n07182003_200307181.

References

Abell, Charles S. 2003. Principal Deputy Under Secretary of Defense's Statement before the Military Personnel Subcommittee, Senate Armed Services Committee (Personnel and Readiness), March 27.

Asch, Beth J., James R. Hosek, and Craig W. Martin. 2002. *A Look at Cash Compensation for Active-Duty Military Personnel.* Santa Monica, CA: RAND, xv, 8–10.

Asch, Beth J., and John T. Warner. 1996. "Should the Military Retirement System Be Reformed?" In *Professionals on the Front Line: Two Decades of the All-Volunteer Force,* eds. J. Eric Friedland, Curtis Gilroy, Roger D. Little, and W.S. Sellman. Washington, DC: Brassey's, 175–206.

Avant, Deborah. 2002. "Privatizing Military Training: A Challenge to U.S. Army Professionalism?" In *The Future of the Army Profession,* eds. Don M. Snider and Gayle L. Watkins. Boston, MA: McGraw Hill, 179–198.

Chu, David S.C., and John P. White. 2001. "Ensuring Quality People in Defense." In *Keeping the Edge: Managing Defense for the Future,* eds. Ashton B. Carter and John P. White. Cambridge: MIT Press, pp. 203–234.

Congressional Budget Office (CBO). 2003a. "An Analysis of the U.S. Military's Ability to Sustain an Occupation of Iraq." September 3: 3.

———. 2003b. "Budget Options." March: 36.

———. 2004. "Military Compensation: Balancing Cash and Noncash Benefits." Economic and Budget Issue Brief, January 16.

Crawley, Vince. 2004. "Proposals Aim to Extend Senior Officers' Careers." *Navy Times* (March 29): 18.

Cymrot, Donald J., and Michael L. Hansen. 2004. "Overhauling Enlisted Careers and Compensation." In Williams, ed. 2004, 119–44.

Department of Defense (DOD). 2004. "Land Forces Programs." News Briefing Slide, February 2.

Garamone, Jim. 2003. "New Personnel System Needed to Meet New Challenges." American Forces Press Service, Washington, DC, July 18.

Gotz, Glenn A. 2004. "Restructuring Reserve Compensation." In Williams, ed. 2004, 167–88.

Jeremiah, Adm. David (ret.). 2001. "Special DoD News Briefing on Morale and Quality of Life." Department of Defense News Transcript, June 13.

Josar, David. 2003. "Voices on the Ground: Stars and Stripes Surveys Troops on Morale in Iraq." *Stars and Stripes* European edition (October 15).

Krepinevich, Andrew F. 2002. *Lighting the Path Ahead: Field Exercises and Transformation.* Washington, DC: Center for Strategic and Budgetary Assessments (CSBA).

Kutz, Gregory D. 2004. "Financial and Business Management Transformation Hindered by Long-Standing Problems," GAO-04-941T. Testimony before the Subcommittee on Financial Management, the Budget, and International Security, Senate Committee on Governmental Affairs, July 8, 5.

Lee, Christopher. 2003. "Rumsfeld Urges Overhaul of Pentagon Civil Service." *Washington Post* (April 22).

Lewis, Mark R. 2002. "Army Transformation, the Exodus, and the Cycle of Decay." Unpublished article, December 31.

Lien, Diana, and Aline O. Quester. 2004. "Developing Tools to Assess Future Choices." In Williams, ed. 2004, 239–64.

Moniz, Dave. 2003a. "Guard, Reserve Short on Recruits." *USA Today* (June 9).
———. 2003b. "Realities Push Bush Back to U.N." *USA Today* (September 3).

Murray, Carla Tighe. 2004. "Transforming In-Kind Compensation and Benefits." In Williams, ed. 2004, 189–212.

Naval Studies Board. 2002. *The Role of Experimentation in Building Future Naval Forces.* Washington, DC: National Academies Press.

Punaro, Arnold L. 2004. "Leadership and Perseverance: Overcoming the Barriers to Change." In Williams, ed. 2004, 265–88.

Raezer, Joyce Wessel. 2004. "Transforming Support to Military Families and Communities." In Williams, ed. 2004, 213–38.

Rees, Raymond F. 2004. "Prosecuting the Global War on Terrorism." in *2004 National Guard Posture Statement.*

Ricks, Thomas E. 2004. "In Army Survey, Troops in Iraq Report Low Morale." *Washington Post* (March 26), 18.

Rosen, Stephen Peter. 2004. "Implementing Changes in U.S. Military Personnel Policy." In Williams, ed. 2004, 288–302.

Rostker, Bernard. 2004. "Changing the Officer Personnel System." In Williams, ed. 2004, 145–66.

Schmitt, Eric, and Thom Shanker. 2004. "Big Pay Luring Military's Elite to Private Jobs." *New York Times* (March 30), 1.

Schwartz, Nelson D. 2003. "The War Business." *Fortune* (March 3).

Singer, Peter W. 2001. "Corporate Warriors: The Rise of the Privatized Military Industry and Its Ramifications." *International Security* 26 (Winter): 186–220.

Svitak, Amy. 2003. "Rumsfeld Wades into Senate Fray over Army Troop Strength." *National Journal's Congress Daily/AM* (October 17).

Tillson, John C.F. 2001. "It's the Personnel System." In *Spirit, Blood, and Treasure,* ed. Donald E. Vandergriff. Novato, CA: Presidio Press.

Trefry,Richard G. 2003. Interview on May 15. Army Force Management School, Ft. Belvoir, Virginia.

Trowbridge, Gordon, and Jim Tice. 2004. "The Army of One Could Be You: Cuts in Manpower Could Send Airmen, Sailors to the Army." *Air Force Times* 10 (May), 14–15.

2004 National Guard Posture Statement. Available at www.arng.army.mil/publications
  _resources/posture_statements/2004/index.html.
United States Commission on National Security/21st Century. 2001. *Road Map for National Security: Imperative for Change; The Phase III Report,* February 15.
U.S. Department of Defense. 2003. "National Guard and Reserve Mobilized as of September 24, 2003." News Release, September 24.
Williams, Cindy. 2001. "Holding the Line on Infrastructure Spending." In *Holding the Line: U.S. Defense Alternatives for the Early 21st Century,* ed. Cindy Williams. Cambridge, MA: MIT Press, 55–77.
———. 2004. "Transforming the Rewards for Military Service." Project sponsored in 2002–2004 by the Smith Richardson Foundation.
Williams, Cindy, ed. 2004. *Filling the Ranks: Transforming the U.S. Military Personnel System.* Cambridge, MA: MIT Press.
Wood, David. 2003. "Some of Army's Civilian Contractors Are No-Shows in Iraq." *Newhouse News Service* (July 31).

12

Will Homeland Security Transform Intergovernmental Management?

Enid Beaumont and Bruce D. McDowell

The events of September 11, 2001, have been transformative for U.S. government. They have brought us the most significant reorganization of the federal government, both in size and complexity, since the Department of Defense (DOD) was created in 1947. In fact, Don Kettl has suggested that the creation of the new Department of Homeland Security (DHS) continues to be even more difficult than setting up the DOD because of the huge number of diverse functions being combined and the "enormous rush to do it without in any way sacrificing any of the pieces that were already being done" (Kettl 2003a, 3; Kettl 2003b). In the process, significant amounts of money have been added to this newly emphasized high-priority function of government right at a time of growing federal deficits fueled by a lackluster economy and the demands of the Iraq War. To complicate matters, many of the twenty-two agencies consolidated into the new department are administered and managed intergovernmentally.

Intergovernmental Challenges and Opportunities

The events of 9/11 have created a large new set of intergovernmental management challenges and a series of red flags warning of potential dangers for our federal system of government. But this unique situation also provides new opportunities to explore and raises vital questions about how to proceed. These opportunities deserve attention because they are not likely to be equaled for many years in the potential they provide to improve the system. As Paul Light has documented, the nation's domestic agenda has been shrinking and fresh new ideas have been included less often in recent years (Light 1999). The central question in this chapter is whether this transforming event will become an instrument to improve the nation's whole system of intergovernmental management, or whether it will simply generate an isolated adaptation to a unique and separate function of government or, at worst, degrade the whole system.

The current era of government, with its downsizing of the career workforce—which has been going on for some time, as Dan Guttman documents in chapter 10—the economic downturn, the rising federal deficit, revenue gaps in state and local governments, and growing demands for governmental services, gives reason to worry that this may not be a good time to take on new homeland security activities. The natural tendency of such activities to centralize government could exacerbate other broader tendencies already leading in that direction. This is a time for increased vigilance not just against terrorism but also against the erosion of U.S. traditions of cooperative federalism.

A major debate is underway among scholars of U.S. intergovernmental relations and federalism concerning the extent to which the nation has moved from cooperative federalism (i.e., more decentralized government) toward more competitive and coercive models of federalism (more centralized). This is a contest between two different philosophies of government. One philosophy espouses partnerships in which the federal, state, and local governments work together cooperatively and collaboratively to achieve complementary goals. The other philosophy suggests that the various governments should work independently within the framework of the Constitution to secure the greatest competitive advantage for themselves. Neither model, of course, is likely to dominate exclusively, but the balance between them shifts from one era and one program to the next.

Many observers see U.S. federalism today as being farther on the competitive/coercive side of the scale, where it has been moving for the last quarter century, than on the cooperative/collaborative side, where it was for the preceding two or three decades. Further shifts in the future are possible. Intergovernmental systems tend to be fluid because of the complex dynamics within them, so what one sees today is not necessarily what one will get tomorrow.

With a system change as large as the Department of Homeland Security's consolidation of twenty-two agencies, many bringing intergovernmental relations with them, it is unlikely that there would be no change in the intergovernmental system. Time will tell the direction in which the balance will shift between types of federal relations.

The Intergovernmental Setting

Government in the United States is heavily decentralized. Although the federal government's share of revenues collected was still, relative to the state and local shares, the largest in 1992, it has been declining steadily since the early 1950s (Conlan 1988, 308). When federal aid to state and local governments is combined with state and local own-source revenues, the two sectors were roughly equivalent in 1992 (U.S. ACIR 1994, 44). Federal revenues rose until 2000, but then declined while federal grants to state and local governments continued to rise (U.S. OMB 2003, 26, 219). Although comparable state and local revenue figures for later years are not readily available, their growth very likely continued even through the recent recession, because of the anti-deficit requirements under which state and local governments operate.

From an employment standpoint, local governments have roughly as many employees—including military personnel—as state and federal governments combined (U.S. ACIR 1994, 151). Over recent decades, federal employment has remained approximately steady, while states have grown somewhat and local governments have grown even faster (U.S. ACIR 1991, 41). Although the federal government predominates in the military sphere—including the state-run National Guard during times of national emergency, as Cindy Williams discusses in chapter 11—it is the primary player in few other functions besides the Postal Service and space programs. Measured by employment—as an indicator of direct service provision—state and local governments dominate such Homeland Security–related functions as health (80 percent), hospitals (85 percent), police (90 percent), fire protection (100 percent), corrections (97 percent), and judicial/legal (88 percent) (U.S. ACIR 1991, 79).

Intergovernmental Management

Decentralization magnifies the importance of intergovernmental management in the federal system. This is not traditional hierarchical management with clear lines of policymaking, accountability, rewards, and punishments. Rather, it is a specialized and highly nuanced form of management, as Thomas Stanton suggests in chapter 13.

Some evaluators have judged intergovernmental management to be ineffective and inefficient. Yet there is no alternative to trying to make it work better. This reality has been recognized for many years (Wright 1988, 449–51). Deil Wright finds that the three main tools of intergovernmental management are (1) problem solving, (2) coping capabilities, and (3) networking (Wright 1988, 450). Robert Agranoff observes that much of this work takes place at the margins between governments, where clear lines of authority are difficult to discern (Agranoff 1986, 1). Mediation, negotiation, and bargained compromises are essential, along with requirements for managing grants, dealing with multiplying regulations, providing for adequate public involvement, and much more.

Pressman and Wildavsky took a detailed look at what it took to implement a federal economic development grant in Oakland, California, with all the diverse and conflicting policies, requirements, and other complexities attached to it, and were amazed that anything at all could get done under those conditions (Pressman and Wildavsky 1973). Over its thirty-seven-year lifespan (1959 to 1996), the U.S. Advisory Commission on Intergovernmental Relations (ACIR) addressed many of these problems and made hundreds of recommendations to simplify intergovernmental management. Although many ACIR recommendations were implemented, this aspect of U.S. government remains one of the most challenging today.

In the extraordinarily complex 9/11 context, Louise Comfort's research suggests using an "auto-adaptive" model of intergovernmental management requiring increased "public investment in development of an information infrastructure that can support the intense demand for communication, information research, exchange, and feedback" (Comfort 2002, 29). This approach "acknowledges that change in performance needs to occur within organizations, among organizations within a single jurisdiction, and between jurisdictions engaged in response to an extreme event" (Comfort 2002, 49). McDowell lays out the case for this approach in reducing wildfire hazards and responding to wildfire events (McDowell 2003).

Early Dialogues on Homeland Security

This chapter has benefited from transcripts of two symposia on homeland security published by the Rockefeller Institute of Government (Kettl 2003b; Rockefeller Institute 2003a, 2003b) and a third symposium convened at the Brookings Institution (Campbell Public Affairs Institute 2003). The degree to which intergovernmental management permeates homeland security was strikingly revealed by Paul Posner in one of the Rockefeller symposia when he explained how "state and local governments are critical players in each of the six major mission areas defined by [the new department's 2002 strategic] plan" (Posner 2003b, 21–22). These mission areas are:

- *Intelligence and warning* involves getting information from state and local governments and advising them about threats to their communities so they can take real-time action.
- *Border and transportation security* involves numerous state- and locally controlled transportation facilities.
- *Domestic counterterrorism* involves intelligence information from state and local sources, as well as help from them with interdiction and advance warnings.

- *Protecting critical infrastructure* involves numerous types of public works and other state and local assets that are essential to keeping civil society working.
- *Defense against catastrophic threats and bioterrorism* centrally involves the newly appreciated roles of state and local health departments.
- *Emergency preparedness and response* involves the bulk of first responders to an incident who are state and local, plus their emergency management command centers, response plans, training programs, and preparedness exercises.

Politically, these intergovernmental issues have gotten some attention also, especially with respect to emergency preparedness and response. There are about 650,000 local police officers on the job, compared to only about 11,000 FBI agents, and the benefit of a larger number of eyes is obvious. Likewise, the number of federal firefighters (16,000) is miniscule compared to the more than one million local firefighters who are usually much closer at hand when the call for first response comes (NAPA, Panel on Managing Wildland Fire 2003, iii).

But it will take some time and effort, plus more federal resources, to integrate these independent forces. And more federal aid to state and local first responders has become a key political subplot in the Homeland Security drama, which includes not just law enforcement and fire departments but also emergency medical teams, emergency management offices, and public health personnel.

Both houses of Congress held hearings in 2003 on the homeland security challenges facing state and local governments (U.S. House of Representatives 2003; U.S. Senate 2003b,; 2003a). In these hearings, the Government Accountability Office (GAO) set forth options for reducing the fragmentation of the highly fragmented grants for first responders; the National Governors Association made the case for coordinating intergovernmental investments in Homeland Security through comprehensive and integrated state plans developed collaboratively by federal, state, local, and nongovernmental parties; and members of Congress, city and county officials, and state emergency management offices called for increased federal aid, along with better coordination, more flexible administration, and reductions of current unnecessary administrative burdens.

Homeland Security Secretary Tom Ridge—the former Pennsylvania congressman and governor—went out of his way to address audiences of state, local, and regional officials who were key to the success of the new department. Thus, he praised the nation's governors, at their annual conference in August 2003, for being such good partners for his department, reported on how well the new nationwide emergency communications system for maintaining contact with mayors and governors was performing, and reminded them how important it would be for them to finish their new emergency response plans and submit them by the end of the year as the basis for allocating the additional intergovernmental funding he expected Congress to provide for the next fiscal year (Broder and Balz 2003). He also supported a proposal to colocate funding programs for state and local first responders within the office directly responsible to him for maintaining communications and coordination with state and local governments (U.S. Senate 2003b).

Thus, it seems everyone recognizes that homeland security is presenting challenges to the intergovernmental system needing prompt high-level attention. Yet there is concern that the system will not live up to these challenges. There are warnings of potential trouble ahead.

Red Flags

Everything is happening so quickly that there is a risk that needed programs and policies may not be well thought out. Will reorganization pressures drive out sound intergovernmental policy innovation? Will first-responder grants be consolidated, rationalized, and simplified, or just patched together to get by? Will overly classified information and secrecy drive out essential collaborations? What about new federal mandates and preemptions, in the name of national security; will they drive out cooperation and joint intergovernmental action? In these times of scarce funding at all levels of government, will the state and local governments be tempted to subordinate themselves excessively to obtain new Homeland Security money that seems the only source of new, vitally needed federal funding on the horizon?

It is too early to know the answers to these questions. The new department is addressing them, but its record to date has been mixed—as might be expected early in its history (Khademian 2004). The following three sections explore these issues.

Reorganization vs. Sound Policy

The urgency of the DHS mission does not allow for much contemplation, debate, and careful vetting of new ideas. The departmental reorganization, as complex and difficult as it is, went into effect immediately. Existing programs, new programs, and expanded programs must keep functioning. The urgency of the situation means that action will be taken, whether the right answers are known or not.

As the recent experience of establishing the Transportation Security Administration (TSA) showed, tight deadlines can cause problems. Huge numbers of new federal employees were hired in a very short period of time to handle airport security, and the congressional deadline was met—largely by contracting to a private firm to do it. Only now is it revealed that security checks on many of the new hires were not completed before they were hired. There were trade-offs; meeting the deadline led to cutting corners. It is hard to know whether those trade-offs were worth the haste.

Will this also happen with grant reform? No one wants to delay the flow of new money for first responders, so it will likely go out under the old fragmented program structures for some time to come. There is little choice for now. But, will the trade-offs reveal themselves in future years? If crisis is the mother of invention, action must be taken while the crisis is fresh. So, the question may be, how long is the half-life of this homeland security crisis? Maybe it will be renewed by new events, or maybe we will get comfortable with the way we began patching together the existing fragmented system. Only time will tell, as the DHS and its various stakeholders jockey for position in Congress (Khademian 2004).

Paul Posner's GAO testimony on the current state of grants for first responders makes a strong case for considering ways to reduce the existing fragmentation and streamline the system (Posner 2003a). Figure 12.1 shows how complex the current system is—even without including all of the relevant programs. The figure shows six major federal agencies that provide first-responder grants to four different types of local first responders. Very often, these programs work through some combination of state, city, and county governments. Although one might not expect to see a clean chart for such a diverse governmental function, it is natural to wonder whether the structure could be improved—especially since there is plenty of evidence that the existing nature of coordination among federal agencies may leave as much to be desired as the current coordination among local responders.

The GAO testimony also shows how much overlap there is in the purposes that sixteen of the main first-responder grants must serve. As Table 12.1 shows, funding of seven of the sixteen programs can be used for equipment; twelve for training; eight for exercises; and twelve for planning.

This is not a new problem. Grant reform has been a major issue for decades, and proposed solutions are plentiful. Still, as illustrated by this case, progress is slow. Overall, the intergovernmental grant system continues to grow more complex almost every year, despite the best efforts of the reformers.

The president's fiscal year 2007 Budget, sent to Congress on February 6, 2006, again proposes some reforms in the first-responder grants at Homeland Security, which have been under discussion in previous years. These current

Figure 12.1   Web of Federal Homeland Security Grant Programs

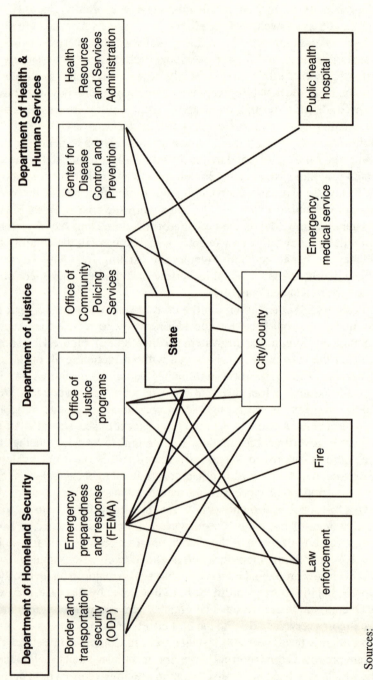

Sources:
GAO Analysis.
U.S. General Accounting Office 2003. *Federal Assistance: Grant System Continues to Be Highly Fragmented,* Congressional Testimony by
Paul L. Posner, managing director, Federal Budget Issues and Intergovernmental Relations, April 29 (GAO-03-718T), Figure 4, p. 9.

Table 12.1

Overlap and Duplication in Homeland Security Grant Program

Grant	Equipment	Training	Exercises	Planning
State Domestic Preparedness Equipment Support Program	•			•
Local Law Enforcement Block Grants Program (LLEBG)	•			
Emergency Management Performance Grants (EMPG)				•
Edward Byrne Memorial State and Local Law Enforcement Assistance (Byrne Formula Grant Program)	•	•	•	•
State Homeland Security Grant Program (SHSGP)	•	•	•	•
State and Local Domestic Preparedness Training Program		•	•	•
State and Local Domestic Preparedness Exercise Support			•	
State and Local Domestic Preparedness Technical Assistance		•		•
First Responder Counter-Terrorism Assistance		•		
State Fire Training Systems Grants (National Fire Academy Training Grants)		•		
Hazardous Materials Assistance Program	•	•		
Assistance to Firefighters Grant			•	•
Edward Byrne Memorial State and Local Law Enforcement Discretionary Grants Program	•		•	•
Public Safety Partnership and Community Policing Grants (COPS)		•	•	•
CDC—Investigations & Technical Assistance				•
Public Health and Social Services Emergency Fund—Bioterrorism Hospital Preparedness Program	•	•		•

Sources:
Catalogue of Federal Domestic Assistance, 2002.
U. S. General Accounting Office. 2003. *Federal Assistance: Grant System Continues to Be Highly Fragmented,* Congressional Testimony by Paul L. Posner, managing director, Federal Budget Issues and Intergovernmental Relations, April 29 (GAO-03-718T), Table 2, p. 13.

proposals would, for example, increase the proportion of funding for state and local governments that would be based on the relative severity of the risks being faced, but they would also make more of the funding discretionary, would reduce the overall amount available, and would remove the requirement that states pass through 80 percent of the money to local governments within sixty days after they receive it. The President's proposal would also change the segmented amounts available for firefighters, law enforcement, emergency management agencies, and infrastructure protection. At the same time, FEMA aid programs would increase overall, and a small new one is proposed for statewide preparedness integration planning. Related proposals for the Department of Justice would cut or eliminate several state and local law enforcement assistance programs, and consolidate thirty-five others. Some of these, or similar, proposals were also considered by Congress for FY 2006, but were not adopted. So, the dialogue continues.

Secrecy vs. Open Government

Homeland security and national security are closely related, if not the same. National security has provided a primary justification for classifying government information as secret, and secrecy interferes with intergovernmental collaboration, cooperation, and joint action. It also creates an obstacle to citizen action and support of governmental objectives.

There is likely to be more secrecy in the Department of Homeland Security than in other intergovernmental programs, and greater contact between officials at all levels of government who are used to operating in the open, and those—on the other hand—who regularly operate in secrecy. This culture clash is likely to get worse before it gets better. That may be the nature of this function of government. Then again, it may not be (Blanton 2003).

Tom Blanton, director of the National Security Archive at George Washington University, commenting on how this issue is rolling out in the United States compared to other countries, suggests a new way of thinking about security—"openness is security," he says. He explains:

> The current climate is one of information phobia. But information is security and openness is our best defense. Americans . . . need to know when airport security is lethally porous. They need to know if and when and where we are vulnerable to biological or nuclear attack. Only when the public is fully informed about such vulnerabilities will there be sufficient pressure to move our leaders to act. . . .
>
> Secrecy is the enemy of efficiency, as well. . . . Just listen to the testimony before Congress from . . . Mayor Rudy Giuliani himself, complaining

that the big problem is the federal government does not share information with the locals. . . .

Openness empowers citizens, weeds out the worst policy proposals, ensures the most efficient flow of information to all levels of law enforcement, makes a little more honest the despots who are our temporary allies against terrorism. Openness keeps our means more consistent with our ends. . . .

We need to place openness where it belongs, not only at the center of our values, but also at the center of our strategy for security. (Blanton 2003, 62–64)

Intergovernmental Shift of Power to the Center

The power to make decisions continues to move toward Washington and away from state and local governments. In spite of the rhetoric about moving power away from Washington, three strong forces are interacting to make the continued movement of power toward the center a reality. They are federal mandates, federal preemption, and the scarcity of governmental funds. Homeland security is accentuating these trends because homeland security responsibilities must be shared so widely within the intergovernmental system. Even some of the formerly most independent state and local activities, such as police and fire protection, must now respond to increasing numbers of direct orders from Washington, particularly when terrorism is involved.

Homeland security is also placing additional fiscal demands on the federal, state, and local governments. As security needs have increased, they have absorbed funds from other functions of government (Krane 2003, 43–44) even when the extant political philosophy is calling for many governments, not just the federal government, to significantly reduce their expenditures (Krane 2003, 32–33). Although some observers have criticized state governments for having been "spendthrifts" in the roaring nineties (Krane 2003, 27–34), changes in the federal tax system, and the serious decline in the value of stocks and bonds, have profoundly dampened state revenues. Even the best efforts of some states to offset this decline by increasing taxes have not been able to stop the short-term decline (Krane 2003, 24). Because the federal government has faced rapidly rising deficits over the last several years (U.S. OMB 2003, 21–22), it is trimming aid to state and local governments in many programs. In the case of highways and transit, to cite just one current example, the authorization ran out long ago and these vital surface transportation programs have been continuing under a series of short-term extensions (Orski 2004) even as they have been absorbing new demands for security on bridges, at borders, and in trucks and transit systems.

These factors together mean that almost all states are showing large gaps between expenses and revenues at the same time that they are being asked to pay more for homeland security out of their own pockets, as, for example, when un-reimbursed police overtime is triggered by a federal decision to declare a Code Orange threat level. With the states desperate to get their expected shares of shrinking federal funds, the financial dialogue has become one of pleading by states for more support from the federal government, accompanied by less concern for maintaining their independent roles in the system. It is difficult to know just how much money state and local governments will need for homeland security and all the other functions of government where federal requirements are raising performance standards, such as education, prisons, and health care, and how much federal control they will accept in return for increased federal funding. Because states are required by their constitutions to balance their budgets, they have little choice other than to make major cost reductions in many programs.

State independence is also threatened by the continued addition of regulations in new and old intergovernmental programs. The federal government continues to press for greater regulatory compliance and fiscal control. Congress continues to mandate activities for states, which then place more requirements on their local governments.

Since the grant system continues to favor categorical grants, a high proportion of federal aid offers limited flexibility for state and local governments. This requires states to administer the federal programs despite inadequate funding, making up the difference themselves to cover federal regulatory requirements.

In the last two years, the federal government has placed many new responsibilities on states and localities. There are new educational standards, new requirements to change voting systems, and new environmental protection standards. These added rules require significant new efforts, even while national government calls for more limited government.

These issues arise in the context of the possible change in the definition of federalism coming from the U.S. Supreme Court (Pickerill and Clayton 2004). After a series of decisions supporting states in the division of power with the federal government, a recent ruling that allows states to be sued about family emergencies might indicate that the Supreme Court now seeks to strengthen federal power. This would be consistent with the Court's view of preemption, under which it tends to shift the balance from the state governments toward the federal government. A keen observer of federal preemption has documented the "sharply increased use of preemption powers by Congress since 1965," including "21 new ones between 2000 and 2004" (Zimmerman 2004, 17, 6). Looking to the future, Zimmerman sees the states' regulatory powers increasingly displaced by congressional action that finances national policies "by imposing burdensome mandates and restraints on subnational governments" (Zimmerman 2004, 21).

The demands of homeland security, the government-wide fiscal crises, and the continued regulation of states through grant conditions, Supreme Court rulings, unfunded federal mandates, and congressional preemptions, all combine to suggest a significant movement of power toward the federal government and away from states. Federal regulation of state and local governments is not new, of course.[1] Most observers conclude that regulatory federalism is gaining momentum and taking new forms (May 2002), often at the expense of the former emphasis on grants and technical assistance.

Surveying this scene, Paul Posner reluctantly joins many other observers in predicting that homeland security will push our nation away from the traditional model of cooperative federalism and toward coercive federalism (Posner 2003b, 28–29). As they resist this greater degree of federal control, many state and local officials may grasp for a middle ground that Posner calls "protective federalism." This could take the form of increased federal funding combined with national performance standards (Posner 2003b, 29–30). Posner describes the motives of these state and local officials as a desire to immunize and indemnify themselves from political risk. By joining networks, including regions, and meeting federal standards, they would try to avoid unstable partners who might increase their liabilities for disasters and "shift blame before the crisis occurs." They might even see the value of:

> Seeking cover in performance standards and measures . . . relying on professionals to develop an expert consensus on how much protection is sufficient, on what kinds of measures define best practices, and on what kinds of reports can best showcase for the public the level of protections that local or state governments are committed to achieving. Ideally, standards and measures and perhaps even a readiness index of sorts would be a far better way of defining accountability and preparedness than the presence or absence of a terrorist event. (Posner 2003a)

New Opportunities

What is most new about homeland security is the urgency and seriousness it brings to a host of old intergovernmental issues. Issues of fragmentation and administrative burdens in the federal grant system have existed for decades (Beam and Conlan 2002; Glendening and Reeves 1984; Walker 1995; Wright and White 1984). So too have issues of growing federal mandates and preemption (Conlan 1998; Zimmerman 2004). Even the issue of inadequate communications between different first-responder teams that are working on the same event is decades old. The nation did not learn about these issues on September 11, 2001, or after Hurricane Katrina. What it learned then was how little had been done to solve these long-recognized problems.

Homeland security provides a new opportunity now to revisit these long-standing issues. Maybe they can be fixed this time, or maybe not. The speakers at the second Rockefeller symposium agreed that coordinating these programs, and the diverse professional disciplines and political players involved, would require many people to perform "unnatural acts," and it is not likely to happen without significant federal financial incentives (Rockefeller Institute 2003a, 11–12, 35). As noted, with rising federal deficits, this is not the best time for incentives to appear.

If the intergovernmental relationship can be structured correctly, however, the issue of homeland security may transform the entire intergovernmental management system by example. If not, the nation may end up merely with some essential quick fixes that will allow the DHS to get by with a fragmented and burdensome system similar to most other federal-aid programs.

What Should We Try?

Don Kettl's conclusion about these new intergovernmental challenges being brought to a head by homeland security is correct. In his words, "Homeland security is primarily an issue of coordination, but coordination is fundamentally a problem in intergovernmental relations and federalism" (Kettl 2003b, 15). He suggests the following four-point strategy, specifically tuned to the current challenge (Kettl 2003b, 12–15):

- *Create a minimum level of protection* as a baseline for what the public can expect.
- *Strengthen local coordination* with adequate incentives, an important state role, and probably some state and regional coordinating bodies.
- *Modify systems for funding* to channel federal aid through the states to local responders, using national minimum standards, best practices, and considerable flexibility for adjusting to unique circumstances.
- *Test new systems* to make sure they will work well when a crisis occurs.

This strategy is consistent with what many other scholars have suggested. However, recent studies by the National Academy of Public Administration suggest some additional thoughts. These studies explore some of the fundamental dynamics that occur when diverse groups work together successfully.

They involve trust building, special boundary-crossing skills, flexible funding authorizations and practices, and the all-hazards approach that the Federal Emergency Management Agency champions. These four dynamics will be essential for success.

Trust Building

Trust building is different from capacity building. It deals more with cultural understanding than with hard skills and formal organizations. Michael Maccoby discusses cultural issues in chapter 9. The different levels of government and the different professional disciplines involved in the DHS possess different ways of thinking about the same issues. Officials from these different organizations and disciplines need to interact with each other, working closely together for some time to begin to understand each other and to be able to communicate with each other effectively (Bardach 1998, 252–68). This is team building in a certain sense, but perhaps in a more diverse setting than normally occurs. The secrecy versus open government discussion above illustrates one of the more extreme aspects of this task (Blanton 2003; NAPA, Panel on Disaster Information 1999). The difference in approaches known as the command-and-control and the boundary-crosser methods of problem solving illustrate another (Peirce and Johnson 1997). The command-and-control approach is well understood. By contrast, people with boundary-crossing skills are experts in getting others with diverse backgrounds, interests, and jurisdictional responsibilities to work together toward common purposes. These people know how to run effective meetings, nurture policy boards and many other types of groups, hold effective consultations (see NAPA, Panel on Rural Transportation Consultation 2000), develop win-win scenarios, facilitate difficult discussions, present facts persuasively to diverse parties, and develop consensus under difficult circumstances. These command-and-control and boundary-crossing approaches are divergent philosophically; bringing them together on the same team will present a significant challenge, but it needs to be done (Bardach 1998, 130–43). If not bridged, these differences will fester to the detriment of the whole enterprise. This problem is identified in the academy's wildfire studies, where the cultural differences between different federal agencies have slowed progress in implementing established interagency policies (NAPA, Panel on Managing Wildland Fire 2001).

Skills

Building new coordination skills is more similar to traditional capacity building than trust building, but it also needs special attention in two respects for

Box 12.1

Six Principles of Effective Consultation

1. Inclusive and well-known process
2. Stakeholder assistance provided
3. Two-way information exchange
4. Timely access to decision makers and timely feedback to stakeholders
5. Satisfaction with the process
6. Influence on results

homeland security. One is the need to create a large supply of a highly specialized skill that is now in very short supply. This skill is "boundary crossing," a name borrowed from a recent book of that title (Peirce and Johnson 1997).

Second is the need for people who can guide effective consultations. A recent NAPA panel developed the six principles of effective consultation summarized in Box 12.1. These principles can be used here and in many other program fields to enhance the collaborative process. Although these principles may appear to be little more than common sense, they are profoundly important to success, yet are very commonly ignored or violated.

Consultation skills are very different from those that most program people possess, but they often are not recognized as separate skills. For example, NAPA's wildfire study recently explained these skills, and the need for them that NAPA research identified unmistakably, to the federal land management agencies. In response, the agencies told NAPA that they don't need these skills because "they collaborate every day." When NAPA asked to see the collaborative products the agencies produced, it was revealed that the agencies and NAPA were talking about completely different levels of collaboration.

Most federal managers are ill equipped to participate in collaborative processes. They are used to being in charge rather than being a member of an intergovernmental group that is developing a group product, such as a homeland security strategy that integrates federal, state, local, and nongovernmental elements. NAPA's report *Principles for Federal Managers of Community-Based Programs* is designed to help federal managers become more productive members of collaborative processes than they usually are. This is a greatly needed skill that rests on a very different way of thinking than the usual regulatory/compliance mind-set that federal officials too often take into the field with them (NAPA, Panel on Community-Based Programs 1997a).

In addition to training specialists with these skills, all people working on collaborative programs should be taught the basic partnering concepts, and this is especially true of federal managers who may be in a position to make progress more difficult if they do not understand how to apply them. In local governments, collaborative approaches are becoming firmly established out of necessity (Agranoff and McGuire 2003), and also because they are often required and financed by such federal programs as transportation, economic development, and disaster hazard mitigation. However, NAPA research and other sources indicate that this approach has not yet penetrated the federal bureaucracy to nearly the same extent (NAPA 2004; U.S. ACIR 1995b). It does little good for some of the intergovernmental partners to be collaborative if the others are not.

Flexible Funding Practices

The number and breadth of grants for functions related to homeland security are such that program consolidations, desirable as they may be, can address only a small part of the fragmentation problem. For example, the last tally of federal grant programs for state and local governments found 11 for national defense, 106 for public health, and 24 for law enforcement (U.S. ACIR 1995a). Finding ways to use grants together helps to develop the needed flexibility to achieve intergovernmental goals in diverse situations. Valuable lessons for homeland security can be found in human services integration experiences (Ragan 2003) and flexible-funding provisions in the federal-aid highway and transit programs (Edner and McDowell 2002). Long years of experience are available to draw upon from both programs, and ACIR thoroughly reviewed the experience with many of these options in the mid-1970s (U.S. ACIR 1977). A thorough update of this work is long overdue.

Taking an All-Hazards Approach

First responders, in particular, need to stay active and well practiced to maintain their qualifications and certifications. The best way to do that is to be involved in whatever disasters and emergency incidents come their way. The same is true for planning and mitigating hazards. There is a significant danger of allowing readiness to decline and funding to slip away when incidents are not frequent enough to be readily remembered.

Taking an all-hazards approach to preparedness and mitigation programs provides a way of avoiding this danger. NAPA found this to be true for seismic safety planning in areas of the nation where earthquake dangers are very serious but not frequent. Emergency managers in those areas were anxious to merge their earthquake preparedness programs with those of other hazards in order to sustain them (NAPA, Panel on Seismic Safety 1997). If the nation is fortunate, or especially effective in deterring terrorism, first respond-ers may have the same problem as the earthquake people, who must remain vigilant enough over the long period of time between significant events to be prepared for "the big one."

Conclusion

Homeland security will test the intergovernmental system as no other pro-gram has tested it before. Although there are well over six hundred federal grants-in-aid programs for a wide variety of purposes (U.S. ACIR 1995a), homeland security is arguably broader in scope and depth than any other program created so far. Furthermore, the homeland security function is inherently intergovernmental. No level of government can possibly ac-complish by itself the myriad of tasks that will be required, and no single jurisdiction will have enough resources to accomplish its own responsi-bilities by itself. A "national" approach will be needed, not just a federal government approach (Krane 2002, 7). Whether the current fragmented system will be able to coordinate sufficiently to provide an acceptable level of protection is an unanswered question. All of the intergovernmen-tal partners will need to work hard for many years to get it right. No easy solution is likely to emerge suddenly from the monumental tugs and pulls in the system.

Some observers have already suggested that regional cooperation will be an essential element of homeland security. Regions often cross boundaries between states and localities. Since the funds from the federal government will be sent through the states to localities, can the grant mechanisms be sensitive enough to work well back and forth across these challenging bound-aries? Since the nation consists of an intricately balanced system of 19,000 municipalities, 3,000 counties, and altogether 87,500 governmental units including school and special districts, how will the new homeland security responsibilities be accounted for within the existing governmental system (U.S. Bureau of the Census 1997, Tables 496 and 497)?

The past has shown that success in regional efforts takes considerable time and energy (So, Hand, and McDowell 1986). The Metropolitan Wash-ington Council of Governments recently completed an unprecedented effort to put in place for the nation's capital a regional communication and coordi-nation process following the 9/11 attack on the Pentagon. Because of its location, this effort had significant support from the federal government (Robertson 2003). The New Orleans, Seattle, and Denver areas have taken similar steps (Krane 2002, 8). Will comparable determination and support for regional cooperation be replicated across the entire nation?

Kettl pointed out that "the work of homeland security necessarily involves multiple federal agencies, complex partnerships with state and local governments, and intricate ties between the public and nongovernmental sectors" (Kettl undated, 4). This must be coupled with the long-standing reality that federal preparedness programs are duplicative, confusing, and poorly focused. Fulfilling the hope that creating the Department of Homeland Security can fix these problems will take a long time.

In addition, the role of the states in homeland security remains unclear. Can states determine which areas are most in need? What will they do to cross-jurisdictional boundaries, including state lines, when and where needed? Should and can the federal government supervise the work of the local governments directly? All of these issues are part of the complex mosaic of the U.S. federal system.

These trends suggest that matters increasingly may be determined by the federal government rather than by states or localities—simply to cut through the delays and uncertainties inherent in developing intergovernmental consensus. Therefore, if left to its own proclivities, homeland security is likely to have a significant centralizing influence in the future. There will be tension between state and local governments to achieve greater independence, and this too will lead to strengthening of the federal government. The United States is so large and has so many governments that the need for the central government to exercise strong leadership in the critical area of homeland security is undeniable. Nevertheless, that leadership can endanger open and responsive governance if it is not consultative and collaborative. All of the governmental partners will need to be extraordinarily vigilant as this new program unfolds to make sure that its centralizing tendencies do not overrun and dampen the vitality and essential capabilities that come with the dispersed responsibilities in our federal system of government.

Note

1. ACIR catalogued its many forms in 1984, and updated this work in 1993 (U.S. ACIR 1993).

References

Agranoff, Robert. 1986. *Intergovernmental Management: Human Services Problem Solving in Six Metropolitan Areas*. Albany: State University of New York Press.

Agranoff, Robert, and Michael McGuire. 2003. *Collaborative Public Management: New Strategies for Local Government*. Washington, DC: Georgetown University.

Bardach, Eugene. 1998. *Getting Agencies to Work Together: The Practice and Theory of Managerial Craftsmanship*. Washington, DC: Brookings Institution Press.

Beam, David R., and Timothy J. Conlan. 2002. "Grants." In *The Tools of Government: A Guide to the New Governance*, ed. Lester M. Salamon, 340–80. New York: Oxford.

Blanton, Thomas F. 2003. "National Security and Open Government in the United States." In *National Security and Open Government*, 31–71. Syracuse, NY: Campbell Public Affairs Institute, The Maxwell School of Syracuse University.

Brinkley, Joel. 2004. "Out of Spotlight, Bush Overhauls U.S. Regulations." *New York Times* (August 14), A1.

Broder, David S., and Dan Balz. 2003. "Ridge Tells Governors They Passed First Test but Must Do More." *Washington Post* (August 19), A05.

Campbell Public Affairs Institute, The Maxwell School of Syracuse University. 2003. *National Security and Open Government: Striking the Right Balance.* Syracuse, NY.

Comfort, Louise K. 2002. "Managing Intergovernmental Reponses to Terrorism and Other Extreme Events." *Publius: The Journal of Federalism* 32 (Fall): 29–49.

Conlan, Timothy. 1998. *From New Federalism to Devolution: Twenty-Five Years of Intergovernmental Reform.* Washington, DC: Brookings Institution Press.

Edner, Sheldon, and Bruce D. McDowell. 2002. "Surface-Transportation Funding in a New Century: Assessing One Slice of the Federal Marble Cake." *Publius: The Journal of Federalism* 32 (Winter): 7–24.

Glendening, Parris N., and Mavis Mann Reeves. 1984. *Pragmatic Federalism: An Intergovernmental View of American Government*, 2d ed. Pacific Palisades, CA: Palisades.

Kettl, Donald. 2003a. "Contingent Coordination: Practical and Theoretical Puzzles for Homeland Security." *American Review of Public Administration* 33 (September): 253–77.

———. 2003b. "Speakers Remarks." In Rockefeller Institute of Government 2003a.

———. Undated brochure. "Promoting State and Local Government Performance for Homeland Security." Project on Federalism and Homeland Security. Washington, DC: The Century Foundation.

Khademian, Anne M. 2004. "Strengthening State and Local Terrorism Prevention and Response." In *The Department of Homeland Security's First Year: A Report Card.* New York: The Century Foundation.

Kinghorn, C. Morgan, president, National Academy of Public Administration. 2004. Testimony before the Subcommittee on Energy Policy, Natural Resources and Regulatory Affairs and the Subcommittee on National Security, Emerging Threats and International Relations; Committee on Government Reform; U.S. House of Representatives, March 24.

Krane, Dale. 2002. "The State of American Federalism, 2001–2002: Resilience in Response to Crisis." *Publius: The Journal of Federalism* 32 (Fall): 1–28.

———. 2003. "The State of American Federalism, 2002–2003: Division Replaces Unity." *Publius: The Journal of Federalism* 33 (Summer): 1–44.

Light, Paul C. 1999. *The President's Agenda: Domestic Policy Choice from Kennedy to Clinton*, 3d ed. Baltimore, MD: Johns Hopkins University Press.

May, Peter J. 2002. "Social Regulation." In *The Tools of Government: A Guide to the New Governance*, ed. Lester M. Salamon, 117–55. New York: Oxford University Press.

McDowell, Bruce D. 2003. "Wildfires Create New Intergovernmental Challenges." *Publius: The Journal of Federalism* 33(3): 45–61.

National Academy of Public Administration (NAPA). 2004. *Advancing the Management of Homeland Security: Managing Intergovernmental Relations for Homeland Security.* Washington, DC.

National Academy of Public Administration, Panel on Community-Based Programs. 1993. *Coping with Catastrophe: Building an Emergency Management System to Meet People's Needs in Natural and Manmade Disaster.* Washington, DC.

———. 1997a. *Principles for Federal Managers of Community-Based Programs.* Washington, DC.

————. 1997b. *The Role of the National Guard in Emergency Preparedness and Response*. Washington, DC.

National Academy of Public Administration, Panel on Disaster Information. 1999. *Legal Limits on Access to and Disclosure of Disaster Information: Summary Report*. Washington, DC.

National Academy of Public Administration, Panel on Managing Wildland Fire. 2001. *Managing Wildland Fire: Enhancing Capacity to Implement the Federal Interagency Policy*. Washington, DC.

————. 2003. *Containing Wildland Fire Costs: Utilizing Local Firefighting Forces*. Washington, DC.

National Academy of Public Administration, Panel on Rural Transportation Consultation. 2000. *Rural Transportation Consultation Processes*. Washington, DC.

National Academy of Public Administration, Panel on Seismic Safety. 1997. *Reducing Seismic Risks in Existing Buildings*. Washington, DC.

Orski, C. Kenneth. 2004. "The Impasse Continues." *An Innovative Briefs Advisory* (July 23). www.innobriefs.com.

Peirce, Neil, and Curtis Johnson. 1997. *Boundary Crossers: Community Leadership for a Global Age*. College Park, MD: The Academy of Leadership.

Pickerill, J. Mitchell, and Cornell W. Clayton. 2004. "The Rehnquist Court and the Political Dynamics of Federalism." *Perspectives in Politics* 2 (June): 233–48.

Posner, Paul, managing director, Federal Budget Issues and Intergovernmental Relations, U.S. General Accounting Office. 2003a. Congressional Testimony before the Subcommittee on Technology, Information Policy, Intergovernmental Relations and the Census; Committee on Government Reform; U.S. House of Representatives, April 29. In U.S. General Accounting Office, *Federal Assistance: Grant System Continues to be Highly Fragmented* (GAO-03-718T). Washington, DC.

————. 2003b. "Speaker's Remarks." In *The Role of "Home" in Homeland Security: The Federalism Challenge: The Challenge for State and Local Government*, Symposium Series No. 2, 16–30, March 24. Albany, NY: The Rockefeller Institute of Government.

Pressman, Jeffrey L., and Aaron Wildavsky. 1973. *Implementation: How Great Expectations in Washington Are Dashed in Oakland; Or, Why It's Amazing that Federal Programs Work at All*. Berkeley: University of California Press.

Ragan, Mark. 2003. *Building Better Human Service Systems: Integrating Services for Income Support and Related Programs*. Albany, NY: The Rockefeller Institute of Government.

Robertson, David J. 2003. "Securing the Homeland across Jurisdictional Boundaries." *Public Manager* (Spring): 31–33.

Rockefeller Institute of Government. 2003a. *The Role of "Home" in Homeland Security: The Federalism Challenge: The Challenge for State and Local Government*, Symposium Series No. 2, March 24. Albany, NY.

————. 2003b. *The Role of "Home" in Homeland Security: The Prevention and Detection of Terrorist Attacks: The Challenge for State and Local Government*, Symposium Series No. 3, June 12. Albany, NY.

Seidman, Harold. 1998. *Politics, Position, and Power*. New York: Oxford.

So, Frank S., Irving Hand, and Bruce D. McDowell, eds. 1986. *The Practice of State and Regional Planning*. Chicago, IL: American Planning Association.

U.S. Advisory Commission on Intergovernmental Relations (ACIR). 1977. *Improving Federal Grants Management*. Washington, DC: U.S. Advisory Commission on Intergovernmental Relations.

————. 1991. *The Changing Public Sector: Shifts in Governmental Spending and Employment*. Washington, DC: U.S. Advisory Commission on Intergovernmental Relations.

————. 1993. *Federal Regulation of State and Local Governments: The Mixed Record of the 1980s*. Washington, DC: U.S. Advisory Commission on Intergovernmental Relations.

————. 1994. *Significant Features of Fiscal Federalism: Volume 2, Revenues and Expenditures*. Washington, DC: U.S. Advisory Commission on Intergovernmental Relations.

————. 1995a. *Characteristics of Federal Grant-in-Aid Programs to State and Local Governments; Grants Funded FY 1995*. Washington, DC: U.S. Advisory Commission on Intergovernmental Relations.

————. 1995b. *MPO Capacity: Improving the Capacity of Metropolitan Planning Organizations to Help Implement National Planning Policies*. Washington, DC: U.S. Advisory Commission on Intergovernmental Relations.

U.S. Bureau of the Census. 1997. *1997 Census of Governments*. Tables 496 and 497. Washington, DC: U.S. Bureau of the Census.

U.S. House of Representatives. 2003. "Federal Grants Management: A Progress Report on Streamlining and Simplifying the Federal Grants Process." Hearing before the Subcommittee on Technology, Information Policy, Intergovernmental Relations, and the Census; Committee on Government Reform, April 29.

U.S. Office of Management and Budget (OMB). 2003. *Fiscal Year 2004 Budget of the U.S. Government: Historical Tables*. Washington, DC: U.S. Government Printing Office.

U.S. Senate. 2003a. "Investing in Homeland Security: Challenges Facing State and Local Governments." Hearing before the Committee on Governmental Affairs, May 15.

————. 2003b. "Investing in Homeland Security: Streamlining and Enhancing Homeland Security Grant Programs." Hearing before the Committee on Governmental Affairs, May 1.

Walker, David B. 1995. *The Rebirth of Federalism: Slouching Toward Washington*. Chatham, NJ: Chatham House.

Wright, Deil S. 1988. *Understanding Intergovernmental Relations*, 3d ed. Belmont, CA: Wadsworth.

Wright, Deil S., ed., with Harvey L. White. 1984. *Federalism and Intergovernmental Relations*. Washington, DC: American Society for Public Administration.

Zimmerman, Joseph F. 2004. "Congressional Preemption: Regulatory Federalism." Paper presented at the annual conference of the American Political Science Association, Chicago, IL, September 4.

13

Improving Federal Relations with States, Localities, and Private Organizations on Matters of Homeland Security

The Stakeholder Council Model

Thomas H. Stanton

The challenge of homeland security has brought to the fore the observation of Lester Salamon that the administration of government services is moving from a hierarchical structure to the management of organizational networks (Salamon 2002). Homeland security requires (1) detection of potential threats, (2) effective incident response, and (3) improvement of systems and infrastructure to prevent or mitigate hostile acts. In each of these areas, the federal government must act through what Salamon has called third-party government, including state and local governments and private actors. Even in areas where a hierarchical model of governance may be called for, such as security of air travel, "high-reliability organizations depend on effective management of their horizontal boundaries with other organizations" (Fredrickson and LaPorte 2002).

Third-party government is significant in all aspects of administering homeland security: detection, response, and prevention. Detection of potential threats involves (besides international intelligence work) state, local, or private policing of critical facilities and infrastructure; monitoring of borders; and monitoring of public health, for example. Effective incident response depends on local police and firefighters and public health officials. Improvement of systems and infrastructure depends on coordination of activities of numerous state or local government organizations and private parties.

It is not comforting that, as Salamon and others point out, third-party government poses major management challenges whose contours are not completely understood either by practitioners or by academics in the field of public administration (Fredrickson and LaPorte 2002, 41). As Harold Seidman has observed:

> The principles developed by the President's Committee on Administrative Management and the first Hoover Commission which call for straight lines of authority from the President down through department heads with no entity exercising power independent of its superior are not adapted to current circumstance. Straight lines of authority and accountability cannot be established in what has become in major degree a non-hierarchical system. Federal agencies now rely for service delivery on third parties who are not legally responsible to the President and subject to his direction. Federal powers are limited to those agreed upon and specified in grants and contracts. (Seidman 2004)

The problem is more than one of power and control. Third-party government also involves information asymmetries: The states, localities, and private parties that must address homeland security and other matters are often closer to events and may have a much more sophisticated understanding of many critical facts that the federal government must know to do its job. Enid Beaumont and Bruce McDowell document this point for states and localities in chapter 12.

This chapter tries to begin to fill the conceptual gap highlighted by Seidman and Salamon. The hierarchical model of federal administration involves the imposition of rules, often based on limited consultation with the affected parties. This is unlikely to be effective in dealing with complex problems, those of homeland security, that call for management of organizational networks. There are too many stakeholder positions and countervailing values for government or private parties to succeed with a purely mandatory approach to many important issues (O'Harrow Jr. 2003). The "Stakeholder Council Model,"[1] an alternative approach for federal interaction with states, localities, and private parties, provides a forum and a process for bringing different stakeholders together to develop solutions in defined areas of federal concern.

The chapter then shows how the Stakeholder Council Model might be applied to an important and complex area of homeland security, the development of comprehensive identity management systems. As proposed here, the Stakeholder Council Model seeks to combine the strengths of the traditional hierarchical model of public administration, that is, application of resources in a timely manner to the achievement of a specified goal, with those of the new organizational network model, that is, the gaining of essential information about a problem and devising of a solution that incorporates the strengths, needs, and incentives of multiple third parties. Finally, the appendix to this chapter, written by Dwight Ink, provides some useful insights about coordination, many of which relate well to the principles of the Stakeholder Council Model.

Two important questions that this chapter raises, and that need to be addressed in the future both conceptually and in pilot programs, are (1) where the Stakeholder Council Model is most applicable and (2) under what conditions. For the federal government, Harold Seidman cautions that "Agencies are most likely to collaborate and network when they are in agreement on common objectives, operate under the same laws and regulations, and do not compete for scarce resources" (Seidman 2004).

For collaboration by stakeholders that include both agencies and non-agencies of all levels of government, the Stakeholder Council Model seems applicable when common goals have been defined but divergent approaches must be reconciled. The issue of interoperability of systems, discussed below with respect to identity management, seems particularly suited to the model. Especially at early stages of development when no one stakeholder has developed the ideal system, interoperability offers potentially fruitful collaboration because of benefits that can flow from development of systems that interact across federal, state, and local agencies, and private organizations.

Experience suggests some useful preconditions for effective management of the Stakeholder Council Model. First, the alternative to collaboration needs to be visibly worse from the perspective of the major participants than collaboration. Second, there needs to be a strong advocate of collaboration in a key policy position—at the Office of Management and Budget (OMB), for example—who has the ability to bring the parties to the table and keep them there. The process may work well if the parties are motivated in the context of a powerful champion who both (1) has the authority to impose an unpleasant alternative and (2) is willing to forego that imposition on the condition that the parties themselves devise a superior outcome in a reasonable period of time. Third, the process requires that leaders and key participants have leadership skills, vision, and willingness to compromise in their greater self-interest.

The author wishes to acknowledge the value of the insights gained from a symposium on "Developing and Implementing Comprehensive Identity Management Systems," held at the Johns Hopkins University Center for the Study of American Government on December 10, 2002. That meeting was cosponsored by the Johns Hopkins Center, the General Services Administration (GSA), the National Association of Clearinghouse Administrators (NACHA), and the Maximus Corporation. Over two dozen people, including representatives from several federal agencies; state and local governments; the government of Canada; parts of the private sector such as transportation, credit cards, and food retailing; academia; advocacy groups; consortia with an interest in identity management; and vendors of technology systems and consulting systems relating to identity management, participated on an off-the-record basis. The dynamics of that symposium, and the writing of the subsequent report, involving stakeholders from many perspectives, provided an opportunity to understand how a more extended Stakeholder Council approach might help to fashion federal policies with respect to aspects of homeland security that are based on a more sophisticated comprehension of the underlying issues than would be possible through a more directive hierarchical approach.

The Stakeholder Council Model

The Stakeholder Council Model is based on years of experience with standards-setting groups in many sectors of the economy. The particular antecedent of most relevance is the NACHA Electronic Benefits Transfer (EBT) Council. The EBT Council began in September 1995 as an organization composed of federal agencies, states, merchants, payments networks, financial institutions, and other EBT service providers, including consultants and processors. The federal government, through the Office of Management and Budget, encouraged these stakeholders to meet in a deliberative group to develop operating rules for the electronic delivery of government benefits, including food stamp and cash benefits. Instead of giving beneficiaries food stamp coupons or paper checks, state governments provide them with a debit-type card that contains the value of their food stamp or cash benefits and that can be used at retailers and in ATMs.

The history of the EBT Council is instructive. In the 1980s, each state with an EBT system operated it on a proprietary basis so that one state's system would not accept another state's EBT cards. Although paper food stamps, for example, were valid in any state in the union, the lack of interoperability of EBT systems meant that recipients lost portability of their benefits. The states, food retailers, and the federal Office of Management and Budget sought a means of promoting interoperability among state EBT systems. It is useful to note that leadership from the states had laid the groundwork for federal involvement.

The EBT Council obtained a common mark that appears on participating state cards and developed operating rules and agreements as to rights, responsibilities, and liability to govern transactions using the EBT card. In 2005 forty-eight states offered statewide EBT programs and thirty-six of those used the rules developed by the EBT Council. As the use of the EBT Council's operating rules has expanded, states are adding to the functions that are served through their EBT card systems, including payments for Temporary Assistance for Needy Families (TANF), Medicaid, and child care (Sims undated). The U.S. Department of Agriculture (USDA) announced in 2004 that the delivery of food stamps has now moved completely to electronic form. USDA is seeking to rename the program because the term "food stamps" has become an anachronism (Pear 2004).

To achieve interoperability is not easy. The EBT Council needed to adopt technical standards that allow for a rapid response when an EBT card is presented at a retailer or an ATM. Also, operating guidelines were required that specify how the receiving retailer is to use the card, and what to do in special circumstances such as if the system goes down. Finally, the EBT Council needed to develop a set of legal operating rules that set forth the liability of the parties issuing, using, and receiving the EBT card, that govern the operating standards, and that prescribe the rules for dispute resolution. Fortunately, the EBT Council was able to acquire an initial set of operating rules and subsequently purchased a national service mark to help speed its work.

One participant in the Johns Hopkins symposium described the federal government's perspective on the EBT Council as follows:

> [L]et me describe a little bit the federal government's thinking on EBT. We could have written a regulation, and we know how to write rules—but we weren't sure that ... regulating [was appropriate]. However, in order to get a broad base of participants to participate together, there really did need to be a common set of rules, and defined set of rules. And we felt that it would work best if it was an industry-based set of rules that the government had a seat at the table, participated in, [and] endorsed.
>
> [T]he government always has veto power. The government can always say no, but it's proven very successful from our standpoint in that the program is administered on a standardized basis. It's efficient for our administration, and we have the industry participation in this government program, because it makes business sense, it makes good business sense because there's a common set of rules that is administered by an industry-based group.[2]

In other words, the structure of the EBT Council is such that no government, federal or state, gives up its authority to make decisions. Rather, the EBT Council provides an opportunity for the participating government and private parties to fashion a set of rules that may be more suitable for participating parties than what the federal government might have been able to devise by itself or through a formal notice-and-comment rule making. If the federal government declines to accept the work product of the EBT Council it always retains the option to issue its own regulation. Similarly, if states do not want to accept the work of the EBT Council, they are not required to use the council's system or operating rules in their own EBT systems.

The deliberate denial of independent power to a coordinating group can be a source of strength for the coordination process. This helps to focus stakeholders on persuasion rather than efforts to direct the other parties in the process. The process of disaster recovery described by Dwight Ink in chapter 7 relied on such a body, called the Field Committee, which was organized to coordinate rather than wield independent power. The result was that "[t]he committee's task was to coordinate, and help expedite, the operations of the various [federal] agencies with one another and with their counterparts at the state and local level. Under no circumstances was it to become another decision-making layer in the federal system" (Ink and Dean 2004).

The legitimacy of the EBT Council also rests on its openness and inclusion of a broad range of stakeholders. The EBT Council is governed by a Representative Board, consisting of twenty-five members. Each of the five main stakeholder groups is limited to a maximum of five seats, so that balance is maintained on the Representative Board. If an impasse arises concerning the EBT rules, the Representative Board can break it with a two-thirds majority of the votes cast. Under the voting rules, government entities have a special ability to block changes to the EBT operating rules that they as a group find objectionable.

The EBT Council has two categories of dues-paying members, full members, who pay $6,000 per year and who have voting rights and can serve on the Representative Board, and associates, who pay $2,000 per year and have no voting rights but may attend all meetings and participate in calls. The largest group of dues-paying members comes from state governments. The only federal agency to pay dues, as a nonvoting associate, is the General Services Administration. Other federal agencies may participate as advisers in EBT Council meetings and calls. The Food and Nutrition Service of the U.S. Department of Agriculture participates as a non-voting, non-dues-paying adviser and attends meetings and participates in conference calls. Although the federal advisers do not vote, they do exercise influence because the EBT Council is concerned with assuring that its operating rules are consistent with federal laws and regulations (Sims 2003).

This relates to another important issue: Given the frequently frayed relations between the federal government on the one hand and state and local governments on the other, as Beaumont and McDowell show in chapter 12, all participants in the Stakeholder Council Model must make repeated efforts to assure that the process is not merely another top-down federal exercise. Although positive results depend on the participants' joining in a *nationwide* perspective, the process depends on all parties' seeing themselves as coequal in their potential contributions to the process. The inclusion of nongovernmental stakeholders, who also have major contributions to make, helps to reduce the perception of a top-down process. On the other hand, the Stakeholder Council Model does not involve the blurring of public-private boundaries that Ronald Moe and Dan Guttman warn against in chapters 5 and 10; the process respects the different roles of each sector and preserves for all governmental entities the ability to exercise their legal responsibilities.

The EBT Council is not an expensive undertaking, especially compared to the magnitude of the benefits that pass through the EBT system. While the system rules were being developed, the council required support from perhaps two staff persons and an annual budget of about $350,000; currently, with the rules written but in a process of continuing revision, the council requires support from two people half-time each and a total budget of about $225,000. These funds come from assessed dues on participating members, who, in addition, each pay the costs of their own participation.

Identity Management as a Case Study of the Complexities of Intergovernmental Coordination

Since September 11, identity management has been of special concern at airports, other vulnerable facilities, and points of entry to the United States. Identity management is also important in the commercial world, for example, to prevent identity theft and fraudulent use of credit cards. The development of comprehensive identity management systems in the current environment is challenging and complex, involving many different parties that issue credentials, rely on them, and use them for a variety of purposes that may be different from the purposes for which they were issued.

To be effective, a comprehensive identity management system must respect trade-offs against other values, such as privacy. Often countervailing values can coexist, as is seen in a number of democratic countries with effective identity management systems that also have high privacy standards. To make such trade-offs properly requires a forum in which representatives of the affected interests can work together to determine whether common ground can be found on which to build a reasonable accommodation. For example, by taking the issue of privacy to a deeper level, it may be that a resolution could be found in distinguishing between (1) effective identification and (2) the recording of information about particular transactions and activities. In other words, it may be possible to create an ID credential that establishes a person's identity but that cannot be used to track that person's activities. Other accommodations may also be possible.

Effective identity management is complicated by the need for source documents, such as birth and death certificates, that provide information relied upon by issuers of other credentials, such as driver's licenses and identity cards. These source documents (traditionally called "breeder" documents) are gathered and maintained with variable quality by different states. The presence of about 100 million visitors to the United States further complicates effective identity management. Ultimately, the problems of identity management relate to systems and the people who use those systems. Too often the people issuing identity documents, including visas, driver's licenses, and Social Security cards, may be among the least compensated, skilled, or motivated people in the issuing organization.

Issues of identity management involve several different analytical levels:

- *ID Validation.* The person who receives an identity document must be the right person. This involves some level of background check and ability to rely on source documents or, for foreigners, other credible information.
- *Authentication.* When a person presents an identity document, it must be demonstrably genuine.
- *Verification.* When a person presents an identity document, they should currently be eligible to do so. Documents should be properly revoked when a person changes employment or other status that means that they are no longer eligible for the benefits that relate to the document they present.

Governments are under pressure to upgrade the quality of their identity documents. State motor vehicle departments are attempting to coordinate improvements in the documentation required for obtaining a driver's license. The federal government enacted the "Real ID Act" (included in Public Law No. 109–13), a new law that sets standards for state-issued identification cards and driver's licenses, on May 11, 2005. The government of Canada has undertaken a far-reaching improvement in identity management. Perhaps the most interesting example of improved credentials has been the initiative of the Government of Mexico to issue a special identity card, the Matricula Consular, to over a million illegal aliens from Mexico who reside in the United States. This identity card enables the alien to obtain a bank account, a driver's license, and other benefits that are unavailable to an undocumented person. (On the other hand, the General Services Administration has announced that a Matricula Consular may not be used to gain access to a federal building without further investigation into its authenticity.)

The effort of state governments to improve the quality of their credentials has shone a bright light on the variable quality of the source documents, such as birth and death records, that native-born Americans use to prove their eligibility for driver's licenses and other documents. Although some states, such as Iowa, have made significant progress, there is wide variation in the quality of these source documents across states and localities. Even though some states improve their source document systems, the sovereignty of state governments means that they resist being directed to do so. The absence of a sound system of death records, for example, results in the Social Security Administration's sending benefit checks to some people long after they are deceased.

Cleaning up the data behind the source documents and maintaining high-quality data are difficult tasks. When Canada improved its identity management system, it addressed the problem of inadequate source documents both by eliminating some especially loose forms of documentation and by establishing a guarantor system so that a person is required to obtain a certification of identity from a licensed professional (e.g., a lawyer, banker, engineer, or notary) who has known the person for a number of years and who will vouch for their source documents, before the Canadian government will issue a passport.

An important issue of identity management relates to interoperability. As federal and state governments move toward an eGovernment model for the provision of services, they are seeking to invest in technologies that can be used across government agencies and that are, to the extent possible, consistent with commercial standards used in the private sector. Otherwise, a set of inconsistent identity management systems is likely to emerge, for airline and airport workers, for hazardous materials truck drivers, for maritime workers, and for security at border crossings. To implement these laws private employers, as well as federal, state, local, and nongovernmental organizations, will need to issue their own credentials. A plethora of systems has already developed as governments and private organizations attempt to upgrade the quality of their identity management systems. The disparate systems somehow require coordination if they are to eliminate wide gaps.

The creation of a system of national identity documents probably does not mean the development of a single national ID credential for the United States. U.S. cultural values would militate against such a single card. In Britain, where similar cultural values prevail, the U.K. government is considering a system of reliance on three documents: a driver's license, a passport, or—for those with neither of those documents—a new "entitlement card." Although everyone would be obligated to possess one of these documents, no one would be obligated to carry it. It is not clear how much information the entitlement card would contain or even whether the U.K. government ultimately will adopt such a system ("Identity Cards" 2002). Canada, another country with a common cultural heritage, also has resisted the adoption of a single identity credential. Instead, the government of Canada is working to build a common technology platform to support the range of uses for a number of different identifying credentials.

One approach to government identity management might be to design credentials with various levels, so that a credential could be upgraded, or could build on other information systems, as an individual has need for a higher level or different type of access. When the need no longer exists, the higher level or different type of access could be suspended or terminated.

The Johns Hopkins conference concluded with a number of observations about the need for a process to help bring agencies of the federal government together with state and local agencies and private parties that require effective identity management to develop interoperable identity management systems:

1. The federal government must play a leadership role along with the states.[3] Otherwise, in the colorful metaphor of one participant, "you're going to have a thousand flowers blooming that don't talk to each other." Different identity management systems will be more effective to the extent that they are consistent and compatible.

2. Federal leadership is essential also because of the major stake of the federal government in developing identity management systems that govern access to critical federal facilities and facilities that will be subject to federal regulations or rules.

3. On the other hand, the federal government cannot dictate a single solution for identity management. Instead, the federal government should provide leadership and, to use the word of one participant, "sponsorship" and should establish a sense of the direction in which identity management should develop. This can help to guide the states and private-sector organizations that also have a stake in the development of consistent systems of identity management.

4. The federal government, working with the states and other stakeholders, can help to establish standards that incorporate the concerns and needs of states and private organizations and create an assurance that credentials that meet the federal standards will be acceptable for specified governmental purposes.

5. It is important to use a collaborative process along the lines of the Stakeholder Council Model to make progress. Critical elements of the process are that the right groups must be involved, working with a clear agenda and goals as well as a commitment to implement whatever recommendations and solutions are proposed.

6. Some participants urged specific action: that the Office of Management and Budget or perhaps the Department of Homeland Security should promptly convene and support the establishment of a public/private process along the lines of the Stakeholder Council

Model with the goal of developing a single interoperable architecture and a set of standards and rules for comprehensive identity management systems.

Applying the Stakeholder Council Model to the Development of Comprehensive Identity Management Systems

Helena Sims, who played a major role in the successful EBT process, has summarized some of the important characteristics of a successful Stakeholder Council: (1) commitment by the federal government, (2) a strong business case for using common rules, (3) a clear vision of the goals and process by the participating parties, (4) attainable goals, (5) a consistent message, and (6) involvement of the key stakeholders (Sims 2004). These elements would seem to be present in the area of identity management systems.

Applying the Stakeholder Council Model to identity management systems can help to highlight the strengths and limitations of the Stakeholder Council approach. Consider the following framework:

- The federal government, through the Office of Management and Budget, the Department of Homeland Security, or the General Services Administration (responsible for many of the federal government's electronic government initiatives) would announce that it seeks to encourage development of interoperable systems of identity management, to be applied to federal (nondefense) facilities, airports, and other high-priority uses.
- After discussions with the states and other stakeholders, the federal government would set forth specific issues that require resolution. These issues should be potentially susceptible to solution through consideration of fairly technical issues. Interoperability is such an issue.
- The process should have a timetable. One of the costs of a deliberative process along the lines of the Stakeholder Council Model is that the deliberations can be time consuming. The participants should try to mitigate this problem by setting fairly clear goals and setting realistic but firm deadlines.
- It will be important to assure that the right parties are at the table. This calls for judgment and also raises the possibility that the funded participants would need to provide stipends to some of the less-affluent advocacy groups, for example, those that represent consumer or privacy interests. If stipends are awarded, they must be designed carefully so that payment does not affect, or create the appearance of affecting, the substantive contributions made by the groups receiving stipends.

- For the first year, the federal government is likely to be required to pay some or all of the costs of the process. Ordinarily state governments could be expected to pay start-up costs as well; however, this may be difficult, given the current fiscal condition of the states.
- Ultimately, if an issue such as interoperability is successfully addressed, the Stakeholder Council Model is likely to turn into an ongoing activity. It has been the experience of the EBT Council, and other standards-setting groups, that standards must be maintained once they are developed. Changing technologies and patterns of application make such a continuing process necessary. Funding for that ongoing activity will be required. The experience of the EBT Council (and other standards groups) shows how the costs of the ongoing process can be paid through dues by the participating members.

The Stakeholder Council Model is potentially also applicable to other homeland security issues. For example, the Maritime Transportation Security Act of 2002 (MTSA) requires the secretary of transportation (or the secretary of homeland security since the responsibilities were transferred to the new department) to enhance maritime cargo security, and in particular to reduce the security risks of containerized cargo shipments. The MTSA also directs the commissioner of customs to issue regulations providing for the electronic transmission to Customs of information pertaining to cargo to be brought into the United States or to be sent from the United States prior to the arrival or departure of the cargo.

The implementation of these responsibilities cannot be done by federal fiat alone. It may be that the Stakeholder Council Model could provide a forum to allow for the necessary exchange of information among the countervailing interests such as carriers, shippers, technology vendors, ports, the Transportation Security Administration, and the commissioner of customs. This could help avoid the fashioning of solutions that rely on inappropriate technologies or that impose unnecessary burdens on commerce in the effort to enhance port security. Once again, interoperability may be an important goal for cargo security systems developed through the Stakeholder Council Model.[4]

Conclusion: Making the Stakeholder Council Model Work

This analysis does not intend to suggest that the Stakeholder Council Model is a universal panacea. The contention rather is that homeland security involves countervailing values that often cannot best be addressed by solutions dictated from Washington. The Stakeholder Council Model presents an alternative approach that, although potentially more time consuming in the deliberative phase, may allow for the development of more effective and comprehensive solutions for the longer term. Needed now are consideration of the areas where the Stakeholder Council Model might be most applicable, development of a framework for applying the model, and implementation of one or more pilot tests.

Notes

The author would like to thank the many people who shared information for this chapter, including Richard Gluck, partner of Garvey, Schubert & Barer; Helena Sims, NACHA senior director for public/private partnerships and executive director of the EBT Council; Thomas P. Stack, vice president of the Maximus Corporation; and other participants in the Johns Hopkins University Symposium on Comprehensive Identity Management Systems. The author also appreciates the insights of reviewers of an earlier paper on this subject, presented at the Panel Session on Homeland Security of the 64th National Conference of the American Society of Public Administration, Washington, D.C., March 18, 2003, including H. George Frederickson, the Edwin O. Stene Distinguished Professor at the University of Kansas; Dan Guttman, fellow of the National Academy of Public Administration; and John Palguta, vice president of the Partnership for Public Service. Sole responsibility for this chapter rests with the author.

1. Benjamin Miller first proposed this term in comments on an early draft.

2. Cited in Johns Hopkins 2003. Recall that all comments from the symposium are not attributable by name to particular speakers.

3. Symposium participants focused on identity management systems broadly and did not seek to express a view of the potential role of smart cards or other specific technologies in identity management systems. However, the symposium's emphasis on the need for federal leadership in identity management did presage a GAO report on smart cards that calls for government leadership and specifically for the OMB director to issue government-wide policy and guidance after consulting with the relevant federal agencies. See U.S. GAO 2003, 35.

4. The author would like to thank Richard Gluck of the law firm of Garvey, Schubert & Barer, a participant in the Johns Hopkins symposium, for this example.

References

Frederickson, H. George, and Todd R. LaPorte. 2002. "Airport Security, High Reliability, and the Problem of Rationality." *Public Administration Review* 62 (September): 33–43.

"Identity Cards: Papers Please." 2002. *The Economist* (December 14): 51.

Ink, Dwight, and Alan L. Dean. 2004. "Modernizing Federal Field Operations." In *Making Government Manageable*, eds. Thomas H. Stanton and Benjamin Ginsberg. Baltimore, MD: Johns Hopkins University Press, 194.

Johns Hopkins Center for the Study of American Government. 2003. "Developing and Implementing Comprehensive Identity Management Systems: Insights from a Symposium at the Johns Hopkins University."

O'Harrow, Robert, Jr. 2003. "Aviation ID System Stirs Doubts: Senate Panel Wants Data on Impact on Passenger Privacy." *Washington Post* (March 14), A16.

Pear, Robert. 2004. "Electronic Cards Replace Coupons for Food Stamps." *New York Times* (June 23), 1.

Salamon, Lester M. 2002. "The New Governance and the Tools of Public Action: An Introduction." In *Tools of Government: A Guide to the New Governance*, ed. Lester M. Salamon. New York: Oxford University Press, 11–14.

Seidman, Harold. 2004. "Foreword." In *Making Government Manageable*, eds. Thomas H. Stanton and Benjamin Ginsberg. Baltimore, MD: Johns Hopkins University Press, x.

Sims, Helena. 2003. Personal communication to the author, NACHA senior director for public/private partnerships of NACHA and executive director of the EBT Council, March 10.

———. 2004. Presentation to the NAPA Standing Panel on Executive Organization. October 15.

———. Undated. "The EBT Council: A Model for e-Government Projects." National Association of Clearinghouse Administrators.

U.S. General Accounting Office (GAO). 2003. *Electronic Government: Progress in Promoting Adoption of Smart Card Technology*, GAO-03-144, January, 35.

Appendix 13.1. Coordination Concepts
by Dwight Ink

Over the years I have had a number of federal assignments from different presidents that involved extensive coordination within the federal government and often with state and local agencies. Here are several concepts that have been especially useful to me in the course of these experiences.

1. Joint Efforts Where Possible

We often discuss "top-down" versus "bottom-up" or "roll-up" approaches, and both have their place. However, I found it very important to address domestic problems on a joint or team basis to the extent possible. In Alaska, for example, discussed in chapter 7, there were no separate federal plans, no separate state plans, and no separate local-government plans. Officials of all three levels literally sat around a large table, generally in a high school gym, and agreed on a plan that would be called a Kodiak Plan, a Seward Plan, an Anchorage Plan, etc. Obviously, this is easier in emergency situations, and in low-population areas. Nevertheless, we were fortunate in extending the "team" concept to a surprising extent throughout the nation in the first three years of President Nixon's New Federalism. Later, this concept stayed in the rhetoric, but faded in reality as the OMB lost its management leadership capacity and federal field career leaders were replaced with political appointees.

2. Preserve Accountability

Too often the team concept results in a loss of accountability and the capacity to act, two concepts I regard as linked. Coordinating bodies such as regional councils can be very useful for exchanging information, facilitating planning, and coordinating action. But they generally become counterproductive if they are given authority. This too often results in their becoming just another layer that further complicates the system. Instead, I have found it more useful to rely upon the authority of the individual members that comes from their agency role. As parts of a coordinating body they can exercise their individual agency authorities in concert, and they are more likely to supplement each other rather than compete or leave unintended gaps. Decision making then can be considerably expedited, as compared to networking groups that grow into formal bodies with power to approve or disapprove actions. In the latter case they then turn into bottlenecks rather than expediters of coordinated activity.

3. Openness a Virtue

In the Alaska Recovery, I served as executive director of the Reconstruction Commission described in chapter 7. Despite the fact that I spent twelve years in the secretive Atomic Energy Commission, I quickly found it very useful to run nondefense operations as openly as one possibly can. In Alaska I never once had a closed meeting except in discussing personnel issues. The media were always there, and the public was not only invited but permitted to speak (briefly), even though this meant at times finishing after sunrise. The Alaskan attorney general was given an office next to mine in Washington. He and the state disaster coordinator participated in my Washington staff meetings, to which key Hill staff were invited. My weekly reports were designed for internal operations, but President Johnson ordered them released to the press even though I was quite candid about the relative performance of federal and state agencies. The combination of participation and open meetings eliminated all of the typical suspicion and questions of hidden motives in a fast-moving operation. More important, opposition to adverse decisions was greatly reduced in intensity, and the debates focused on substantive issues.

As every city manager knows, open, participatory operations require an ability to move forward and not get bogged down. They also require the confidence to meet opposition face to face, and the courage to act when consensus is not attainable.

Contrary to the thinking of some, I found that the time invested in broad participation and open operations saved time in the end. In Alaska, for example, I told the agencies that we did not have time for the formal public hearing procedures embedded in a number of our programs, especially urban renewal. We had not one complaint, because our open approach provided them with an even greater chance to keep informed and to voice their views as the planning and execution moved forward. In view of the much larger populations involved, and the absence of an emergency environment, we could not accommodate the open participatory process as much in President Nixon's New Federalism, but we did provide far more than had been the prior practice.

4. Value of Streamlined Management

Minimize the formal processes as much as possible, a concept that is much easier to apply in emergencies than in continuing operations, but essential in both cases. Some will remember the A-95 circular the Bureau of the Budget (BOB, the predecessor organization to the Office of Management and Budget) issued in 1969 that stimulated considerable cooperation among local governments and triggered much of the birth of councils of government

(COGs) across the nation. As director of the BOB Office of Executive Management, I would not permit more than one-third of one staff person's time to be devoted to central management of the circular and I imposed a severe limit on the length of this highly successful circular. Later, when the procedures grew significantly and several people were added to central direction, its usefulness declined and eventually disappeared.

Despite the complexity of the operation, I established only one procedure in leading the rebuilding of Alaska, that of a system of reporting from the Alaskan field offices directly to me concurrently with their reports to their agency leadership. I, and all levels of the agencies, including members of the cabinet, received the field information at the same time without the time required for sequential forwarding up through the ranks. The reports to me and the agencies were identical, except that additional detail was added to their agency reports.

With this one exception, we relied upon existing processes to the extent they were retained. Many were not. I received tacit approval from both the president and the congressional leadership to authorize all the departments to waive any existing procedures (but not laws) that got in the way of meeting our program objectives. In the case of the New Federalism, we did some waiving of procedures, but the bulk of our effort was directed toward a radical elimination and streamlining of processes that had smothered programs of assistance to state and local governments. (One problem we never solved satisfactorily was the tendency of some states to substitute state requirements for those we eliminated at the federal level. Another was our inability to prevent new red tape and unfunded mandates from evolving in subsequent years.)

5. Necessity of Institutional Support

The presidential support that I had from Johnson in Alaska and Nixon in the New Federalism clearly made my job easier. What may be less obvious is the key role played by BOB and OMB management staff in every interagency or intergovernmental task I was assigned. In some aspects of this work, there was useful cooperation with the budget staff, but the independence of the management staff enabled it to provide the president with the management leadership on his behalf to ensure that the federal agencies would work together, especially in the field, and that the three levels of government could function in concert on implementing national policies. The OMB is now essentially a budget organization with only a limited management shell still in existence, and there is nothing in the federal government to replace the OMB management staff, making coordination far more difficult today.

About the Editor and Contributors

Enid Beaumont was director of the Academy for State and Local Government for over a dozen years. Dr. Beaumont is a fellow of the National Academy of Public Administration (NAPA) and has been vice president of NAPA, executive director of the National Institute of Public Affairs, and president of the American Society for Public Administration. Dr. Beaumont is the former director of the Public Administration Program, New York University; chief of party, Macedonia Project, USAID; assistant administrator, Human Resources Administration, New York City; personnel administrator, U.S. Agency for International Development; and manager, Port Authority of New York and New Jersey. She currently teaches at George Mason University.

James D. Carroll has served as a budget analyst, the U.S. Department of Housing and Urban Development; director, Government Research Division, the Congressional Research Service, the Library of Congress; professor and chair of the Department of Public Administration, the Maxwell School; and director, the advanced study program, the Brookings Institution. He recently wrote "The Future of Public Action: From the Administrative to the Entitlement to the Domestic Security State," in David Rejeski, ed., *Government Foresight,* 2003. He holds a PhD from the Maxwell School and has been a member of the New York State and federal bars. He is a professor of public policy and administration, Florida International University, Miami, Florida.

Murray Comarow is a Washington, D.C., attorney, vice chair of the Standing Panel on Executive Organization and Management, and senior fellow of the National Academy of Public Administration. He has served as a member of the Academy's Board of Directors. He was executive director of President Johnson's Commission on Postal Organization in 1967–68, executive director of President Nixon's Advisory Council on Executive Organization in 1970-71, and served as Assistant Postmaster General of the United States. He was Distinguished Adjunct Professor in Residence at the American University from 1975 to 1995 and Acting Dean of the College of Public and International Affairs.

Alan L. Dean has devoted over fifty-five years to the study of how best to organize and manage federal executive departments, independent agencies, and government enterprises. He is the former chair of the Board of Trustees of the National Academy of Public Administration. He has held numerous senior positions in the executive branch, including vice president for administration of the U.S. Railway Corporation, management adviser to the secretary and undersecretary of the Department of Health, Education and Welfare, assistant director for management of the Office of Management and Budget, assistant secretary for administration of the Department of Transportation, and associate administrator for administration of the Federal Aviation Agency.

Dan Guttman, a fellow at the Center for the Study of American Government at Johns Hopkins University and of the National Academy of Public Administration, served as special counsel to Senator David Pryor in the oversight of "government by third party," and coauthored *The Shadow Government* (1976). Now an attorney in private practice in Washington, D.C., he also served as executive director of the Presidential Advisory Commission on Human Radiation Experiments, and commissioner of the U.S. Occupational Safety Health and Review Commission. In 2004 he was awarded a Fulbright scholarship to teach on the law faculty at Shanghai Jiao Tong University in China.

Dwight Ink is president emeritus and former president of the Institute of Public Administration. He has held numerous executive positions in the federal government, including assistant administrator, Bureau for Latin America and the Caribbean, U.S. Agency for International Development; acting administrator, General Services Administration; director, U.S. Community Services Agency; and assistant director for executive management of the Office of Management and Budget.

Frederick M. Kaiser is a specialist in American National Government at the Congressional Research Service. His work with congressional committees and offices over three decades has dealt with executive-legislative relations and executive reorganization, homeland security agencies, and many other areas. He has served as a consultant to government commissions, including the President's Reorganization Project. A frequent participant in national and international conferences, he has also published extensively, for example, on "Federal Law Enforcement: Structure and Reorganization," *Criminal Justice Review;* "Congress and National Security Policy," *Comparative Studies;* and "Congressional Control of Administrative Action," *Administrative Law Review.*

Michael Maccoby is an anthropologist, psychoanalyst, and consultant on leadership strategy and organization. He is president of the Maccoby Group in Washington, D.C., and has a PhD from Harvard University, where he directed the Program on Technology, Public Policy and Human Development from 1978 to 1990. Dr. Maccoby has been a consultant and coach to leaders in many corporations, unions, and universities; the World Bank; and the State and Commerce departments of the U.S. government. His books include *The Gamesman, The Leader,* and *Why Work? Motivating the New Work Force.* He is coauthor of *Agents of Change: Crossing the Post Industrial Divide* (2003), which describes his approach to making organizations more effective.

Bruce D. McDowell, FAICP, has had a forty-five-year career as a city and regional planner, intergovernmental analyst, federal executive, widely published author, and consultant, including jobs with the Maryland–National Capital Park and Planning Commission, Metropolitan Washington Council of Governments, U.S. Advisory Commission on Intergovernmental Relations, U.S. Housing and Home Finance Agency, and National Council on Public Works Improvement. Dr. McDowell's wide variety of consultant clients includes the National Academy of Public Administration. McDowell is a fellow of the academy and a fellow of the American Institute of Certified Planners.

Ronald C. Moe is a fellow at the Washington Center for the Study of American Government of Johns Hopkins University. In 2002, he retired after thirty years as the specialist in government organization and management at the Congressional Research Service of the Library of Congress. During this period he worked closely with lawmakers and staff on governmental management issues. In support of this responsibility, Dr. Moe wrote scholarly books and articles and four times received the Brownlow Award for the best management article to appear in the *Public Administration Review.* His latest book is *Administrative Renewal: Reorganization Commissions in the 20th Century* (2003). Moe is a fellow of the National Academy of Public Administration.

Beryl A. Radin is professor of Government and Public Administration at the University of Baltimore. A fellow of the National Academy of Public Administration, she is the managing editor of the *Journal of Public Administration Research and Theory.* She has written a number of books and articles on public policy and public management issues, focusing on management issues in the federal government. Her latest book is *The Accountable Juggler: The Art of Leadership in a Federal Agency,* published by CQ Press in 2002. She served as a special adviser and consultant to the assistant secretary for management and budget in the Department of Health and Human Services (HHS) from 1995 to 1999.

Thomas H. Stanton, a Washington, D.C., attorney, advises the federal government, state and local governments, and international organizations on improving the design and capacity of public institutions. He is a member of the NAPA board of directors and a fellow of the Center for the Study of American Government at Johns Hopkins University, where he received the Award for Excellence in Teaching. He is a former member of the federal Senior Executive Service. His writings on government include several books and many articles. The concerns he expressed in *A State of Risk* (HarperCollins, 1991) helped lead to enactment of legislation and the creation of a new federal financial regulator in 1992. Stanton edited (with Benjamin Ginsberg) *Making Government Manageable: Executive Organization and Management in the 21st Century* (Johns Hopkins University Press, 2004).

Cindy L. Williams is a principal research scientist in the Security Studies Program at the Massachusetts Institute of Technology. Formerly she served as assistant director for national security in the Congressional Budget Office, as a director at the MITRE Corporation, and in the Senior Executive Service. Dr. Williams is the editor of *Filling the Ranks: Transforming the U.S. Military Personnel System* (2004) and *Holding the Line: U.S. Defense Alternatives for the Early 21st Century* (2001). A fellow of the National Academy of Public Administration, Dr. Williams also serves on the Naval Studies Board, the editorial board of *International Security,* and the advisory board of Women in International Security (WIIS). She is a member of the Council on Foreign Relations.

Index